CHIVALRY AND VIOLENCE IN
MEDIEVAL EUROPE

CHIVALRY
AND
VIOLENCE
IN MEDIEVAL EUROPE

RICHARD W. KAEUPER

OXFORD
UNIVERSITY PRESS

*This book has been printed digitally and produced in a standard specification
in order to ensure its continuing availability*

OXFORD
UNIVERSITY PRESS

Great Clarendon Street, Oxford OX2 6DP

Oxford University Press is a department of the University of Oxford.
It furthers the University's objective of excellence in research, scholarship,
and education by publishing worldwide in

Oxford New York

Auckland Cape Town Dar es Salaam Hong Kong Karachi
Kuala Lumpur Madrid Melbourne Mexico City Nairobi
New Delhi Shanghai Taipei Toronto
With offices in
Argentina Austria Brazil Chile Czech Republic France Greece
Guatemala Hungary Italy Japan South Korea Poland Portugal
Singapore Switzerland Thailand Turkey Ukraine Vietnam

Oxford is a registered trade mark of Oxford University Press
in the UK and in certain other countries

Published in the United States
by Oxford University Press Inc., New York

Oxford is a registered trade mark of Oxford University Press
in the UK and in certain other countries

Published in the United States
by Oxford University Press Inc., New York

© Richard W. Kaeuper 1999

The moral rights of the author have been asserted

Database right Oxford University Press (maker)

Reprinted 2006

ISBN 0-19-924458-8

to Seth, Geoffrey, and John

ACKNOWLEDGEMENTS

✦✦✦

Essential support for launching this project came from awards granted by the Harry Frank Guggenheim Foundation in 1989–91. Their generous financial and moral support is gratefully acknowledged. The University of Rochester gave me one-semester academic leaves in 1991, 1993, and 1997, for which I am likewise grateful.

Warm thanks go to the anonymous Clarendon Press readers, and to William Calin, John Maddicott, Jeffrey Ravel, and Roberta Krueger, who read large parts of the book manuscript and gave helpful critiques. Tony Morris encouraged the project and saw the book through the contract stage at the Press with much appreciated skill and enthusiasm. Ruth Parr, Anna Illingworth, and Dorothy McLean directed the crucial process by which a large manuscript became a book. Sarah Dancy did the truly heroic work of copy-editing. The staff in Reference and Interlibrary Loan, Rush Rhees Library, University of Rochester, obtained even the most obscure French sources. The index was skilfully prepared by Nicholas Waddy.

Responding to my ideas as I formulated them was one gift from my wife Margaret. Even more important was her splendidly sound advice as I shaped the book and her unfailing capacity to ask the hard questions.

This book is dedicated to my sons, Seth, Geoffrey, and John, with love and pride.

Richard W. Kaeuper

University of Rochester

CONTENTS

✦✦✦

PROLOGUE

✦✦✦

M ARK TWAIN'S Connecticut Yankee, finding himself suddenly transported across centuries into the strange world of Camelot, manages, despite the shock of time travel, to preserve his acute sense of observation. From the start he views the Arthurian court ambivalently, feeling horror at its failure to anticipate the democratic and technological glories of his own nineteenth century, mixed with a somewhat reluctant dash of romantic admiration for its very otherness, exhibited with such vigour and colour, especially in the quaint richness of its verbal expression.

If the Yankee thus drops substantial weights onto the pans swinging on each side of the scales of judgement, the balance arm tips heavily toward the negative. His early conclusion is that Camelot must be an insane asylum, its denizens virtual savages who can be dismissed as 'white Indians'. Listening to the talk in court for the first time, he reports:

As a rule the speech and behavior of these people were gracious and courtly; and I noticed that they were good and serious listeners when anybody was telling anything— I mean in a dogfightless interval. And plainly, too, they were a childlike and innocent lot; telling lies of the stateliest pattern with a most gentle and winning naivety, and ready and willing to listen to anybody else's lie, and believe it, too. It was hard to associate them with anything cruel or dreadful; and yet they dealt in tales of blood and suffering with a guileless relish that made me almost forget to shudder.[1]

This passage, of course, shows us much that we try to avoid as historians. Here the Yankee shares the prejudices of his age and wears the racial blinkers of his creator; he also reveals the sour suspicion of all things venerably European that periodically appeared in Twain's books.[2]

Yet we can more easily read on past the prejudices and culturally smug comments about childlike natives when we observe that the passage and the book, whatever their obvious failures in cultural relativism, present a thoroughly

---

[1] *A Connecticut Yankee*, 13. Twain would have appreciated Clausewitz telling his wife that it would be years before he could recall the scenes of Napoleon's Russian campaign 'without a shuddering horror'. Quoted in Keegan, *A History of Warfare*, 8.

[2] The complex, shifting, even contradictory relationship between Twain and European culture is noted in Kaplan's fascinating study, *Mr Clemens and Mark Twain*.

salutary admonition to us as modern analysers of the medieval phenomenon of chivalry. For the great danger in the study of chivalry is to view this important phenomenon through the rose-tinted lenses of romanticism, to read chivalry in terms of what we want it to be rather than what it was. However glorious and refined its literature, however elevated its ideals, however enduring its link with Western ideas of gentlemanliness—and whatever we think of that—we must not forget that knighthood was nourished on aggressive impulses, that it existed to use its shining armour and sharp-edged weaponry in acts of showy and bloody violence. As Twain reminds us succinctly, we must not forget to shudder.

To avoid romanticism should enable analysis, of course, not prevent it. An occasional, salutary shudder does not mean we must judge chivalry—as Twain does here—by modern liberal standards, nor indeed that we must judge it at all, but simply that we should take care not to be blinded by the light reflected off shining armour; we should try instead to look at the social effects of chivalry as dispassionately as possible, and now and then manage to write of chivalry in a tone other than the reverential. Such efforts in no way diminish an appreciation of the vast investment in chivalry by medieval people or of the vast importance attributed to chivalry by modern analyses that may go well beyond the particularly medieval range of vision. In fact, the most compelling reason to avoid romanticizing chivalry is that taking a view through rose-tinted lenses distorts and finally trivializes this extraordinarily powerful force in early European history.

Significant benefits accrue if we follow Twain's advice and avoid romanticism. We can better evaluate the mixture of the ideal and the actual in the medieval past. We can consider chivalry as a range of ideals closely and complexly intertwined with a set of practices and problems, noting always the context which required this fusion. By escaping romanticism we can better recognize the linkage between chivalry and major issues in medieval society, especially the crucial issue of violence and public order.

In any romanticized reading, chivalry becomes a purely positive and uncomplicated factor in securing order. Such a reading holds, in essence, that chivalry brought about the internalization of necessary restraints in a vigorous group of men—valorous and violent men, to be sure, but potentially the finest of fellows their society could produce. These stout men learned the ideal, used their weapons in the name of God and in aid of the weak and oppressed. If violence and the prevalence of war in medieval society caused any problems of order, some modern scholars imply, these problems could not be inherent in chivalry itself, nor could they even be encouraged by chivalry. Rather, the trouble stemmed from the insufficient generalization of chivalry in society, from the unfortunate fact of limited diffusion, with chivalry unable to touch all warriors with its simultaneously elevating and restraining hand.

A preference for reading texts in this fashion is surely understandable. Scholars' tasks are so much easier, so much more hopeful, if the tone of the texts is considered unproblematically upbeat, if these texts are considered to favour values scholars themselves hold dear. Most denizens of the groves of academe, after all, tend to be mild-mannered (except for the verbal violence of departmental meetings, long footnotes, reviews, and the institutional cocktail party); they sometimes also show a certain emotional commitment to positive value judgements about their particular era and field of study.

An element of modern scholarly identification with the upper social layers in the distant past may even lie buried now and then within this line of argument, for should any slightly distasteful issues about warlike violence arise in analysis, the locus of trouble is quickly identified and the terminology is quickly changed. 'Soldiers', whose very name implies wage-taking rather than the true calling (and the right social status) might, granted, be hard for the knights to control; they might get out of hand, might ride, pillage, burn, and rape on a scale sufficient to constitute a social problem; but the problem of the soldiery was that they were not knights and had yet to acquire the internalized restraints of chivalry. War on the home front, the 'private war' of knight against knight, or of knight against the sub-knightly, was apparently either uncommon or simply the means of asserting needed hierarchical order.

This study argues, to the contrary, that in the problem of public order the knights themselves played an ambivalent, problematic role and that the guides to their conduct that chivalry provided were in themselves complex and problematic. The issues are built into some of the very ideals of chivalry, not merely in the lamentable inability of fallible men to attain them. This approach is not simply a self-consciously hard-nosed brand of realism or even some species of cynicism. It takes as a given the yawning gap between a knightly practice that is recoverable (if we only look diligently) and the impossibly high ideals expressed for it in one major text after another. This gap is unsurprising and need spawn no modern moralizing.

Upon discovering this divergence, beginning students, of course, often decide to debunk chivalry: the cads did not live up to the high ideals after all. Any slice of human history could, however, show groups of people more or less professing one course and more or less following another; surely that discovery cannot be the point of serious study. Nor need it be the point in a study of chivalry and order. The chivalry that knights practised upheld the high ideals of a demanding code of honour; as we will see, these ideals were probably achieved as nearly as any set of human ideals ever can be in an imperfect world. Yet even when achieved, their ideals may not have been fully compatible with the ideal of a more ordered and peaceful society also being advanced during 'the age of chivalry'.

The issues analysed in this book are thus as much social as individual and the questions concern political and social order more than any judgement of knighthood. Of course, competing investments of meaning will compel us to think of chivalry throughout this book as a concept working under constant tension. The goal is to discover the mixture of ideals and practices knights followed in an atmosphere of reform, and to learn how this process affected the effort to secure public order in a society just coming to its mature formation.

It will not prove helpful to analyse chivalry in terms of an unreflective and rough practice of knights confronted by a glowing theory or high ideal that outsiders all agreed upon and wanted to impose. Each competing ideal sought to bend chivalry to its plan; knights took up some of these ideas, rejected others, and were sure they had ideals of their own.

Use of the term chivalry by the medievals themselves suggests a blurring of such simplistic categories as theory and practice. When they spoke or wrote of chivalry (*militia* in Latin, *chevalerie* in French), any of three related meanings may have been in their minds. First, the term could mean nothing more theoretical or ethical than deeds of great valour and endurance on some field of combat, that is, heroic work with sword, shield, and lance. Second, the term could mean a group of knights. In the simplest sense this may be the body of elite warriors present on some particular field of battle. In a more abstract sense the term might refer to the entire social body of knights considered as a group stretching across space and time. Third, chivalry might be used to mean a knightly code of behaviour.

Just what that code should be was not clear in detail, sometimes not in fundamentals. Idealist critics wanted to change much in the knightly mixture of ideals and practices; some of these idealistic reformers were knights themselves. Chivalry can only be interpreted, in other words, as a mixture of ideals and practices constantly critiqued by those who wanted to change both.

PART I

✦✦✦

ISSUES AND APPROACHES

HALF a century after Twain's *Connecticut Yankee* appeared, Norbert Elias, a German sociologist, published *Über den Prozess der Zivilisation*, a massive study of changing manners and of the 'civilizing process' in European history.[1] The present book shares certain basic questions with his. Was the medieval world (in its mentality and practice) significantly troubled by violence? Were knights in particular a source of violence? How and when did Europeans begin to internalize restraint and edge away from disruptive personal violence? What role was played by kings and the civilizing influence of their courts?

Medievalists who read Elias will find his questions thoughtful and important; they are likely to be less satisfied with the range of evidence and the view that significant signs of change appear only in post-medieval Europe. For the medieval centuries Elias's questions could stimulate further close investigation along many lines of enquiry, at least one of which is taken up in the chapters that follow: the complex connections of chivalry and violence.

Emphasizing these problems of order is scarcely a denigration of medieval civilization and does not align us with those for whom 'medieval' has always been a term of abuse. On the contrary, such an enquiry emphasizes how deeply medieval people worked at solving a fundamental problem—one which, even with our greater resources, we have not quite managed to figure out in the long span of post-medieval centuries.

The issue of violence was always present, either obvious and in the foreground or more subtly present behind the scenes and between the lines. To be sure, chivalry created elaborate codes designed to refine knightly behaviour and to set knights apart from others. Showing elegant manners became increasingly important; knowing how to talk and act in refined company and especially with ladies was added to knowing how best to drive a sword-edge through a mail coif into a man's brain. These 'courtly' qualities are of much obvious importance in early European history.

Yet scholars have studied and emphasized these courtly qualities so enthusiastically that they threaten to claim exclusive right to the large mantle of chivalry, blocking from our vision the prickly sense of honour, the insistence

---

[1] *Über den Prozess der Zivilisation* (1939; reissued 1997); English translation in 2 vols: Edmund Jephcott, tr., *The Civilizing Process. Volume I: The History of Manners* (1978), and *Volume II: Power and Civility* (1982). Cf. final section of Chapter 9.

on autonomy, the quick recourse to violence. Chivalry was not simply a code integrating generic individual and society, not simply an ideal for relations between the sexes or a means for knocking off the rough warrior edges in preparation for the European gentleman to come. The bloody-minded side of the code—even if it seems to moderns, as Twain might say, a shuddering matter—was of the essence of chivalry. The knight was a warrior and not Everyman.

After all, the division of high medieval society outlined in spoken or written word was always threefold: the imagined world divided into those who fight, those who pray, and those who work.[2] The fighting, let us remember, was not merely defensive, not simply carried out at the royal behest in defence of recognized national borders, not only on crusade, not really (despite their self-deceptions) in the defence of widows, orphans, and the weak, never (so far as the historian can discover) against giants, ogres, or dragons. They fought each other as enthusiastically as any common foe; perhaps even more often they brought violence to villagers, clerics, townspeople, and merchants.

The lay elite cherished as a defining privilege this right to violence in any matter touching their prickly sense of honour. 'Because I like it (*pour ce qu'il me plest*)' was the belligerent motto of the late fourteenth-century Breton lord Olivier de Clisson.[3] Such a combative sense of autonomy is encountered time and again in all the evidence relating to chivalry; the sense of honour it conveys was secured with edged weapons and bloodshed. In the provincial leagues that formed in 1314, French lords demanded that the Capetian crown recognize their right of private war; a generation earlier they had pointedly reminded clerics that the French kingdom itself had been founded 'by the sweat of war'.[4] 'I will be justice this day', exults Gamelyn in the fourteenth-century English romance; he has just recovered right and honour by violently overwhelming the meeting of a corrupt royal court, has hanged the sheriff and jurors, and will shortly hang the king's justice, after cleaving his cheekbone and breaking his arm.[5] English and French judicial records can produce parallels from life to this violent scene of autonomy imaginatively realized in literature.[6] The identity of chivalry and status with proud violence will continue throughout the medieval centuries and into those we call early modern.[7]

---

[2] See Duby, *Les Trois Ordres*.   [3] His life is examined in Henneman, *Olivier de Clisson*.
[4] Paris, *Chronica Majora*, iv, 593: 'regnum non per jus scriptum, nec per clericorum arrogantiam, sed per sudores bellicos fuerit adquisitum'; cited in Clanchy, 'Law and Love', 51.
[5] Sands, *Middle English Verse Romances*, 178–81.
[6] See the examples in Kaeuper, 'Law and Order' and *War, Justice, and Public Order*, 225–68.
[7] See, e.g., Mervyn James, 'English Politics and the Concept of Honour'; Billacois, *Le Duel dans la société française des XVIe–XVIIe siècles*; Kiernan, *The Duel in European History*; Schalk, *From Valor to Pedigree*.

Of course we need no more believe that most knights were constantly out of control, moved by sheer glandular urges to cut and thrust, than to believe that most of them had happily experienced a complete taming of such impulses simply by learning courtesy. The problem that distinguishes the medieval chapter of the story of public order, however, is that (as we will see) the right and personal practice of warlike violence has fused with honour, high status, religious piety, and claims about love, so that those knights who are inclined, or who see opportunity, will be likely to act with whatever force they can muster, confident in their course of action. This ethos, moreover, will inevitably and understandably extend beyond the caste of knights to play a role in society generally. It will be a long time, indeed, before confidence in the role of heroic violence is truly shaken.

I

THE PROBLEM OF PUBLIC ORDER AND THE KNIGHTS

✦✦✦

The High Middle Ages and Order

The millennium of European history we call medieval has known more than one scheme for subdivision into shorter thematic and chronological periods. Charles Homer Haskins's *Renaissance of the Twelfth Century* stands among the most enduring, fruitful, and debated of these plans.[1] However polemical its chosen title, however excessive we may think the book's untiring emphasis on revived classicism as the key indicator and engine of change, Haskins's book was one of the key works to focus our attention on the period beginning in roughly the mid-eleventh century (or even earlier, as many scholars would now insist), often termed the Central or High Middle Ages. A distinguished body of scholarship emphasizes the fundamental importance of this period of European history: to Henri Pirenne, Roberto Lopez, M. M. Postan, it represented the transformation of economic and urban life; it was the influential 'second feudal age' for Marc Bloch; for R. W. Southern the age embodied 'medieval humanism'; for Robert Fossier it was 'the beginnings of Europe', for Georges Duby it brought the 'early growth of the European economy' and the 'age of the cathedrals'; for Joseph Strayer it created the 'origins of the modern state'; for Karl Leyser its early decades marked 'the ascent of Latin Europe'.[2] The list could be considerably extended, but the basic point remains that many historians have argued that in so many varied and important dimensions of life the generations between something like the eleventh and the early fourteenth centuries saw change and accomplishment on a scale truly important for the long course of Western history.

[1] Hasking, *The Renaissance of the Twelfth Century*.
[2] Pirenne, *Economic and Social History of Medieval Europe*; Lopez, *The Commercial Revolution of the Middle Ages*; Postan, *Medieval Trade and Finance* and *Medieval Society and Economy*; Marc Bloch, *Société Féodale*; Southern, *Medieval Humanism and Other Studies*; Fossier, *Enfance de l'Europe*; Duby, *Early Growth of the European Economy* and *Age of the Cathedrals*: Strayer, *Medieval Origins*; Leyser, *Ascent of Latin Europe* .

Change on this scale inevitably produces tensions, many of which have been explored by medievalists. The uneasy coexistence of spirituality and commercial expansion is an excellent case in point.[3] Yet in all of the discussion of this central period of medieval history one of the most significant issues has attracted less close analysis than it deserves. This basic issue is public order. We have studied ecclesiastical and lay government in detail, we have analysed war, and, more recently, crime; chivalry as an ideal has long attracted scholars, and some have even descended to consider it in daily life; but we cannot truly understand public order by studying any one of these topics in isolation.

Working to create and sustain the order, the regularity, the acceptable degree of peacefulness that make civilized life possible is, of course, a fundamental need of all societies. The effort will always raise significant questions. What violence is licit or even sanctified? What violence is considered destructive of necessary order? Who has the power to decide these questions and how are such decisions actually secured?

If these questions are universal, however, Western Europeans in the High Middle Ages confronted the issues with particular urgency; they had quite specific and compelling reasons to concern themselves with issues of violence and order. How do we know this?

We can be certain of their concerns because they so clearly uttered them and because they effected broad changes in the institutions and ideas by which they lived. Looking at the views of several twelfth-century historical writers can give us an initial sense of this evidence; then, after briefly considering some well-known evidence about social and institutional change, we will turn to the rich field of imaginative literature.[4]

Three Witnesses

The first of our three historians, Orderic Vitalis, though born in England, spent his life as a Norman monk at Saint-Évroul. His wide-ranging chronicle, *The Ecclesiastical History*[5] shows that monastic walls formed no impenetrable

---

[3] Little, 'Pride Goes Before Avarice', 16–49; Southern, *Western Society* .

[4] This is, of course, not the only evidence that could be used. The books of miracle stories of St Benedict which were compiled in the eleventh and twelfth centuries 'are very much concerned with men who appear to be knights and are almost invariably represented as agents of violence': Rollason, 'The Miracles of St Benedict', 82–7. Though the topic is little investigated, Europeans of this period may even have painted their concerns; see Raynaud's study of the portrayal of violence in manuscript illuminations, *La Violence au Moyen Âge*. Canon law also reflects a concern over violence: Gaudemet, 'Les collections canoniques'; Richard M. Fraher, 'Theoretical Justification' and 'Preventing Crime in the High Middle Ages'.

[5] Chibnall, ed., *Ecclesiastical History*. For general discussion of this work in context, see Chibnall's introduction, and her article, 'Feudal Society in Orderic Vitalis'; Holdsworth, 'Ideas and Reality'; Strickland, *War and Chivalry*, especially 12–16.

barrier to a genuine understanding of the outside world or to writing an account of its major features; in roughly 1123–37 Orderic, in fact, wrote one of our most useful accounts of the society taking shape around him.[6] In the sections of his history dealing with northwestern Europe, as opposed to his derivative accounts of the first crusade, Orderic reveals an almost obsessive concern for order and the elusive goal of a more peaceful society. As a monk, he shows a thoroughly professional distaste for sexual laxity in any form, as we might expect; but a more consistent and urgent leitmotiv in his history, highly significant for our purposes, is the need for firm, authoritative action against the violence, disorder, and constant warfare that so characterized his world.[7]

Orderic is no pacifist. Violence in the right cause, carried out by the proper people, can cause him to wax eloquent, as, for example, he does frequently when narrating the crusade.[8] Violence of Christian against Christian troubles him more, but even here he can show approval if the goal and end result seem to be a more orderly society. His language describing even the monastic life can take on the martial tonality not uncommon for religious writers of his time: monks are 'soldiers of Christ' battling demons; they use the 'weapon of prayer'. But looking out over monastic walls at the violence in his own society, he repeatedly laments the impulse to war in such terms as: 'The turbulent are chafed by peace and general tranquillity and, while they attempt to destroy the pride of others, are themselves through God's just judgement very often slain by their own weapons. How blind and foolish are the men who desire war in times of peace.' When a marriage alliance ended one of these local wars, he is relieved 'that multiple crime did not proliferate from the root of evil and put out new and worse shoots continually in future generations'.[9]

He is certain that the cure for such disorder rests with proper authorities who can at least attempt to restrict the practice of major acts of violence to their own capable hands. In an ideal world there would perhaps be no need for violence at all, but in a speech he puts into the mouth of Count Helias at the time Henry I is establishing his rule in Normandy, Orderic says, 'as the popular saying goes, "wrong must be done to put an end to a worse thing." This

---

[6] Chibnall, ed., *Ecclesiastical History*, I, 32. Duby says that Orderic has given us 'du premier XIIe siècle la meilleure vision, sans doute': 'Guerre et société', 474. Orderic comments on the frequent conversations between monks and visiting knights: see, e.g., Chibnall, *Ecclesiastical History*, III, 206–7, and Chibnall's helpful comments in I, 36–8; also see her article, 'Feudal Society in Orderic Vitalis'. Cf. Flori, *L'Essor de chevalerie*, 271–4.

[7] Orderic, for example, praises Henry I to the skies for his role as a provider of peace, despite the king's record number of illegitimate offspring. William Rufus and Robert Curthose, much less successful kings, are scorched by Orderic for their sexual laxity: Chibnall, *Ecclesiastical History*, V, 286–7, 300–1. For general comments on Orderic's concerns, see sources cited in note 5.

[8] See, e.g., ibid., V, 68–9. Examples abound throughout all Orderic's crusade accounts.

[9] E.g. ibid., III, 260–1, 292–3; VI, 328–9; IV, 200–3.

indeed I repeat as a common proverb, I do not claim divine authority for it.'
Orderic imagines his hero Henry I speaking in similar terms: 'I saw with sorrow the affliction of my ancestral inheritance, but could bring no help to the
needy except by force of arms.'[10]

Believing in right order secured, if necessary, by the coercive violence of the
right authorities, Orderic speaks high praise for the stern governance of both
William I and Henry I as dukes of Normandy. A deathbed speech he puts into
the mouth of William the Conqueror has the king confess: 'I was brought up
in arms from childhood, and am deeply stained with all the blood I have shed',
but he pictures the king going on to justify his action on the grounds that his
Norman subjects 'need to be restrained by the severe penalties of law, and
forced by the curb of discipline to keep to the path of justice'.[11] Praising this
firm and just rule of William, Orderic provides at one point a wonderfully concise statement of his belief. The king/duke, he tells us, 'forbade disorders, murder and plunder, restraining the people by arms and the arms by laws'.
Narrating one of William's visit to Normandy, he elaborates on this capsule
assertion of one of his major themes:

At the news of the king's coming peace-lovers everywhere rejoiced, but trouble-makers
and criminals trembled in their evil hearts and quailed before the coming avenger. He
assembled all the nobles of Normandy and Maine and used all his royal powers of per-
suasion to move them to peace and just government.[12]

Vivid accounts of disorder after William's death and again after Henry's death
underscore the importance of authoritative curbs on lordly violence.[13] Orderic
has no kind words for Robert, William's eldest son and heir in Normandy,
who was unable to suppress local warfare and brigandage. In a speech which
Orderic creates for Henry, Robert's brother and supplanter, Henry tells Pope
Calixtus that he actually wrested Normandy not from Robert but from the
robbers and evildoers who effectively controlled it. Orderic's blessing on this
work is clear: Henry has 'calmed the tempests of war by his royal might'.[14]

---

[10] Chibnall, ed., *Ecclesiastical History*, VI, 96–7; ibid., VI, 284–7. Henry continues: 'I did not
wish to refuse my service to holy mother Church, but endeavoured to use the office laid on me by
heaven for the general good. So by taking up arms to fight and spreading fire I . . . recovered the
inheritance of my father . . . and strove to uphold my father's laws according to God's will for the
peace of his people.'

[11] Ibid., IV, 80–1. Compare the deathbed speech of Robert Bruce, thanking God he has been
given time to repent for all of his bloodshed, quoted in McDiarmid and Stevenson, eds, *Barbour's
Bruce*, book XX, ll. 169–81.

[12] Chibnall, *Ecclesiastical History*, IV, 192–3, 284–5.

[13] See the opening of ibid., IV, bk. viii, and ibid., VI, bk. xiii. On Henry's death, Orderic, writing of the local lords, laments 'now they imagine no law will constrain them.' Ibid., VI, 450–3.

[14] Quotation at ibid., IV, 138–9. For his attitude towards Robert and Henry as peacekeepers see
the opening of IV, bk. viii, and VI, bk. xi, passim, especially 32–3, 58–65, 92–3, 98–9, 146–9.

Philip I of France, on the other hand, proved himself unable to restrain 'proud and turbulent men' and so 'allowed his princely power to decline', with the consequence that 'the royal justice had become too lax to punish tyrants'.[15]

The agent of order may be other than a king/duke. Count Geoffrey Martel of Anjou merits Orderic's praise as a punisher of robbers and enforcer of justice; his father, Orderic complains, had by contrast spared such men and shared the loot with them. A ruler at any level, he argues, had to offer God the 'fruit of justice' in order to escape the charge of barren governance. Tyrants, in his view, were thus not hard-driving and efficient kings or dukes but, rather, the feuding local lords who escaped any royal restraints.[16] Robert of Bellême is the classic type; driven from England, he continued his career of disruption and devastation in Normandy. Orderic describes him as

a renowned knight of great enterprise in the field . . . endowed with quick wits and a ready tongue as well as courage; but everything was marred by his excessive pride and cruelty and he hid the talents with which Heaven had endowed him under a sombre mass of evil deeds. He engaged in many wars against his neighbours.[17]

Even Orderic's own monastery found it necessary to pay Robert protection money, as did many other victims, 'for at that time kings and dukes were unable to restrain his ferocity and secure the peace of the Church by any authority of theirs'.[18]

But if Robert of Bellême represents the classic offender, Orderic thinks the violence is endemic within the knightly layers of society. Almost in passing he mentions a Robert of Vitot, knight, who had nearly forty kinsmen, 'all proud of their knightly status, who were continually at war with one another'.[19]

Of course, kings could themselves create disorder through their disputes; then the 'war-shattered people' could only rejoice when the 'long-desired calm serenity of peace' was achieved. Orderic is at one point left marvelling how God 'directs his church amidst the tumults of war and the clash of arms, and preserving and enlarging it in many ways leads it on to safety'.[20] Clearly, the peace of God was something which, in the words of the liturgy, passes human understanding.

---

[15] Ibid., VI, 154–7.   [16] Ibid., VI, 74–5; 86–7; 154–7.

[17] Ibid., 298–9. The parallel to the description of Claudas in the opening of the *Lancelot* is noteworthy: 'Claudas was a king, a very fine knight and clever man, but he was treacherous as well', in Rosenberg, tr., *Lancelot Part I*, 3; Elspeth Kennedy, ed., *Lancelot do Lac*, I, 1.

[18] Chibnall, ed., *Ecclesiastical History*, IV, 298–301. Robert appears prominently in Orderic's book; cf. VI, bk. xi, especially 26–7, 32–3, 58–65. Of Robert, Orderic says, 'he mercilessly sent out his armed bands against all his neighbours and terrorized monks, clerks, and the defenceless populace by his fierce tyranny': IV, bk. viii, 298–9.

[19] Ibid., II, 120–1.   [20] Ibid., II, 288–91; III, 18–19.

Between 1138 and 1145, that is just a few years after Orderic wrote his informative general history, another monk, Suger, Abbot of Saint-Denis just outside Paris, was writing a much more particular but equally informative kind of history, an admiring account of the deeds of King Louis VI of France (Louis le Gros).[21] Abbot Suger was not second to Orderic in his admiration for royal agents of imposed peace, nor in his belief that they might act with force in the interests of order.[22] He praises Orderic's hero Henry I as a man known throughout the world, and pointedly quotes a prophecy of Merlin about the coming of a Lion of Justice; after giving good justice to England as king, he came to Normandy as duke and imposed order there by force. Suger always refers to him approvingly, using some such phrase as 'the illustrious king of the English'. Peacemaking is the great quality in a leader. He even praises Pope Calixtus for the somewhat surprising achievement of clearing brigands out of Italy and Calabria.[23]

But Louis le Gros was his subject as biographer, and it is significant that the king is lauded not only because he is Suger's friend and the benefactor of his monastery, but above all because he was a guarantor of order and, as such, the *imago dei*, the image of God on earth. In fact, Suger tells us, Louis began to play this role even before he came to the throne in 1108 on the death of his father, Philip I, who had been much less active and successful as a promoter of peace and order, a fact noted even by Orderic.[24] Louis, though, as Suger observes approvingly, had always been the proper son and had never brought disorder in the realm 'as is the custom of other young men'.[25] A very great deal of Suger's account in fact consists of colourful vignettes showing Louis, either as prince or as king, moving out into the Île de France (the central royal demesne between Paris and Orleans) to play the policeman, leading his knights and the parish militia against some offending lord, fighting pitched battles, or, more frequently, besieging the castles that served, in Suger's view, as the nodal centre for the spread of the cancer of disorder. Of one of these local strongmen, Eudes, Count of Corbeil, Suger states that his death strengthened the peace of the realm; he then adds, warming to the subject, that Eudes thus transferred his battle to the depths of hell where he could carry on

---

[21] Waquet, *Vie de Louis VI*. In their introduction to their translation, *The Deeds of Louis the Fat*, Cusimano and Moorhead insist, with reason, that this is an account of the deeds of Louis, rather than a biography.

[22] His support for royal peace efforts was not merely chauvinistic. He commended Henry I of England for his judicial organization and could think of him as the Lion of Justice. Ibid., 98–9.

[23] Waquet, *Vie de Louis VI*, 206–7.

[24] Chibnall, ed., *Ecclesiastical History*, VI, 154–7.

[25] Waquet, *Vie de Louis VI*, 82–3. On the turbulence of 'the youth', see Duby, 'Dans la France de Nord-Ouest'.

war eternally.[26] Like Orderic, he reserves the term tyrant for just such terror-izers of some locality, men who 'provoke wars, take pleasure in endless pillage, trouble the poor, destroy churches'; if not restrained, these tyrants would grow more bold still and act 'in the manner of evil spirits'. It pertains to the office of kingship to repress the impudence of tyrants. Against such men, he writes, a king's hand is very strong.[27]

The chief villain in Suger's story is probably Thomas of Marle (though Hugh of Le Puiset runs a close second). Thomas is *homo perditissimus*, a man who, aided by the Devil, devoured the countryside in the region of Laon, Reims, and Amiens 'like a furious wolf', sparing neither clerics out of fear of ecclesiastical sanctions, nor the common folk out of any sentiment for human-ity. Louis moved against him in 1114, backed by the blessing of the Church, which had, under the leadership of a papal legate, declared Thomas excom-municate and unfit to wear the *cingulum militarem*, the belt of knighthood. Seizing the castles of Crécy and Nouvion, Louis 'piously massacred the impi-ous'. Captured at Marle, Thomas offered indemnities to both Church and King, and won a pardon unwisely granted him by Louis. He quickly went back to his old work, requiring a second royal expedition in 1130. By this time the expedition went without the king, since Louis was too fat to mount a horse, but Thomas was again taken, and died in captivity, being at the last, Suger gleefully reports, unable to take the Eucharist.[28]

Thus, however ill Suger's idealized portrait of Louis VI may have matched the imperfect man, the biographer's great concern for order, his worry about grasping strongmen as a source of disorder, and his belief in a royal discipli-nary role are as clearly set forth as Orderic's. The latter would approve Suger's borrowing from Ovid the maxim that kings have long arms.[29]

For a third witness, we can turn to a different sort of historian writing a quite different sort of history. After the murder of Charles the Good, Count of Flanders, in 1127, Galbert of Bruges, a notary (who may have been in minor orders but was apparently not a priest or canon), wrote a strikingly precise and detailed history of events in Bruges and in the surrounding countryside. In *The Murder of Charles the Good (De multro, traditione, et occisione Gloriosi Karoli Comitis Flandriarum)*[30] he narrates the collapse of order, the ensuing, almost

[26] Waquet, *Vie de Louis*, 150–1.
[27] Ibid., 172–3. He later (pp. 232–5) gives the bishop of Clermont a speech accusing the Count of Auvergne of playing the tyrant against him.
[28] Ibid. 30 ff., 174–7.   [29] Ibid., 180–1.
[30] Ross, tr., *Murder of Charles the Good*; her translation is based on the Latin text edited by Pirenne, *Histoire du meurtre de Charles le Bon*, but I will cite Rider, ed., *De multro*. Cf. Nicholas, *Medieval Flanders*, 62–70; Dhondt, 'Les "Solidarités" médiévales'.

universal violence, and the gradual restoration of order. However much his point of view might differ in detail from our monastic writers—he can show a caustic anti-clericalism, for example—his account dovetails with their emphasis on the perils of private war and vengeance, the need for a strong authority figure to repress violence and secure peace.

The murdered Count Charles had been just such a figure. He had taken 'such measures to strengthen the peace, to reaffirm the laws and rights of the realm, [so] that little by little public order was restored . . . everything was flourishing, everything was happy and joyful in the security of peace and justice'. To secure these blessings of peace he had enforced arms legislation, so that his subjects 'should live together in quiet and security without resort to arms; otherwise they would be punished by the very arms they bore'.[31]

The crisis had erupted because of two characteristics of the powerful Erembald clan, the chief plotters of the murder, whose leader, Bertulf, was the count's chief official: they were vulnerable because they were technically of servile status; and they were enthusiastic practitioners of the local violence and warfare Count Charles was committed to stamping out. Galbert tells us that Bertulf had 'armed his kinsmen for strife and discord; and he found enemies for them to fight in order to make it known to everyone that he and his nephews were so powerful and strong that no one in the realm could resist them or prevail against them'. The pillaged country folk (under cover of darkness) appealed to the count, who took vigorous measures, but he was then brutally murdered, on Bertulf's orders, before he could act decisively.[32]

Page after page of Galbert's narrative records the waves and counterwaves of violence that washed over Flanders as contenders fought for the prize of rule, as private quarrels found outlet in the general strife, as merchants were plundered or fled in the nick of time. 'Now in truth,' he lamented, 'the whole land was so torn by dangers, by ravaging, arson, treachery, and deceit that no honest man could live in security.'[33] Like our monastic historians, Galbert is no pacifist, no uncompromising opponent of all violence. Revenge for the murdered count, attacks on his enemies, and, in fact, all violence in a cause he approves receive his full approbation.

Several weeks into his grim story Galbert paused to reflect on the site of the crime, the church of Saint-Donatian. For him it remained a symbol of what the count who had been murdered there had once meant to Flanders:

---

[31] Ross, tr., *Murder*, 82–3; Rider, ed., *De multro*, 5, 7.
[32] Ross, *Murder*, 116, 102–5; Rider, *De multro*, 33, 35; 21–33.
[33] Ross, *Murder*, 291; Rider, *De multro*, 155.

'in the splendor of its beauty like the throne of the realm; in the midst of the fatherland it called for safety and justice everywhere in the land through security and peace, right and laws'.[34]

At the end of his account Galbert is left puzzling over how he might find the dispensation of God in the complex and violent actions of men.

Context: Socio-Economic and Institutional Change

Confidence in the evidence provided by our three witnesses increases when we review two features of the general environment within which they lived and worked. The very pace and consequences of change in the Central Middle Ages forced basic questions about order into the forefront of the thinking and acting of all those in any position of awareness or responsibility, and led to the creation of important institutions. An age vibrant with as much change as noted historians find in these centuries would necessarily devote a good deal of energy to securing order, reducing disruptive violence, and finding ways of resolving disputes. If even calmer times yield such a channelling of energies, the need could only be greater when one social, economic, political, and religious catalyst after another was actively at work speeding the rate of reaction.

The exact measurement of demographic growth (to take an obvious and important example) is likely to continue to elude scholars, but the fact of a significant increase in population commands general agreement.[35] Historians have fought even longer over theories of the nature of urban origins, but the fact of a significant urbanization of Europe in this period stands beyond dispute.[36] That this phenomenon rested on an economic transformation likewise seems established, though the details are again a matter of contention.[37]

By the year 1000, moreover, people over a wide stretch of Europe faced the necessity of political reconstruction almost from the ground up. The order tentatively set in place by the family of Charlemagne had fractured time and again into increasingly localized units, which constituted the only political units retaining anything like effective governing power and what might pass for loyalty or at least acquiescence from those governed.[38] By the age of Orderic, Suger, and Galbert, as we have seen, the work of political

---

[34] Ross, tr., *Murder*, 167; Rider, ed., *De multro*, 86.
[35] Overviews, with many sources cited, in Pounds, *Economic History*, ch. 3, and Fossier, *Enfance de l'Europe*, I, 87–287.
[36] Surveyed in Ennen, *The Medieval Town*.
[37] Duby, *Early Growth of the European Economy*; Fossier, *Enfance de l'Europe*.
[38] Analysis of the scholarship written during the last half century on all aspects of the Carolingian world appears in Sullivan, 'The Carolingian Age'.

reconstruction was well under way in northwestern Europe; in another generation or two it would be considerably advanced.[39]

Growth in political frameworks relied of necessity on supportive public opinion, or at least on the good will of those levels of society whose opinion counted. Measures to secure public order, in other words, could scarcely have been imposed simply from the top down, without the foundation of fairly widespread support, generated by real concern about basic questions of order. Both the reforming Church and the emerging State took on increasingly institutionalized form during the High Middle Ages, and in the process considerably expanded their role as guarantors of acceptable levels of order. Clearly, large numbers of the people whose opinion mattered in this society had some investment in peace and order and often backed institutions of government that might help achieve these goals.[40]

On the early edge of this period the Church, despairing of kings who no longer seemed able to play this role, tried to secure a minimal level of peace through its own councils, generating what historians have long termed the Peace Movement, beginning in the late tenth century.[41]

The movement for reform in the Church which began in the late eleventh century led, among its many significant results, to an increased emphasis on effective papal administration; a growing network of courts and system of appeals brought papal judicial influence across the Alps; the canon law and a framework of ecclesiastical courts grew both in strength and outreach into society; a system of taxation siphoned off some portion of the wealth of field and town to fund—always inadequately though, it seemed to clerical officials—the growth of ecclesiastical administration at all levels. The sheer volume of documentation produced at the centre in Rome, if plotted on a graph, rises inexorably.[42]

At about the same time the growing power of kingship and the equally dramatic extension of its social role have led historians to analyse the medieval origins of the modern state as an outstanding feature of high medieval society.[43]

---

[39] See Hallam, *Capetian France*; Reynolds, *Kingdoms and Communities*; Strayer, *Medieval Origins*; Baldwin, *Philip Augustus*. England, as so often, proves to be a special case, building on Anglo-Saxon foundations: see James Campbell, 'Reflections on the English Government'; Chibnall, *Anglo-Norman England* .

[40] One of the arguments in Kaeuper, *War, Justice, and Public Order*.

[41] Some of the recent scholarship, and the contentions and debates it entails, appear in Head and Landes, eds, *The Peace of God*.

[42] Southern, *Western Society and the Church*; Morris, *The Papal Monarchy*; I. S. Robinson, *The Papacy*; see the graph in Clanchy, *From Memory to Written Record*, 44. The ideological stance of the post-Gregorian ecclesiastical hierarchy with regard to violence, sanctified and otherwise, will concern us later.

[43] See especially Strayer, *Medieval Origins*. Cf. the wide-ranging essays in Gouron and Rigaudiere, eds, *Renaissance du pouvoir legislatif* .

The growth of the English state makes the case most plainly. By their very bulk, increasing year after year, records from the English royal lawcourts preserved in the Public Record Office, London, dramatically document the growth of business; they show us the willingness, even the eagerness, of people to bring their cases before the king's justices, however much they complained about the partiality, delay, and expense that seem the perennial accompaniments of centralized justice in all ages that know them. The 'registers of writs', in which working attorneys and litigious monasteries collected the standard formulas of the royal writs that initiated legal action on the civil side, filled ten or twelve pages with the styles of 50 or 60 writs in the early thirteenth century; they grew to 120 writs by the last quarter of that century and to 890 writs by the first quarter of the following century.[44] On the criminal side, the English crown by the 1170s required local grand juries to name before its circuit justices all those suspected of murder, larceny, harbouring criminals, forgery, and arson. As Alan Harding has cogently argued, the demands of the crown and the press of business thrust by litigants upon these circuit justices across the twelfth and thirteenth centuries finally exhausted the legal work-horse of the general eyre by overuse.[45]

In both England and France litigants could bring a case into a royal court by making the significant charge that an enemy had wronged them by illicit violence: the formula in England stated the wrong was done 'by force and arms and against the king's peace'; one analogous French formula charged the wrongdoer had acted 'by force, violence and by the power of arms'.[46] Royal interest and activity in criminal jurisdiction increased sufficiently in France for the central law court, the *Parlement*, to open a separate criminal register in 1313.[47]

Even the briefest sampling of the evidence, then, shows the concern over disruptive violence and the support which allowed major institutions to increase their roles in an age of widespread growth. In other words, all the evidence we have examined thus far seems congruent: from our three witnesses (and many others we could summon to the stand from the following centuries), from the social and economic setting around them, from the institutions their contemporaries were busily creating.

---

[44] Harding, *Law Courts of Medieval England*, 77.   [45] Ibid, 86–7.
[46] Kaeuper, *War, Justice, and Public Order*, 158, citing sources.
[47] Strayer, *Philip the Fair*, 208–36.

Evidence from Chivalric Literature

One final source of evidence shows perceptions of order and violence: the vast body of chivalric literature.[48] Even a brief, initial sampling can reveal patterns of thought, for these texts drew on the continuous experience of daily life, on collective memories and imagination. Since we can never recover all this particular experience in detail, it is all the more important that we take into account the powerful cumulative traces of experience in literature. Examining this literature puts us in touch with a vast store of relevant human experience; moreover, it obviously attempts to shape attitudes. No simple mirror reflecting society, it is itself an active social force, identifying basic issues, asking probing questions, sometimes suggesting constructive change.

Almost without fail these works give prominence to acts of disruptive violence and problems of control. Complexity characterizes the point of view: even more than in the histories we have already sampled, attitudes about violence come strongly mixed. Belief in the right kind of violence carried out vigorously by the right people is a cornerstone of this literature. Yet aggression and the disruptive potentiality of violence is a serious issue for these writers no less than for the historians. This significant fact has seldom been analysed.

What troubles these writers (echoing our three historians) is not usually violence in the abstract, nor war simply conceived as one sovereign or even one seigneur marshalling his forces against another. Rather, the issue is how to carry on daily living with enough security and peacefulness to make civilized life possible; the world seems almost Hobbesian, with violence carried out on any scale possible to achieve any end desired.

In confronting such issues, a writer sometimes creates an image of unusual power and vividness, conveying across the centuries the elemental fear created by knightly violence. The author of the *Perlesvaus* (written in the early years of the thirteenth century) produces just such an image in the huge knights in black armour who appear more than once in the pages of his romance.[49] We

---

[48] The issues involved in using this literature are discussed in the second section of Chapter 2.

[49] The several quotations that follow come from Bryant, tr., *Perlesvaus*, 144, 176–8, 221; for the original French, see Nitze and Jenkins, eds, *Perlesvaus*, 222–3; 274–8; 344. The earliest appearance of these knights, or some men very much like them, comes near the opening of the romance when King Arthur fights a black knight with a flaming lance at the Chapel of St Augustine. Mysterious knights appear on the scene to hack this knight into fragments after Arthur defeats him; they similarly cut apart one of their company who failed to kill or capture Arthur. This company is not, however, described as being black, nor carrying flaming weaponry. Bryant, *Perlesvaus*, 27–30; Nitze and Jenkins, *Perlesvaus*, 38–40. Black knights on black horses appear again, issuing from the Castle of the Black Hermit, later identified as Hell. Bryant, *Perlesvaus*, 37, 73, Nitze and Jenkins, *Perlesvaus*, 55, 109. The black knights are later identified as spirits of those who died 'sanz repentance' or as 'ungodly demons'. Nitze and Jenkins, *Perlesvaus*, 222, 345.

first see these dread figures through the eyes of Perceval's sister when she comes to the Perilous Cemetery:

As the maiden peered around the graveyard from where she stood among the tombs, she saw that it was surrounded by knights, all black, with burning, flaming lances, and they came at each other with such a din and tumult that it seemed as though the whole forest were crumbling. Many wielded swords as red as flame, and were attacking one another and hewing off hands and feet and noses and heads and faces; the sound of their blows was great indeed.

Later in the story, when Arthur, Lancelot, and Gawain journey on a Grail pilgrimage, they find themselves in the midst of a dense forest without the accommodation that usually appears in such stories as if on cue. After sending a squire up a tree to try to discover some sign of civilized life and hospitality in the engulfing darkness, they move towards an open fire he has sighted in the distance. The fire is burning inexplicably, they find, in the ruined courtyard of a fortified but deserted manor house.

When they send the squire in search of food for the horses, he returns in utter terror, having in the dark stumbled into a chamber filled with fragments of butchered knights' bodies. Suddenly a maiden appears in the courtyard, bearing on her shoulders half a dead man, the latest addition to the grisly collection the squire discovered within. For her sins against knighthood this unfortunate maiden has had to 'carry to that chamber all the knights who were killed in this forest and guard them here at the manor, all alone without company'. She warns the Round Table companions against a fearsome band of knights who will come at night, 'black they are, and foul and terrible, and no-one knows where they come from. They fight one another furiously, and the combat is long.' On her advice, Lancelot draws a circle all around the house with his sword—just in time, for the demon knights

came galloping through the forest, at such a furious speed that it sounded as though the forest were being uprooted. Then they rode into the manor, clutching blazing firebrands which they hurled at one another; into the house they rode, fighting, and made as if to approach the knights, but they could not go near them, and had to aim the firebrands at the king and his company from a distance.

Though the maiden warns Lancelot not to step outside the protective magic of his circle, with characteristic valour he attacks the knights. Inspired by his example, Arthur and Gawain join in; swords swing, sparks and hot coals fly, the evil is defeated. As the swords of the heroes cut through them, 'they screamed like demons and the whole forest resounded, and as they fell to the ground and could endure no more, both they and their horses turned to filth and ashes, and black demons rose from their bodies in the form of crows'.

With hardly a moment's rest Arthur, Lancelot, and Gawain confront another band, 'even blacker men, bearing blazing lances wrapped in flames, and many were carrying the bodies of knights whom they had killed in the forest'. Flinging down the bodies, they demand of the maiden that she deal with them as with all the others. She refuses, declaring her penance done. They attack the three companions, seeking revenge for their defeated fellows and the combat is terrible until a bell (which we later learn is sounded by a hermit saying mass) rings out in the forest and they flee suddenly.

Towards the end of the story, shapes that are apparently these same demon knights put in a final, chilling appearance. Lancelot at the Perilous Chapel 'came to the door of the chapel, and there in the graveyard he thought he saw huge and terrible knights mounted on horseback, ready for combat, and they seemed to be staring at him, watching him'. Though these astonishing and terrifying images could be fitted into the elaborate religious symbolism in this romance (which has generated much interesting scholarship), this imagery works in another dimension as well.[50] The 'dark side of the force' of knighthood (to borrow the familiar language of the popular *Star Wars* films) could scarcely be rendered more powerfully than in the portrayal of these demon knights lurking in the forest shadows or suddenly emerging to hack at each other and at the innocent with their flaming weaponry.[51]

Their appearance in the *Perlesvaus* takes on even more force when we consider that the author seems to be drawing the raw material of his images from a folkloristic tradition known as 'la Mesnie Hellequin', or Herlequin's Hunt, a wild nocturnal ride by a hunting party or armed host across the countryside.[52] The use of such images in this romance calls to mind 'one of the most unforgettable passages in the *Ecclesiastical History*' of Orderic,[53] thus linking, once again, our chronicles with imaginative literary sources.

Orderic tells us the story given to him in person by Walchelin, a priest who claimed to have witnessed the fearful procession on the first night of January

---

[50] See Carman, 'Symbolism of the *Perlesvaus*'; Kelly, *A Structural Study*, 91–194, with many citations to earlier studies. Kelly sees this text as addressed primarily to lay males as an encouragement to them to conduct their chivalry in accordance with divine will. The preoccupation of the text with almost macabre violence and cruelty seems to him a reflection of actual issues in this society (20–3, 95, 158–61, 171–8). Saly, 'Perceval-Perlesvaus', emphasizes the role of lignage and vengeance in Perceval's quest.

[51] Writers on fantasy have noted that accounts like this test social truths and reveal the 'dark side' of the dominant order in society: Jackson, *Fantasy*, 4, 15.

[52] Sainéan, 'La Mesnie Hellequin', shows how widespread the tradition was in medieval Europe, the image of nocturnal army being older, the image of hunt being more widespread; Lot, 'La Mesnie Hellequin'. Both are cited in Chibnall, ed., *Ecclesiastical History*, IV, xxxviii–xl, where she discusses this phenomenon and the available scholarship.

[53] Chibnall, *Ecclesiastical History*, IV, xxxix–xl; the following quotations appear in the text, pp. 236–51.

1091, while returning from a visit to a sick parishioner. Hearing them approach, Walchelin mistook the noise to mean a troublesome contemporary force, the household troops of Robert of Bellême (Orderic's *bête noire*), on their way to the siege of Courcy, and feared being 'shamefully robbed'. His initial fear is useful evidence in itself.

What happened was yet more terrifying, however, for he saw pass before him in the clear moonlight not an army of mortals, but four troops of tormented spirits: first commoners on foot, then women riding sidesaddle, then a great troop of clergy and monks, all groaning under torments. The last troop was 'a great army of knights, in which no colour was visible save blackness and flickering fire. All rode upon huge horses, fully armed as if they were galloping to battle and carrying jet-black standards.' Wanting proof that he had actually seen 'Herlechin's rabble'. Walchelin foolishly tried to seize one of the coal-black horses, which easily galloped off. His yet more foolish second attempt provoked an attack by four of the demon knights. Orderic assures us that he saw the scar on the priest's throat caused by the knight's grasp, 'burning him like fire'. One of the knights proved to be the cleric's dead brother, who spared Walchelin, told him of the torments the ghostly knights suffer, and begged for his priestly prayers as his hope for relief:

I have endured severe punishment for the great sins with which I am heavily burdened. The arms which we bear are red-hot, and offend us with an appalling stench, weighing us down with intolerable weight, and burning with everlasting fire. Up to now I have suffered unspeakable torture from those punishments. But when you were ordained in England and sang your first Mass for the faithful departed your father Ralph escaped from his punishments and my shield, which caused me great pain, fell from me. As you see I still carry this sword, but I look in faith for release from this burden within the year.

Walchelin noticed what seemed to him 'a mass of blood like a human head' around his brother's heels where his knightly spurs would attach. It is not blood, he learns, but fire, burning and weighing down the knight as if he were carrying the Mont Saint-Michel. His brother explains: 'Because I used bright, sharp spurs in my eager haste to shed blood I am justly condemned to carry this enormous load on my heels, which is such an intolerable burden that I cannot convey to anyone the extent of my sufferings.' The knight's message is clear: 'Living men should constantly have these things in mind.' It seems likely that the author of the *Perlesvaus*, a century later, had them much in mind. Both he and Orderic testify vividly to a fear of knightly violence at the deepest level of human psychology.

Another image of similar vividness and power is much better known. The incident of a 'dolorous stroke' with frightful consequences to whole kingdoms appears in more than one romance, often in connection with the theme of wasteland. As portrayed in the story of Balain, contained within the Post-Vulgate *Merlin Continuation* (written probably soon after 1240),[54] the dolorous stroke gives us particularly useful evidence of fears generated by knightly violence and the devastation it caused.

This story is all the more powerful for being a part of a major structural contrast built into this widely read cycle of romances. The contrast is embodied in two knights. Both possess undoubted and praised prowess; but the results of their knighthood could scarcely be more different. Balain, source of misery and misfortune, is set opposite Galahad, bringer of joy and release; the Unfortunate Knight stands on one side, the Good Knight on the other. Balain brings into being the oppressive 'adventures' of the Grail when he wounds King Pellehan; Galahad lifts this curse when he cures him. In a society accustomed to thinking about Fall and Redemption, it seems significant that Balain is compared to Eve, Perceval to Christ.

The story of Balain's misadventures is compelling. Doggedly pursued by an invisible knight who repeatedly kills his companions without warning, Balain finally finds the man in conveniently visible form at the castle where King Pellehan is holding court. Wasting no time, Balain kills his enemy with a sword stroke, splitting the man from his head down through his chest. King Pellehan is even more outraged at this act of vengeance in his court that was Arthur when Balain had similarly killed a lady in his presence. In his hot wrath the king attacks Balain with a great pole and breaks the knight's sword. A wild chase through the castle ensues, with Balain searching in desperation for any weapon to resist the pursuing king.

Disregarding an unearthly voice warning him not to enter so holy a place, Balain rushes into a marvellous and sweet-smelling room containing a silver table upon which stands a gold and silver vessel. A lance suspended miraculously in mid-air, point down, is poised over this vessel. Ignoring another voice of warning, Balain seizes the lance just in time to thrust it through both thighs of King Pellehan, who falls to the floor grievously wounded. Although it first seemed to Balain that this stroke was justified, his monumental error becomes progressively clear. This time, he cannot ignore the voice, which trumpets the following sentence, the entire castle trembling all the while as if the world were coming to an end:

[54] Asher, tr., *Merlin Continuation*, chs 8, 10–13, 16–23; Paris and Uhlric, eds, *Merlin*, I, 212–25, 233–61, 276–80; II, 1–60. For Balain's story in most recent French edition, see Roussineau, ed., *Merlin*, I, 65–111, 129–97. David Campbell has also translated these passages: see *Tale of Balain*.

Now begin the adventures and marvels of the Kingdom of Adventures which will not cease until a high price is paid, for soiled, befouled hands having touched the Holy Lance and wounded the most honored of princes and the High Master will avenge it on those who have not deserved it.[55]

Balain has, of course, seized the sacred lance that pierced the side of Christ, the Lance of Longinus, and has used it against the king into whose care God had entrusted the keeping of the Holy Grail.

What follows may remind modern readers of an atomic bomb explosion, with rings of gradually decreasing devastation. A great part of the castle wall falls; hundreds within the castle die from pure fear; in the surrounding town many die and others are maimed and wounded as houses tumble into rubble; no one dares to enter the castle for several days, as a sense of divine wrath akin to radiation lingers. Merlin finally leads people back into the site, accompanied by a priest wearing 'the armour of Jesus Christ', which alone will guarantee them safe entry. Finding Balain, Merlin leads him out, even providing him with the necessary mount. Everywhere he rides the prospect is cheerless:

As he rode through the land, he found the trees down and broken and grain destroyed and all things laid waste, as if lightning had struck in each place, and unquestionably it had struck in many places, though not everywhere. He found half the people in the villages dead, both bourgeois and knights, and he found laborers dead in the fields. What can I tell you? He found the kingdom of Listinois so totally destroyed that it was later called by everyone the Kingdom of Waste Land and the Kingdom of Strange Land, because everywhere the land had become so strange and wasted.[56]

So powerful and complex an incident as the Dolorous Stroke can only be considered a polyvalent symbol. Yet we can see immediately its significance for our enquiry. A man who is recognized as one of the best knights in the world takes perhaps understandable vengeance for unprovoked attacks. Fleeing for his life, weaponless, he commits the great sin. A knight, whatever his good qualities, has laid profane hands on the weapon that pierced God in the course of divine redemption and has used it in his private quarrel to wound one of his fellow knights and one of God's chosen agents. Devastation, like lightning— like war—blots out or blights the lives of innocent people throughout an entire region. Pure knightly prowess, highly praised at the opening of this story, has produced these stunning results near its close.

Is such evidence representative or merely exceptional? Extensive reading in chivalric literature provides a convincing answer, for these works are filled

---

[55] Asher, tr., *Merlin Continuation*, 212; Bogdanow, *Romance of the Grail*, 246, supplies the passage quoted, on one of the pages of the old French text missing in Paris and Uhlric, eds. *Merlin*, II.

[56] Asher, *Merlin Continuation*, 214; Paris and Uhlric, *Merlin*, II, 30.

with plentiful and consistent evidence along the lines of the passages already noted. As we will see in exploring this literature, almost any text to which we turn shows deep concern over disruptive violence in medieval society.

Conclusion

Medieval writers—historians, authors of vernacular manuals, and creators of the fiction patronized at the most influential levels of society—clearly voiced concerns for order, fears about unrestrained violence, and hopes for some path to improvement. It is important to locate what was the origin, in their view, of the problem of disorder and unfettered force.

Of course, ordinary crimes of the sort to be expected—robbery, assault, and the like—and committed by the most ordinary farmers and carpenters, clearly received much attention in our period; sometimes public outcry or a particularly vigorous lord or lord king generated new measures to stiffen the criminal law to deal with these crimes. Likewise, the seigneurial regime itself produced impositions that might easily lead to fears of popular rebellion, another kind of violence. Sometimes these fears took on frightening reality. As towns increased in size and strength, their demands for a corresponding control over their own governance easily led to urban uprisings, even as the settling of their internal affairs and shifting social and economic hierarchies produced seemingly endless quarrels. Over time the accumulating burdens of governmental taxation, whether royal or regional, would likewise produce fears of popular revolt.

Yet the common concern of our evidence points unmistakably in another direction. What particularly worries all our witnesses is not primarily common or garden crime, not country folk attacking their lordly exploiters, not simply urban unrest, not tax revolt, but the violence of knights. The medieval problem of order took on its particular contours because the lay elite combined autonomy and proud violence in the defence of honour.

Of course the violence of feuding (or 'the peace in the feud', if we choose to look at its ideal benefits)[57] can provide one formula for establishing hierarchy and settling disputes. Yet this pattern, prominent in earlier medieval centuries, was unlikely to continue to satisfy all expectations, especially in an era experiencing as much fundamental growth and change as occurred in Europe in the Central Middle Ages. We will be especially interested in the relationships between this autonomous, violent elite and centralizing authorities, who, on the obvious basis of much popular support, were developing strong views

---

[57] Southall, 'Peace in the Feud'. Many scholars have studied medieval dispute resolution. See, e.g., White, *'Pactum'*; Geary, 'Vivre en conflit'; Davis and Fouracre, eds, *Settlement of Disputes*.

about licit and illicit violence and the authority for setting those categories—
even as they enthusiastically raised banners of war themselves.

As Europeans moved into one of the most significant periods of growth and
change in their early history, they increasingly found the proud, heedless violence of knights, their praise for settling any dispute by force, for acquiring any
desired goal by force on any scale attainable, an intolerable fact of social life.
Such violence and disorder were not easily compatible with other facets of the
civilization they were forming.

We will misunderstand chivalry if we fail to set it squarely in the context of
this knightly violence so evidently in the minds of all our witnesses or if we
miss the linkage of this issue with the broader search for that degree of order
essential to the creation of high medieval society. This context sets the tone,
and, as Maurice Keen has sagely observed, the meaning of chivalry is to a
significant degree tonal.[58] By placing chivalry within this context, we can move
beyond microanalysis, close attention to the evidence of chivalric ideals in the
careers of individual knights, and engage in macroanalysis, considering the
social effects of chivalry and specifically its complex role in public order.

Insisting on the very complexity of that role, this book parts company with
much scholarship that has characterized chivalry in less problematic terms, as
a positive and less ambiguous force for building an ordered society. The following chapters will argue that medieval evidence on chivalry and order is
filled with tension and contradiction. Among its contemporaries, chivalry won
high praise as one of the very pillars of medieval civilization, indeed, of all civilization. At the same time the practitioners of its great virtue, prowess, inspired
fear in the hearts of those committed to certain ideals of order. As they worried about the problem of order in their developing civilization, thoughtful
medieval people argued that chivalry (reformed to their standards) was the
great hope, even as they sensed that unreformed chivalry was somehow the
great cause for fear. How chivalry could be praised to the heavens at the same
time it could be so feared as a dark and sinister force with flaming weaponry
makes a topic worth investigating.

[58] Keen, *Chivalry*, 2.

2

EVIDENCE ON CHIVALRY AND
ITS INTERPRETATION

✦✦✦

OUR investigation can rely in part on the kinds of evidence long used by
historians—chronicles and judicial records, for example. But this book
will draw heavily on the evidence available in the vast body of chivalric literary
texts, a rich source much less frequently (and certainly less comprehensively)
used by historians. It is a species of evidence that can provoke doubts and mis-
givings.[1]

Did Knights Read Romance?

We must first be certain knights actually attended to works of imaginative literature, either by reading or listening.[2] Of the various kinds of writing within
the rubric of chivalric literature only the works traditionally classed as romance
are in question.[3] No one doubts that chivalric biography, *chanson de geste*, and

---

[1] Elspeth Kennedy, 'The Knight as Reader'. See also Duby, preface to Flori, *L'Idéologie du
glaive*. Jacques le Goff, in his introduction to Boutet and Strubel, *Littérature, politique et société*, 18,
argues: '[L]es historiens éprouvent de plus en plus le besoin d'integrer dans leur champ docu-
mentaire le document littéraire et prennent conscience du double caractère de l'oeuvre littéraire, à
la fois comme document spécifique, document de l'imaginaire, et comme document d'histoire
totale, pour peu qu'on sache y démêler les relations compliqués de la société, de la littérature et des
pouvoirs.' As Spiegel writes, 'texts both mirror *and* generate social realities, are constrained by *and*
constitute the social and discursive formations which they may sustain, resist, contest, or seek to
transform': 'History, Historicism', 77. Strohm, discussing problems of reading texts, rightly calls
'literary' and 'historical' texts 'outworn categorization': *Hochon's Arrow*, 3–9. I occasionally use
such terms in this book only as traditional categories.

[2] More may have heard than read. As Asher notes, in the *Merlin Continuation*, 'there are only
two references to reading the story instead of hearing it . . . (273, n. 8).' However, as Clanchy has
demonstrated, lay literacy was much higher than we once thought: *From Memory to Written
Record*. Hindman discusses these issues for Chrétien's romances in *Sealed in Parchment*.

[3] No rigid separation of *chanson* and romance is suggested. Current scholarship blurs older categories of *chanson de geste* and romance, emphasizing rough coincidence in time and space and
increasing broad similarities. Calin provides a good introduction to this theme, with many citations, in *A Muse for Heroes* and in 'Rapport introductif'. Cf. Kibler, 'Chanson d'aventure' and
Maddox, 'Figures romanesques'. Kay argues for essential difference with a dialogic relationship
between genres: *Chansons de Geste*. The relationship of chivalry to growing governmental

vernacular manuals of chivalry were written for knights and read or heard by knights. But what of the extensive body of romance?

As Elspeth Kennedy has shown, knights in the very real world referred frequently and familiarly to these works of literature. A 'two-way traffic' connected these men of war, law, and politics with Arthurian romance no less than *chanson de geste*. Many owned copies of these texts, which seem to have been readily passed from one set of hands to another, often registering considerable wear.[4] Some, such as the father of the famous jurist Philippe de Beaumanoir, even wrote romance themselves.[5] Under Isabella and Mortimer, the English Privy Wardrobe issued works of romance to male and female courtiers alike; Mortimer himself borrowed twenty-three such works and must have sponsored a romance-reading group.[6] Geoffroi de Charny, the leading French knight of the mid-fourteenth century, apparently knew romances like the *Lancelot do Lac* and wrote easily (and disapprovingly) of men who would love Queen Guinevere only if they could boast of it.[7] In addition to borrowing heavily from the imagery of the *Ordene de chevalerie* (*Order of Chivalry*; one of the vernacular manuals for knights), Ramon Llull, the former knight who wrote the most popular book on chivalry in the Middle Ages, likewise drew heavily on thirteenth-century prose romances.[8]

Romance and other categories become indistinguishable in the minds of those who wrote and those who read. The authors of historical works sense no gap between the actions they describe in chronicle or biography and those in imaginative literature; often they stress the links between the types of writing.[9] The author of the Norman-French 'Song of Dermot and the Earl', written around 1200, sometimes says his work is based on a *geste* and refers to it both as *le chansun* and *l'histoire*. He records Maurice FitzGerald defending an Irish king and, like a hero from romance, swearing on his sword that anyone who

---

institutions is especially noticeable in *chansons de geste*. Works traditionally classed as romances focus on a deepening knightly piety which must address the fit of its ideals with those of *clergie*. Yet these themes are far from exclusive and topics inevitably overlap in particular works of chivalric literature. See Chapters 11, 12.

[4] Kelly (*Structural Study*, 20) notes that manuscripts of the *Perlesvaus*, for example, were owned by chivalric figures, not monks. Hindman comments on borrowed and worn manuscripts of Chrétien's romances in *Sealed in Parchment*, 3, 8–9, 46–8.

[5] Gicquel, *'Le Jehan le Blond'*.

[6] Vale, *Edward III*, 49–50; Revard, 'Courtly Romances'.

[7] Kaeuper and Kennedy, *Book of Chivalry*, 118–19.

[8] Elspeth Kennedy, 'Knight as Reader' (typescript kindly provided in advance of publication). An additional example supporting her argument appears in Gutierre Diaz De Gamez, standard-bearer and biographer of Don Pero Niño, who says he has been 'reading . . . many histories of kings and famous knights,' and decides to add the deeds of his master to these accounts of other famous deeds: Evans, tr., *The Unconquered Knight*, 13.

[9] See Keen's useful discussion of the broad question in *Nobles, Knights and Men-at-Arms*, 63–81.

lays a hand on the king would have his head split.[10] John Barbour (d. 1395) terms his chronicle of Robert Bruce a 'romanys'.[11] Both Barbour and Sir Thomas Gray assure us that if all the deeds done in Ireland by Robert's brother Edward Bruce were set down they would make a fine romance.[12] Other active knights shared the sentiment. We even know that Robert Bruce often told 'auld storys' to his men in trying times, to buck them up. During a tedious passage over Loch Lomond, he merrily read out passages from the romance of Fierabras.[13]

Moreover, the very content of the romances leads to the same conclusion. Anyone who has read thousands of pages of chivalric literature knows that either these texts were meant for men as well as women, or that medieval women simply could not get enough of combat and war, of the detailed effects of sword strokes on armour and the human body beneath, of the particulars of tenurial relationships, and of the tactical manouevres that lead to victory. Such evidence suggests that the great body of chivalric literature was aimed at knights even more than at their ladies.[14]

The knights' conduct, of course, also shows that the literature is reaching them, as students of chivalry have shown in case after case.[15] Larry D. Benson's examination of the tournament in the romances of Chrétien de Troyes and in the *Histoire* of William Marshal, for example, concluded that tournament wonderfully illustrates the interplay of life and art—impossible, of course, were knights not deeply steeped in chivalric romance as well as *chanson*.[16]

Knights, in sum, say that they have read this literature, which itself does not distinguish genres closely; they show that they have read it by using it in their

[10] Orpen, ed., tr., *Song of Dermot*, ll. 1065, 1912, 2115–20, 2403.

[11] McDiarmid and Stevenson, eds, *Barbour's Bruce*, bk. I, l. 446.

[12] Maxwell, tr., *Scalacronica*, 57. Gray says Bruce performed there 'feats of arms, inflicting great destruction upon both provender and in other ways, and conquered much territory which would form a romance were it all recounted'. What constitutes proper subject matter for romance is as instructive as the link between romance and history. Barbour says of Edward Bruce, 'off his hey worschip and manheid / Men mycht a myckill romanys mak.' McDiarmid and Stevenson, eds. *Barbour's Bruce*, bk. IX, ll. 496–7.

[13] McDiarmid and Stevenson, eds, *Barbour's Bruce*, bk. IX, ll. 267–70, 405–65. Barbour refers to characters in the 'Romance of Alexander' in bk. III, ll. 72–92.

[14] For the *Perlesvaus*, Kelly reached a similar conclusion: *Structural Study*, 20, 23. As Elspeth Kennedy notes, male interests 'may well have been directed towards different elements within the romance': 'Knight as Reader', 1. Crouch suggests the young William Marshal would have known and perhaps memorized a body of *chanson de geste* and romance. His father was familiar with Geoffrey of Monmouth or one of his imitators: *William Marshal*, 23. Hindman notes that a scene in the romance of *Hunbaut* pictures a group of ten knights and six young ladies listening to the reading of a romance: *Sealed in Parchment*, 86.

[15] Good general accounts in Painter, *French Chivalry* and Keen, *Chivalry*. For specific influences see—in addition to the Benson article cited in fn. 16—three studies by Loomis: 'Arthurian Influence', 'Chivalric and Dramatic Imitations', and 'Edward I'.

[16] Benson, 'The Tournament'. Cf. Barber and Barker, *Tournaments*.

own writings, and they show by their actions that they have read it and are bringing it into their lives.

Is Chivalric Literature Hopelessly Romantic?

Such evidence makes it difficult to dismiss or discount chivalric literature as hopelessly romantic and useless in serious historical enquiry. We cannot expect this literature, or any other, to serve as a simple mirror to social reality in the world in which it emerged. Chivalric literature was an active social force, helping to shape attitudes about basic questions. As such, it has immense usefulness, if read with care.

Above all, we need to remember that these works are, in conscious intent at least, more often prescriptive than descriptive; they advance ideals for what chivalry should become, in other words, more often than they mirror an ideal already transformed into social reality.[17] In *The History of the Holy Grail*, Joseph of Arimathea (considered a great knight of the era of Christ) is ordered by God to sire the son who will continue the line of knightly heroes that will culminate in the perfect knight, Galahad. This son, the text says,

was later such a worthy man that one should certainly recall his deeds and the nobility of his life in the hearing of all worthy men, so that the wicked will abandon their folly and worthy men, who hold the order of chivalry, may better themselves toward the world and God.[18]

The prescriptive impulse of much of this literature could scarcely be stated more openly.

Yet it is often descriptive as well, for the writers of chivalric literature regularly offer up descriptions of actual knightly practices from the world around them. These scenes are either given consciously, to show some behaviour in need of improvement, or unconsciously, while the writer is actually focusing on some other aspect of knightly life and behaviour.

Ordinary practice can always be recovered, if we are prepared to look carefully between lines written either prescriptively or descriptively. Specific critiques are directly revealing; even highly gilded passages of praise are indirectly revealing: we seldom preach virtues to replace non-existent faults. Of course the descriptive and prescriptive often come intertwined, almost sentence by

---

[17] As Barron suggested, 'The paradox of romance in all periods is that it expresses man's need to see life not as it is but as it might be, yet the very formulation of the ideal rests upon his awareness of personal and social imperfections': 'Knighthood on Trial', 103.

[18] Chase, tr., *History of the Holy Grail*, 119; Hucher, ed., *Le Saint Graal*, III, 126–7. Galahad himself is later pictured as listening attentively to the stories told him by a holy hermit about his noble ancestors: see Asher, tr., *Quest*.

sentence. In fact, these categories blur readily into a third, the provocative. Our texts often toss out challenging opinions or incidents bound to spark debate in chamber or hall as more wine is poured and the company settles into a conversation we would give much to hear.[19]

We can, likewise, only regret that no medieval writer went from one castle, tourney field, court, siege camp, battle line, or raiding party to another, observing and interviewing knights of all particular social claims to record their commonplace attitudes and beliefs; with such evidence we could easily differentiate their attitudes in varying degrees from the ideal statements and reform tracts which we possess in abundance.

Lacking such a record, we have no oral history of chivalry, although that is precisely what we want. For most chivalric texts press some ideal about chivalry to the forefront, with bright gold leaf liberally applied to the expressions.[20] Almost unnoticed, our assumption can easily become that this is what chivalry was and how it actually worked in medieval society.

The hard truth is that we must reconstruct the living reality of chivalry from the entire set of texts available: the vast corpus of imaginative chivalric literature, as well as ecclesiastical and lay legislation, legal records, contemporary chronicles, handbooks for knights, the details of chivalric biography. Each piece of evidence we draw into this book will add its witness to our cumulative sense of just what chivalry was and just how knights thought about it. In the process we can gradually reconstruct something like the oral history that we would so much like to have.

Perhaps dazzled by the gold leaf, even the fig leaf of idealization, textbook accounts of chivalry often fail to distinguish between various reform plans and actual practice; taking chivalry at the evaluation of its own idealistic texts, they place perhaps half a dozen ideal qualities for a knight in the spotlight. Anachronistic ideas from post-medieval revivals of chivalry easily creep into the pattern unnoticed. Chivalry thus becomes the composite, enduring ideal represented by courtesy, prowess (easily sanitized as moral courage), largesse, loyalty, 'courtly love', fairness, piety (even 'muscular Christianity'). There is no

---

[19] Scott's paradigm—*Domination*—largely applies to other circumstances; yet his description of a 'public transcript of dominance' fits much chivalric literature. As the 'self-portrait of dominant elites' (p. 18) intended to 'awe and intimidate [subordinates] into a durable and expedient compliance' (p. 67), it is also aimed at 'a kind of self-hypnosis within ruling groups, to buck up their courage, improve their cohesion, display their power, and convince themselves anew of their high moral purpose' (p. 67). The Achilles heel comes from 'critiques within the hegemony' (p. 105) which are hard to deflect because 'they begin by adopting the ideological terms of reference of the elite . . . which now stands accused of hypocrisy if not the violation of a sacred trust' (p. 105).

[20] Morris observes, 'In truth one should think less of a code of chivalry than of conflicting ideals of chivalry': '*Equestris Ordo*', 96.

tension, no contradiction, no sense of any pressing social issues which might have generated criticism and debate in the first place.

This venerable technique cannot be followed if we are to understand the broad societal role chivalry played for centuries. We must identify the major functions of chivalry as a social force, not merely draw up a list of idealized individual qualities, taken largely from works pressing for reforms.

Two straightforward conclusions follow. First, most medieval writing about chivalry will show a tendency to social criticism or even a reformist cast; it will be read more creatively and analytically with this in mind. Second, the direction of much of this writing points us towards the fundamental issue of securing order in society. In other words, if most chivalric literature involves criticism, debate, and reform, much of it was written in the shadow of fears for public order

This is not to suggest that authors of chivalric literature were cheerless critics, taking only the odd, scowling glance out of a study window at actual knighthood—to confirm their dislike—while grinding out works presenting one critique after another. To the contrary, this literature is animated by the diverse energies found in any great literature; every text will celebrate the glories of chivalry and will often overflow with sheer joy and appreciation for the richness, colour, and splendour of chivalric life. In the process, texts instruct knights how to be more suave and urbane, how to play the ideal lover as well as the perfect knight. In fact, they claim that chivalry (if only reformed to their liking) constitutes the very buttress which upholds civilized life.

Yet the steady social criticism, the urging of restraint and reform, can be heard constantly and insistently, despite the variety of other themes—rather like the steady continuo playing behind other instrumental voices in a baroque concerto. This rich and contrapuntal play of praise and critique, hope and fear, emphasizes the powerful tensions as well as the harmonies at work. These tensions give a fascinating complexity to any piece of chivalric literature; the balancing act requires celebration of chivalry as the grand guide to civilized life, while simultaneously pressing with some degree of urgency for the changes that could make chivalry truly that force in the world. These are not purely celebratory or aesthetic works; they do not present merely the splendour of chivalric life as it was, or the diversions of an escapist literature of life as it never could be. These texts spoke to some of the most pressing issues of their day, especially to the issues of social order and knightly violence, to the serious need for chivalric reform in a world much troubled by warlike violence.

We cannot, in other words, take the line that in any problem linking knighthood and order, chivalry was simply the solution. What makes these issues so much more real and infinitely more interesting is that chivalry figures on both sides of the equation of order—both as a part of the problem and as an ideal solution—even if we take chivalry to mean a code, rather than simply certain men or their heroically violent deeds.

The Framework of Institutions and Ideas

If public order is the background issue, what focal points of power and authority should we consider? Analyses of the hierarchical organization of medieval society have focused on the three broad functional categories, the three theoretical 'orders' used by medieval writers themselves: those who pray, those who fight, and those who work. Institutional historians have, of course, emphasized the major governing institutions of Church and State. In trying to understand the basic issues involving order in the sense intended in this book, however, neither of these classic formulations is sufficient.

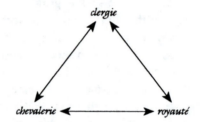

Figure 1. Focal points of power and authority

We must think, instead, of a simple triadic relationship (as illustrated in figure 1). The points on this triangle of relationships are not simply institutions but a rather more complex set of forces: capacities for coercion pure and simple, perhaps, but also ways of looking at the world, means of organizing and justifying a set of answers to the basic questions about order and the conventions or the sheer power and legitimizing authority which might secure it. Gerd Tellenbach's highly useful suggestion that Church reformers of the later eleventh century were seeking to secure 'right order in the world' can, in fact, stand as the goal of each of our focal points of power.[21] This is not to suggest the primacy of abstract conceptions in the minds of those who clustered assertively at each point of our triangle, for if each collectivity of men saw their world ideally organized and run in a particular way, the concomitant fact was their insistence on their own hegemony; to this end they claimed and exercised

---

[21] Tellenbach, *Church, State, and Christian Society.*

specialized functions and elaborated an ideology which spurred and justified their power and responsibility.

Each focal point thus represents through a cluster of enabling powers and ideas, a particular stance regarding the issue of order. Each is distinct, though none stands exclusively, unconnected with the others. In other words, between each pair of focal points (i.e. along each side of the triangle in figure 1) strong bonds of attraction are at work, as well as powerful forces of competition, imitation as well as independence, or even outright opposition.

Clergie indicates the impressive institutional and juridical organization of the Church from the bishop of Rome to the lowliest wearer of the tonsure. It entails the special mediatory relationship of priests, monks, and nuns who stand between God and the mass of humanity, the priests channelling from God the saving means of grace through the sacraments, and all, perhaps especially the regulars, offering up to God especially efficacious prayers about pressing human needs. But *clergie* also entails scholarship, the Latin learning of the schools with all the mysterious and arcane power of books and the resonances from the revered and Latinate world of antiquity.[22] The idea of public order held by these men had been clear for centuries, at least when they thought about conditions within Christendom itself; from the late tenth century clerics had sponsored a peace movement that sought not simply the absence of endless local strife (though it necessarily began thus), but an embodiment of the divine will in a human society animated by harmonious (and hierarchical) social relationships. Organization, a body of special practitioners, special functions, a sphere of ideas glowing with power—all formed part of the world of *clergie*, all contributed to what we will see as its stance regarding proper order.

The second point of the triangle is not so easily labelled. *Royauté* may serve as a term, meaning the emerging lay state with all of its powers, ideology, busy personnel, and important functions in society. These men claimed to secure the peace which represented the divine will for the world by making and

---

[22] The knightly amalgam of awe and suspicion regarding such learning appears regularly in chivalric literature. Marsent and her nuns in *Raoul de Cambrai* try to stop the violence of Raoul by processing outside town walls carrying books, one so venerable it was revered in the age of Solomon. Kay, ed., *Raoul de Cambrai*, 82–3, ll. 1123–32. The power of even Merlin and Morgan le Fay is contained in books. Morgan is at one point termed 'a very good woman clerk': Sommer, ed., *Vulgate Version*, 253, ll. 19–20. Of Gamille, the Saxon Lady of the Rock, it is said, 'with all her books she could make water flow uphill': Carroll, tr., *Lancelot Part II* 236; Micha, ed., *Lancelot*, VIII, 481–2. Sir Kay burns all her books to ashes. The Duke of Cloyes is said to be so old and experienced that 'he had so much knowledge that only a man knowing Latin could have more': Rosenberg, tr., *Lancelot Part III*, 250; Micha, ed., *Lancelot*, I, 79. The lady rescued by Guinglain in *Le Bel Inconnu* had been turned into a serpent by an enchanter who touched her with a book; the text links magic and necromancy with the study of the liberal arts: see Fresco, ed., and Donagher, tr., *Renaut de Bâgé*, ll. 3341, 1931–6, 4933–47.

enforcing laws, by protecting property; in the process, they were beginning to try to secure a working monopoly (or at least a controlling oversight) of licit violence as well as the significant revenues that such powers inevitably entail. They claimed as well that they protected and enabled the practice of true religion as conducted by clerics, whom they cheerfully recognized as legitimate special functionaries. Beyond the borders of the realm their just war would repress wrong as surely as their regular hanging of thieves did at home, one species of violence connected to the other in kind and differing only in scale. These men always successfully claimed divine approval for their role and won enthusiastic clerical approbation for the practical functioning of lay political sovereignty, whatever the current status of the contest between papacy and kingship. In fact, in so far as the first two points of our triangle are grounded in institutions of governance, their shared, even borrowed, features are obvious and need no further comment.

The third point of our triangle must be *chevalerie*, however, and it involves a cluster of a rather different sort. Similarities to the other two clusters exist, of course. Again, we find a collectivity of ideas, a set of special functions, a particular body of practitioners, even a sense of divine approval, in time cautiously recognized by ecclesiastics. Yet *chevalerie* was rooted in different soil, growing not out of the restrained and restraining traditions characteristic of institutions of governance but rather from the ancient social practices and heroic ideals of generations of warriors, fiercely proud of their independence, exulting in their right to violence and in their skill at exercising it.

The chronicler Matthew Paris provides a striking illustration of this independent and martial outlook in an entry for the year 1247. He tells us that the French nobility asserted that their kingdom had been won 'not by the learned written law (*jus scriptum*), nor by the arrogance of clerks, but by the sweat of war'.[23] A British chronicler of the following generation provides an equally vivid vignette. As the English cavalry manouevred at the opening of the battle of Falkirk in 1298, Ralph Bassett, lord of Drayton, told Bishop Bek, who was leading the English right wing: 'It's not for you, bishop, to teach us knights how to fight when you ought to be busy saying mass. Go back to celebrate mass; we shall do all that needs to be done in the way of fighting.'[24]

Of course lawmakers and clerks busily building the institutions of Church and State were neither strangers nor uncompromising opponents of war, even if they did not all personally take the field. Major governing institutions in the

---

[23] Paris, *Chronica Majora*, IV, 593: 'regnum non per jus scriptum, nec per clericorum arrogantiam, sed per sudores bellicos fuerit adquisitum'.

[24] Quoted by Barrow, *Robert Bruce*, 144, from J. de Fordun, *Chronica Gentis Scotorum*, ed. W. F. Skene (Edinburgh, 1871–2), i, 330.

history of Western Europe have always been deeply if ambiguously involved with violence, some forms of which they have legitimized or vigorously practised themselves. But both *clergie* and *royauté* also felt the power of that significant strain in their ideology which stressed peace; it was obviously desirable in the eyes of God; it was no less obviously a congenial compulsion for strong-willed men, whether they were tonsured or carried royal wands of office, to exercise control of the most basic sort, in other words to prohibit illicit violence and to regulate or even practise licit violence themselves. A practice of power rooted in jurisdiction and nourished by revenue was, of course, the very essence of governance. The process would lead vigorous figures from the worlds of both *clergie* and *royauté* to strive, in effect, for the needed reforms which would bring *chevalerie* into consonance with their particular view of right order in the world.

The pattern of interaction is far from simple, however; having established our threefold clusters of men and ideas, we need to remember how porous were the spaces separating them. Churchmen were in theory not only committed to ideas of peace and forgiveness, they were prohibited (again, in theory) from shedding human blood; any coercion requiring this final commitment to force would necessitate cooperation from laymen outside the sphere of *clergie*. Similarly, the upper ranks of royal administrations ran on the skills of not a few clerics willingly serving their kings. These kings, moreover, were knights as well as monarchs, and thus lived, we might almost say, in two worlds. If knights aggressively claimed their own sphere, they were also loyal practitioners of the accepted forms of Christianity, presided over by clerics. They were landlords, busy in the royal courts, as well as warlords. Their service as agents of government and their support of royal governmental efforts for order and the protection of property was real and, in fact, essential for the indisputable growth of the State.

Yet our several focal points with their distinct powers and ways of looking at the world remain. The body of men, practices, and ideals in chivalry was a far from perfect fit with those of the growing institutions. If a vast corpus of literature reflected a fascinating mass of contradictions, attractions, and repulsions where chivalry was concerned, similar ambivalence characterized the relationship of *chevalerie* with *clergie* and *royauté*. In both instances, influential figures struggled to reform chivalry in accordance with their views on right order in the world, secured by the right people.

AFTER he has observed life in Camelot for a time, Mark Twain's Connecticut Yankee delivers an unforgettable judgement, etched in an acidic cynicism that seems to scorch the page: 'I will say this much for the nobility; that, tyrannical, murderous, rapacious and morally rotten as they were, they were deeply and enthusiastically religious.'[1] Although Twain has once again dipped his pen in vitriol to write these lines, his comment (with the sting neutralized to the taste of the individual reader) still has point. We need not, of course, accept his moral condemnation to be intrigued by the ambiguities and potential conflicts in the meaning of religion for the practitioners of prowess.

At first glance the complexity of the bond between religion and the chivalric layers of society may surprise some modern observers. Then or now, it would be comforting to believe that the chivalrous were all truly motivated by religious ideas and that they felt, in a way akin to modern conscience, deeply spiritual impulses. It would be at least clarifyingly simple to believe, to the contrary, that their religion was only a form, that it was no structural component of their lives, that there could have been absolutely no connection between their religion and their life of arms.

What Twain suggests, however sharp and malicious his juxtapositions, is a close connection that requires further thought. A way of life devoted in no small measure to showy acts of bloody violence was combined with an obvious, even ostentatious practice of religion. The modern, hopeful, supposition might be that the latter impulse would cancel the former, but here they are, side by side.

Moreover, the tension doubles when we shift our focus from the knights to the clerics. The view of knightly ideals and practices from the vantage point of *clergie* could only be ambivalent. Clerics knew without doubt that they had to deal with knights as a fact of social life; they relied on knightly benefactions no less than they needed knightly sword blows against the constant menace of pagans; in general, they blessed the legitimate use of force by the knights

---

[1] *A Connecticut Yankee*, 82. Modern historians can also write fairly biting comments along these lines. Emma Mason says: 'In crude terms, they tried to buy off the consequences of their aggression by offering a share of the loot to those whose prayers would hopefully resolve their dilemma. Such a naive attitude cannot, however, be contrasted with any superior spirituality of the cloister, for religious houses were all too ready to cooperate in this cycle': 'Timeo Barones', 67.

acting to preserve order and property. The problem, of course, was that the knights often acted and sometimes thought in ways that made them a part of the problem of order, rather than its solution.

These are the issues explored in Part Two. Chapter 3 examines the tension between an undoubted knightly piety and the considerable force of knightly independence. Chapter 4 looks at chivalry through clerical eyes, documenting both the high praise for ideals of behaviour and the sour condemnation of much that knights said and did in the world.

3

KNIGHTS AND PIETY

✦✦✦

Lay Piety, Lay Independence

In so many ways the chivalric layers of society thought and acted as conventionally pious Christians; they followed the set course for life, from baptism at the church font to the final rites and prayers as their bodies were lowered into sanctified ground. Along the way, cellular acts of piety structured the religious component of their daily lives: they heard mass, they made confession, they said prayers, they gave alms. Many reinforced this lifelong cycle by some major act, going on crusade or founding a religious house. Many, likewise, sought the surety of a religious order as intimations of mortality came forcibly into their consciousness.[1]

Chivalric literature portrayed and reinforced this orthodoxy. It reminded the knights of the undeniable function of priests in the sacramental system of which they were willing, prudent participants. A layman, even a knight, needed priests as conduits for divine grace, especially at critical, liminal points in life. Knights in this literature regularly state their fear of dying without confession.[2]

In Chrétien's *Perceval* one key injunction the hero hears from his mother as he starts out into the world is to go to church or chapel to hear mass regularly.[3] Galahad, as readers of *The Quest of the Holy Grail* learned, 'always chafed if a day passed without his hearing the holy office'.[4] Lancelot in the *Mort Artu* regularly hears mass and says the proper prayers 'as a Christian knight should'; he confesses to an archbishop before his single combat with Gawain.[5] Balain and

---

[1] Chibnall, ed., tr., *Ecclesiastical History*, provides abundant examples. Cf. the excellent article by Harper-Bill, 'Piety of the Anglo-Norman Knightly Class'.

[2] E.g., Carroll, tr., *Lancelot Part II*, 219; Sommer, ed., *Vulgate Version*, III, 396; one of many examples in this text. In the *Lancelot*, Arthur himself, thinking that he is about to die, cries out, 'Oh, God! Confession! The time has come!': Rosenberg, tr., *Lancelot Part III*, 276; Sommer, ed., *Vulgate Version*, IV, 76.

[3] Bryant, tr., *Perceval*, 7; Roach, ed., *Roman de Perceval*, ll. 568–94.

[4] Matarasso, tr., *Quest*, 72; Sommer, ed., *Vulgate Version*, VI, 34.

[5] Cable, tr., *Death of King Arthur*, 32, 178; Frappier, ed., *La Mort*, 12.

his brother, dying tragically from their mutually inflicted wounds, take the sacrament and beg Christ for forgiveness of their sins 'they received their rites, such as Christian knights should have, and . . . asked forgiveness of their Saviour for their sins and misdeeds'.[6] Gautier similarly visits a church to pray before his single combat in *Raoul de Cambrai*, though in this case the author tarnishes the bright ideal image with a realistic comment: on this occasion there was no joking, nothing omitted.[7] In their battlefield prayers, knights themselves (William and Vivian, for example, in the cycle of William of Orange) present mini-sermons complete with summations of basic Christian dogma, or they listen to similar sermons preached to them by clerics, as do the knights of the *Chanson d'Aspremont*.[8]

In fact, in our literary evidence knights seem to swim in a sea of piety, using religious language even in situations that strike modern sensibilities as purely secular. 'In God's name, I am called the marquis William', announces William of Orange to his opponent in *The Crowning of Louis*.[9] 'In God's name, I think you will find him the most comely and well-made youth you have ever seen', Sir Yvain says to the queen, speaking of Lancelot in the *Lancelot do Lac*.[10] King Louis solemnizes over relics his obligations to give Raoul a fief;[11] William of Orange swears over relics to protect King Louis;[12] all knights swear constantly by some favourite saint, or by the relics in some church near at hand; Roland and Ganelon carry weapons bearing sacred relics within their hilts; Gawain, in *The Marvels of Rigomer* has the names of the Trinity inscribed on his sword blade.[13]

The great waves which well up from this sea of piety are not lacking in chivalric literature. Girart founds a monastery for three hundred monks in the *Chanson d'Aspremont*.[14] Of course, crusade features so largely in chivalric literature, especially in works traditionally classed as epic, as almost to defy illustration.

---

[6] Asher, tr., 'Merlin Continuation', 221; Paris and Ulrich, eds, *Merlin*, II, 56.

[7] Kay, ed., tr., *Raoul de Cambrai*, laisse 201.

[8] Muir, tr., *Song of William*; McMillan, ed., *La Chanson de Guillaume*, laisses 67–8; Hoggan, tr., *Crowning of Louis*; Langlois, ed., *Couronnement de Louis*, laisse 22. For basic doctrine in both prayers and sermons, see Newth, ed., tr., *Song of Aspremont* and Brandin, ed., *Chanson d'Aspremont*, laisses 28–9, 118, 235, 385. The hermits in *The Quest of the Holy Grail* sermonize the knights at regular intervals.

[9] Hoggan, *Crowning of Louis*; Langlois, *Couronnement de Louis*, I, laisse 22.

[10] Corley, tr., *Lancelot of the Lake*, 70; Elspeth Kennedy, ed., *Lancelot do Lac*, I, 156.

[11] Kay, *Raoul de Cambrai*, laisse 35.

[12] Hoggan, *Crowning*, Langlois, *Couronnement de Louis*, II, laisse 13.

[13] Brault, ed., tr., *Chanson de Roland*, laisses 46, 173; Vesce, ed., tr., *Marvels of Rigomer*, 275; Foerster, ed., *Mervelles de Rigomer*, ll. 12910–14. The use of relics is not merely a literary conceit. As late as the Tudor period, kings and knights kept pieces of the skull, joints, and bones of St George in their armour and their chapels. See Gunn, 'Chivalry', 110.

[14] Laisse 508, in Brandin, *Chanson d'Aspremont*, and Newth, *Song of Aspremont*.

Imaginative literature is supported by more traditional historical sources. The chivalric example *par excellence* in the late twelfth century, William Marshal went on pilgrimage to Cologne, fought as a crusader, founded a religious house, and died in the robe of a Templar, having made provision to be received into the order years before. His biographer records William's belief that all his knightly achievement was the personal gift of God.[15]

Geoffroi de Charny (more than a century later) similarly went on crusade, and founded a religious house. Through a sheaf of papal licences, granted in response to his requests, we can sense his piety no less than his influence: he had the right to a portable altar, the right to receive from his confessor a plenary indulgence when facing death, the right to hear a first mass of the day before sunrise, the right to have a family cemetery alongside the church he founded.[16] As readers of his *Book of Chivalry*, we know in detail how thoroughly he agreed with William Marshal's belief in God as the fountainhead of all chivalric honour. Charny sets out this formula time and again. A healthy mixture of fear and gratitude can be the only proper response on the part of knights. Charny, in fact, almost floats in pieties on the pages of his book.[17]

Marshal and Charny were model knights, however, and not simply model Christians. In company with all knights, they lived by the sword, and the founder of their religion had said some troubling words about such lives. Their violent vocation necessarily shaped their practice of religion: their piety scarcely could be that of merchants or craftsmen. The tension between the ideal standards of their Christianity and the daily practice of violence brings us back to the issues raised by Twain's harsh dichotomies.

In fact, the knightly solution seems clear and characteristic: they largely appropriated religion; they absorbed such ideas as were broadly compatible with the virtual worship of prowess and with the high sense of their own divinely approved status and mission; they likewise downplayed or simply ignored most strictures that were not compatible with their sense of honour and entitlement.

This seeming paradox in fact formed one of the structural features of chivalric ideology and a great source of its strength. For in one of its essential dimensions chivalry rested on the very fusion of prowess and piety; it functioned as the male, aristocratic form of lay piety; it was itself, in other words, an embodiment of the religious force that worked so powerfully to shape society, at least from the twelfth century. The worship of the demigod prowess—with all the ideas and practices of the quasi-religion of honour—was merged with medieval Christianity. If sometimes the yawning gap separating the two

---

[15] Meyer, ed., *Histoire*, ll. 6171–92, 7274–87, 9285–90, 18216–406.
[16] Kaeuper and Kennedy, *Book of Chivalry*, 38–9. [17] Ibid., passim.

systems of belief stimulated inspired writing (as in *The Quest of the Holy Grail*, or *Sir Gawain and the Green Knight*), more often the gap was simply, willfully, not seen. In a prologue to his translation of Christine de Pisan's *Epistle of Othea* (*c.* 1440), Stephen Scrope assured Sir John Fastolf that God 'ys souuerayn cheyveten and knyght off all cheualrie'. Having spent most of his life in 'dedys of cheualrie and actis of armis', Fastolf should now turn to 'gostly cheuallrie' to prepare himself for 'the ordre of knyghthode that schal perpetuelly endure and encrese in joye and worship endlese'.[18] The key trait of knightly prowess wins divine approbation; disloyalty and anything leading to dishonour becomes sin, a moral and not merely a social blunder.

Earning honour by prowess appears throughout most chivalric literature as complementary to the worship of God. Approval for prowess—at least for prowess in the right causes—comes not only from humans but descends from highest heaven. In fact, God opens wide the doors of paradise for his brave knights. Geoffroi de Charny cannot often enough or forcefully enough preach that prowess, like all good things, comes as a gift of God, that the Lord will welcome his good knights, those who use this great gift well, into paradise.[19] By the time he wrote, in the mid-fourteenth century, the theme had been well developed. Promises of heavenly reward for crusaders punctuate both *chansons de geste* and historical accounts of crusade preaching. This valorization, as we will see, gradually became a blessing on all of knightly life.

The approbation of God appears time and again. Early in *The History of the Holy Grail* Seraphe (though he is still a pagan) receives the gift of great prowess from God. Fighting against the enemies of the early Christians, 'no feat of arms could be compared to his prowess, performed with his hands, for he held a marvellously strong and sharp battle-axe in both hands'. Using this weapon, 'he cut strong shields, sliced thick hauberks, cleaved helmets and visors; he slashed feet, legs and arms; chests, heads, ribs and thighs; he bathed his battle-axe up to the shaft in the blood of men and horses.' Seraphe hero-ically keeps up the work even after he is unhorsed and trampled by two hun-dred horsemen. Christ himself, acting through the White Knight, supplies him with a new and even more efficient axe. As the White Knight announces, hand-ing it over, 'Here, Seraphe, this is sent to you by the True Crucified One.'[20] If God supplies the weapons, he can also direct the blows. In the *Didot Perceval* Arthur splits the Roman emperor down to the waist with a great sword stroke delivered 'with the aid of God'.[21]

[18] Bühler, ed., *Epistle of Othea*, 121–4.   [19] Kaeuper and Kennedy, *Book of Chivalry*, 132–3.
[20] Chase, tr., *History of the Holy Grail*, 36–41. The White Knight himself, of course, performs marvellous 'feats of arms and chivalry': p. 41; see also Sommer, ed., *Vulgate Version*, I, 56–65.
[21] Skells, tr., *Perceval in Prose*, 88; William Roach, ed., *The Didot Perceval*, 271.

The Almighty is pictured as a fine judge as well as a general approver of prowess. The Ship of Faith that he sends to the three companions in *The Quest of the Holy Grail* carries a sword reserved for the knight with the greatest prowess; its blade bears the daunting message, written appropriately in blood-red letters, 'that none should be so bold as to draw the sword unless he was to strike better and more boldly than anyone else'. The penalty for a failed attempt is injury or death.[22] However much we spiritualize such a symbol, we must stop to consider its message at the most apparent level: God provides a test for determining the best knight, that is, the one with the greatest prowess, the divine gift to knighthood.[23]

God, as he appears in chivalric literature, likes knightly doing and daring, even if reformers were careful to picture him on their side. For his worthy knights, moreover, God supplies opportunities. Divine power holding the sunlight to give Charlemagne light for his bloody revenge after the death of Roland is only the most well-known case in point.[24] Finding a beautiful glade, early in the *Perlesvaus*, Perceval's immediate, almost reflexive thought is that 'two knights could joust well and handsomely on that ground'. He prays to God: 'in your gentleness [let a knight appear] with whom I can test whether there is strength or valour or chivalry in me.' God sends one of the best, in fact, for Lancelot appears and the two nearly kill one another, though in 'the great rage that they bore each other and the great ardour of their will . . . they were hardly aware of their wounds'. Providentially, a hermit appears to end this conflict of uncle and nephew who, as always in such fights, recognize each other only after the combat has ended.[25]

Divine approval of prowess is often conveyed by saints or angels. Gabriel appears in *Roland*, for example, not only to carry away Roland's soul to its well-earned rest, but to urge on Charlemagne when his prowess slips a bit in hand-to-hand combat with the pagan Amiral. Dazed, his skull creased by a mighty sword blow, Charles hears Gabriel, standing like a coach by his side, demand, ' "Great King, what are you doing?" ' Charlemagne quickly recovers and spills his opponent's brains.[26] The Virgin Mary retrieves Rainouart's great

---

[22] Chase, tr., *History of the Holy Grail*, 77–8, 83; Sommer, ed., *Vulgate Version*, VI, 121–4, 133–4. This is King David's sword, put on the marvellous ship by King Solomon. Divine power later wounds Nascien for drawing the sword unworthily. Chase, ibid., 97; Sommer, ibid., 163. Cf Matarasso, tr., *Quest*, 212–20; Pauphilet, ed., *Queste*, 200–8. The scabbard also bears a warning that 'He who wears me shall do greater deeds than any other', before it continues with a concise sermon on chastity.

[23] For symbolic interpretations, see Matarasso, *Redemption of Chivalry*, 65–7. Obviously, no unbelievers need apply; yet within the subset of the elect, the test involves prowess as well as piety.

[24] See Brault, ed., tr. *Chanson de Roland*, laisse 176.

[25] Bryant, tr., *Perlesvaus*, 92–3; Nitze and Jenkins, eds, *Perlesvaus*, 139–42.

[26] Brault, *Chanson de Roland*, laise 261.

cudgel for him on a battlefield in the *Chanson de Guillaume*, when he has unfortunately left it behind.[27] In one popular story, the Virgin even jousted for a knight who missed a tournament because of his devotions to her.[28] The military saints similarly do more than approve or enable the warriors, of course: both chronicle and *chanson de geste* depict them joining in the fight.[29]

Such an accommodation of the Christian God within the ideas of knighthood thus provides a third crucial element in the tough metallic alloy of chivalry, adding strength to further fusions we will explore in detail later: prowess alloyed with honour (secured with the catalyst of loyalty), with high status, and with love; knights conceived of chivalry as a practised form of religion, not merely as knighthood with a little pious and restraining overlay. Through the practice of chivalry, the heroic life and ideals, which carried a strong sense of independent moral standards, combined with selected principles of medieval Christianity; through chivalric ideas and practices, warriors fused their violent way of life and their dominance in society with the will of God.

Moreover, there was another benefit to the bargain, powerfully present even if seldom stated explicitly. Knights know that God will understand and forgive the slips that mar their moral scorecards, especially since the very toughness of their lives functions as a form of penance.

This knightly belief appears classically in Gawain's attitude on the Grail quest; Malory tells us Gawain heard more about his sins (especially his killings) from a hermit-confessor than he wanted, and so hurried off, using the excuse that his companion, Sir Ector, was waiting for him. He had already explained to the hermit that he could accept no penance: 'I may do no penaunce, for we knyghtes adventures many tymes suffir grete woo and payne.'[30] The tendency, then, was for knights to believe that they had a private arrangement with the Lord God (not dissimilar from that with the lord king): their hard lives, bravely chosen and followed through all hardships, all but provided penance enough for their inevitable sins. A hermit who hears Gaheriet's confession in the *Merlin Continuation*, for example, 'gave him such penance as he thought he could do along with his labour at arms'.[31]

This attitude is resisted in the thirteenth-century *Quest of the Holy Grail*, probably because it was common. Malory seems much more comfortable with

---

[27] Muir, tr., *Song of William*, McMillan, ed., *Chanson de Guillaume*, laisse 160. Archbishop Turpin rebukes the Virgin (in the Middle English *Sege of Melayne*) when she allows Roland to be temporarily defeated; see the lines quoted in Gist, *Love and War*, 140.

[28] Story cited in Keen, *Chivalry*, 98.

[29] See, e.g., Newth, ed., tr., *Song of Aspremont*, and Brandin, ed. *Chanson d'Aspremont*, laisses 425–6, for military saints helping out on the battlefield.

[30] Vinaver, ed., *Malory. Works*, 535, 563.

[31] Asher, tr., *Merlin Continuation (end)*, 46; Sommer, ed., *Zeitschrift für Romanische Philologie*, 121.

the idea of a bargain between God and merely 'earthly chivalry' than with the insistence on 'heavenly chivalry' in the *Quest*.[32] Geoffroi de Charny, too, would have at least understood Gawain, for all the piety he wrote into his *Book of Chivalry*, for all the reverence of the clergy he insisted upon in its pages.

Knightly lay piety, in short, involved an appreciable degree of practical lay independence; chivalry took on the valorizing mantle of religion without fully accepting the directive role claimed by ecclesiastics; it virtually absorbed religion for its own purposes, in no small measure on its own terms. Knights did not simply and obediently bow before clerical authority and, bereft of any ideas of their own, absorb the lessons and patterns for their lives urged by their brothers, sisters, and cousins bearing tonsures and veils. Knights thought they had an understanding with God, a contract which finally bypassed the troublesome clerics, even while paradoxically acknowledging their essential sacerdotal role.

The particular nature of their piety, then, and the way in which it combined their power in the world with the valorization of other-worldly approval helps explain the strength of chivalry. Admittedly, some men in any age seem to need no justification beyond the imperious surge of their own will; but perhaps most men in most ages act more confidently when they can feel that what they want to do is not so distant from what they should do. Such reassurance in chivalry came largely from the knightly appropriation of religion; chivalric piety acted not simply as a force in opposition to main currents of knightly life, but in consonance with them.

The appropriation shows up clearly in historical texts such as biographies and chronicles, and not merely in those relating crusading history. In the *Song of Dermot and the Earl*, a chronicle of the late twelfth-century English invasion of Ireland, the English leader more than once urges his knights to sally forth 'in the name of the Almighty Father'. The poet himself tells us that as the knights rush into battle from a coastal fort they are sent by 'the good Jesus'. Miles de Cogan calls upon them in another fight (in words that could be borrowed from the *Song of Roland*) to 'Strike, in the name of the Cross! / Strike, barons nor delay at all, / In the name of Jesus the son of Mary!' His countryman Raymond le Gros often invoked St David in his very martial speeches.[33]

This language can be heard century after century. Froissart says the English launched their crossing of the Somme, in the campaign leading to the field at Crécy (1346), invoking 'the name of God and St George.'[34] The Black Prince,

---

[32] See Vinaver's comments in *Malory. Works*, 758–60.

[33] Orpen, ed., tr., *The Song of Dermot*, ll. 1443, 1471, 1883–4, 1924–6, 1937–40. When a cowled monk kills an Irish lord with an arrow, the man is much praised: see ll. 2005–10.

[34] Brereton, tr., *Froissart*, 60.

before his great battle at Najera (1367), uttered an equally revealing prayer, with clasped hands raised to heaven:

True, sovereign Father, who hast made and created us, as truly as Thou dost know that I am not come here save for the maintenance of right, and for prowess and nobility which urge and incite me to gain a life of honour, I beseech Thee that Thou wilt this day guard me and my men.[35]

God, the author of prowess and honour, is expected to understand.

The strong element of lay independence in chivalry appears most blatantly in blistering anticlericalism. Sometimes the imagined attacks even go beyond the verbal to become directly physical.[36] In *The Coronation of Louis*, for example, a cleric tells William that some of his fellow clerics are involved in a plot against the young king Louis. This loyal informer suggests that William behead them, despite their order, and for his part offers to take upon himself the sin of desecrating the Church in this way. 'Blessed be the hour that such a cleric was nurtured', William replies in wonder and gratitude, though he finally decides on a lesser sacrilege: he will simply beat the tonsured traitors and toss them out of the building, commending them to eighty devils.[37]

If the abuse directed at clerics in chivalric literature is more often verbal, it is no less informative. Denunciation of priests as greedy and lecherous is standard practice, but the interesting broader goal in chivalric literature is to demonstrate the equality or even superiority of the loyal and necessary knightly function in society. Chrétien has Gawain say:

> . . . a man can give good advice to another
> who cannot heed advice himself,
> just like those preachers
> who are sinful lechers,
> but who teach and preach the good
> that they have no intention of practising themselves![38]

Rainouart in *Aliscans* tells William, who has just forcibly conquered countless pagans, that he converts so well he should be a cleric; the knife slips in soon, however, for he then describes their soft and dissolute life in terms that bring general laughter.[39] The biography of William Marshal refers pointedly to those standard figures of anticlerical satire, Saints Alfinus and Rubinus (i.e. Blessed Silver and Gold), and says that they are much honoured at the papal court.[40]

[35] Pope and Lodge, eds., *The Black Prince*, ll 3172–83.
[36] Noble provides a highly useful sampling of anti-clerical sentiments in a number of *chansons*: 'Anti-Clericalism', 150–8.
[37] Hoggan, tr., 'Crowning of Louis', 35–7; Langlois, ed., *Couronnement de Louis*, 53–6.
[38] Kibler, ed., tr., *Yvain*, ll. 2537–43.
[39] Ferrante, ed., tr., *Guillaume d'Orange*, 274; Wienbeck *et al.*, eds. *Aliscans*, 505.

The author of the *Song of Roland*, after gazing in wondering admiration at the feats of the knight/archbishop Turpin on the battlefield, asks, rhetorically, 'Where is the priest who drove his body to do such mighty deeds?'[41] The question would appeal to Geoffroi de Charny, who would make the same point in only slightly altered form several centuries later. Comparing the ease of a priestly career with the rigours of the knightly life, Charny notes that the clerics 'are spared the physical danger and the strenuous efforts of going out onto the field of battle to take up arms, and are also spared the threat of death'.[42] The author of *Roland* was even more explicit in his answer, however, and he presents Archbishop Turpin himself to state the case. Asking what a knight is worth who is not strong and fierce in battle, he answers his own question unambiguously, 'not . . . four pennies . . . / Instead he should be in one of those monasteries / Praying all the time for our sins.'[43]

At one point William of Orange similarly and pointedly reminds King Louis that the French thought he was of little worth and wanted to make him a cleric.[44] In another text in the same cycle William tells Louis, who has failed to take up his father's offer of the crown with vigor, that he might as well be a monk.[45] On the arrival of Enide's father for her wedding to Erec, Chrétien assures his audience that the bride's father 'did not have a troop of chaplains / or of silly or gaping folk, / but of good knights.'[46] Never trust a priest except at confession time, says the author of the *Chanson d'Aspremont*.[47] The statement has the ring of a popular maxim.

Chivalric Mythology

Yet the religious strength of chivalry is best seen in the steady confidence expressed in the inherent value of the knightly life rather than in the cut and thrust of anticlericalism. In its sacred mythology chivalry is older than the clerical hierarchy, having emerged in the age and circle of Christ. The element of independence is obvious, as is the associative piety and valorization drawn

[40] Meyer, ed., *Histoire*, ll. 11354 ff.
[41] Brault, ed., tr., *Chanson de Roland* ll. 1606–7. Similar comparisons of the chivalric and monastic life appear in *Moniage du Guillaume*, quoted and discussed in Subrenat, 'Moines mesquins'.
[42] Kaeuper and Kennedy, *Book of Chivalry*, 166–7.
[43] Brault, *Chanson de Roland*, ll. 1876–82. For similarly anti-clerical remarks from Turpin, see Newth, ed., tr., *Song of Aspremont*, 9–10, and Brandin, ed., *Chanson d'Aspremont*, laisse 15.
[44] Price, tr., *The Waggon-Train*, 64; McMillan, ed., *Charroi de Nîmes*, 66. The French text says they wanted to make him 'clers ou abé ou prestres'.
[45] Hoggan, tr., 'Crowning of Louis', 3; Langlois, ed., *Couronnement de Louis*, 4.
[46] Carroll, ed., tr., *Erec*, l. 6530.
[47] Newth, *Song of Aspremont* and Brandin, *Chanson d'Aspremont*, laisse 87.

from links with priestly mythology—correlations and allusions, similarities in typologies.[48]

These links appear vividly in stories about Perceval, Galahad, and the Grail. The blood lines of Perceval and Galahad go back to that great knight Joseph of Arimathea, who cared for the entombment of that most precious relic in the world, the body of Christ, and who cared as well for that most famous sacerdotal object, the Holy Grail. In fact, in the loose and allusive way in which these romances so often suggest parallels with sacred mythology, Perceval and Galahad recall the functions of Christ himself, or at least those of his functions which would appeal most readily to knights. They spread true faith and conquer the forces of evil.

These are knights for whom God performs miracles. Towards the end of the *Quest* Galahad brings healing to a man lame for ten years.[49] Even Lancelot's blood performs, if not quite a miracle, a marvellous cure when it restores Agravain in the *Lancelot do Lac*.[50] In Malory's *Mort Darthur* Lancelot heals the grievously wounded Sir Urré by a laying-on of hands.[51]

Earlier, rough-hewn examples stand behind these Christ-like scenes. The retired William of Orange has learned from his abbot that he must not fight with weapons, but only with flesh and blood. Confronted by robbers in a forest, he rips a leg off a packhorse and uses it as a club. Feeling pity for the packhorse after the fact, he replaces the leg and prays; the horse becomes whole again.[52]

An atmosphere of at least pious power thus hangs over these knights. The result is reverence. In the *Lancelot*, at a time when Lancelot is thought to have perished, his battered shield is kept in the centre of a courtyard, with crowds of ladies, maidens, and knights dancing round it; 'and every time the knights or ladies came to face it, they would bow before it as before a holy relic'.[53] Again, in the *Mort Artu*, Lancelot's shield becomes an object of veneration. Sent to the cathedral in Camelot before he leaves Logres, it soon hangs by a silver chain in the middle of the church where it is 'honoured as if it had been a holy relic' by the populace which flocks to see it. The value of this evidence

---

[48] Ecclesiastics must have felt deep ambiguity about the independent directions knightly piety could take, an uneasiness similar to the reception clerics gave mysticism, which also claimed authentic religious inspiration irritatingly free from direct clerical control. Burns comments on clerical opposition to stories about Lancelot and the Grail in Lacy, ed., *Lancelot-Grail*, I, xxx.

[49] Matarasso, tr., *Quest*, 281; Pauphilet, ed., *Queste*, 275–6.

[50] Corley, tr., *Lancelot of the Lake*, 370; Elspeth Kennedy, ed., *Lancelot do Lac*, I, 539.

[51] Vinaver, ed., *Malory. Works*, 663–71.

[52] Ferrante, ed., tr., *Guillaume d'Orange* and Cloetta, ed., *Deux Redactions*, laisse 25.

[53] Rosenberg, tr., *Lancelot Part III*, 326; Sommer, ed., *Vulgate Version*, IV, 144. Characteristically, a quarrel over its possession leads to a fight, which brings to mind the fights that broke out over the possession of relics.

increases when we realize that some battered shields and banners from the very real world hung in churches in memory of knights who carried them.[54]

The knights themselves can receive such veneration. After Galescalin has freed the castle of Pintadol, in the *Lancelot*, he is greeted 'with the greatest possible joy' by a thankful crowd. 'And as he passed in front of them, they all fell to their knees as if before an altar.'[55] Those freed by Lancelot's splendid success at Escalon the Dark, in the same romance, welcome him 'as joyously as they would have hailed God himself'.[56]

The same could be said of the Grail, which (whatever Chrétien de Troyes intended), later writers identify with the platter that served Christ's Passover lamb, the vessel for the wine, or the vessel that received his blood; they likewise identify the bleeding lance with the lance of Longinus which pierced Christ's side as he hung on the cross. In other words, the objective of this imagined knightly questing is nothing less than attainment of Eucharistic or mystical union with the divine; the knights strive to come to the Lord's table, there to feed on the bread of heaven dispensed by Christ himself.

This quest and union are effected by the knights and their God, with only minimal sacramental mediation by priests. As we will see shortly, hermits stand like signposts on the way, pointing questing knights in the right directions, spiritually as well as spacially. But in the final moments a few elect knights who have earned the apotheosis meet God and commune with him in a blaze of light.

We have been prepared for this moment by the unmistakable lay Pentecosts and Grail appearances in *The History of the Holy Grail* and especially in *The Quest of the Holy Grail*.[57] In the latter text, at dinner on the feast of Pentecost, 'After they had eaten the first course, an extraordinary event took place; all the doors and windows of the palace closed by themselves, without anyone touching them. However, the room was not darkened.' A venerable man in white appears, leading into the company of veteran knights a young knight dressed in red and white, the colours of Christ. 'Peace be with you', is his greeting. The

[54] Cable, tr., *Death of King Arthur*, 152–3; Frappier, ed., *La Mort*, 162. Joinville hung his crusading uncle's shield in his chapel, with a tablet of explanation: Shaw, tr., *Joinville and Villehardouin*, 18. Coss notes that 'English churches seem to have been literally festooned with armorial glass and depictions of donors': *The Knight*, 89. Ayton cites banners deposited in churches, in addition to representations in windows, altar cloths, and the like: Ayton and Price, eds., *Medieval Military Revolution*, 87. The practice is illustrated inversely in the five hundred pairs of gilded spurs Froissart says the Flemings hung in the church of Notre Dame of Courtrai, having taken them from dead French knights on the field of battle outside that city in 1302: see Brereton, tr., *Froissart*, 251.

[55] Rosenberg, tr., *Lancelot Part III*, 294; Micha, ed., *Lancelot*, I, 227. Holdsworth cites a case from life: 'Ideas and Reality', 76.

[56] Rosenberg, *Lancelot Part III*, 303; Micha, *Lancelot*, I, 265.

[57] Chase, tr., *History of the Holy Grail*, 23; Hucher, ed., *Saint Graal*, II, 168–72.

young newcomer soon establishes his unique status by taking the Perilous Seat at the Round Table (doom for anyone else), by drawing the sword from the stone floating in the river beside the palace, and by defeating all comers in a celebratory tournament. At the end of the day, announced by a thunderclap and illuminated by intense rays of light, the Grail appears and provides each knight with his most desired food. The knights swear to quest for the Holy Grail.[58]

Medieval Christians would not miss the parallel between this scene in chivalric myth and scenes from sacred history—a blending of the first appearance of the risen Christ to the disciples in the upper room with the original Pentecost, when the Holy Spirit came in a rushing wind to the apostles in a closed room, to set them on their great mission in the world. Christ's colours were red and white; his greeting in the upper room was 'Peace be with you'. In fact, the author later makes the parallelism explicit, more than once. Perceval's aunt, a pious recluse, draws the connections for him point by point.[59]

Near the end of the romance another lay Pentecost combines with a remarkable Eucharist. Galahad, Perceval, and Bors, the three elite companions on the quest (soon joined somewhat awkwardly by nine knights to make up the required apostolic twelve), are seated in the castle of Corbenic. The sky darkens, the stormy wind makes a great hot rush through the hall and the Grail appears. The companions, 'their faces wet with tears of awe and love', see Christ appear from the Grail, miraculously to offer them the heavenly food of his own body. They soon hear the voice of the Lord telling them:

you resemble my apostles. For just as they ate with me at the Last Supper, now you will eat with me now at the table of the Holy Grail. . . . Just as I dispersed them throughout the world to preach the true law, so too will I disperse your group, some here, others there.[60]

Religious valorization of this intensity comes from texts which walk the border—only as thick as a penstroke—between the pious and the unthinkable. The essential actors in this drama are God and his knights. Christ himself participates not only as sacrifice but as officiating agent, assisted by Josephus who dramatically descends into the scene from heaven, seated on a throne carried by four angels. This son of Joseph of Arimathea is here called (in full disregard of sacred priestly history) the first bishop. Josephus conducts at least the consecration of the host (drawn from the Grail) into which Christ descends from above in the form of a shining child who becomes a mature human form.

---

[58] Burns, tr., *Quest*, 5–8; Matarasso, tr., *Quest*, 36–45; Sommer, ed., *Vulgate Version*, VI, 7–14.
[59] Ibid., 36–7; 100–1; 56–7. [60] Ibid., 84–5; 273–7; 189–91.

Josephus places this consecrated host in the Grail, kisses Galahad, and vanishes. Christ himself emerges from the Grail to give each knight present 'his Saviour'.

Lay independence hovers about this wondrous scene. If a quasi-priest officiates here, he is surely an unusual specimen. He has, for one thing, been dead for three centuries, as the marvelling knights recognize when he descends from heaven. Moreover an inscription on his brow informs the knights that he was 'consecrated by our Lord in Sarras, in the spiritual palace'. Josephus is decidedly not one of the clerics recognized by the priestly tradition in which the authority of God came to Peter and subsequently, by the laying on of hands, to each bishop and priest across the centuries. Even if he descends clothed in bishops robes, holding a crozier, wearing a mitre, Josephus is a figure created by knightly lay piety to begin a ritual which ends with the appearance of Christ to feed his best knights with his own body from his own hands.[61]

The Quest of the Holy Grail is far from a simple valorization of knighthood, whatever the striking parallels with sacred myth it creates for chivalry. Yet the degree to which such a work praised an idealized knighthood is fascinating and informative. Powerful ideas crackled like high voltage alternating current along lines connecting *chevalerie* and *clergie*. If, as we will see, the pattern proposed for knighthood in a text like this soared beyond actual knights, the sacralization of their idealized work, replete with concessions to their sense of independence, remains important.[62]

Knights and Hermits

The spectacular Grail scene at Corbenic is a culminating experience, the apotheosis of an imagined spiritual quest. Lay assertion of independence from clerical authority appears much more regularly in the prominence of hermits in all chivalric literature, particularly in the romances. Hermits are clearly the chivalric cleric of choice. In the forests which are the setting for adventure, hermits seem to have established their dwellings at convenient intervals of one day's ride in order to accommodate knights errant who lodge with them regularly. They are figures of wisdom as well as keepers of plain hostelries for the

---

[61] For the consecration of Josephus, see Chase, tr., *History of the Holy Grail*, 25–8; Sommer, ed., *Vulgate Version* I, 30–6. Here, Josephus is termed 'sovereign bishop' over his sheep, is dressed in all the 'things a bishop should have', is attended by angels, and is anointed and consecrated by God 'in the way a bishop should be'. He wears a mitre, holds a crozier, has a ring on his hand. He performs the first mass. Later he ordains priests and bishops. Chase, ibid., 49; Sommer, ibid., 78.

[62] Clerical ideas of reform are discussed in Chapter 4, further discussion of the *The Quest* appears in Chapter 12.

chivalrous; a knight can find an explanation for his recent adventures or his troublesome dreams and a sure guide for his future conduct, as well as a bed, and at least barley bread and water.

Hermits are ubiquitous in chivalric literature. A hermit starts Yvain on his road to recovery after madness in Chrétien's *Yvain*;[63] another speaks the key advice to Perceval on Good Friday in his *Perceval*.[64] Scores of hermits nourish and direct the knights throughout *The Quest of the Holy Grail*. In fact, hermits will play a key religious role in romance for the next several centuries.[65] And not only in romance. The spoken advice that becomes Llull's important manual on chivalry, we must remember, likewise comes from an old hermit who is instructing a candidate for knighthood. The chronicler Orderic Vitalis pictures a hermit foreseeing the future at the request of Queen Matilda, consort of William the Conqueror. His elaborate vision could come from the pages of *The Quest*.[66]

To realize why this knightly preference for hermits is significant to the lay piety of chivalry we need to understand the kind of figure hermits represent. Two key facts seem to stand at the heart of an answer. First, both as we find them in medieval society and as they were represented in chivalric literature, hermits were closely integrated with the world around them; they were part of lay society. In England hermits were sometimes expected to take on such mundane functions as hospitality, chapel tending, work on roads and bridges, as well as the spiritual counselling and advice to laypeople we might expect.[67] In literature they appear as especially attuned and sympathetic to knighthood, and often have come from the same social milieu as knights, indeed have often been knights themselves until age and waning capacity closed a chivalric career.

A second characteristic is of equal importance. Hermits were, in Angus Kennedy's words, 'not opposed to but rather on the outskirts of the ecclesiastical hierarchy proper'.[68] The combination is perfect for making them ideal purveyors of religion to the practitioners of chivalry. With thoughts of lay independence and suspicions of clerical aggrandizement in their heads, knights could readily appreciate the somewhat marginal position of pious hermits within the ranks of the clergy.[69]

---

[63] Kibler, ed., tr., *Yvain*, ll. 2831–90.

[64] Bryant, tr., *Perceval*, 67–70; Roach, ed., *Perceval*, ll. 6217–517. The didactic role plays on unabated through the continuations to this latter romance.

[65] Angus Kennedy provides an especially helpful overview: 'The Hermit's Role'. Cf. Frappier, 'Le Graal'.

[66] Chibnall ed., tr., *Ecclesiastical History*, III, 104–9.

[67] Ann Warren, 'Self-Exclusion and Outsidership in Medieval Society: The English Medieval Hermit', paper read at the University of Rochester, 1991.

[68] Angus Kennedy, 'The Hermit's Role', 83.

[69] If Henrietta Leyser is correct, the hermits in the world at the time chivalric romances were being written were already forming institutions and had moved some distance from the more solitary life pictured in these texts: see *Hermits and the New Monasticism*.

Benedictine monks and some clerics understandably took offence at the hermits' claims and their criticisms of older monastic forms; they sometimes directed sarcastic attacks at what they considered anarchic, orderless, headless (i.e. leaderless) hermits.[70] Their scorn and criticism, of course, make the same point as the knightly endorsement, from an opposing direction: these men are outsiders, not fully citizens of the world of *clergie*. Not all hermits were, in fact, priests, and even those who were priests seemed more engaged in the life of the laity and less entrenched in *clergie* than their fellows in monastery, parish church, or episcopal court. As Jean Becquet wrote, if Western eremiticism was clearly clerical, it was also lay, finding its recruits among laymen as well as monastics, and combining them in 'a perfect symbiosis'. He notes that the master of one of the prominent eremitical orders in mid-twelfth-century France, the order of Grandmont, was Pierre Bernard, a former knight who had only recently become a priest.[71] Some scholars are not sure that all hermits had even received the licence from the bishop theoretically necessary for entering the eremitical life.[72]

In fact, there is always a faint scent of the protest movement lingering about hermits. Jean Leclercq notes that in the eleventh and twelfth century they represented something of a movement or reaction, especially against contemporary monasticism; Angus Kennedy argues that by the fourteenth century hermits in literary works took on the role of critics of the Church of their day.[73] In short, hermits combined a maximum of recognized piety and involvement in the life of the laity with a minimal possession or exercise of ecclesiastical authority; to this potent brew they added a dash of criticism of the church establishment.

Their undoubted piety was buttressed by the asceticism that always registered as authentic piety in medieval consciousness. This very asceticism showed the heroic character of the hermits, a quality which, of course, struck a responsive chord in knights; each group undertook its characteristic adventures and put the body in peril for a higher goal. Knightly recognition and approval of this asceticism appears regularly in chivalric literature. A hermit in the *Perlesvaus*, we learn, has not stepped outside his hermitage for forty years.[74] Llull's hermit patently shows his holy life in his worn clothing, worn body,

---

[70] See the examples in Leclercq, 'Le poème de Payen Bolotin'; this article discusses and prints a twelfth-century satire directed against hermits. See also Flori, *L'Essor de chevalerie*, 262–3, citing Geroh of Reichersberg.

[71] Becquet, 'L'Érémitisme'.

[72] G. G. Meersseman, commenting on Becquet's paper in *L'Eremitismo in Occidente*, 207; Becquet's agreement appears at ibid., 209.

[73] Ibid., 210, 594; Angus Kennedy, 'The Hermit's Role', 76–82.

[74] Bryant, tr., *Perlesvaus*, 75; Nitze and Jenkins, eds, *Perlesvaus*, 112.

many tears. In the 'first Continuation' of the *Perceval*, a hermit keeps a vow of silence through each night, visited by a helpful angel.[75] Ascetic discipline wins for the hermits particularly clear and direct channels to God and his angels. Through this efficient access to divine power hermits can foretell the future, explain the past, heal the injured.[76] The *Mort Artu* even explains Gawain's mysterious increase of prowess at noon by the fact of his baptism by a holy hermit at that hour.[77] In the *Perlesvaus*, Lancelot receives from a hermit the tempting offer to take upon himself Lancelot's sin with the queen. The gesture is noble, but Lancelot declines, confident that God will understand.[78]

Such powers are all the more attractive to knights when the hermits have actually known the chivalric life and come from the proper social class. The continuation of Chrétien's *Perceval* by Gerbert shows us a band of twelve hermits led by a hermit king, all former knights.[79] Lancelot and Yvain stop at a hermitage in the *Lancelot* and find 'two good men, one who was a priest and another who had been a knight and was the uncle of the two knights' guide'.[80] The hermit who gives Lancelot useful information early in the *Lancelot* 'was very old and had been a knight, one of the handsomest in the world. He had turned to religion in his prime, when he had lost within one year all twelve of his sons.'[81] A hermit in the *Perlesvaus* had been a knight in King Uther's household for forty years and then a hermit for another thirty years.[82] Time and again romance authors show us hermits who have long been knights and who can thus speak to other knights on a level plane of social equality and shared vocation.[83] A hermit whom Yvain meets (in the *Lancelot*) had been a knight errant even before Arthur was crowned: 'And I'd have been a member of the Round Table, but I refused to join because of a knight member for whom I bore a mortal hatred, and whose arms I later cut off. So after he was crowned, King Arthur disinherited me.'[84]

One hermit after another is presented as a former knight. In the *Lancelot do Lac*, to pick an example almost at random, we meet a hermit who had in his previous profession been one of the finest knights in the world.[85] The hermits

---

[75] 'first Continuation' in Bryant, *Perceval*, 152.
[76] Many examples in Angus Kennedy, 'Portrayal of the Hermit-Saint'.
[77] Cable, tr., *Death of King Arthur*, 181; Frappier, ed., *La Mort*, 173. Cf. the highly effective prayers of Perceval's hermit uncle in Roach, ed., *Didot Perceval*, 180.
[78] Bryant, tr., *Perlesvaus*, 110–11; Nitze and Jenkins, eds, *Perlesvaus*, 168.
[79] Bryant, *Perceval*, 239–43; Williams and Oswald, eds, *Gerbert de Montreuil*, I, ll. 8906–10153.
[80] Rosenberg, tr., *Lancelot Part III*, 301; Sommer, ed., *Vulgate Version*, IV, 110.
[81] Rosenberg, *Lancelot Part III*, 86; Sommer, *Vulgate Version*, III, 163.
[82] Bryant, *Perlesvaus*, 41; Nitze and Jenkins, *Perlesvaus*, I, 60–1.
[83] Many examples in Angus Kennedy, 'Portrayal of the Hermit-Saint'.
[84] Kibler, tr., *Lancelot Part V*, 174; Micha, ed., *Lancelot*, IV, 248.
[85] Corley, tr., *Lancelot of the Lake*, 139; Elspeth Kennedy, *Lancelot do Lac*, 209.

who are so thick on the ground in *The Quest of the Holy Grail* likewise prove often to have been knights; the hermit who hears Lancelot's confession in this text at least has a brother who is a knight and who can be called upon for the essential horse and armour Lancelot has lost.[86] In the *Perlesvaus* a hermit does one better and keeps a stable of warhorses ready for use by worthy knights in need; this is the sort of cleric a chivalrous audience could really appreciate.[87]

Some of the hermits never quite block out the trumpet calls of their former calling. One who keeps arms to fight against robbers and villains appears in the *Perlesvaus* and later in that romance hermits enthusiastically join with Perceval in battle.[88] It is more common, of course, for hermits to consider that warfare continues in their new lives but takes a different form; in singing their masses, they are often said to wear 'the armor of Our Lord'.[89]

The link becomes even stronger when we note how many heroes themselves end their lives as hermits. Perceval becomes a hermit at the end of *The Quest of the Holy Grail*; Lancelot, Bleoberis, Girflet, Hector (as well as the Archbishop of Canterbury) are all hermits in the closing pages of the *Mort Artu* and, again, in Malory's great book.[90] William of Orange, who has retired from knighthood to become a rather unhappy monk in *William in the Monastery*, hears the voice of God telling him in a dream to leave that community and become a hermit.[91]

Some hermits even reverse the usual pattern and turn to the greatest knights for advice or even spiritual intercession. In the *Perlesvaus*, for example, a hermit takes counsel of Perceval because of his good life, and another asks Galahad (in *The Quest of the Holy Grail*) to intercede with God for him.[92] The projection of knightly lay independence in chivalric literature could scarcely be clearer.

Did this portrayal of hermits and the elaboration of mythology and learning really mean anything to a knight setting out on a countryside campaign or

[86] Knights become hermits, see Matarasso, tr., *Quest*, 138, 209; Sommer, ed., *Vulgate Version*, VI, 86, 142; the hermit's brother and Lancelot's equipment, see Matarasso, ibid., 94; Sommer, ibid., 51.

[87] Bryant, tr., *Perlesvaus*, 236; Nitze and Jenkins, eds, *Perlesvaus*, I, 367. The *Post-Vulgate Quest for the Holy Grail* notes that in the good old days the kingdom was full of hermits, many of them former knights. The custom was to bear arms for thirty or forty years and then go off into mountainous solitude where they 'performed pennance for their sins and sensuality': Asher, tr., *Quest*, 177; Bogdanow, ed., *Version Post-Vulgate*, 302.

[88] Bryant, *Perlesvaus*, 108, 168–71; Nitze and Jenkins, *Perlesvaus*, I, 164–5, 262–8.

[89] e.g. Matarasso, *Quest*, 86, 103; Sommer, *Vulgate Version*, VI, 45, 59.

[90] Matarasso, *Quest*, 284; Sommer, *Vulgate Version*, 198–9; Cable, tr., *Death of King Arthur*, 226, 231–2; Frappier, ed., *La Mort*, 227, 232–5; Vinaver, ed., *Malory. Works*, 722.

[91] Ferrante, ed., tr., *Guillaume d'Orange*, 304–5; Cloetta, ed., *Deux redactions*, laisse 30.

[92] Bryant, *Perlesvaus*, 264; Nitze and Jenkins, *Perlesvaus*, I, 407 ; Matarasso, *Quest*, 256; Sommer, *Vulgate Version*, VI, 176. A priest asks Bors for his prayers when the knight comes before the Holy Grail and an abbot also asks for his prayers. Matarasso, ibid., 180, 199; Sommer, ibid., 120, 134.

even on a crusade? Would any particular knight care about an some imagined hermit's advice, about Joseph of Arimathea, the shield of Lancelot, or the miracles of Galahad?

Knights need not have been primarily men of ideals to have ideals that mattered to them. If chivalric literature presents critiques and hopes for the reform of chivalry, it also reveals a good deal of the basic religious attitudes commonly held by knights. Their piety may have been thoroughly formal and from a modern, ideal perspective may look distressingly devoid of deep spirituality; but it need not have been less real for all that, nor less a guide to their conduct. These attitudes constitute a form of lay piety that was eminently practical. The knights wanted to be pious, orthodox Christians; they also insisted on a valorization of their profession of arms which would link them, finally, with divine order. Ideas that carried such weight mattered to them.

4

CLERGIE, CHEVALERIE, AND REFORM

✦✦✦

SHEER necessity as well as intellectual heritage gave the medieval Church a tradition of ideas which opposed some but not all violence. The very survival of Christian society was no mere abstraction for people with vivid memories of the break-up of the Carolingian order, if not of the break-up of the parent order of Rome. Continuing might of Islam, made so painfully evident in the Holy Land, brought their memories and fears quite up to date.[1] Even within Christendom none could doubt that the evils inherent in an imperfect world would require the use of armed force in their solution, as they always had.[2]

These ever-present problems were redoubled by the interlocking set of changes taking place so rapidly and to such significant effect in high medieval Europe. All three apexes of our triangle of power relationships, *clergie, royauté*, and *chevalerie*, were by the late eleventh and twelfth centuries coming into full vigour and were taking on sharper intellectual focus. The Church was confronted by the rise of knighthood, the emergence of a parent form of the Western European State, and new socio-economic, urban, demographic patterns in society (as noted in Chapter 1). Finding the right role for violence in general and for knighthood in particular thus gave churchmen sleepless nights.

The context within which clerical ideas on violence took shape may thus be as important as the ideas themselves, considered in the abstract. Despite the intellectual precedents available, the actual situation in the world of the late eleventh century seems dramatically new. The great heritage from the patristic and Carolingian past, even Augustine's ideas on just war, would have to find

---

[1] Pagans of some sort frequently appear as the threat in *chansons* and even in works more traditionally classed as romance.

[2] The ultimate statement came from Honoré Bonet: '[I]t is no great marvel if in this world there arise wars and battles, since they existed first in Heaven.' He has in mind the rebel angels who fought against God: see Coupland, ed., tr., *Tree of Battles*, 81. Bonet later notes (pp. 118–19) that the world can never be at peace, since conflict is built into heavenly bodies, animals, and humans, and argues that even if evil is done in war it is not in itself evil 'but is good and virtuous' (p. 125).

their proper fit in this brave new world of papal power, crusade, and canon law. From this complex mix of theological ideas with the exigencies of socio-political change emerged a range of ideologies with high praise for an ideal knighthood at one end, bitter denunciation of the evils of knighthood at the other.

If over time more and more influential voices added their significant opinion at the positive end of the scale, clerical views on chivalry were always reform views, constantly mixing praise and denunciation to produce a society in which the Church could live, and an armed force with which the Church could work. With their bookish love of wordplay, the clerics perfectly captured the stark endpoints on the scale of their thought by using two terms of opposite tenor, differing in only one letter. Was chivalry, they liked to ask, the ideal service of God—*militia*—or was it simply badness—*malitia*?

Clerical Praise for Knightly Militia

After the Gregorian Reform, led by a vigorous line of eleventh-century popes, had notionally drawn the world of *clergie* out of the somewhat smothering embrace of secular society, papal reformers found themselves confronted by issues of violence in all of their starkness. Could the leadership of the Church coerce enemies who opposed its realization of the will of God? Could the pope, only now achieving effective authority even within the Church, declare and direct war? Should churchmen personally bear arms in good causes? If they could not participate directly, how could ecclesiastical leadership guide the coercive power and violence of laymen?

Scholars generally hold that the Gregorians wrought significant changes in ecclesiastical views on such questions; many even consider the reformers' views, in particular those of Leo IX (1049–54) and Gregory VII (1073–85), truly revolutionary in their willingness to consider violence and warfare in a good cause not merely regrettable but even praiseworthy.[3] Peter Damian and Cardinal Humbert, chief counsellors of Gregory VII, argued against the use of force even in defence of the faith or in the struggle with heretics.

Yet if both points of view continued to find defenders, Gregory is commonly considered the principal single architect of subsequent medieval Christian ideas of holy war. If soldier-saints had been canonized in earlier

---

[3] As Brundage notes: 'The really radical change in papal policy toward warfare . . . occurred during the reign of that most warlike of pontiffs, pope Gregory VII. . . . It has been argued, with considerable justice, that Gregory VII revolutionized the Christian view of warfare and that he was the principal inventor of the holy war idea in medieval Christendom': 'Holy War', 104. Cf. Erdmann, *Crusade*; I. S. Robinson, 'Gregory VII'; Cowdrey, 'Genesis of the Crusades'.

times, this was usually despite their military calling; significantly, Gregory considered some contemporary knights, such as Erlembald of Milan ('martyred' in the very physical struggle against clergy who resisted papal reform measures), to be virtual saints because of their warring for right order in the world. His letters crackle with martial terminology: 'the warfare of Christ', 'the service of St Peter', 'the vassals of St Peter'. His enemies—St Peter's enemies, God's enemies—have to be resisted, 'even to blood'.[4]

At one point he chastised Abbot Hugh of Cluny for having dragged, or at least received, Duke Hugh of Burgundy into the peace of the Cluniac order; the abbot should rather, the pope wrote, have permitted the duke to remain in the world to carry out his much-needed service of another sort, the legitimate military function of a layman.[5] At least briefly he tried to enlist the knighthood of Europe in a grandiose campaign to overawe the old Norman enemies of the papacy in Italy and then to march off triumphantly to Eastern lands. There they could aid the Christians in Constantinople against the unbelievers and, in the process, enforce Roman supremacy over the Eastern church.[6]

Even before his calls to arms in the famous struggle with the Emperor Henry IV, calls which a hostile archbishop characterized as declaring war against the whole world,[7] Gregory VII found his enemies accusing him of unheard-of uses of force. The accusations could only increase during that struggle. The antipope Wibert of Ravenna, who pictured Gregory standing abashed at the Last Judgement asked, rhetorically, what defence he could give 'when the blood of the many slaughtered cries out against him, "Avenge our blood, O Lord!" ' Reporting the accusations circulating against Gregory, Wenrich of Trier wrote to the pope:

They declare that . . . you incite to bloodshed secular men seeking pardon for their sins; that murder, for whatever reason it is committed, is of small account; that the property of St Peter must be defended by force; and to whomsoever dies in this defence you promise freedom from all his sins, and you will render account for any man who does not fear to kill a Christian in Christ's name.[8]

One of these critics, Sigebert of Gembloux, presented the anti-Gregorian position with even greater succinctness in a sharp rhetorical thrust:

---

[4] On military saints, see Cowdrey, 'Genesis of the Crusades', 20. I. S. Robinson comments on Gregory's military imagery: 'Gregory VII', 177. Brooke notes that ' "[b]lood" was a word often on his lips': *Medieval Church and Society*, 62.

[5] Letter quoted in I. S. Robinson, 'Gregory VII', 190.

[6] Cowdrey, 'Gregory VII's Crusading Plans', 27–40; I. S. Robinson, 'Gregory VII'.

[7] Quoted in I. S. Robinson, 'Gregory VII', 174.

[8] Ibid., 180, 183. For a general discussion, with many citations, see Erdmann, *Crusade*, 229–68.

[W]here does it come from, this novel authority by which sinners are offered freedom from punishment for sins which they have committed, and licence to commit fresh ones, without confession and penance? What a window of wickedness you have thus opened up to mankind![9]

Gregory and his supporters would, of course, deny and counter such charges, but another feature of their ideology would have brought no denials from their lips or pens. They pressed forward an effort to disarm the clergy as a complement to directing the armed might of knighthood. The clerics might rightly direct righteous war; they were not to participate, sword in hand.

Legislation in councils striving to reform the Church often aimed to take weapons from the sacred hands of clerics no less than to remove women from their eager arms. Apparently the former effort was much more successful than the latter. In his account of the beginnings of the Gregorian movement, Orderic Vitalis, for example, links the evil of clerical sexuality with the bearing of arms by the clergy. He complains with practised monastic indignity that the clerks could more readily be parted from their weapons than from their women. The aftermath of the visit of Leo IX to Reims in 1049 made this result clear to him: 'From that time the fatal custom [of clerics bearing arms] began to wither away little by little. The priests were ready enough to give up bearing arms but even now they are loath to part with their mistresses or to live chaste lives.'[10]

One of the most significant conductors for the high voltage of reforming ideas was the emerging science of canon law. The positive Gregorian concept of Christian warfare entered canon law through the writings of Bishop Anselm of Lucca, papal legate in Lombardy and publicist for the Gregorian cause. By 1140 these ideas had then moved forward another and even longer step. Combining Anselm's ideas with those of the slightly later Ivo of Chartres, and drawing heavily on the Church fathers (Augustine in particular), the monk Gratian created an ecclesiastical law of war 'as a particular species of violence' in his influential *Decretum*, a work which later theologians and writers on the canon law had always to take into account.[11]

In *Causa* 23 of this work, the first *quaestio* asks pointedly, 'Is military service a sin?' Although here and elsewhere in his work Gratian quotes authorities who would answer in the affirmative, his conclusion follows Augustine in asserting that such service is not inherently sinful. In fact, truly just warfare was not simply acceptable, it could be pleasing in the eyes of the Almighty. Well in advance of enthusiastic writers of vernacular manuals on chivalry and of the great chivalric *chanson* and romances, Gratian even proclaimed prowess a gift

[9] Quoted in Housley, 'Crusades Against Christians', 19.
[10] Chibnall, ed., *Ecclesiastical History*, III, 120–3.
[11] Brundage, 'Holy War', 106; cf I. S. Robinson, 'Gregory VII', 184–90.

of God; such prowess exercised in just warfare became an instrument leading to the blessed goal of peace. If the warriors had the right motives, if the war was called by proper authority in order to right a wrong or injury, then all was well. Gratian was especially concerned about proper authority, but his list of such authorities, reflecting the situation in his world, seems to have been fairly comprehensive: it did not absolutely exclude anyone 'from the Emperor or king down to the most lowly vassal'. Clerics were prohibited from direct participation by bearing arms themselves, and even from directly ordering bloodshed; but they could encourage others to defend right, correct wrongs, protect the Church. God was, of course, the ultimate authority for violence, but his Church could direct just war on his behalf.[12]

Canonists would work to fill in these broad outlines (and to confront the myriad of questions Gratian left unanswered) for generations to come. For our purposes, the window of opportunity opened for a clerical valorization of knighthood is immediately obvious. The law of the Church, though with many qualifications and caveats, accepted the need for knightly violence.

For all of its fears of the *milites*, the cloister, too, proved to be a source of ideas valorizing emerging chivalry. A much-discussed parallel between knights on the one hand and monks and hermits on the other provided one of the most venerable means by which blessings descended upon knighthood. Churchmen frequently asserted that knights and monks were both called to serve; significantly, the Latin verb they used, *militare*, could mean to fight as well to serve and, in fact, they easily considered the service of both knights and monks a form of warfare against evil, in one dimension conducted in the spirit, in the other in physical battle.[13] All the *milites Christi*, monks and knights alike, in other words, were warriors engaged one way or another in battle against evil, even as Christ himself had been.[14]

In a scene of wonderful symbolic content, white-robed monks in *The Quest of the Holy Grail* literally pull the knight errant Galahad into their religious house to enjoy their hospitality; on his part, he recognizes them, the author tells us, as brothers. In this same text the hermits who so prominently dispense religious advice regularly put on 'the armour of Holy Church' or 'the armour of Our Lord', when saying mass for the knights.[15]

[12] See the discussions in Russell, *Just War*, 55–85, and Chodorow, *Christian Political Theory*, 234–46. For Gratian's text, see Richter, ed., *Decretum Magistri Gratiani*, I, 890–965.

[13] As noted by Holdsworth, 'Ideas and Reality', 77.

[14] This parallel is not confined to comparisons of monks and knights, though that is its usual form. Clerics other than monks might feel the basic similarity of roles, as John of Salisbury notes: Dickinson, ed., tr., *Statesman's Book*, 190.

[15] E.g. Matarasso, tr., *Quest*, 53, 86, 103; Pauphilet, ed., *Queste*, 26–7, 62, 81–2.

Orderic Vitalis draws upon the world of war to write of monks using 'the weapon of prayer (*arma orationis*)'. He can use the term martyr for knights who suffer death on their crusade. When he pens the phrase 'soldiers of Christ (*milites Christi*)' he sometimes means monks, sometimes crusading knights.[16]

Writing in praise of a man named Gerold, a pious clerk in the household of the Earl of Chester, Orderic says:

[He] did his best to convert the men of the court to a better way of life by showing them the examples of their forebears. He rightly condemned the worldly wantonness that he saw in many and deplored the great negligence that most of them showed for the worship of God. To great lords, simple knights, and noble boys alike he gave salutary counsel; and he made a great collection of tales of the combats of holy knights, drawn from the Old Testament and more recent records of Christian achievements, for them to imitate. He told them vivid stories of the conflicts of Demetrius and George, of Theodore and Sebastian, of the Theban legion and Maurice its leader, and of Eustace, supreme commander of the army and his companions, who won the crown of martyrdom in heaven. He also told them of the holy champion, William [of Orange], who after long service in war renounced the world and fought gloriously for the Lord under the monastic rule. And many profited from his exhortations, for he brought them from the wide ocean of the world to the safe harbour of life under the Rule.[17]

Orderic presents a fascinating compromise here, suggesting, indirectly, the validity of a knightly life in the world, so long as religion is not neglected and the battles are fought for good causes, but ending conventionally with the ultimate monastic solution: it would be better for the knights to become monks, at least at the end of an active life in the world. Of course many knights in fact heard this call, William Marshal only the most famous of them.[18]

In the writings of St Bernard, himself the son of a knight, these military metaphors appear regularly. An Augustinian canon, who had given up his religious vocation and returned to the world, was admonished in a letter from Bernard: 'Show yourself in the fight. If Christ recognizes you in battle he will recognize you . . . on the Last Day.' He wrote to Robert de Châtillon to return to his 'fellow-soldiers' in the monastery at Clairvaux: 'Arise, soldier of Christ, I say arise! Shake off the dust and return to the battle.' Bernard tells Robert he is sleeping, while his house is invaded by armed men scaling the walls, pouring in at every entrance.[19]

---

[16] Chibnall, ed., *Ecclesiastical History*, III, bk. VI 260–1, 292–3, 298–9; V, bk. IX, 6–7, 52–7, bk. X, 340–1.

[17] Chibnall, *Ecclesiastical History*, III, bk. VI, 216–17.

[18] Even Bertran de Born, famous warrior/poet, retired to a religious house he had patronized: Paden *et al.*, eds, *Poems of the Troubadour*, 24–6.

[19] Quoted in Evans, *Bernard of Clairvaux*, 24.

Crusade was clearly another conduit for transmitting clerical valorization of knightly violence.[20] In the era of crusade, as Christian society was being divided by clerical intellectuals into three distinct 'orders'—those who pray, those who fight, and those who work—knighthood became, in clerical minds, an *ordo*. Knights became, that is, one of these divisions of society approved by God, one of the orders within which one might achieve salvation.[21]

At a time when much cultural attention was likewise focused on penance and the means of achieving salvation,[22] when salvation may have appeared to many almost as a treasure securely kept behind monastic walls, contemporaries sensed the novelty of creating this new order not simply for laymen, but specifically for knights, with all their enthusiasm for killing. In the early twelfth century Guibert of Nogent, a monk and supporter of Gregorian ideals, wrote that knights who wore the crusader's cross could now find salvation without taking the traditional path of giving up their way of life and entering a monastery:

God in our time has introduced the holy war so that the knighthood and the unstable people, who shed each other's blood in the way of pagans, might have a new way to win salvation. They need not choose the life of a monk and abandon the world in accordance with the vows of a rule, but can obtain God's grace through their own profession, in their accustomed freedom and secular dress.[23]

Otto of Freising, writing towards the middle of the twelfth century, thought of crusaders in similar terms. At a time of senseless war at home,

some, for Christ's sake, despising their own interests and considering that it was not for naught that they were wearing the girdle of knighthood, set out for Jerusalem and there, undertaking a new kind of warfare, so conducted themselves against the enemies of the Cross of Christ that, continually bearing about in their bodies the death of the cross, they appeared by their life and conversation to be not soldiers but monks.[24]

The special service of crusade thus covered the sins of the knights and could pry open the doors of paradise itself. The troubadour Aimeric de Pégulhan exults that knights 'can obtain honour down here and joy in Paradise' and manage all this 'without renouncing our rich garments, our station in life, courtesy and all that pleases and charms'. He is wonderfully relieved that '[n]o more is there need to be tonsured or shaved and lead a hard life in the most

---

[20] Convincing views in Keen, *Chivalry*, 44–63.
[21] See Duby, *Les Trois Ordres*; Flori, *L'Ideologie du glaive*.
[22] Cowdrey, 'Genesis of the Crusades', 21–4.
[23] Quoted in Erdmann, *Crusade*, 336–7.
[24] Otto of Freising, *Chronica*, in Hofmeister, ed., *Scriptores Rerum Germanicarum*, 320, Mierow, tr., *Two Cities*, 414–15.

strict order if we can revenge the shame which the Turks have done us'.[25] The exchange is explicit and explicitly stated in some *chansons*: Christ died for the knights, they must be willing to die for him.[26]

The most influential monastic voice speaking to knighthood as crusade ideas gathered force was that of Bernard of Clairvaux, perhaps the most influential churchman of the first half of the twelfth century. Bernard was willing to recognize a role for the hermaphroditic fusion of monk and knight in a special body of crusaders, the Order of the Knights Templar, for whom he wrote 'Praise of the New Knighthood'.[27] His approval of this new knighthood, 'unknown to ages gone by', is fulsome, but specific: the order 'ceaselessly wages a twofold war both against flesh and blood and against a spiritual army of evil in the heavens'. The Templars can, he assures them, fight secure in their moral stature as God's warriors:

The knight of Christ, I say, may strike with confidence and die yet more confidently, for he serves Christ when he strikes, and serves himself when he falls. Neither does he bear the sword in vain, for he is God's minister, for the punishment of evildoers and for the praise of the good. If he kills an evildoer, he is not a mankiller, but, if I may so put it, a killer of evil [*non homicidia, sed ut ita dixerim, malicidia*].[28]

Bernard's last phrase recalls the wordplay with *militia* and *malitia* of which he and other clerics made such telling use; but here the game elevates his ideal knights at the expense of their brothers among merely 'worldly chivalry'.

Some years later he granted his blessing to an even larger subset of the knightly (admittedly somewhat slowly at first) in his preaching of the Second Crusade. At Vezelay in 1146, Bernard issued an eloquent call for crusaders, using the 'heavenly instrument' of his voice to praise the work they would do, even modifying on behalf of these knights his usual preference for the fight of the monk, whose warfare for the good was spiritual and interior, not physical and exterior. Contemporaries noted that his eloquence on behalf of crusading warfare won the approval of God, as the many miracles that took place at Vezeley witnessed. In the preaching campaign that followed, Bernard travelled many miles through the Kingdom of France and the Empire.[29]

[25] Quoted in Painter, *French Chivalry*, 87, and linked to Guibert's statement, quoted above, by Keen, *Nobles, Knights*, 3.

[26] See, for example, ll. 9380–1 in Newth, ed., tr., *Song of Aspremont* and Brandin, ed., *Chanson d'Aspremont*. For an example from romance, see Bryant, tr., *Perlesvaus*, 236; Nitze and Jenkins, eds, *Perlesvaus*, I, 370.

[27] In Greenia, tr., *Bernard of Clairvaux*, 127–67. For the Latin version, see Leclercq and Rochais, eds, *Bernard of Clairvaux*, III, 213–39.

[28] Greenia, *Bernard of Clairvaux*, 129, 134; Leclercq and Rochais, *Bernard of Clairvaux*, III, 214, 217.

[29] Berry, ed, tr., *Odo of Deuil*, 9–10, describes the scene at Vezeley. Riley-Smith provides a map of St Bernard's preaching tour: *Atlas of the Crusades*, 48. For the rather slow development of his

Finally we should note that clerics gradually became willing to transfer the blessings they had long reserved for kingship to the *ordo* of knights, shifting the heavy mantle of praise and high responsibility from one set of shoulders to another. Jean Flori's detailed studies of knighting ceremonies, of church ritual and liturgy, of the legislation of church councils, and the ideas of clerical intellectuals and popularizers, have skilfully illuminated this revealing change.[30] The clerical tradition which had praised and legitimized the necessary societal role of Christian Roman emperors, sub-Roman Germanic kings, Carolingian emperors and their successors, came in the course of the High Middle Ages to bless and praise the ideal role of knights. The knights were needed in hard times. Like kings, and even in place of kings who were failing to fulfil their function, they could defend the Church, keep the peace, protect the weak.

Idealistic reformers assigned knights particular responsibility for defending widows and orphans.[31] If originally and ultimately such responsibility rested with God, it had devolved in turn upon the Jewish people, the Christian Church, and then, more specifically and exclusively, Christian kingship. When the power of post-Carolingian kings slipped over much of Europe, the knights came to share this aspect of royal responsibility.

Over time this more generous view of knighthood not only predominated but generalized to cover the entire order of the chivalrous. A form of sacralization—even though it always carried significant qualifications—came to rest on the knighthood which clerics so decidedly needed for all of the business of life sadly requiring force. Descendants of the knights whose excesses were condemned by the leaders of the peace movement (discussed below) heard their praises sung as at least potentially blessed warriors. They could become the 'knights of St Peter' at the time of Gregory VII, or the 'knights of Christ' when fighting under later crusade banners, whether the foe consisted of Muslims in the Holy Land or heretics or declared papal enemies within Christendom.

Finally, the blessing spread from the select few to the generality of knights, as knighthood began to be more or less equated with nobility over much of Europe, as clerics attributed major aspects of royal power and responsibility to the *ordo* of knights. Not just crusaders, but all knights could be saved within this order if only they carried out their mission faithfully, listened to each sermonette from their clerical betters, and heeded the warnings. The formula of

enthusiasm for the crusade, and his efforts to explain its complete failure, see Evans, *Bernard of Clairvaux*, 24–36.

[30] Flori, *L'Idéologie du glaive* and *L'Essor de chevalerie*. Flori's numerous articles appear in the bibliographies to these books.

[31] As Flori notes, however, 'Le service de la Dame prime peu à peu sur celui de l'Eglise et la "protection" plus flatteuse, de la pucelle l'emporte sur celle de la veuve et de l'orphelin. A l'idéologie cléricale se mêle l'idéologie profane': *L'Essor de chevalerie*, 302.

willingness to die for Christ, who was willing to die for humanity, shifts easily—chivalric literature shows us—to a willingness to die for the lord or king who puts his body at risk for his men.[32] This laicization and generalization of crusade valorization is sometimes quite explicit. In the *Lancelot do Lac* and in the *Lancelot*, the knight Pharian explains to his fellow vassals why they must fight for their liege lords, the young Bors and Lionel:

> if we die for them it will be to our honour in the world and to our renown as warriors, because for the sake of rescuing his liege lord from death a man is duty-bound to put his own life ungrudgingly at risk. If anyone then dies, he dies as sure of salvation as if he were slain fighting the Saracens, the enemies of Our Lord Jesus Christ![33]

Fighting for one's lord has taken on the aura of fighting for the Lord. The point is made even more broadly and strikingly later in the *Lancelot*. A former knight, who leaves the religious life he has adopted to return to the world to fight against an enemy troubling his son, argues this case in discussion with Gawain:

> is he who destroys life without justification not worse than a Saracen? If I went overseas to fight against the destroyers of Christendom, it would be judged praiseworthy, for I must do all in my power to avenge the death of Jesus Christ, since I am a Christian. Therefore I'll go to avenge my son, who is a Christian, and help him against those who are in the place of the unbelievers.[34]

Such views had a long future.[35]

Clerics must have had their doubts about the logic as well as the behaviour of the knights; but they had few alternatives. They crossed their fingers and kept preaching their ideals, excepting from the blessings they bestowed on the High Order of Chivalry only those (in theory a minority) who burned churches, looted and raped the poor, and caused general mayhem through unjust warfare.

The Order of Knighthood (*Ordene de chevalerie*, c. 1220) seems to sum up clerical valorization. Evidently written by a cleric and possibly a priest, this manual provides what its editor, Keith Busby, terms a mystico-religious meaning for the ceremony by which a knight is made. Each step, each piece of equip-

---

[32] See, for example, Pickens, tr., *Story of Merlin*, 291; Sommer, ed., *Vulgate Version*, II, 226–7.

[33] Rosenberg, tr., *Lancelot Part I*, 32; Sommer, *Vulgate Version*, III, 60; Elspeth Kennedy, ed., *Lancelot do Lac*, I, 73.

[34] Carroll, tr., *Lancelot Part II*, 199; Sommer, *Vulgate Version*, III, 359; Kennedy, *Lancelot do Lac*, I, 476.

[35] They also had a recent past. The account of the crusade of Richard the Lion-Heart, written around the turn of the thirteenth century, says that Richard, fighting hostile Cypriots en route to the Holy Land, 'forbore to seek worse Saracens' than these enemies: ('*Peors Sarazins ne volt guerre*'): Paris, ed., *L'Histoire de la guerre sainte*.

ment is given a moral or religious meaning. The bath shows the knight cleansed from sin; the bed on which he rests figures the bed he will earn in paradise, etc. The intent to praise knighthood and fit it into medieval Christian society is obvious. The audience whom the author seems to be addressing is clerical, as the following statement near the end of the manual indicates:

knights, whom everybody should honour . . . have us all to guard; and if it were not for knighthood, our lordship would be of little worth, for they defend Holy Church, and they uphold justice for us against those who would do us harm. . . . Our chalices would be stolen from before us at the table of God, and nothing would ever stop it. But their justice which defends us in their persons is decisive. The good would never be able to endure if the wicked did not fear knights, and if there were only Saracens, Albigensians, and Barbarians, and people of evil faith.

The clerical case for the necessity of knighthood and the justification of their swords could scarcely be made more clearly.[36]

Clerical Strictures on Knightly Malitia

Clerics balanced approval of chivalry, as an ideal type with the most blistering criticism of the ideals and practices of chivalry actually encountered in the world.

The peace movement, at work between the late tenth and twelfth centuries, overlapped the gestational age of chivalry.[37] Despite much debate, most historians think that the warriors of middling and lesser rank, the castellans (masters of fortifications), and their subordinate *milites* were the targets of much of the legislation. Clerics wanted licit war to be limited to the higher authorities, which meant that the bishops and abbots pinned their hopes for social order on the great lords, at least in the absence of effective royal control (which to them would have been preferable still).

In the specific form known as the Truce of God (which sought, from the second quarter of the eleventh century, to outlaw fighting during times of religious significance), the prohibition against fighting was often relaxed in favour of the lay authority considered licit by the churchmen. A count or duke could thus licitly fight against those engaged in acts of illicit violence. Not surprisingly, at least in Normandy, Flanders, and Catalonia, the Peace of God had, before the end of the eleventh century, become the Peace of the Count

---

[36] Busby, ed., *Ordene de chevalerie*, tr., 174–5; French text, 117.
[37] The debates over interpretations of the Peace of God are surveyed and sampled in Head and Landes, eds, *Peace of God*. See also Duby, *Chivalrous Society*, 123–33; Cowdrey, 'Peace and Truce'; Jean Flori, *Idéologie du glaive*, 135–57.

or Duke; by the mid-twelfth century it had become the King's Peace in France.[38]

Some scholarship takes us beyond major peace councils to informal efforts, which are no less significant for our themes. With the approval of the count, the monks of the monastery of Lobbes in Flanders, for example, left their house, ruined by war, to take the relics of their patron saint, Ursmer, on a tour in 1060. Among the many miracles recorded by the monks on this tour, the greatest was that the saint brought peace to the region in which interlocking feuds were everywhere. At Strazeele, the writer noted, 'some knights were so hostile to each other that no mortal man could bring them to peace'. At Lissewege, the problem centred on a young man named Robert who had a large following of knights; he would not reconcile with his enemy. Pressed by the monks and locals (including older knights, we should note), he and this enemy lay prostrate before the saint for three hours. Robert gnashed his teeth, groaned, turned alternately pale and red, clawed the ground and ate dirt in sheer frustration with those who would rob him of revenge. Finally, the saint's reliquary dramatically spewed smoke and levitated: Robert pardoned his enemy and peace was made.[39]

The solemn rigours of the canon law—some distance from smoking, levitating reliquaries in a Flemish village—can likewise show us clerical doubts and fears about the *milites*. Although, as we have seen, Gratian's influential *Decretum* created safe canonical space for just warfare, he seems to have sensed how hard it would be to make Christian charity the motivating force for fighting, how unlikely it would be for the knightly ranks of his day to give up such sinful motives as private revenge or plentiful booty. Frederick Russell argues, for example, that the prolix and pompous exhortations that Gratian and so many later canonists addressed to the knights (against their 'lust for doing harm, cruelty of punishment, implacable and unsatisfied vehemence, savagery, and lust for domination') show deep fears on just these points. As Russell writes, 'Against the well-known greed, rapacity, and ferocity of the knightly class of his time Gratian opposed the patristic portraits of the Christian soldier, thereby striking at the core of knightly practice.'[40] The canonists, with hope in their hearts, praised the military virtues, in other words, but they recognized and feared the military vices so evident in their world; and they spoke to that fear.

---

[38] Flori, *Idéologie du glaive*, 154; Head and Landes eds, *Peace of God*, 8. The capacity of royal government in England eliminated the need for this infusion of support.

[39] Koziol, 'The Making of Peace', 250–1. Koziol notes that the castellans must have welcomed the monks into their regions, hoping for some increment to their own prestige.

[40] Russell, *Just War*, 61.

Though crusading epitomized knightly lay piety, most knights for most of their lives were not crusaders; the majority of their fighting was done at home against their fellow knights (or at least their enemies' peasantry). Clerics constantly drew the sharpest contrast between the ordinary conduct of knighthood and the special service of crusade.

Even Urban II, as he preached the crusade at Clermont in 1095, took this approach, if we can at all trust later accounts of his famous crusade sermon. He seems to have stressed the evils inherent in the knightly life and presented crusading as a means of atonement. The chronicler Fulcher of Chartres pictures Urban saying, 'Now will those who once were robbers become *Christi milites*; those who once fought brothers and relatives will justly fight barbarians; those who once were mercenaries for a few farthings will obtain eternal reward.'[41] Baldric of Dol gives the pope an even more outspoken speech of condemnation with a smaller escape hatch of virtue opened for the knights:

You are proud; you tear your brothers to pieces and fight among yourselves. The battle that rends the flock of the Redeemer is not the *militia Christi*. Holy church has reserved knighthood for itself, for the defence of its people, but you pervert it in wickedness . . . you oppressors of orphans and widows, you murderers, you temple-defilers, you lawbreakers, who seek the rewards of rapacity from spilling Christian blood. . . . If you wish to save your souls, either abandon the profession of arms or go boldly forth as *Christi milites* and hasten to the defence of the Eastern church.[42]

Whether or not these are words actually spoken by Urban from his platform at Clermont, they clearly establish the continuing clerical criticism of knighthood and the strait gate through which it had to pass to meet the approval of *clergie*.

If chroniclers wrote the pope's words for him, their own words flowed in the same vein. William of Tyre thought the crusaders needed the opportunity to redeem themselves by pious work: their habit was to commit theft, arson, rape, murder. William of Malmesbury agreed; he thought that the departure of the *milites* as crusaders meant that Christians at home could now live in peace.[43]

Views from the knights' 'fellow warriors' in the cloisters had long been fearful and condemnatory about knightly practice, however much they liked to imagine a brotherly parallel between knights and monks in theory. We have already noted some expression of these monastic fears when we looked at Orderic's chronicle and Suger's biography of Louis VI. To their witness we should add that great voice of monasticism, Bernard de Clairvaux. If he sang

---

[41] Quoted in Erdmann, *Crusade*, 339–40.   [42] Ibid., 340.
[43] Quoted in Flori, *L'Essor de la chevalerie*, 199.

the praises of the select company of Knights Templar, and of the larger body of those who went on the Second Crusade, for ordinary knights—which of course means the overwhelming majority of the knights of his day—St Bernard could scarcely restrain his contempt.[44] To these men, 'fighting for the devil', go plain words of warning:

If you happen to be killed while you are seeking only to kill another, you die a murderer. If you succeed, and by your will to overcome and to conquer you perchance kill a man, you live a murderer. . . . What an unhappy victory—to have conquered a man while yielding to vice, and to indulge in an empty glory at his fall when wrath and pride have gotten the better of you!

Warming to his subject, Bernard heaps scorn on the combination of vanity and violence in chivalry as it was practised all around him:

What then, O knights, is this monstrous error and what this unbearable urge which bids you fight with such pomp and labor, and all to no purpose except death and sin. You cover your horses with silk, and plume your armor with I know not what sort of rags; you paint your shields and your saddles; you adorn your bits and spurs with gold and silver and precious stones, and then in all this glory you rush to your ruin with fearful wrath and fearless folly.

Since most knights, he is convinced, are fighting for the devil rather than for God, he does not hesitate to call them 'impious rogues, sacrilegious thieves, murderers, perjurers and adulterers'. When they are converted to the new knighthood of the Temple, there will be twofold joy: 'A twofold joy and a twofold benefit, since their countrymen are as glad to be rid of them as their new comrades are to receive them. Both sides have profited from this exchange, since the latter are strengthened and the former are now left in peace.'[45] On one occasion Bernard backed up his ideas with dramatic effects on some knights who visited Clairvaux, but refused his entreaties to put down their arms and give up tourneying for the Lenten season. After Bernard gave them beer which he had blessed, they soon left the secular *militia* and became monks.[46]

The voice from the schools could be no less critical, or at least no less demanding than that from the cloister. In writings such as his sermon 'Ad Milites' the noted scholar Alain de Lille (d. 1203) wields a pen as effective and almost as

[44] Grabois, '*Militia* and *Malitia*'. Cf. Buist-Thiele, 'Bernard of Clairvaux', 57–65. Leclercq notes that Bernard's purpose in his treatise was not simply to promote the Knights Templar, but 'to find expression for his own ideal of knighthood': *Monks and Love*, 21.

[45] Greenia, tr., *Bernard of Clairvaux*, 138, 131, 132, 143; Leclercq and Rochais, eds, *Bernard of Clairvaux*, 219, 215, 216, 213.

[46] Leclercq tells the story in *Monks and Love*, 89.

sharply pointed as that of St Bernard.[47] In one important sense his position is more comprehensively tolerant than that of Bernard; he sees a valid knightly role extending well beyond that of knight-monks as a special subset of crusaders. In an unusual reinterpretation of the famous image of two swords (often used to refer to the powers of Church and State) he even suggests that knights possess them both. They belt on the physical sword to secure temporal peace; the second sword, he says, is spiritual, an interior weapon by which they can secure the peace of their own hearts.[48]

But he charges knighthood in general with terrible sins of omission and commission. They should be devoted followers of the military saints; they should defend their homeland and the Church their mother; they should fight her enemies boldly; they should protect widows and orphans. But how do they act in fact? They show only the outward appearance of knighthood, not realizing that these exterior signs are but figures of the true knighthood within, that which is nourished by the word of God in their breasts. Their knighthood becomes utterly empty, only a shell. Thus, what they practise is not true knightly service, but plundering; not *militia*, but *rapina*. In short, they become thieves, devastating the poor. They avoid fighting the enemies of Christ (out of sloth or fear), but make fellow Christians the victims of their swords. In his most telling phrase Alain denounces knights for sharpening their swords in the viscera of their mother, the Church.[49]

His criticism of knightly pillaging and looting appears vividly in a story told of knights from the region bursting into Alain's theology classroom at Montpellier. The knights (obviously motivated by intellectual curiosity and some respect for the learning of *clergie*) demanded that he tell them what constituted the highest degree of courtesy. An unruffled Alain pronounced the opinion that it lay in giving liberally and beneficently. Though the knights all liked this answer, they could only have been less pleased as Alain turned the tables with much didactic coolness and asked them what, correspondingly, was the deepest degree of villainy (*rusticitas*). When the knights failed to agree on an answer, he explained archly that it lay in living by looting the poor as they did.[50] Of course, no professor easily tolerates a rude invasion of his classroom, but, as we have already seen, Alain gave similar views on the evils of

---

[47] *Patrologia Latina*, 210, cols 185–7. Cf his 'Sermo de cruce domini'—in d'Alverny, *Alain de Lille*, 279–82—in which he insists that crusaders must perform their service in a spirit of penitence, not anger, and must wear this penitence as an inward cross, parallelling in a more meaningful form their exterior crusading cross. They must imitate the thief to Christ's right on Calvary, not the angry thief to his left. Was this thief imagery chosen purely by chance? For a general discussion of Alain's views on knighthood see Flori, *L'Essor de chevalerie*, 291–4.

[48] 'Ad milites,' *Patrologia Latina* 210, col. 186.   [49] Ibid.

[50] Two versions of the story are quoted in d'Alverny, *Alain de Lille*, 16–17, n. 30.

knighthood, from the uninterrupted quiet of his study, in his sermon 'Ad Milites'.

John of Salisbury is generally more accepting. Since he clothes knights in the classical drapery of his self-conscious learning, his view allows for more talk of the loyal service owed by *milites* to 'the prince' and to 'the commonwealth'. He wants his readers to know he is not hostile to military men or the military life.[51] He tries to think of contemporary knights as the Roman soldiers he so admires in his books on antiquity, fitted into a world properly directed by *clergie*. The armed soldier, in fact, 'no less than the spiritual one is limited by the requirements of office to religion and the worship of God, since he must faithfully and according to God obey the prince and vigilantly serve the republic'. Given such a military force, he announces his willingness to 'undertake its defence against whoever attacks it and will fully justify it on the authority of God'.[52]

He knows, though, that the world in which he lives is not the world of his books. He would that the knights of his own day were a stalwart, ideal soldiery selected by careful examination, disciplined in constant drill, and enlisted for true public service. He is thus disappointed and critical on two levels. First, he confronts the knights on their own ground, on the level of sheer professionalism: the knights of his day are simply not good enough at their tasks as warriors, not bold enough, not truly committed to their high and necessary vocation. The Roman discipline is gone, he laments, largely because of effeminacy and luxury.[53]

But his second criticism is more pointed, even if John, ever cautious, gives it less space. The wrong people hold the swords and use them in wrongful pursuits. Many of those who call themselves *milites* 'are in reality no more soldiers than men are priests and clerics whom the Church has never called into orders'. He knows, from his books, what to call these men, 'for in old writings those who use arms outside the decree of law are called murderers and bandits.' These untrue *milites*,

believe that the glory of their military service grows if the priesthood is humiliated, if the authority of the Church becomes worthless, if they would so expand the kingdom of man that the empire of God contracts, if they declare their own praises and flatter and extol themselves by false eulogy. . . . Their courage manifests itself mainly if either their weapons or their words pierce the clergy or the unarmed soldiers [i.e. the other servants of the republic].

---

[51] What follows draws on his *Policraticus*: see Webb, ed., *Ioannis Saresberiensis* and Nederman, tr., *Policraticus*. The insistence that he appreciates the military appears at the opening of Book VI, chapter v.

[52] *Policraticus*, VI, chs viii and v.

[53] Ibid., Book VI, ch. vi.

Such men serve 'rage or vanity or avarice or their own private will' rather than defending the Church and the poor, pacifying the land, and even giving their lives, if needed.[54] Though *milites* ideally offer their service to the republic and Church,

the number is legion of those who when they offer their belt upon the altar for the purpose of consecrating themselves to military service, their evil works seem to cry aloud and proclaim that they have approached the altar with the intention of declaring war against it and its ministers and even against God Himself who is worshipped there.

They are more like practitioners of *malitia* than members of the true *militia*.[55] In such passages, John seems to step away from the classical backdrop that so often formed the stage-set for his writing and to speak plainly about his own age.

Gerald of Wales, a bridge figure connecting this world of scholarship with the busy world of clerical administrators, often adopts the mores of the world he describes in his historical writing. Yet even he can slip in telling critiques. If he praises the knights from England and the Welsh Marches who invaded Ireland in the reign of Henry II, he can note archly that their work were better done if they

had paid due reverence to the church of Christ, not only by preserving its ancient rights and privileges inviolate, but also by hallowing their new and sanguinary conquest, in which so much blood had been shed, and which was stained by the slaughter of a christian people, by liberally contributing some portion of their spoils for religious use. But ... this has been the common failing of all our countrymen engaged in these wars from their first coming over to the present day.[56]

Gerald's contemporary, Etienne de Fougères, chaplain to Henry II and bishop of Rennes (1168–78), was even more outspoken and pointed in the criticisms. His *Livre des manières*, which excoriates all the divisions of society, states that knights should provide justice, extinguish violence and plundering:

But most knights are usually lax about their duties,
So I hear complaints all day long (from those the knights should protect)
That little remains to them
That they can own or obtain (with surety).

The great eat and drink up the hard-won fruits of peasant labour, turning chivalry into faithless debauchery. Though loyal knights can be saved in their own order of society, the evil knights who will not cooperate with Holy

[54] Ibid., VI, ch. viii.   [55] Ibid., chs ix and xiii; quotation from the close of chapter xiii.
[56] Wright, tr., *Historical Works*, 266.

Church, who joust and tourney and misuse the power of the sword given them by God, should be stripped of sword and spurs and expelled.[57]

How did clerics respond to the important phenomenon of tournament? At first, clerical writers universally took a censorious view of this most character-istic and popular sport of chivalry, fulminating against what St Bernard of Clairvaux termed 'those accursed tournaments'.[58] Chronicle, chivalric biogra-phy, and imaginative chivalric literature all show that participation in tourna-ment was for knights the very affirmation of *chevalerie*. But in clerical eyes these mock wars imperilled soul as well as body, encouraged pride, occasioned the risk of homicide, and, in a more general sense, deflected martial energies bet-ter spent on crusade. After the initial interdiction issued at the council of Clermont in 1130, this condemnation would scarcely slacken in principle for the better part of two centuries.

At the highest level churchmen gave ground slowly and only yielded to the inevitable, finally, in 1316, when Pope John XXII revoked the ban on tourna-ments. Local ecclesiastical authorities had probably compromised much sooner: in 1281 Pope Martin IV had commented with resignation that some-times custom is stronger than law.[59] He was thinking of tournaments, of knightly custom, and papal law.

One eminent scholar has emphasized the general shift in clerical position symbolized by the acceptance of tournament. Georges Duby has, in fact, sug-gested that the clerical critique of chivalry emerged from an essentially monas-tic Church and so became muted, or rather transmuted, after the crisis in Western monasticism so evident by roughly the mid-twelfth century. The more worldly clerks and canons who dominated the Church from the later twelfth century were men more attuned to military activity and were even more personally involved in it; they thus turned away from monastic hostility to chivalry and created for knights '*la nouvelle morale des guerriers*'.[60]

The present chapter argues that both impulses, the hostile and the valoriz-ing, were actually present in a clerical ideology of reform throughout the lifes-pan of chivalry, and that they both appeared not only in the cloister, but in the papal circle, in episcopal courts, and in the schools. Both impulses continued through the undoubted twelfth-century transformations which took place in monasticism and its role within the Church at large. The crucial valorizing role

[57] Lodge, ed., *Etienne de Fougères*, ll. 537–676. Translation from Switten, '*Chevalier*'. Cf. Flori, *L'Essor de chevalerie*, 315–19.

[58] For what follows see Barker, *Tournament*, 139–51; Barber and Barker, *Tournaments*, 139–46; Keen, *Chivalry*, 83–102. For St Bernard's comment, see Bruno Scott James, tr., *Bernard of Clairvaux*, letter 405.

[59] Quoted in Langlois, *Philippe III*, 199.

[60] Duby, 'Guerre et société'. For overviews of this monastic change, see John van Engen, 'Crisis of Cenobitism', and Leclercq, 'Monastic Crisis'.

of the Gregorians, who represent the ecclesiastical world moving beyond the cloister, after all, stands on the early side of a mid-twelfth-century line, and the continuing influence of stringent Cistercian critics, the most powerful and effective monastic force of their day, was written into such powerful works as *The Quest for the Holy Grail* in the early thirteenth century, on the later side of that line. Criticism was never simply monastic, as we have seen in looking at the ideas of schoolmen such as Alain de Lille and John of Salisbury. Clerics and intellectuals of the later twelfth and thirteenth centuries did not simply create a new morale for knights; most of them also continued to condemn the chief and characteristic knightly sport of tournament, and many of them set standards for ideal chivalry so high as to be almost unreachable by the generality of knights.

But Duby's argument serves as a highly useful reminder of an important fact. If both valorization and criticism were structural elements of the clerical stance on chivalry, over time both the tenor of the discussion and the relative weights on the balance beam of clerical opinion shifted significantly. Stated in its simplest form, knighthood became a given in high medieval society, an accepted building block in the structure of civilization, imagined by Chrétien de Troyes, for example, to be as old as civilization itself. As chivalry came to signify the identifying set of values of the nobility in society, it became an *ordo* in clerical thought. The rhetorical vitriol attributed to Urban II and that of a certainty written by St Bernard and Alain de Lille thus gave way to a more balanced, steady stream of didactic, reformist exhortation. Not the rightful existence of chivalry, but its rightful practice came to be the issue. More in knightly life and practice was understood or tactfully overlooked; more— finally, by the fourteenth century, even tournament—was overlooked or forgiven.

The Church and Governing Power

'Enforcement of the law', as Richard M. Fraher notes, 'stands with diplomacy, defense, and taxation as one of the functions which modern observers associate with the state.'[61] In a famous passage, F. W. Maitland pointed to clear similarities between the medieval Church and our contemporary idea of a state:

The medieval church was a state. Convenience may forbid us to call it a state very often, but we ought to do so from time to time, for we can frame no acceptable definition of a state which would not comprehend the church. What has it not that a state should have? It has laws, lawgivers, law courts, lawyers. It uses physical force to compel men

---

[61] Fraher, 'Theoretical Justification', 579.

to obey its laws. It keeps prisons. In the thirteenth century, though with squeamish phrases, it pronounces sentence of death.[62]

In fact, as it dealt with the chivalrous, the institutional Church lacked one characteristic feature of a state which is crucial for our analysis. Although clerics had articulated an ideology concerning chivalry and order, although (as Maitland states so elegantly) they possessed an elaborate system of courts, codes, and practitioners of law, they lacked direct means of enforcing these ideas or even these laws.[63]

The clerical hierarchy was not in any position, in other words, to use physical force to compel knights to obey its laws or to follow its more general guidelines about licit and illicit violence. The paradoxical constitution of the medieval Church comes sharply into focus on just such a point.[64] In the broadest conception, of course, Christian society and the Church were coterminous; the knights were the armed force of the church, the armed force within the Church. In the more hierarchical and strictly clerical conception of the Church, so influential following the Gregorian reform, however, the knights represented a somewhat more alien force, one with ideas and standards of an independent nature; they constituted a force, moreover, with weapons which were thoroughly physical—the only such force after the disarming of the clergy, which had been another great goal of church reformers.

For peace, for right order in the world, churchmen turned from long-accustomed habit to the upper reaches of the hierarchy of lay powers, to kings above all, and to great lords. A colourful case in point appears in the early twelfth-century efforts of Louis VI against the castle of Crécy belonging to Thomas of Marle, the warlord who was so disliked, as we have seen, by Abbot Suger and characterized by Guibert of Nogent as 'the proudest and most wicked of men'. Having called upon the king to destroy the power of this man, the prelates gave the king's forces their most enthusiastic blessing. Guibert tells us that

the archbishop and the bishops, going up on high platforms, united the crowd, gave them their instructions for the affair, absolved them from their sins, and ordered them as an act of penitence in full assurance of the salvation of their souls to attack that castle.[65]

The blessing is important; but the point to note is that the armed force relied upon was royal.

In England the reality and continuity of royal power made a peace move-

[62] Maitland, *Roman Canon Law*, 100.
[63] Useful discussions in Rodes, *Ecclesiastical Administration*, 99, and Helmholz, 'Crime'.
[64] See discussions in Strayer, 'State and Religion', and Southern, *Western Society*, 19, and Smalley 'Capetian France', 63.
[65] Quoted and discussed in Benton, *Self and Society*, 204–5.

ment virtually unnecessary; and, in what was becoming France, such a convergence of the concern for public order and a belief in holy war directed by the Church faded gradually but significantly before the advance of Capetian royal power.

In the south, Norman Housley notes, the fusion of clerical activism with the peace movement went from strength to strength, 'because of the absence of such [lay] authority, coupled with the alarming spread of mercenary violence and, later, heresy'. But '[i]n northern France, the incorporation of crusading ideas into peace-enforcement had no long term future because of the rapidity with which Capetian authority was growing'.[66]

Thus no coercive ecclesiastical role regarding violence developed in northwestern Europe. By the thirteenth century ecclesiastical authorities so generally relied on 'the secular arm' that in England a specific royal writ offered a regular means by which clerics secured the coercion of those offenders who ignored even sentences of excommunication; the spiritual sentence was enforced, in effect, by the king's officer, the sheriff, when the chancery sent him the writ *de excommunicato capiendo* ordering him to arrest the resisting excommunicate.[67] Relying on this writ is not the act of a competing form of state, whatever the sophistication of its laws, however significant its treasure-store of ideas.

The same point appears in the famous thirteenth-century French legal treatise, *The Customs of the Beauvaisis*, by Philippe de Beaumanoir. He insists that lay officials must use the secular arm to protect Holy Church, and he says why: 'For the spiritual sword would not be much feared by wrong doers if they did not believe that the temporal sword would get involved; this in spite of the fact that the spiritual sword is incomparably more to be feared'.[68] Evidently, ecclesiastics recognized that the coercive force exercised by lay government was, in fact, much more effective than spiritual censures in France, as it was in England.

Of course this recognition on the part of ecclesiastical authorities was not some lamentable or reprehensible failure on their part. The Church had for many centuries placed hope and confidence in Christian Roman emperors and, later, pious kings or at least great Christian lords. If Gregorian radicals had briefly considered taking the task in hand personally, even they, and certainly their successors—while they continued to assert their leadership of Christian society—knew that for tasks involving coercion, physical force, and blood, they had to work through the power of kingship (sometimes in the

---

[66] Housley, 'Crusades Against Christians', 25.   [67] Logan, *Excommunication*.
[68] Akehurst, tr., *Coutumes de Beauvaisis*, 29–30; Salmon, ed., *Philippe de Beaumanoir*, I, 39. The final statement is wonderfully theoretical in view of the plain words with which he begins.

hands of great lords), and finally the power of knights themselves. These lay powers were at once necessary and dangerous, worthy of sacralization and in need of constant correction.

The Force of Ideas

Was the clerical ideology of reform absorbed by the knights themselves; in other words, was this external ideology to any significant degree internalized by knights, who (as we have already noted) displayed a high degree of independence of thought? Academics inclined to believe in the force of ideas—especially scholars who rely primarily on the evidence of idealizing texts—are likely to utter statements of hope in approaching this difficult issue. The medieval world knew much violence, to be sure, but at least clerical ideas set the terms of the discourse and began to make a difference, to civilize the brutal warriors, and help them make their world a better place. Along with John of Salisbury, some scholars tend to link advancing civilization and restraint with the admixture of classical and clerical ideas in chivalric culture.

Scholars who have spent years among court records and chronicles, on the other hand, are less likely to think the knights stepped, transformed, out of the soft hues of pre-Raphaelite paintings; the most hard-boiled are more likely to argue that clerical efforts in fact—however unintentionally—pulled the thinnest veil of decency over knightly behaviour that often went on largely as before. In such a view, knights simply absorbed and laicized the clerical valorization of all the violence they carried on with such enthusiasm, while filtering out most of the criticism.

The difficulty, of course, lies not only in finding sufficient evidence but in calibrating a standard for judging the effectiveness of reform ideas in the world. How could we know in how many instances knights refrained from burning a church or pillaging an opponent's peasantry out of a fear and love of God inculcated by clerical instruction on ideal chivalry?

Some evidence is suggestive. We might recall that Orderic Vitalis thought it highly commendable and worthy of mention that Richer of Laigle hesitated to attack peasants whom he had already plundered and who had prostrated themselves before a roadside crucifix in terror. Such unusual restraint, praised so highly ('something that deserves to be remembered forever') at least indirectly suggests what was a common view of early twelfth-century Norman knights.[69] A passage in the contemporary *Crowning of Louis* pointedly reminded its audience that Jesus liked knights who spared churches from the torch, a theme that

---

[69] Chibnall, ed., tr., *Ecclesiastical History*, VI, 250–1.

might have special meaning for John Marshal (father of the more famous William), whose face had been disfigured by molten lead dripping from the roof of an abbey church burned by one of his enemies during the twelfth-century period of civil war in England.[70]

Major characters in chivalric literature occasionally speak out in a surprisingly self-critical vein. In the prose romances of the early thirteenth century Queen Guinevere, Lancelot, and Galehaut confess fascinating and revealing doubts about the moral solidity of chivalric life as they live it. The queen, in conversation with Lancelot, says that it is 'too bad Our Lord pays no heed to our courtly ways, and a person whom the world sees as good is wicked to God'. A little earlier, Galehaut, learning from a dream that his death may be close, decides to amend his life. He admits: 'I have committed many wrongs in my life, destroying cities, killing people, dispossessing and banishing people.'[71] This confession comes from a man continually praised as an exemplar of all excellent chivalric qualities.

If such evidence is problematic and at best suggestive, other evidence is indisputable. Wars without clerical sanction continued throughout the Middle Ages and subjected 'non-combatants' to the entire scale of violence available, especially to the indiscriminate force of fire.

It seems equally important that clerics themselves were not satisfied with the reception and internalization of their ideas by knights; even crusaders suffered bitter criticisms from disappointed ecclesiastical enthusiasts. Certainly, the knights showed no great inclination to listen to clerical condemnations of their characteristic sport of tournament. In a letter to Abbot Suger, St Bernard complained in bitter tones:

The men who have returned from the Crusade have arranged to hold again those accursed tournaments after Easter, and the lord Henry, son of the count, and the lord Robert, brother of the king, have agreed regardless of all law to attack and slay each other. Notice with what sort of dispositions they must have taken the road to Jerusalem when they return in this frame of mind![72]

Nor did knights accept clerical claims regarding the dubbing ceremony. To control these ceremonies would obviously win the clerics an excellent opportunity for inculcating their ideas of true chivalry at one of the more significant moments in a knight's life. An ecclesiastical strand is undeniably present in the historical and literary accounts of dubbing ceremonies. Yet, as Maurice Keen has argued convincingly, the Church, which managed to establish its role in

---

[70] Hoggan, tr., 'Crowning of Louis', 43; Langlois, ed., *Couronnement de Louis*, 64. The John Marshal incident is discussed by Crouch, *William Marshal*, 13; John lost one of his eyes.

[71] Rosenberg, tr., *Lancelot Part III*, 275, 254, Micha, ed., *Lancelot*, I, 152, 61.

[72] Bruno Scott James, tr., *Bernard of Clairvaux*, letter 405.

the coronation ceremony, achieved much less success when it came to the dubbing of knights.[73] In fact, dubbing to knighthood looks very much like a classic example of independent lay piety, an appropriation or laicizing of the
clerical entry into knightly practice; once again, knights more readily took on
religious legitimation than the element of sacerdotal control intended from
the sphere of *clergie*.

   None of these estimates needs to be read judgementally, of course. If
medieval churchmen did not cut through the Gordian knot binding violence
and religion, neither have thoughtful people before or since—at least not to general satisfaction. Nor must we take up the ecclesiastical scales of judgement on
knighthood in this matter. Knights surely did not passively absorb restraining
and improving clerical ideas and then fail deplorably to reach the high standards.
They had ideas of their own, as we have seen, even ideas along religious lines.
They considered themselves competent judges as to which clerical ideas about
chivalry they would accept and may not even have wished to accord their lives
with many others. Our task is not to award or withhold good behaviour points
for knights, but to recognize how selectively they absorbed clerical ideology.

   Their particular form of lay piety probably gave knights the confidence that
God understood them and appreciated their hard service, even if further transactions were necessary to secure formal approval via his touchy worldly repre-
sentatives—likely to be their brothers, sisters, and cousins who had entered the
clergy. Valorization of holy war, of course, spread easily at a time when any
war could, with minimal effort or sophistry, be considered holy.[74] But the simpler truth could be that knights needed very little valorization of their warfare
by clerics at all, though undoubtedly they would prefer to have it.

   Their hard lives and their good service covered most of the tab for their
morally risky violence. If their hands were bloody, was it not because—as even
the clerics recognized—some blood had to be spilled in a world spoiled by sin?
Whether loyally smiting the king's enemies or merely troubling their neighbours, whether they fought before or after a crusade, they were doing what
they had to do in the confidence that they could settle any accounts with the
fussy clerics through donations or deathbed contrition, even deathbed conversion to the religious life. 'In crude terms', Emma Mason writes, 'they tried
to buy off the consequences of their aggression by offering a share of the loot
to those whose prayers would hopefully resolve their dilemma.'[75] Christopher
Holdsworth makes a similar observation: 'Standards were held up, but at the

---

[73] See the discussion in Keen, *Chivalry*, 64–82.   [74] See Russell, *Just War*.
[75] Mason, 'Timeo Barones', 67. Mason continues, 'Such a naive attitude cannot, however, be
contrasted with any superior spirituality of the cloister, for religious houses were all too ready to
cooperate in this cycle.'

last one lot of soldiers would take the others in, provided they received an adequate payment.'[76] This certainly was the view of the Anglo-Norman knight Rodolf Pinellus, when his violent way of life was criticized by Abbot Herluin of Westminster; only after he had had his fill of worldly pleasure and was tired of fighting, he coolly told the abbot, would he give it up to become a monk.[77] Likewise, Gerald of Wales tells us that the Anglo-Norman invaders of Ireland were great men; but they had failed to give enough in payments to the Church to offset their slaughters.[78]

William Marshal in the early thirteenth century and Geoffroi de Charny in the mid-fourteenth century took what probably seems to us a less crude view, but they both showed the same spirit of lay independence when the matter in question was the knightly right to fight, to take pleasure in the display of prowess and the winning of honour and profit. William's flattering biography, primarily a study of war and, secondarily, of the quasi-war of tournament, shows no evident qualms about warfare; instead, one comment after another reveals an easy assumption of the knightly right to violence in causes any knight would consider right.[79] His unceasing piety hardly keeps Charny, similarly, from paeans of praise for prowess and assertions of the religious character of the knightly life *per se*. Charny is especially sure that the sheer suffering endured by knights in their demanding calling wins them favour with God.[80]

In fact, we must remember that ideological influence flowed both ways between *clergie* and *chevalerie*, or at least that churchmen found it necessary and sometimes even congenial to accept more of the self-estimate of the knightly role than strict clerical ideology would suggest. In his sermon delivered at William Marshal's funeral, for example, the Archbishop of Canterbury waxed eloquent about the 'finest knight in the world' in language not very different from that used to praise the Marshal at the French royal court. The Templar sent shortly before William's death to receive him into the order had announced unambiguously that, as the greatest knight in the world, possessed of the most prowess, 'sens', and loyalty, Marshal could be sure that God would receive him.[81]

---

[76] Holdsworth, 'Ideas and Reality', 78. See his further comment on pp. 76–7: 'The work of a knight, the work of Christ, the work of a monk, were all inextricably linked because they seemed varieties of battle.'

[77] Vita Herluini, in J. A. Robinson, *Gilbert Crispin*, 94–5.

[78] Wright, ed., tr., *Historical Works*, 266. Orderic would undoubtedly not have appreciated this stark formulation, yet in praising the benefactors of his own house he tells us that a former knight, Arnold (now one of the monks), travelled as far as Apulia and Calabria 'to ask for support for his church from the loot acquired by his kinsmen in Italy': Chibnall, ed., *Ecclesiastical History*, IV, bk. VIII, 142–3.

[79] Gillingham, 'War and Chivalry'. [80] Kaeuper and Kennedy, *Book of Chivalry*, 176–7.

[81] Meyer, ed., *Histoire*, II, ll. 18387–406, 19072–165.

Such unqualified praise is easily understandable. Men who have acted largely in the world brought great honour and legitimacy to a way of life with which they were closely identified, or which, as in William's case, they personified. The need for knighthood was undeniable; churchmen knew that knighthood could be the armed force of God. When that force acted heroically on the battlefield (even if not in strict accord with clerical standards) or when it acted beneficently in a court, giving gifts to religious foundations, the concept of an *ordo* of knighthood was available as a vehicle for thought. It was likely to loom much larger in both lay and clerical minds than the formal qualifications and particular strictures attached to the idea.

PART III

✦✦✦

THE LINK WITH *ROYAUTÉ*

W E have seen that clerical theory accepted violence for right causes and not for wrong—a distinction that is tricky to make at the best of times, and especially so in an imperfect world. Kings and royal administrators, no less than their counterparts in the clerical hierarchy, had mixed feelings about basic issues of war, violence, and rightful authority. They had two goals: to move in the direction of a working monopoly—or at least a royal supervision—of war-like violence within their realm, and to maintain vigorous leadership of the violence exported beyond the realm in the form of organized war. These royal goals inevitably entailed a complex pattern of cooperation and conflict between emerging kingship and emerging chivalry. Like powerful bar magnets turning at different speeds in close proximity, chivalry and kingship now drew each other together, now forced each other apart.

Yet on either side of the Channel—or at least within spheres dominated by the Capetians and the Plantagenets—kingship was rooted in specific historical circumstances and gathered its strengths and capacities on differing timetables. These important differences, as well as many shared characteristics, shape the chapters of Part Three. Common features, particularly well illustrated in French chivalric literature, appear in Chapter 5, which only begins to sketch out differences between Capetian and Plantagenet political culture. Chapter 6 takes up the case of chivalry and English kingship, emphasizing differences. As so often, the particularities of English political and social circumstances repay separate, close investigation.

5

CHEVALERIE AND *ROYAUTÉ*

✦✦✦

Royal Stance on War and Violence

Powerful images of the fellowship of Arthur and his companions gathered at the Round Table point us towards the genuine shared interests of kings and knights. Yet this Arthurian literature, with its dénouement of destructive conflict, likewise suggests tensions and contradictions between royalty and chivalry. This chapter examines both lines of force.

By right and duty kings were assumed to work to secure basic order in society. Even though they might prove ineffectual or even troublesome in that role, they settled disputes, were supposed to protect property, and promoted honour; they operated a legal system of courts and officials that knights clearly found useful.

Chivalric literature openly endorses this royal role in law and justice.[1] A wise man-at-arms in the *Lancelot do Lac* provides a classic statement of the right and responsibility of royalty: '[E]veryone would be disinherited and ruined if King Arthur were overthrown,' he says, 'because the stability of all of us is his concern.'[2] The *Story of Merlin*, takes the same line, asserting that able kings secure order. The text relates that rebellions against Arthur's father, Uther Pendragon, had increased with the king's age and weakness.[3] The *Lancelot* makes a similar point: the land was sorely troubled by disorders, while Arthur was imprisoned by the False Guinevere: 'Now seeing their land without a master, the barons began to war with one another, though this was unbearable to the worthy and noble among them who sought only the general good.'[4] On his quest in *The Marvels of Rigomer*, Lancelot enters a land he learns is rife with

---

[1] In addition to the texts cited below, see two fascinating discussions: Elspeth Kennedy on issues of royalty, chivalry, lineage, and prowess in the *Lancelot do Lac* in 'Quest for Identity', and Roussineau on the *Perceforest*, chivalry, and the founding of the order of the Garter by Edward III in 'Ethique chevaleresque'.

[2] Elspeth Kennedy, ed., *Lancelot do Lac*, I, 35. The same sentiment is repeated in the cyclic version of the Lancelot story: Rosenberg, tr., *Lancelot Part I*, 17; Sommer, ed., *Vulgate Version*, II, 31.

[3] Sommer, *Vulgate Version*, II, 77.

[4] Rosenberg, tr., *Lancelot Part III*, 265: Sommer, *Vulgate Version*, IV, 51.

terror and conflict because of weak governance. The message is doubled when he is told that he should travel in a neighbouring land ruled well by a powerful king who is also a brave and noble knight who hangs robbers enthusiastically.[5]

The king as ideal fount of justice can blend with the king as ideal patron of chivalry. *The Romance of Silence* imagines this ideal partnership as its story opens:

> Once upon a time Evan was king of England.
> He maintained peace in his land;
> with the sole exception of King Arthur,
> there never was his equal
> in the land of the English.
> His rules were not just idle talk. . . .
> He upheld justice in his realm;
> his people were no criminals.
> He maintained chivalry
> and sustained young warriors
> by gifts, not empty promises.[6]

If they shared some ideals about peace and justice, kings and knights also shared war. Persistently, on both sides of the Channel, rulers and those who clustered around them acted on bellicose impulses, to which the political and military history of the period stands as plain witness. War involved the king as knight, with his knights. Of course it was never as simple as this. War also involved money, ships, mercenaries, and specialist engineers for the inevitable, grinding sieges; moreover, it did not closely involve all of the king's knights. At the level of basic patterns of thought, however, *royauté* and *chevalerie* agreed on the inevitability and importance, even the desirability, of war. If kings thought more of politics where some knights were more concerned with prowess, both considered the profits—a completely honorable motive—and both thought war a characteristic and defining activity of their respective spheres, here joined in basic cooperation.

What becomes more interesting, then, is to ask about royal and chivalric attitudes towards war *within* the realm. What rules, if any, governed the possession of fortifications, the open display of arms and the assertion of the right

---

[5] Vesce, tr., *Marvels of Rigomer*, 53; Wendelin Foerster, ed., *Mervelles de Rigomer*, ll. 2365–84. Later in this romance a body of British knights overwhelms both sides in a private war and imposes peace: Vesce, ibid., 163; Foerster, ibid., ll. 7484–604. Giants who issue forth from their castle to ravage the countryside could easily be a symbol of lordly ravaging: Vesce, ibid., 192–3; Foerster, ibid., ll. 8869–9102.

[6] Roche-Mahdi, ed., tr., *Silence*, 6–7.

to use them in 'private' war? And what of tournament, which basically amounted to a form of war as chivalric sport?

Such topics involve fundamental issues of sovereignty, for kings increasingly claimed that warlike violence undoubtedly ranked among the significant areas over which they wanted some control.[7]

On both sides of the Channel successive kings worked sporadically, but with something like a sense of mission, to enforce a conception of peace that stemmed from a developing royal prerogative as well as a sense of duty rooted, finally, in the will of God.

Some scholars find no tension at all, denying that kings could have much effect on issues of public order, or even took them seriously. Of course, no medieval government could truly supervise justice and guarantee public order throughout the realm, nor, for that matter, could any other government for a long time thereafter. Fears about governmental inability on this score have even surfaced in the contemporary world. Yet an essential dimension of the problem of public order drops from sight if we neglect the obvious royal impulse on both sides of the Channel to read sovereignty in no small measure in terms of the control of warlike violence, or at least to insist on a royal role in its direction and channelling. Whatever their success rate, whatever the complications of their own complicity, kings surely tried to effect a royal monopoly over licit violence, and the attempt is an undeniably important fact in early European history. Their work as sovereigns was complicated by two significant facts: kings, too, were knights and generally believed in a code that enshrined violence; and they needed the knights as part of their administrations and as a key element in their military force.

Yet the sense of responsibility for public order and the drive for sovereignty were real enough and brought royal encroachment on the independence of knights, especially those inclined to engage in heroic violence.[8] In the biography of William Marshal the author moans that, in his day, chivalry has been imprisoned; the life of the knight errant, he charges, has been reduced to that of the litigant in courts.[9]

Even when desired and accepted, royal justice could be partial and imperfect. Caution is especially strong in earlier French works, as effective kingship is just emerging. The king, who in many a *chanson* reigns even when he does not effectively rule, creates endless problems by unwise and immoral

---

[7] See Strayer, *Medieval Origins* and Kaeuper, *War, Justice, and Public Order*.

[8] The anthropologist Julian Pitt-Rivers catches the ambiguity nicely by noting that 'while the sovereign is the "fount of honour" in one sense, he is also the enemy of honour in another, since he claims to arbitrate in regard to it': 'Honour and Social Status', 30.

[9] Meyer, ed., *Histoire*, ll. 2686–92.

distribution of fiefs; his foolishness sets up the seemingly endless cycles of violence in *Raoul de Cambrai*, for example.[10] Arthur himself sometimes needs reminding of his royal role in the maintenance of justice. In the crisis of his quarrel with Galehaut, the Wise Man tells Arthur he must truly give the justice God entrusted to him with the dominion he holds. Later in this same romance we find a chastened Arthur dutifully holding admirable courts of law: 'as soon as the case was heard, the right had to be upheld'.[11]

Even when impartial, royal justice could intrude on knightly honour defended by prowess. More than one knight finds himself charged with murder in a case of killing he considers fully justified and honourable. Even the poor but honourable knight whom Robin Hood helps in the *Geste of Robyn Hood* was impoverished as a result of defending his son in court after the young man had killed another knight and a squire in a tournament.[12]

An even more revealing case appears when Guinevere's father, King Leodagan, 'who was a good ruler and lawgiver', condemns the knight Bertelay. Though Bertelay had slain another knight, it was only after following the proper forms—breaking faith with the man and openly threatening him with death.[13] Asked about the killing,

[Bertelay] answered that he would indeed defend himself against anyone who called him a criminal: 'I do not say I did not kill him, but I did break faith with him first. . . . So, as I see it, a man should harm his deadly enemy in all the ways he can—after he has broken faith with him.'

The defence is, of course, that of Ganelon in the *Chanson de Roland* of perhaps a century earlier: taking revenge against an enemy openly is no crime against a king. What have kings to do with this anyway? Charlemagne's answer in the great epic, validated by a trial by combat which reveals the will of God, emphasizes public good over private revenge and leads to Ganelon's terrible death as a traitor.[14] King Leodagan's position, though milder, would have pleased Charlemagne; the king told Bertelay 'that he was mistaken, "but if you had come to me and brought suit against him, I would not have ruled against you; then you could have taken vengeance. But you did not find me worthy enough to seek justice from me." ' Bertelay's reply assures personal loyalty but asserts private right: ' "Sir," he said, "say what you will, but I have never done you any

---

[10] Kay, ed., tr., *Raoul de Cambrai*. Any of the *chansons* in the Cycle of Rebel Barons could make the point, as could many from the Cycle of William of Orange.

[11] See Carroll tr., *Lancelot Part II*, 120–1, 150–1; Sommer, ed., *Vulgate Version*, III, 217–20, 271.

[12] See the *Geste of Robyn Hood*, Fytte One, stanzas 52–3 in Knight and Ohlgren, eds, *Robin Hood*.

[13] The following is drawn from Pickens, tr., *Story of Merlin*, 339–41; Sommer, *Vulgate Version*, II, 310–13.

[14] Brault, ed., tr., *Chanson de Roland*, laisses 270–91.

wrong, nor will I ever, God willing." ' But King Leodagan's court, made up
for this case of King Arthur, King Ban, King Bors, and seven distinguished
knights, orders Bertelay to be disinherited and exiled. King Ban, speaking for
the court, states the key to their decision: 'The reason is that he took it upon
himself to judge the knight he killed, and at night, but justice was not his to
mete out.' Bertelay goes off into exile, accompanied by 'a most handsome following of knights to whom he had many times given fine gifts, for he had been
a good and strong knight'.[15]

Other leading characters are occasionally drafted to speak out on behalf of a
recourse to the courts. Though the false Guinevere episode puts her in peril,
the true queen upholds the ideal monarchical role regarding justice, even
against her own immediate interests. When Galehaut offers to solve all her
problems by taking the false queen by force, Guinevere stoutly speaks up for a
system of justice administered in the courts and against violent self-help: 'I will
not, please God, allow that. I don't seek to be defended against her accusation
by anything but the law, and I won't ever, please God, be tempted by sinful
means but will wholly accept the king's judgement.'[16]

Even Lancelot informs a knight whom he encounters that it is not right for
one knight to pass judgement on another single-handedly; he should prove his
case in a court.[17] The principle is interesting, and runs directly counter to
Ramon Llull's assertion that good knights should simply eliminate the bad.[18]
Of course Lancelot gives advice he does not follow himself, for he marks the
trail of his adventures with the broken bodies of evildoers.

Early in the *Merlin Continuation* (much concerned with 'firsts', with the origins of chivalric customs) a squire asks Arthur to take vengeance for his lord,
killed in what the king calls the first of 'these trials of one knight against
another'. The squire tells Arthur that as king, by God's grace, he has sworn to
right 'the misdeeds that anyone—a knight or any other person—did in the
land'. Arthur goes in person to confront the killer, who turns out to be
Pellinor. Before the inevitable joust, Arthur and Pellinor assert contradictory
views about individual right and royal responsibility: 'Sir knight, who told
you to keep the passage of this forest in such a way that no knight, native or

---

[15] Cf. Rosenberg, tr., *Lancelot Part III*, 263 and Sommer, ed., *Vulgate Version*, ed., IV, 46,
where Bertelay's hatred is connected with his role in the False Guenevere episode. In *Lancelot Part
I* King Bors of Gaunes, who disinherited Pharian because of such a death, is called 'of all men one
of the most bent on justice': Rosenberg, tr., *Lancelot Part I*, 10; Sommer, *Vulgate Version*, III, 17.

[16] Rosenberg, tr., *Lancelot Part III*, 264; Sommer, *Vulgate Version*, IV, 48.

[17] Rosenberg, *Lancelot Part I*, 91; Sommer, *Vulgate Version*, III, 172; Elspeth Kennedy, ed.,
Lancelot do Lac, I, 222.

[18] Byles, ed., *Book of the Ordre of Chyvalry*, 27–30, 49. Llull thought of knights as governors
themselves, and gave little attention to any mechanisms by which their own excesses or crimes
might be checked.

foreign, may take the way through the forest but he must joust with you?' If Arthur has raised the fundamental question of licit violence, Pellinor, addressing Arthur as a knight, asserts a knight's right: 'Sir knight . . . I gave myself leave to do this, without authority or grace from anyone else.' Arthur will not accept such a sense of private right: 'You have done a great wrong . . . in that you didn't obtain leave at least from the lord of the land. I command you on his behalf to remove your tent from here and never again be so bold as to undertake such a thing.'[19]

The tension emerges openly again when Lancelot proposes to make kings of Hector, Bors, and Lionel in the victorious aftermath of the war against the usurper Claudas. Bors will have none of it, and explains why:

What is this, my lord, that you wish to do? Truly if I wanted to receive the honor of kingship, you should not permit it, for as soon as I have a kingdom, I'll be obligated to give up all knighthood, whether I wish to or not, and I'd have more honor as a landless man but a good knight than as a rich king who had given up knighthood. And what I say concerning myself, I say about your brother Hector, for it will be a mortal sin if, from the ranks of prowess and great knighthood where he now is, you remove him so that he may become king.[20]

The worlds of kingship and of pure knightly prowess obviously seem incompatible here.

More than a century later, these issues likewise bothered Honoré Bonet. In his *Tree of Battles*, sent to Charles VI in 1387, he takes the royalist line:

a person other than a prince cannot order general war. The reason for this is that no man should, or may, bear arms without the license of the prince. And another reason is that a man cannot take upon himself to do justice on another who has wronged him, but the prince must do justice between these men. But nowadays every man wishes to have the right of making war, even simple knights, and by the law this cannot be.[21]

Capetian Kingship and Chivalry

If the relationship of *royauté* and *chevalerie* was everywhere complex and ambivalent, it was not everywhere the same. Monarchy, in England and France in particular, followed different timetables, and these differences shaped the interaction between kingship and chivalry in each realm. Baldly stated, precocious growth characterized the English State; the French state (the model for most other realms) developed more slowly.[22] It is worth mak-

---

[19] Asher, tr., *Merlin Continuation*, 175, 179; Roussineau, ed., *Merlin*, I, 28, 41–2.
[20] Carroll, tr., *Lancelot Part VI*, 319; Micha, ed., *Lancelot*, VI, 169–70.
[21] Coupland, ed., tr., *Tree of Battles*, 129.
[22] This theme is developed in Kaeuper, *War, Justice, and Public Order*.

ing two separate examinations: we will look just at the Capetians here, then, in Chapter 6, at the Plantagenets.

At one level, it is true, the ideology of kingship as formally expressed in treatises and colourful ceremony would show broad similarities over much of high medieval Europe. On questions of controlling and channelling warlike violence, kings of France and their cousins in England shared a substratum of ideas from earlier medieval centuries; they formally linked regality with a justice impartially dispensed at all levels, and with the assurance of the sort of order within the realm that would allow the peaceful practice of Christianity. They came to view some violence as an affront to their sovereignty.

The similarities in oaths and responses spoken by the kings of England and France in their coronation ceremonies, for example, or the general agreement of ideas about the royal role expressed by ecclesiastical writers, easily demonstrate this fact.[23] Generic forms of coronation oath even appear in chivalric literature. In *The Story of Merlin*, for example, Arthur, recognized as king after he has repeatedly drawn the sword from the stone, is told by the archbishop:

if you are willing to swear and promise all the saints that you will safeguard the rights of Holy Church, keep lawful order and peace in the land, give help to the defenseless as best you can, and uphold all rights, feudal obligations, and lawful rule, then step forward and take the sword with which Our Lord has shown that you are His elect.

Weeping with joy, Arthur asks for God's help in providing 'the strength and the might to do what is right and to uphold all the things that you have told me and I have heard'.[24]

Promises which eventually hardened into formal coronation oaths show these basic ideas in Capetian France. Three traditional precepts bound the new king: to 'preserve through all time true peace for the church of God and all Christian people, to forbid rapine and iniquities of all sorts, and to enforce equity and mercy in all judgements'.[25]

Ideas even more closely focused on public order came from the gradual royal cooption of the peace movement. Although the *pax dei*, the Peace of God, originally looked to the greater lords to secure a measure of peace which weak kings were unable to manage, as effective Capetian power grew in the twelfth century the movement became the king's peace, *pax regis*.[26] Within this overall peace movement the effort to establish specific times of truce, a *treuga*

---

[23] These themes can be followed with much profit in Flori, *L'Idéologie du glaive*, especially 65–103.

[24] Pickens, tr., *Story of Merlin*, 216; Sommer, ed., *Vulgate Version*, II, 88.

[25] Quoting from Baldwin, *Philip Augustus*, pp. 375; see his discussion of the coronation promises and oaths, 374–5, and the many sources cited there.

[26] Grabois, 'Trêve de Dieu'.

dei when all fighting was prohibited, may have been particularly significant. As Head and Landes suggest,

over the course of the twelfth century, the Truce of God was inexorably co-opted by secular authorities and became part of the emerging constitutional order of governance and peacekeeping. By the mid-twelfth century in France the Peace of God had become the King's Peace.[27]

That the kings of England, by contrast, did not need the buttress of the peace movement reinforces the importance of cross-Channel differences. The work of kings of France had to be different, constrained as it was by different circumstances, especially the size and growth of the realm, the slow emergence of a hierarchy of courts and appeals, and the crucial factor of timing.

Ideology, in short, does not simply equate with actual capacity; beyond royal ideology, abstractly expressed, lies another important layer of operative ideas: justifications that royal officials gave for measures actually taken, day-to-day assertions found not only in coronation oaths or treatises but in the working documents of busy administrations. At this level the differences between English and French kingship retain significance and demand attention.

The ordinance or testament of 1190, which Philip II had drawn up before departure on crusade, speaks in its preface in bold terms of public utility, and states that the kingly office consists in securing his subjects' well-being. The document that follows this preamble outlines active measures: the *baillis* (regional officials) are to set aside one day a month to hold assizes at which they would receive appeals, and give prompt justice. Yet one clause establishes a formal procedure in case anyone made war against Philip's son, the young king, while the crusade lasted.[28] Clearly, this significant document embodies a sense of justice as a key function of regality; just as clearly, the reality and legitimacy of noble war within the realm, and even war against royalty itself, had to be recognized.

Louis IX (St Louis), half a century later, greatly strengthened the royal stance against violence within the realm. Perhaps he affected opinion most by his general unhappiness with 'private' war and duel and by his preference for peace, at least for peace among Christians. For each of his specific measures the exact timing, mechanisms, and generality within the realm remains uncertain; but at least within the royal domain the evidence suggests a serious pro-

---

[27] Head and Landes, eds, *Peace of God*, 8.
[28] *Ordonnances*, I, 18. See the discussion in Baldwin, *Philip Augustus*, 137–44. The difference between the statement about war against the young king in France and the closing of the Magna Carta (which licenses war against King John in case of non-compliance with the Charter) is that in England such war was formally illicit and was royally licensed by the Charter in this exceptional case; in France such war was not formally illicit and was simply expected.

gramme: Louis prohibited trial by battle in both 'civil' and 'criminal' cases; he instituted the 'quarantaine le roi' (a forty-day truce in private wars during which relatives of the combatants could have a chance to choose not to involve themselves); he restricted tournaments, and even prohibited private war itself and the carrying of offensive weapons. On the other hand, that he sometimes demolished castles belonging to lords under sentence of his court is a matter of record.[29]

The great reform ordinance of 1256 announced that his officials were to do justice to rich and poor alike and declared that they must preserve good laws. Louis probably believed in these principles, which could all too easily be dismissed. Joinville's story of the good king sitting beneath an oak at Vincennes, dispensing justice, is famous; but he also twice tells the story of the king listening intently to a friar's sermon and never forgetting its message: the only kingdoms lost to their kings were those in which justice was ignored. In a letter to his son, the future Philip III, these same themes reappear.[30]

Though he was a strenuous knight himself, so that Joinville could open his biography by saying he will tell of Louis's 'great deeds of chivalry (*de ses granz chevaleries*)', the king also revealed significant reservations about the devoted elevation of prowess, a key element of knighthood. Joinville once heard him state that a great distance stands between the man of prowess and the worthy man: '*il a grant différence entre preu home et preudome*'.[31] Behind the king's play on words lies the serious point that prowess cannot reign untempered and alone, the very point so often made in works of literature.

The last Capetians, Philip IV and his sons, advanced the programme of St Louis in a series of well-documented court decisions and *ordonnances*, which announced that the king's war must take precedence over all other warlike violence; while he fought his enemies, no private wars, judicial duels, or tournaments were to be tolerated.[32] The special relationship of royalty to warlike violence could scarcely be more clearly drawn: the king would lead war abroad and regulate it—in all its manifestations—within the realm. In fact, these late Capetian kings claimed rights to regulate warlike violence even in peacetime. As Philip IV announced in a 1292 ordinance: '[T]hroughout the entire realm of France, [cases involving] breaking the peace, carrying arms . . . generally

---

[29] *Ordonnances*, I, 56–8, 84, 86. See discussion and sources cited in Jordan, *Louis IX*, 140, 203–4; Ducoudray, *Origines du Parlement*, 329–32; Kaeuper, *War, Justice, and Public Order*, 214–15, 231–5. Cf. Wailly, ed., *Historie de Saint Louis*, 55, where a castle of a robber baron is pulled down by Louis on his way to take ship for the crusade.

[30] Wailly, *Histoire de Saint Louis*, 24, 25, 288–9, 308–9. In *Louis IX*, passim, Jordan has argued that in his great reform initiatives Louis was eliminating wrongs in his governance that had turned divine blessing away from his central crusading mission.

[31] Wailly, *Histoire de Saint Louis*, 235.

[32] E.g. *Ordonnances* I, 328–9, 342–5, 390, 421–2, 492–3, 538–9, 562, 643, 655–6, 701–2.

belong wholly to the lord king, by reason of his superiority, even in places where other lords hold high justice.'[33]

Whenever needed, French kings could draw upon an arsenal of legal measures: they could provide royal safeguards (*sauveguardes*) to particular religious houses or individuals, they could impose assured truces (*asseurements*) on quarreling parties, grant the royal *panonceaux* (signs of the king's protection) to be affixed almost anywhere, on houses, ships, even gallows.[34] In their day-by-day work the royal courts continued, in theory, to provide swift and impartial justice to great and small, the most basic royal service in the interests of peace within the realm.[35]

Did the French crown really act on the ideas expressed so often in its legal and administrative documents? *Ordonnances* announced in the most uncompromising language may not, to be sure, have covered the entire realm, and were often violated where they did in theory apply; but the direction of the working royal ideology and royal efforts at actual enforcement can scarcely be denied. No reader of the records of the highest French court, the *Parlement* of Paris, can doubt that the crown prosecuted knights for assault and murder, theft and pillage, breaking of truces, and private war.[36] No reader of French chivalric literature can doubt the knights' sensitivity to the intrusion.

The Balance Sheet

For all the tensions, chivalric literature in France never seriously challenged the existence of kingship. Some epics in their frustration, it is true, may edge close to the idea of doing without the troublesome fact of kings. The *Charroi de Nîmes* (in the cycle of twelfth-century *chansons* about William of Orange) at one point imagines that this great knight angrily tells King Louis that he could kill all of Louis' men and even kill Louis himself. A little later in this same *chanson* William pointedly reminds the king that he had himself placed the crown on Louis' head and warns that he now feels like knocking it off.[37] In *Aliscans*, another of his *chansons*, an irate William again threatens to kill King Louis, who has here scorned William in his great need.[38] Would William have replaced him as king, rather than leaving the kingdom without its titular head?

---

[33] *Ordonnances*, VII, 611, quoted in Strayer, *Philip the Fair*, 195: 'pacis fractio, portacio armorum . . . generaliter pertinent domino rege in solidum per totum regnum Francie racione sue superioritatis, eciam in locis ubi alii domini habent merum imperium.'

[34] Discussed, with sources cited, in Kaeuper, *War, Justice, and Public Order*, 231–60.

[35] As in Philip IV's great reform ordinance, 1302: *Ordonnances*, I, 354–6.

[36] Evidence provided in Kaeuper, *War, Justice, and Public Order*, 184–268.

[37] Price, tr., *Wagon-Train*, laisses 11, 17; McMillan, ed., *Charroi de Nîmes*.

[38] Ferrante, ed., tr., *Guillaume d'Orange*, laisse lxv; Wienbeck *et al.*, eds, *Aliscans*.

In *Raoul de Cambrai* the erring King Louis is cursed as the cause of trouble and told by a baron he is 'not worth a button'.[39]

Yet such statements represent the growlings of particular dissatisfaction more than any sober attempts at a theory of governance. In fact, learned studies have argued that many of the *chansons de geste* must be linked to the waxing of royal power which these texts support.[40] Some romances show the same ideological inclination, a good example being Chrétien's *Erec*, with its self-conscious associations with Angevin kingship in its famous coronation scene.[41] Kings are accepted; these works simply projected characteristics essential to an ideal and emphasized them by vividly illustrating the problems caused by their absence. The problem of governance, in short, was not located in the very fact of kingship, but was blamed, instead. on bad or inept men trying to fill the role.[42]

Of course, a true king was in no small degree welcomed in this literature because he possessed one of the chief chivalric qualities: prowess. A good king was a good knight and could cleave helmets and thrust lances with the best. The *Perlesvaus* presents a classic scene of Arthur and Gawain riding side by side into the action of a great tournament:

Their horses were now decked in their trappings, and the king and Sir Gawain mounted, fully armed, and charged into the tournament with such fury that they smashed right through the biggest companies, felling horses and knights and whatever they met. Then the king caught sight of Nabigan who was riding forward in all of his finery; the king struck him such a furious blow that he sent him crashing from his horse and broke his collar-bone.[43]

Riding side by side into actual war is, of course, better still. In the *Mort Artu*, as Arthur and his knights fight their tragic battle against the forces of Lancelot, Arthur proves his worth as a knight in the best manner:

That day King Arthur bore arms, and did it so well that there was no man of his age in the world who could have equalled him; indeed the story affirms that on his side there was no knight, old or young, who bore arms as well as he did. Through the example of

---

[39] Kay, ed., tr. *Raoul de Cambrai*, laisses CCXXV, CCXXIV.

[40] General discussions in Boutet and Strubel, *Littérature, politique et société*, 39–67; Boutet, 'La politique et l'histoire'; and 'Chansons de geste'. The theme in particular works: Hunt, 'L'inspiration idéologique'; Combarieu, 'La violence'; Flori, 'Sémantique et idéologie'.

[41] Topsfield, *Chrétien de Troyes*, 52; Schmolke-Hasselmann, 'Henry II Plantagenêt'. Cf. Holzermayr, 'Le "mythe" d'Arthur'; Boutet, 'Carrefours idéologique'.

[42] Peters discusses the complexities and tensions associated with the *rex inutilis* theme in *The Shadow King*; for tensions in the portrayal of King Arthur (and Charlemagne), see Elspeth Kennedy, 'King Arthur'.

[43] Bryant, tr., *Perlesvaus*, 189; Nitze and Jenkins, eds, *Perlesvaus*, II, 294.

his fine chivalry all his men fought so well that the men from the castle would have been conquered if it had not been for Lancelot.[44]

Another royal trait idealized in chivalric writing may seem merely unremarkable piety. Who could be surprised to read time and again that a king must be a good Christian? The Duke of Burgundy, in the *Song of Aspremont*, begins his speech on ideal kingship along just these lines: 'The type of man who seeks a crown on earth, / Should look to God and in his faith be firm; / He should both honor and serve the Holy Church.'[45] Is this insistence, encountered so often, simply the reflex response of the cleric or quasi-cleric who penned the text?

This trait is unlikely to be rooted in clericalism alone. More likely, it also reflects age-old beliefs that the religious standing of the king significantly determines the fate of the group or, in time, of the kingdom.[46] Such beliefs were much older than the Gregorian Reform that sought to diminish their force; they also proved to be more durable than clerical critics expected. In chivalric literature, kings, in company with other great laymen, often dominate churchmen and church property in just the ways the Gregorians had vigorously denounced for a century or more. We need only recall how dominant and even sacerdotal a role Charlemagne plays in *The Song of Roland* — blessing in Jesus's name and in his own, conversing with his companion angels, convincing God to extend the daylight (in order to effect his revenge).[47] As Marc Bloch pointedly observed, 'Clearly the Gregorian reform had not yet passed that way.'[48]

Royal piety is, moreover, often linked with the basic obligation of the king to right fundamental wrongs in human society, especially to succour widows and orphans. Significantly, such duties were also a staple of the chivalric ethos. In the *Lancelot do Lac* the Worthy Man's blistering critique of Arthur's kingship includes the charge that '[t]he right of widows and orphans has perished under your dominions'. He threatens Arthur with the warning: 'God will call you most cruelly to account for this, for He Himself said through the mouth of His prophet David that He is the guardian of the poor and sustains the orphans and will destroy the ways of the sinners.'[49]

---

[44] Cable, tr., *Death of King Arthur*, 144; Frappier, ed., *La Mort*, 115.

[45] See ll. 7160–62 in Newth, ed., tr., *Song of Aspremont*, and Brandin, ed., *Chanson d'Aspremont*.

[46] Bloch, *Société Féodale*, tr. Manyon, II, 379–83; Chaney provides an interesting case study in *Cult of Kingship*.

[47] Laisses 26, 179 in Brault, ed., tr., *Chanson de Roland*, For the anti-Gregorianism in the *Chanson d'Aspremont*, see the opening section of Chapter 11 below.

[48] *Société Féodale*, I, 96 n.

[49] Corley, tr., *Lancelot of the Lake*, 238; Elspeth Kennedy, ed., *Lancelot do Lac*, I, 283.

The idea that the king must do his utmost to give impartial justice to all, regardless of rank, is tirelessly emphasized in *chansons* and romances. Arthur states the position plainly in Chrétien's *Erec*:

> I am the king . . .
> I should not wish in any way
> to commit disloyalty or wrong,
> no more to the weak than the strong;
> it is not right that any should complain of me . . .[50]

In fact, chivalric authors' interest in the full social range of impartial royal just-ice often quickly narrowed to the ranks of privileged society and to the specifics of feudal relationships.[51] More than one poem in the Cycle of William of Orange turns on that point, and it is a similar failure of the king to provide feudal justice that animates the savage cycles of knightly feuding in *Raoul de Cambrai*.[52]

One key policy is for the king to free himself of low-born advisers and rely solely on the only people who count, that is, on men of 'the right blood', whether they are clerics or laymen. In the *Crowning of Louis*, Charlemagne advises his son Louis 'not to take a lowborn man as your counsellor, the son of a lord's agent or of a bailiff. These would betray their trust in a minute for money.'[53] The Duke of Burgundy in the *Song of Aspremont* speaks to the choice of both clerical and lay officials and counsellors; combining self-conscious anti-Gregorianism with chivalric rectitude, he insists that all come from 'good family':

> You should keep by your side men of good birth;
> From their good counsel you may find out and learn
> The way to govern your own soul and self first: . . .
> Make not a bishop of the son of your shepherd;
> Take a king's son, or duke's or count's, I tell you.
> Or vavassor's, though his family be penniless . . .
> Archbishops seven bear office in my shires
> And there's not one, so strict I've scrutinized,
> Whom either king or high duke has not sired . . .[54]

This ideal must have produced sage nods of agreement from those assembled in a royal or baronial hall—some low-born officials perhaps prudently paying more attention to their wine goblets for a moment.

---

[50] Carroll, ed., tr., *Erec*, ll. 1757, 1764–7. [51] Larmat, 'L'orphelin.

[52] Larmat recognizes the social constrictions on the royal concern for orphans and widows: see ibid. *Raoul de Cambrai* will be discussed below, Chapter 11.

[53] Hoggan, tr., 'Crowning of Louis' 5; Langlois, ed., *Couronnement de Louis*, 7.

[54] See ll. 11236–8, 11214–16, 11310–12, in Newth, ed., tr., *Song of Aspremont*, and Brandin, ed., *Chanson d'Aspremont*. *Dignités* is the word translated as 'shires'.

Yet if this ideal court is a centre of fine chivalry and a useful forum, in all instances disputes are brought to the king by a suitor's choice, not by royal claims to jurisdiction. Supervised arbitration is the process, not clearly sovereign adjudication, a picture that largely matches twelfth-century political and legal reality. As John Baldwin has shown, slightly more than a third of the cases coming into the royal court under Philip II between 1179 and 1223 received imposed royal judgements; somewhat more than half were settled by simple agreements between the parties.[55] Like Charlemagne or Arthur, Philip Augustus offered a service to those who chose to take advantage of it. Yet Philip's reign was, as Baldwin also argues, a turning-point in French history: 'The French king was no longer merely reacting to his great vassals . . . He was now able to seize the initiative to win supremacy. . . . Benefiting from the resources of a rich kingdom, Philip laid the foundations of French royal power in the Middle Ages.'[56]

Chivalric literature was highly reluctant to recognize such direct royal jurisdiction over major issues of justice and even more reluctant to recognize a working royal monopoly over licit violence.[57] The pages of *chanson* and romance generally refuse even to register the existence of a centralizing, bureaucratic administration with a system of courts energized by insistent and expanding jurisdiction, with proceeds of taxation collected through administrative mechanisms looming ever larger over the local horizon. Historical records occasionally preserve the puzzled and offended surprise which greets royal constraint. On the way to the gallows in 1323, at the end of a remarkable career of defiant private warfare, Jourdain de l'Isle Jourdain confessed that his actions on several counts merited the death penalty; yet, the record reveals, he added a significant coda of failed self-justification in each case: 'but he said that it was in war'.[58]

---

[55] Baldwin, *Philip Augustus*, 37–44. 'We can only conclude that the technique of allowing contending parties to arrive at their own decisions, then to be confirmed by royal authority, was the preferred method for resolving disputes in the royal courts' (p. 43).

[56] Ibid., 423.

[57] Coming to terms with royalty was a particular theme in the *chansons de geste*. Kaeuper, *War, Justice, and Public Order*, 315–25.

[58] Statement in Langlois and Lanhers eds, *Confessions et jugements*, 37–9. Discussion of the case and career in Cutler, *Law of Treason*, 46, 144–5; Kicklighter, 'Nobility of English Gascony'.

6

ENGLISH KINGSHIP, CHIVALRY AND LITERATURE

✦✦✦

ALTHOUGH a part of common patterns of medieval civilization, England regularly shows fascinating and instructive differences from societies across the Channel. By the 'age of chivalry' one of the most significant differences is the long-term growth of royal power. Real meaning infused the widespread idea that the king of England was responsible for order and justice in his realm; from an early date this royalist ideal appeared regularly in documents by which officials remembered and acted.

Royal Ideology and Enforcement

Statements announcing the beginning of a king's reign provide a rich source. At his somewhat uncertain accession to the throne in 1100, Henry I trumpeted his intention in terms of royal peace: 'I establish my firm peace through my entire realm and order it to be kept henceforth.'[1] When Edward I acceded, on his father's death in 1272, his administrators unambiguously announced on his behalf (since he was on crusade): 'We are and will be prepared, by the authority of God, to give full justice to each and every person in all cases and matters concerning them against any others great or small.'[2] Similarly, the administration of Edward III, at the time of his father's supposed abdication in 1327, stated on behalf of the young king:

We command and firmly enjoin each and every one, on pain of disherison and loss of life or members, not to break the peace of our said lord the king; for he is and shall be ready to enforce right for each and every one of the said kingdom in all matters and against all persons, both great and small. So if any one has some demand to make of another, let him make it by means of [legal] action, without resorting to force of violence.[3]

---

[1] Stubbs, *Select Charters*, 119.   [2] Stubbs, *Select Charters*, 439.
[3] Stephenson and Marcham, *English Constitutional History*, 205.

Such sentiments echo throughout the *Dialogue of the Exchequer*, by Richard FitzNigel, the first administrative treatise written in Western European history (*c.* 1179). Although the work is mainly concerned with the technical operation of the royal exchequer, comments on the king's role in keeping the peace surface frequently. Of Henry II, the author says: 'from the beginning of his rule he gave his whole mind to crushing by all possible means those who rebelled against peace and were "froward" '.[4] Rebelling against the king appears to this official as rebellion against peace itself. Of the Assize of Clarendon, FitzNigel says: 'nobody must venture to oppose the king's ordinance, made as it is in the interest of peace'.[5] He is sure royal power is sufficient to see that offenders will be punished and quotes approvingly a rhetorical question first asked by Ovid and picked up by more than one medieval writer: 'Have you forgotten that kings' arms are long?'[6]

Preambles to statutes offer the carrot as well as the stick. Henry III announced in the Statute of Marlborough (1267) his intention to 'provide for the better estate of his realm of England, and for the more speedy administration of justice, as belongs to the office of a king'. Henry's son, Edward I, likewise announced in his Statute of Gloucester (1278) a fuller administration of justice 'as the good of the kingly office demands'. The first Statute of Westminster (1285) worried over 'the peace less kept and the laws less used, and the offenders less punished than they ought to be, so that the people feared the less to offend'. The king announced in the opening clause that the peace of the Church and of the land will henceforth be guarded and that common right will be done to all, rich and poor.[7]

When royal authority had been challenged, as in the mid-century baronial wars of the reign of Henry III, the language recording a recovery of the royal powers can become especially forceful and specific. The Dictum of Kenilworth (1266) declared in its first clause:

the most noble prince Henry, illustrious king of England shall have, fully receive and freely exercise his dominion, authority and royal power without impediment or contradiction of any one, whereby, contrary to the approved rights and laws and long established customs of the kingdom, the regal dignity might be offended; and that to the same lord king and to his lawful mandates and precepts full obedience and humble attention shall be given by all and singular the men of the same kingdom, both greater and lesser. And all and singular shall through writs seek justice in the court of the lord

---

[4] Johnson, ed., tr., *Dialogus de Scaccario*, 75. The text contains many passing references on the royal duty of preserving the peace; e.g., p. 63.
[5] Ibid., 101. See also p. 102 where the king is again identified with the interests of peace.
[6] Ibid., 84. As we saw in Chapter 1, Suger also used this image.
[7] *Statutes of the Realm*, I, 19, 45, 26.

king and shall be answerable for justice, as was accustomed to be done up to the time of the recent disorders.

Clause 38 of this document is even more explicit about private quarrels. The royal government asserts: 'no one will take private revenge on account of the disorders, nor will he procure or consent or tolerate that private revenge should be taken. And if any one takes private revenge, let him be punished by the court of the lord king.'[8]

The most revealing piece of evidence comes, however, from a simple phrase which began to appear during the first quarter of the thirteenth century in writs of trespass and in informal legal complaints asking the crown to provide justice. One prospective plaintiff after another stated that some wrongdoer had come 'by force and arms and against the lord king's peace (*vi et armis et contra pacem domini regis*)'. Such litigants knew that these magic words would bring their cases into the royal courts.[9] The message had filtered through: the king would maintain his peace throughout the realm; his governance would supervise the use of arms within the realm.

Of course it was not really true; the king's government could not do all that it claimed. The phrase came sometimes to be used as a key to open courtroom doors for cases that involved mere gentle fraud or illegal apple-picking, with no edged weapons glinting in the sunlight.[10] The point remains, however, that royal claims became quite clearly recognized, even if only partially enforced. *Royauté* within the realm of England meant sovereignty and a working monopoly of the means of violence associated with war.

That the English crown was serious about sovereignty of this sort appears in its efforts to control tournaments, to require licences for building castles, and to outlaw any insular version of the continental practice of 'private' war. For a time it succeeded in making England seem to the high-spirited and chivalrous a dreary place without a good tournament circuit, as the oft-quoted passages from the biography of William Marshal state explicitly.[11] But the maintenance of so hard a royal line was only temporary; by the fourteenth century English kings were joining in and leading the sport rather than continuing to prohibit so powerful a practice.[12] Nevertheless, the English crown had at least taken steps to regulate this simulacrum of war.[13]

The royal insistence on licences 'to crenelate'—that is, to fortify—had more long-range success. A staggering number of illicit or 'adulterine' castles were pulled down, especially in the reign of Henry II; the policy of formal licences,

---

[8] Ibid., I, 12–17.   [9] Harding, 'Plaints and Bills'.   [10] Ibid.
[11] Meyer, ed., *Histoire*, II, ll. 1533–48. Cf. Barber and Barker, *Tournaments*, 19–26.
[12] Kaeuper, *War, Justice, and Public Order*, 199–211, and the sources cited there.
[13] Keen, *Nobles, Knights*, 83–99. Cf. Kaeuper, *War, Justice, and Public Order*, 199–211.

a recognition of the royal right to regulate, had become viable by the time of Henry III.[14]

The policy against war within the realm—that is, open warlike violence or even carrying offensive arms and riding with unfurled banners in full and joyous expectation of combat—met with greater success still, except, of course, for those times when an over-governed England erupted in civil war. With that exception, however, the concept of the king's peace had real content and showed (within limitations inherent in medieval government) a genuine effort to translate royal ideals into fact.[15]

Did English knights cooperate? Chivalric ideas, whatever qualifications about royal control they embodied, did little to prevent English knighthood from serving the crown regularly and loyally. If their military service is obvious, they also gave essential and unpaid help in law and administration; they sat on juries and inquests, on commissions of oyer and terminer, on commissions of roads and dikes, or of array; they acted as tax assessors and collectors. Some served as sheriffs, some as justices. Many of them eventually went to Westminster to sit in Parliament as Knights of the Shire. This range of services has been fully investigated in many historical studies.

Other facets of English knightly life, however, have been less often treated and have sometimes been denied. Although English knighthood could not claim a legal right of war within the realm, as in France, lords and knights turned to formally illegal acts of violence, on any scale they could manage, when the law did not serve or when the sense of urgency was simply too great. The results for public order could look rather like those we have noted for France.

In late thirteenth-century England three particular witnesses—King Edward I, the chronicler Pierre Langtoft, and the anonymous author of a broadside poem—commented from their quite different vantage points that the violence troubling the country seemed like the outbreak of war. Edward I added, significantly, that this illicit warlike violence 'flouted the lordship of the king'.[16]

Legal records show us that the knightly violence so prevalent in chivalric literature was (in somewhat more prosaic form, but without loss of essential enthusiasm) practised in everyday life, with serious consequences for public order. Only very slowly, only with mixed success, could the crown declare such action illegal; only more slowly still could the crown take effective action actually to restrict knightly violence within the realm.

[14] Kaeuper, *War, Justice, and Public Order*, 211–25.
[15] Ibid., 225–67. Waugh provides a good case study in 'Profits of Violence'.
[16] Sources and discussion in Kaeuper, 'Law and Order'.

Of course, a search of records surviving from royal courts uncovers case after case of some villager or townsman attacking another with varying degrees of success and consequence; the margins of the parchment rolls are dotted with the letter 's' combined with a ligature, indicating that the accused was hanged (*suspendatur*) after conviction. These unfortunates were assuredly of sub-knightly status. In fact there can be no suggestion that court records on either side of the Channel mainly document crown action against the knightly.

We need feel no surprise. The dockets of courts in most societies are surely not filled with cases against those occupying the highest ranks in that society, charging them with some form of behaviour that they stoutly maintain is licit. Rather, we should take note that such cases appear at all in medieval royal records. The crown gradually sought to define the warlike violence of the privileged as illicit and to take steps against it. Chivalric literature records the obvious sensitivities to such control.[17]

The Evidence of Literature

The particularities of medieval civilization in England produced not only a unique *royauté* and *chevalerie*, they generated a literature written in three languages: Latin, Anglo-Norman French, and Middle English. This literary evidence is complicated by questions about the groups or social levels that enjoyed these stories about kings, knights, and yeomen.[18]

Understanding this issue of audience means again recognizing a unique feature of medieval England: social structure was much more fluid, much less rigidly hierarchical than that across the Channel. Lines of demarcation in the upper social ranks tended to blur, producing more community of feeling among all ranks of the privileged, from great lords through country knights and squires (sometimes even a notch below) and not excluding the more important mercantile layers.[19] The pattern of landholding helps to explain this characteristic of English society; even the great held estates scattered widely by continental standards, where relatively compact territorial holdings were more common. A lord or a lordling who held a single manor here, partial rights to

---

[17] See the evidence and interpretation in Harding, 'Early Trailbaston Proceedings'; Kaeuper, *War, Justice, and Public Order*, 184–268.

[18] The theme of England's differences is developed in Maddicott, 'Why was England Different?' and in Kaeuper, *War, Justice, and Public Order*, 315–47. The theme of audience is discussed in Mehl, *Middle English Romances*, 2–13; Barron, *English Medieval Romance*; Crane, *Insular Romance*; Green, *Poets and Princepleasers*; and Coss, 'Cultural Diffusion'.

[19] It is striking, for instance, to note the ease with which Sir John Clanvowe, a knight at the court of Edward III and Richard II, used mercantile images in his treatise, 'The Two Ways': see Scattergood, ed., *Sir John Clanvowe*, 60–1.

another there, and half a mill in another county would have a highly developed interest in the royal role in peacekeeping and in the details of the emerging common law. Kingship, the common law coming into being and into effect through royal courts, a particular pattern of estates—all helped to make the social and political context in England different from that on the other side of the Channel.

It comes as no surprise, then, to find that the literature of this society reflected and helped to generate and generalize this unusual degree of royal capacity and social fluidity. These factors surely help to explain, in turn, why there is less attention paid in English than in French literature to those troublesome, talented men of modest social status who carried wands of office and issued orders, no doubt in a voice just a bit too shrill. It certainly helps to explain why English literature, unlike French romances, does not stress the social and cultural separation of knights from everyone else.

The unusual qualities of the literature, however, have led some scholars to suggest that romances were written in twelfth- and thirteenth-century England for bourgeois audiences, or for even humbler groups raising tankards in some tavern. Others have suggested, more convincingly, that the influence, as so often in the Middle Ages, came from the top of society, but that it is here mediated and diffused downward throughout privileged society generally by unique features of English social, tenurial, and political life.[20]

If we step aside from the details of such discussions, the important fact seems to be that there was not an exclusively chivalric literature in England on the pattern we have just considered in France, a literature which reinforced a strong sense of a caste or class of knights as different as they could imagine themselves to be from the sub-knightly. To the contrary, in England a 'knightly' point of view must be considered within a broader consensus of views informing the minds of those in the upper social layers, from substantial village landowners up the scale to the very great. In short, we must ask what privileged society in general—knights included—thought of the power of kingship advancing so inexorably and of the framework of law that kings and their advisers at least claimed to elaborate and enforce. Framing our questions in these terms, the literature patronized can show us the ideas celebrated, the questions debated.

This reading recalls another important historical fact: though kings and knights had differing agendas, only their cooperation allowed the early construction of something like sovereign power in England. Whatever quarrels

---

[20] This is one of the themes of Crane, *Insular Romance*. For extended discussion of this issue in a single romance, see Bunt, ed., *William of Palerne*, 17–19.

were writ large in tumults and civil wars, kings and knights found much common ground, in concert with all other privileged groups in society.

The most famous tale from medieval Britain provides our best evidence. The oldest surviving tale of Robin Hood, the *Geste*, merges the social ranks of the knights with sturdy yeomen and places issues of law and justice firmly in the foreground.[21] Robin Hood is not a knight; the text pointedly calls him 'a gode yeman'. But he shows many qualities we associate with ideal knighthood. His prowess is constantly displayed and is never in question. His loyalty, seen in his steadfastness, contrasts with the Sheriff of Nottingham who breaks his sworn word. Robin dispenses largesse with an open hand, never mind that the wherewithal comes from others' purses. The text shows—and comments on— his courtesy time and again; he regularly removes his hood and drops to one knee in the presence of those of more exalted rank. He is devoted to the Blessed Virgin and will harm no company in which ladies are present. He dines not only on the royal venison, but on swans, pheasants, and other fowl— all elegant fare. In a faint parallel to King Arthur himself (who always delayed dinner until he learned of some marvel or adventure), he will not sit down to table before he has found some guest. His piety also requires him to hear three masses before dining.

Moreover, one axis around which the story revolves is Robin's aiding a knight, Sir Richard atte Lee, who, if poor, is clearly the genuine article, much admired. When Robin Hood, learning of his poverty, thinks out loud that his entry into knighthood must have been recent, that he has been forced into the rank (by 'distraint of knighthood') or has wasted his resources foolishly or wickedly, Sir Richard answers stoutly:

> 'I am none of those.' sayd the knyght.
> 'By God that made me;
> An hundred wynter here before
> Myn auncestres knyghtes have be.'[22]

It comes as no surprise that Sir Richard's prowess, and that of his family, is quickly asserted. Financial troubles arose because his son killed 'a knyght of Lancaster and a squyer bolde' in a tournament; the financial drain of the effort 'For to save hym in his right'—legal costs, bribes, or an out-of-court settlement, we must assume—has devastated his resources. The father has matched his son's valour. Sir Richard has been a crusader and is considering it as an honourable outlet should he lose his lands to the wicked Abbot of St Mary's, as he fears. Called a false knight by the Abbot, he bristles:

---

[21] Knight and Ohlgren, eds, *Robin Hood*.   [22] Ibid., fit 47.

> 'Thou lyest,' then sayd the gentyll knyght,
> Abbot, in thy hall;
> False knyght was I never. . . .
> In ioustes and in tournement
> Full ferre than have I be,
> And put my selfe as ferre in press
> As ony that ever I se.'[23]

He has endangered his body with the best, thrusting himself into the press of opposing warriors in the most worshipful way. Who can justly call a man of prowess false?[26]

Yet justice is far to seek, a state of affairs which has, of course, made Robin and his men outlaws in the first place. The effective agents of the king in the region, the sheriff of the county, and the 'hye justyce of Englonde' are false to the core; the latter is even in the pay of Sir Richard's dread enemy, the Abbot of St Mary's, and wears his livery, as he openly tells the knight: 'I am holde with the abbot, sayd the justyce, / Bothe with cloth and fee.'[25] Robin Hood's largesse saves Sir Richard from ruin and their combined righteous violence checks the sheriff and his men. Yet the only hope for a lasting solution, even after Robin has put a clothyard shaft through the sheriff's body, rests with the king himself, with 'Edward our comly kynge'.[26]

Of course, once the king and the king of outlaws meet, in famous scenes of disguise and game-playing, all goes well. The king, recognizing Robin's qualities and his unfeigned devotion, forgives all and takes him back to court. Despite all local corruptions, the fountain of justice runs pure at the centre. Good yeomen (marked by chivalric qualities), a good knight, a good king, have brought right order back into the world.[27]

This concern for justice within several layers of society, coupled with an abiding belief in the role of the king, also appears prominently in the body of tales traditionally known as the Matter of England romances. These tales, written in the thirteenth and fourteenth centuries, show a consistent fascination with political arrangements and a concern for good royal governance grounded in law. In no small measure they are stories about kingship.[28]

---

23 Knight and Ohlgren, eds, *Robin Hood*, fits 114, 116.
24 For prowess linked to loyalty and other qualities, see the discussion in Chapter 7.
25 Knight and Ohlgren, *Robin Hood*, fit 107.
26 Ibid., fit 353.
27 This being an outlaw tale, Robin tires of court and goes back to the greenwood, and to his murky end as a victim of the Prioress of Kirklees. Yet the sense of basic resolution of justice and of peace between Robin and the king remains.
28 For general discussions see Barron, *English Medieval Romance*, 63–89, and Crane, *Insular Romance* 1–92.

Order is secured by strong and wise kings: the theme appears indirectly, in speeches by leading characters, or directly, in outright admonitions to the audience. The author of *Havelok the Dane*, in a classic example that merits extensive quotation, gives his audience an idyllic picture of the conditions obtaining in a well-governed realm:

> It was a king by are dawes,
> That in his time were gode lawes
> He dede maken and full well holden;
>
> . . .
>
> He lovede God with all his might,
> And holy kirke and soth and right
>
> . . .
>
> Wreyeres and wrobberes made he falle
> And hated hem so man doth galle:
> Utlawes and theves made he binde,
> Alle that he might finde,
> And heye hengen on gallwe-tree;
> For hem ne yede gold ne fee;
> In that time a man that bore
> Well fifty pund, I wot, or more,
> Of red gold upon his back,
> In a male white or black,
> Ne funde he non that him missaide,
> Ne with ivele on hond layde.
>
> . . .
>
> Thanne was Engelond at aise;
> Michel was swich a king to praise
> That held so Englond in grith!

(There was a king in former days who made and fully kept good laws. . . . With all his might he loved God and Holy Church and truth and right. . . . Traitors and robbers he brought low and hated them as much as gall; he bound all the thieves and outlaws he could catch and hanged them high on gallows, taking no gold or goods [in bribes]; at that time a man carrying fifty pounds of gold or more in a black or white bag on his back found no one troubled him nor lay an evil hand on him. . . . Then was England at ease; such a king should be much praised, who held England in peace.)[29]

This imagined flower of English kingship ('Engelondes blome', l. 63) so loved right himself and so hated wrong in others that he did uncompromising justice on anyone who dared trouble the fatherless, 'Were it clerk or were it

---

[29] Sands, *Middle English Verse Romances*, ll. 27–30, 35–6, 39–50, 59–61; my translation. An interesting argument for the importance of local legend in the origins of the text is given by Bradbury, 'Traditional Origins'.

knight' (l. 77). Any man who troubled widows, 'Were he nevre knight so strong' (l. 80), was soon fettered and jailed. Whoever shamed virgins swiftly suffered castration.

The references to knights catch our eye, and they continue. The king himself was 'the beste knight at nede / That evere mighte riden on stede / Or wepne wagge or folk ut lede' (or bear weapons or lead folk out to war).[30] Yet his licit mastery over other knights is explicitly and fulsomely praised:

> Of knight ne havede he nevere drede
> That he ne sprong forth so sparke of glede,
> And lete him knawe of his hand-dede
> Hu he couthe with wepne spede;
> And other he refte him hors or wede,
> Or made him sone handes sprede
> And 'Loverd merci! loude grede.'

(He feared no knight, so that he could spring forth like a spark from the coals and make him know the strength of his hand and how he handled weapons; he either deprived the knight of horse or harness or made him cry out loudly, with hands outspread [in submission], 'Mercy, Lord!')[31]

In these passages royal correction of wrong serves to stabilize medieval English society. Yet many Anglo-Norman and Middle English poems dealing with kingship stress the other side of the coin and show instead the dangers of strong kings distorting the framework of the law as they blatantly effect their private will rather than communal good. In these tales, the hero, not the king, embodies this common good even as he pursues his own private ambition; only his triumph will bring back ideal stability and the good old law.[32]

Yet the hero usually becomes king himself, in the process reinforcing the valid and essential role of kingship: only let the right man wear the gold crown. Havelok's right could scarcely be in doubt: he emits a marvellous light while sleeping and bears a glowing birthmark in the shape of a cross on his right shoulder.[33]

---

[30] Sands, *Middle English Verse Romances*, ll. 87–99. The poem similarly praises Birkabein, King of Denmark, as 'A riche king and swithe stark. / . . . He havede many knight and swain; / He was fair man and wight, / Of body he was the beste knight / That evere mighte leded ut here / Or stede onne ride or handlen spere.' (ll. 341–470)

[31] Ibid., ll. 90–7; my translation. The importance of hands as agents of prowess (or of submission) is noteworthy. See the discussion in Chapter 7.

[32] A more complex and much darker view appears in the *Alliterative Morte Arthure*, written in the late fourteenth century. See Brock, ed., *Alliterative Morte Arthure*. A good introductory sample of scholarly opinion appears in Göller, *Alliterative Morte Arthure*.

[33] Sands, *Verse Romances*, ll. 586–610.

Villains often hold the throne at the start of the tales, however, and they can use the powerful and characteristic English machinery of government to flatten all opposition. Early in *Havelok*, on the death of good king Athelwold, the throne is seized by Earl Goodrich (intended, perhaps, to evoke memories of the historical Earl Godwin and his son Harold late in Edward the Confessor's reign). He puts trusted knights into key castles, and requires oaths of loyalty from 'erles, baruns, lef and loth, / Of knightes, cherles, free and thewe'. The administrative apparatus is then oiled and set in motion to trans-mit his will from the centre out into the green countryside:

> Justises dede he maken newe
> All Engelond to faren thorw
> Fro Dovere into Rokesborw.
> Schireves he sette, bedels, and greives,
> Grith-sergeans with long gleives,
> To yemen wilde wodes and pathes
> Fro wicke men, that wolde don scathes,
> And forto haven alle at his cry,
> At his wille, at hise mercy,
> That non durste been him again,
> Erl ne barun, knight ne swain.

(He made new justices to ride through all England from Dover to Roxbourgh. He established sheriffs, beadles and stewards, peace serjeants with long swords to control wild woods and roads against evil men who would do harm, and to have all at his word, at his will, at his mercy, that none dare be against him, earl, baron, knight, or servant.)[34]

Here is the problem in a nutshell: a king who provides justices, sheriffs, peace-keepers, an entire force against 'wicke men', is himself one of the wicked. In effect, the plot reinforces the point, for Denmark, which also figures largely in the tale, represents a kingdom ruled by a wicked regent, Godard. It requires a remarkable hero to right matters on both sides of the seas, as Havelok does, in the end killing the wicked regent and burning Goodrich on earth as he was undoubtedly expected to burn in eternity.

The king may in other tales be legitimate and of good will, but badly informed or ill-served by local officials and corrupted law in the countryside. In the mid-fourteenth-century *Tale of Gamelyn*, for example, a hero whose birth puts him just at the margins of knightly status can only recover his landed heritage by three heroic displays of violence, finally overwhelming his evil brother John, who can manipulate the local agents of royal administration and

---

[34] Ibid., ll. 263–73; my translation.

justice. In the process, the tale manages to hint at some complexities of attitude regarding the violence so integral to its story.[35]

Yet a belief in licit violence carried out by the right people and rewarded in
the end by the highest authority was surely the overwhelming sentiment. The
parallels with tales in which bold Robin Hood, outlaw and vanquisher of the
sheriff, receives the king's forgiveness, friendship, and royal office are obvious
and informative.

Thus the message of all of these texts is clear: a proper king is good; his law
properly enforced is good for society as a whole. This is the advice to his
daughter put into the mouth of the Roman Emperor in *William of Palerne*:

> bi þi lif, as þou me lovest dere,
> þt never þe pore porayle be piled for þy sake,
> ne taxed to taliage; but tentyfli þou help
> þat al þs lond be lad in lawe as it ouȝt
> þan wol al þe pore puple preie for þe ȝerne.

(on your life, as you love me, you will never rob the poor for your own ends, nor tal-
lage them, but attentively see to it that all this land be led in law as it should be; then
all the common people will gladly pray for you.)[36]

Yet violent self-help, a show of prowess carried out even against local royal
officials and law, is licit, even praiseworthy, whenever the king or the law does
not merit obedience. If the English framework of powerful kingship and common law was widely approved; that is, its operation and especially its personnel needed occasional adjustment carried out with sword, staff, noose, or
longbow.

Matter of England romances and Robin Hood tales have shown a basic
respect for kingship and royal law, a reserved sphere of licit violence despite
the king's law or its agents, and worries over the balance between recourse to
courts and outright brutality. The same pattern emerges clearly from the
Arthurian tradition in Geoffrey of Monmouth's *History of the Kings of Britain*
(c. 1136, Latin), refashioned especially in Wace's *Roman de Brut* (1155, French)
and Lawman's *Brut* (c. 1199–1225, Middle English).

Each book sings the praises of wise kings who provide good laws and secure
order. One imagined king after another works this causal sequence, culminating in the great Arthur, of whom Geoffrey says '[he] fostered justice and peace,
the maintenance of the laws and decent behaviour in all matters throughout
his kingdom'. Constantine, according to Geoffrey, 'maintained justice among
his people, moderated the rapacity of footpads, put an end to the oppressive

---

[35] Text and analysis in Knight and Ohlgren, eds, *Robin Hood*. Cf. Kaeuper, 'Tale of Gamelyn'.
[36] Bunt, ed., *William of Palerne*, ll. 5123–6; cf. this theme in ll. 1311–15, 1371, 5238–49, 5475–84.

behaviour of local tyrants and did his utmost to foster peace everywhere'.[37] Wace pictures Arthur, in conquered France, spending nine fruitful years putting down the proud (*mainte orguillus home*) and restraining felons.[38] Writing about actual historical time in his *Roman de Rou*, he pictures Anglo-Saxon courtiers similarly stressing kingship in the maintenance of peace and justice.[39] Lawman is even more enthusiastically positive.[40] Of the dawn of British kingship under Dunwallo he notes,

> [He] was the first man whom they put a golden crown on,
> Here within Britain since Brutus's men came here.
> He made such a peace, he made such a truce,
> And laws which were good and [long] afterwards stood;
> He established a settlement and with oaths he secured it,
> So that each peasant at his plough had peace like the king himself.[44]

Lawman links proud and competitive knighthood with disorder. One early king, he says, disliked his knights because they kept desiring war. Another king lost his good fortune when all his noble earls and all his great barons fomented unrest: 'they refused altogether to keep the king's peace'—a phrase echoing the *pax domini regis* from the legal language of Lawman's own day, of course. The succeeding ruler then

> settled the land, he worked for peacefulness.
> He established strong laws; he was stern with the foolish
> But he loved those people whose lives were law-abiding;
> Every single good man he honoured with property;
> He enforced peace and truce upon pain of limb and life.[42]

Lawman's most striking passage about knights and order comes in his explanation of the origin of the Round Table. Before its construction, Arthur's midwinter feast had been disrupted by quarrels over precedence: blows were struck, loaves of bread and even goblets full of wine flew through the air as missiles; knight seized knight by the throat. Arthur retired to his chamber to think of a solution and the knights got their hands on the carving knives; severed heads hit the floor amidst 'an enormous blood-shed, consternation in the

---

[37] Thorpe, tr, *Geoffrey of Monmouth*, 124, 132. Local tyrants appear more than once in the writing of this period. See the comments of Suger on tyrants in Chapter 1 above.

[38] Arnold, ed., *Brut de Wace*, II, 532–3: 'Es nuef anz que il France tint / Mainte merveille le avint, / Maint orguillus home danta / E meint felun amesura.'

[39] Holden, ed., *Rou de Wace*, II, 100–1.

[40] Allen notes that Lawman's contribution to the story creates 'a picture of "merry Britain" where law and order create a world in which populations thrive and society achieves stability and security'. *Lawman, Brut*, xxiii.

[41] Ibid., ll. 2121–6.   [42] Ibid., ll. 1311 ff; 1391 ff; 1403 ff.

court'. A stern and kingly Arthur ordered justice done on all offenders (and even on their female relatives). All must swear to take no revenge, to take part in no future brawls. Weeks later he introduced his solution: a Round Table which could seat 1,600 knights, so that none should have precedence over another. The craftsman who has made it assures Arthur, 'you never need be afraid in all the wide world / That ever any proud knight would at your table start a fight.'[43] The Round Table came into being as both a sign of the unity between king and knights and a means to stop disruptive knightly violence.

The poet who wrote the *Life of William Marshal* at one point complains that his world is being spoiled by the decay of chivalry, meaning the very reforms praised by Lawman; what worries him is a shift away from prowess and largesse and a commitment to mere courtroom litigation:

But now the high lords have imprisoned chivalry for us; by their lethargy and because of greed, largesse is thrown into prison. And the knights errant and the tourneyers have been transformed into courtroom litigants.[44]

This image of chivalry wrongly imprisoned and prowess confined to the court-room contrasts strongly with Lawman's praise of Arthurian royalism suppressing knightly violence in his own house. The gold of chivalry has been transmuted into lead, so it seems.[45] This sentiment anticipates by four centuries a seventeenth-century complaint that the country was so well governed there was 'no employment for heroickal spirits'.[46]

Yet if Marshal began life as a knight errant, hurrying from England to the continent, where knighthood was less restrained, he ended his career as regent of England and chief prop to the crown in a time of crisis. Alongside complaint against royal restrictions on chivalry, we must set the broad course of William's life to illuminate the complex pattern of chivalry, literature, and kingship we have found in England.

---

[43] Allen, tr., *Lawman, Brut,* 11367 ff.
[44] My translation, from Meyer, ed., *Histoire,* I, ll. 2686–92:

> Mais or nos ront mise en prison
> Chevalerie le halt home:
> Par perece qui les asome
> E par conseil de coveitise
> Nos ront largesse en prison mise,
> E l'esrer e le torneir
> Si sunt torné al plaidier

[45] Lawman is, of course, no pacifist; he waxes enthusiastic for the right kind of violence, at the right time, by the right people.
[46] Quoted in Benson, *Malory's Morte Darthur,* 177.

PART IV

✦✦✦

THE AMBIVALENT FORCE OF CHIVALRY

NEAR the opening of his *Cliges*, Chrétien de Troyes, speaking directly to his audience in words now become famous, confidently announces the *translatio* of ancient civilization to the world of medieval France via the linked agencies of chivalry and learning:

These books of ours have taught us that Greece once stood pre-eminent in both chivalry and learning. Then chivalry proceeded to Rome in company with the highest learning. Now they have come into France. God grant that they be sustained here and their stay be so pleasing that the honour that has stopped here in France never depart.[1]

Speaking for many in his age, this influential author declares chivalry an essential element of civilization; he even suggests that it functions as one of the two components which take the measure of a civilization. He is enough a citizen of the world of *clergie* to include learning (the learning of the clerks, that is) alongside chivalry, but he gives chivalry equal rank, and first mention, as the key to honour.

Several centuries later the biography of the much-admired Jean de Boucicaut, marshal of France, *Le Livre des fais du bon messire Jehan le Maingre, dit Boucicaut*, announced, in words clearly recalling Chrétien's:

Two things have been established in the world, by the will of God, like two pillars to sustain the orders of divine and human laws . . . and without which the world would be like a confused thing and without any order . . . These two flawless pillars are Chivalry and Learning, which go very well together.[2]

For something like half a millennium of European history such evaluations of the importance of chivalry produced basic agreement among virtually all the laity whose opinion counted in this society and among most clerics as well; beneath helmets and tonsures, wimples and mitres, all heads nodded sagely, all thought chivalry was virtually equivalent to civilization, or at least stood as one

---

[1] Staines, tr., *Romances of Chrétien de Troyes*, 87; Luttrell and Gregory, eds, *Chrétien de Troyes*, ll. 30–9.

[2] Lalande, ed., *Jehan le Maingre*, 6–7: 'Deux choses sont, par la volunté de Dieu, establies au monde ainsi comme .II. pillers a soustenir les ordres des loys divines et humaines . . . et sanz lesquielz seroit le monde ainsi comme chose confuse et sanz nul ordre. . . . Yceulz .II. pillers, sanz faille, sont Chevalerie et Science qui moult bien se couviennent ensemble.' Lalande notes somewhat similar expressions appear elsewhere in the book. We will see below (Chapter 13) that in the thirteenth century Ramon Llull took a similar view in his much-read book on chivalry.

of its essential components, certainly that it was the model for the lives of lay males.

Characteristic praise flows in the biography of William Marshal. In the final scenes, as William lay dying, the monk-knight who came to receive him into the Order of the Temple praised him unstintingly as the greatest knight in the world, with the most prowess, 'sens', and loyalty. He announced with certainty that God would receive William in heaven. Similar praise for William's ideal chivalric career echoed in the laudatory sermon preached by an archbishop beside his bier and, again, in the approving oral obituary composed in the conversation of the French royal court. He was, simply, 'the best knight in the world (*Le meillor chevalier del monde*)'.[3] For all of these speakers it seemed that no more need be said.

Yet of course there was much more to be said on the subject of chivalry; medieval writers regularly spoke, however more subtly and indirectly, to their fundamental fears of the violence and disruption carried out in the world by 'the chivalry'. Early in his *Perceval* Chrétien de Troyes provides a classic case in point. The young, absolutely naive, and primitive hero, hunting alone in the forest, for the first time sees knights in splendid and shining armour emerge from the green curtain of trees. Almost stunned, Perceval asks their spokesman the arresting question, 'Are you God? (N'iestes vos Dieux?)'[4] Was this a question Chrétien wanted the knights of his society to consider? Were they, like the first sinners in Eden, setting themselves up in the place of divinity, arrogating to themselves God-like power? The danger certainly seems to have been in the mind of Perceval's mother, for when he tells her he has seen shining angels in the forest she replies, 'I commend you to God, dear son, for I'm deeply afraid for you. I do believe you've seen the angels who cause people such grief, killing whoever they come across.' He assures her that she is wrong, that the strangers told him they were knights. Hearing this word, she faints.[5] It is hard not to read this passage as a telling criticism of the chivalry of Chrétien's own day; his romances abound in trenchant social criticism and suggestions for an

---

[3] See Meyer, ed., *Histoire*, II, ll. 18351–end of text.
[4] Bryant, tr., *Perceval*, 3; Roach, ed., *Roman de Perceval*, 6. This attraction is elaborated in the Post-Vulgate Cycle: see Asher, tr., *Merlin Continuation (end)*, 8; Bogdanow, ed., 'Folie Lancelot', 83.
[5] Bryant, *Perceval*, 5; Roach, *Roman du Perceval*, ll. 306–400. She has good reason to fear: her husband has been maimed in knightly combat and her two older sons killed the very day of their knighting. Similar evaluations can be found in much lesser works. A questing Lancelot, seeking shelter in *The Marvels of Rigomer*, comes upon a monstrous old woman beside a fire he is sure is magical. Snoring on all fours like a beast, she badly frightens both Lancelot and his horse. When he identifies himself as a knight she threatens him, declaring that for a thousand years she has heard that knights are the worst things in the world who kill just as they like. Kay notes that women are often given a role as social critics and counter-narrative agents: *Chansons de Geste*, 138, 176.

improved *chevalerie* that might truly stand alongside ideal *clergie* as a prop to civilized life.[6]

The tensions are inherent: chivalry will be praised as a solution to the problem of which it is so integral an element. The grounds for this widespread pattern become immediately apparent if we consider chivalry in its broadest sense of ethos or ideal. A code to guide dominant laymen would necessarily do major social work: it would provide guidelines for basic questions confronting a society that was expanding its intellectual as well as its physical, social, and economic boundaries.

Did chivalry in fact address basic social questions? As an experiment, I have for years asked students in seminars to draw up a list of the primary issues that societies must confront, once they have secured the fundamentals of living space and sustenance. Although the list produced by such a discussion varies somewhat, it regularly includes the following social needs: principles of distributive justice, means for resolving disputes, rules about licit and illicit violence and its practitioners, guides for regulating social hierarchy, standards for relationships between the sexes, means both for satisfying spiritual longings and regulating the authority of the spiritual in the temporal world.

Such a list is fascinating and instructive, for we can see at once that all of these issues closely involve chivalry. How were the dominant layfolk to live, love, fight, practise piety, merit their high status and its considerable rewards? All such lines of thought led to chivalry. Like some social analogue to the molecular structures of organic chemistry, chivalry results from the powerful bonding of prowess to honour, piety, status, and love. Yet these bonds, if strong, are complex and even conflicted; medieval people interpreted them in particular ways and argued over their ideal nature and content. Is prowess an unalloyed good? Does it unerringly reveal status? Is it blessed by God? Does it lead to love? Simply to state a few such questions points to the issues in the chapters to follow. The importance of such questions helps us to understand how chivalry could for so many centuries stand at the centre of so much belief and debate. Any medieval writer interested in any one of these issues might well want to valorize his or her point of view by identifying it with the great code which formed a capstone of the arch of civilization.

Was there, then, only one point of view, the single 'ideal chivalry' of university survey courses, against which any thought or action could be measured? Medieval Europe, despite what some textbook writers and some romantics want to imagine, does not look like a society with a single set of answers with regard to chivalry—or much else. The extensive literature of

---

[6] For Chrétien's work as social criticism or reform, see Topsfield, *Chrétien de Troyes*; Frappier, *Chrétien de Troyes*; Krueger, *Women Readers*, 33–68.

chivalry scarcely appears as an unproblematic literature of agreement or celebration, of praise for a single code, universally accepted as 'true chivalry'.
Debate, criticism, and competing reform ideas surge through these texts.

The subject need not thus disintegrate or slip from our hands. As scholars
such as Maurice Keen, Georges Duby, and Jean Flori have argued, there is
enough continuity to allow us to discuss chivalry as a recognizable phenomenon
over the centuries. From some point in the twelfth century a core of ideas and
practices persisted among knights. William Marshal in the late twelfth century,
Geoffroi de Charny in the mid-fourteenth century, and Thomas Malory at the
end of the fifteenth century can be imagined sitting down together to discuss
such a core of ideal beliefs and practices rather comfortably.[7]

Yet their works criticize as well as praise the ideas and practices of fellow
knights; and others, too, would have their say. When we move beyond the
inner circle of practising knights into the vast realms of chivalric literature of
all stripes, we can hear polyphony—at times, perhaps, cacophony; the tension
crackles, and we encounter fears, doubts, and debate, as well as agreeable celebration. This is surely a literature of contending views on basic issues.

Of course, debate encouraged valorization: chivalry won social power not
only as the framework for the ideals of dominant laymen, but from repeated
efforts at reform, each praising an ideal to meet some set of interests.
Dissatisfaction with chivalry in the sense of a body of men who wielded very
real weapons in the world, or with the disruptive nature of their violent work
in an emerging civilization, could be most usefully and discretely expressed as
praise for the ideal code favoured by the writer. But we will do well to remember that social criticism and ideas of reform are as real as the praise, even if less
obvious.

Chapter 7 helps to explain why. Knights worshipped at the shrine of the
demi-god prowess and practised violence as an esteemed and defining entitlement. The primary constituent in chivalry was prowess which wins honour,
weapons in hand. What this meant on the tourney field, in a raiding party, on
the battlefield, is taken up in Chapter 8.

The fundamental bond of prowess and honour was strengthened, as noted
above, by the addition of three further bonds: a practised form of piety
(already explored in Chapter 3), an assertion of high status (Chapter 9), and a
troubled link with love and gendered relations (Chapter 10). The lavish eulogies sung to chivalry—and the worries more prudently expressed—can
scarcely be understood without recognizing its bonds to these crucially important social issues.

---

[7] Discussed in Chapter 13.

Chapters 11 and 12 take up *chanson de geste* and quest patterns, respectively, with a double goal: first, to get a closer look into highly useful evidence and, second, to demonstrate that the ambivalent role of chivalry in issues or order appears forcefully in entire works no less than in passages selected from many works.

Finally, Chapter 13 considers the critical and reformist views of the knights themselves. Again using specific works, we can see that ideas for change and improvement did not all come from the non-knightly. If model knights loudly and predictably praised chivalry, their fears and reformist ideals were real and their carefully chosen words are audible and significant.

7

THE PRIVILEGED PRACTICE OF VIOLENCE: WORSHIP OF THE DEMI-GOD PROWESS

✦✦✦

DURING the Battle of Mansourah in the crusade of Louis IX (1250), Joinville, St Louis's companion and biographer, sought refuge with his men in a ruined house surrounded by their enemies. Saracens who climbed the broken roof thrust lances literally into the French knights' faces. Two knights suffered multiple facial wounds and another took a lance blow between the shoulders 'which made so large a wound that the blood poured from his body as if from the bung-hole of a barrel'. In this crisis, Érard de Siverey spied French forces in neighbouring fields; but before riding for help he asked Joinville if he could do this without loss of honour, repeating his earnest question to all the others. 'I said to him,' Joinville reports, ' "My dear man, it seems to me you would win great honour for yourself if you went for help to save our lives," ' adding, ' "your own, by the way, is also in great danger." ' Érard brought help, but later died from a wound that had left his nose dangling over his lips.[1]

The vivid story told by Joinville rushes us into the vortex of the world of chivalry: we see bloody hand-to-hand combat, and hear serious talk of honour. Prowess and honour are closely linked in the knights' minds, for the practice of the one produces the other, a theme tirelessly expounded in all chivalric literature. Malory (as always, an ideal spokesman) writes repeatedly and enthusiastically of the *worshyppe* owed to men of valour and won by them.[2] Honour is the veritable currency of chivalric life, the glittering reward earned

[1] Wailly, ed., *Histoire de Saint Louis*, 93–5; Shaw, tr., *Joinville and Villehardouin*, 220–1.

[2] Tristram, preparing to fight two Round Table knights who have beaten his cousin, says 'have ye no doute but I woll have ado with them bothe to encrece my worshyp, for hit is many day sythen I dud any armys': Vinaver, ed., *Malory. Works*, 248. Malory is not alone. In the *Stanzaic Morte Arthur*, Bors calls for his companions to test their worship 'With spere and sheld and armes bright': Benson, ed., *Morte Arthur*, ll. 1550–5. In the Post-Vulgate *Merlin Continuation* Gawain wonderingly observes a stranger knight knock ten challengers from their saddles, each with a single blow. He not only proclaims the victor 'the best jouster I may ever see', but adds, 'For indeed, he should never lack honor, since he wins it so well'. Asher, tr., *Merlin Continuation (end)*, 3; Sommer, ed., *Zeitschrift*, 20.

by the valorous as a result of their exertions, their hazarding of their bodies. It is worth more than life itself.

Yet even if we keep the importance of honour firmly in our minds, we should not forget that the prowess from which it springs is the fundamental quality of chivalry. Prowess was truly the demi-god in the quasi-religion of chivalric honour; knights were indeed the privileged practitioners of violence in their society.

In the *Lancelot do Lac* the young hero learns from the Lady of the Lake that 'knighthood was not created and set up . . . because some men were originally more noble or of higher lineage than others, for all people are descended from one father and one mother'. Given this common descent, he asks rhetorically, how would one become noble except through prowess? Once evil had entered this world, the corrective could only be found by selecting as knights 'the big and the strong and the handsome and the nimble and the loyal and the valorous and the courageous'.[3] Nearly two centuries later Froissart, the ardent chronicler of chivalry at work in the Hundred Years War, asserted that, 'as firewood cannot burn without flame, neither can a gentleman achieve perfect honour nor worldly renown without prowess'.[4]

In the real world, to be sure, overweight lords with rusting armour but vast acreage and good lineage might command the respect given to rich and lordly patrons in any age. And important clerics who were lords of men and lands could be quite clear about their honour, even though they were formally prevented by their order from the display of prowess in combat. But in chivalric ideology, tension between lineage and prowess is suppressed; the assumption, almost without exception, is that honour originates, is merited, proved, and increased sword in hand by those whose lineage leads them to such deeds.[5] Pharian, in *Lancelot*, speaks of 'the honour of this world, towards which all prowess struggles'.[6] Youths of noble birth, such as the young Gareth or Perceval, are drawn almost mystically to the armour and weapons of knighthood.[7] Havelok the Dane, nearly lost beneath kitchen grease and soot, soon comes to his true vocation, warrior as well as king.[8] In the *chansons*, even a

---

[3] Elspeth Kennedy, ed., *Lancelot do Lac*, I, 110–11, 142; tr. from Corley, *Lancelot of the Lake*, 52.

[4] Luce, *Chroniques*, I, 2: 'Si comme la busce ne poet ardoir sans feu, ne poet le gentilz homs venir a parfait honneur ne a la glore dou monde sans proece.'

[5] See the useful discussion in Elspeth Kennedy, 'Quest for Identity'.

[6] Rosenberg, tr., *Lancelot Part I*, 39; Micha, ed., *Lancelot*, VII, 164. Elspeth Kennedy's text reads somewhat differently at this point: *Lancelot do Lac*, 92.

[7] Malory pictures the young Gareth arriving at court eager to witness jousting. Kay is unimpressed by his first humble request for sustenance: 'for and he had be come of jantyllmen, he wolde have axed horse and armour': Vinaver, ed., *Malory. Works*, 178–9. Gist provides a number of Middle English examples of the noble urge to exercise prowess overcoming circumstances of upbringing: *Love and War*, 140, n. 13.

[8] 'Havelock the Dane', in Sands, ed., *Middle English Verse Romances*.

great cleric such as Archbishop Turpin must fight as a knight (contrary to the prohibitions of church reformers) and is valued accordingly.[9]

A knight's nobility or worth is proved by his hearty strokes in battle. Seeing Oliver cut a pagan in half, for example, Roland sings out 'The Emperor loves us for such blows.'[10] Seeing Rainouart in *Aliscans* throw a squire who has tormented him against a pillar, breaking all the young man's limbs at once, William of Orange says in admiring wonder, 'By St Denis, he's to be respected.'[11] Wounded by Hector in a tournament, in the *Stanzaic Morte Arthur*, Lancelot at first promises repayment (causing Hector to blanche in fear), but soon forgives Hector and tells him he loves him more for his hard blow: 'But ever the betyter love I thee, / Such a dint that thou can smite.'[12] Kay and Bedevere, Arthur's court officials, hit so hard in battle in *The Story of Merlin* that their Roman opponents cry out, 'God, what a seneschal! . . . God, what a constable! Here are goodly ministers for a king's court!' Gawain (called here by his affectionate diminutive, Gawainet) makes a similar estimate of the status of the warrior who is in fact the Saxon king Brandon:

And when Sir Gawainet saw what he was doing and the great slaughter of his people, he was certain that he was a highborn man of mighty stock, and he showed by the way he fought that he was a king or a prince; Sir Gawainet highly esteemed him, and would have been very glad if he had been a Christian.[13]

In one of his earliest combats Lancelot 'admired the prowess of the man who had just dealt him the best blow that he had ever received'.[14] Later, a kind host who takes in Lancelot (temporarily fallen into madness) knows him to be a noble knight because of the blow he receives: 'he dealt me a blow on my helmet, the like of which I never received from any man since I was knighted. For that reason I'm sure he used to be a good knight and of noble condition.'[15]

Malory tells us in the *Morte Darthur* that when Lamorak's strokes fail to defeat his opponent (a disguised King Mark) quickly, he 'doubled his strokys, for he was of the nobelyste of the worlde'.[16] As Lancelot and Gawain fight near the end of the *Mort Artu*, 'whoever could have seen the blows given and

[9] See classic expressions of Turpin's prowess in Brault, ed., tr., *Chanson de Roland, laisses* 114, 121, 155, and in Newth, ed., tr., the *Song of Aspremont*, especially 202–3, 222.

[10] Brault, *Chanson de Roland*, l. 1377.

[11] Ferrante, ed., tr., *Guillaume d'Orange*, 231; Wienbeck *et al.*, eds., *Aliscans*, 184.

[12] Benson, ed., *Morte Arthure*, ll. 464–500.

[13] Pickens, tr., *Story of Merlin*, 409, 385; Sommer, ed., *Vulgate Version*, II, 438, 394.

[14] Rosenberg, tr., *Lancelot Part I*, 93; Sommer, *Vulgate Version*, III, 174–5; Elspeth Kennedy, ed., *Lancelot do Lac*, I, 225. Lancelot is, in fact, sorry that he has killed the man, putting his lance right through his 'insides'.

[15] Carroll, tr., *Lancelot Part VI*, 320; Micha, ed., *Lancelot*, VI, 211.

[16] Vinaver, ed., *Malory. Works*, 355.

received would have realized that the two men were of great nobility'.[17] An exceptionally strong and able lance thrust or sword stroke, in fact, often reveals a hero's identity despite his attempt at disguise by wearing unaccustomed armour. Lancelot's great prowess regularly puts him in this situation. Tristram and others have the same problem.

Galahad delivers what may be the ultimate sword blow in the complex fighting between incognito knights in the Post-Vulgate *Quest*. Bors, unhorsed by Galahad, challenges him to a sword fight: 'Come test me with the sword, and then I will see that you are a knight.' He gets more than he bargained for. Galahad's blow

cut through his shield, the pommel of his saddle, and the horse's withers, so that half the horse fell one way and half the other in the middle of the road, and Bors was left on foot, holding his naked sword, and half his shield, the other half having fallen in the road.

A badly frightened Bors calls out, 'I see by this blow you're the best knight I ever saw.'[18]

To be the best knight in the world, as we can read time and again in chivalric literature, means not to be the greatest landlord but to show the greatest prowess. The wise Merlin tells Arthur, about to choose new knights for the Round Table:

King, choose from all the land the fifty best knights you know, and if you know any poor knight, valiant in person and courage, do not fail to include him because of his poverty. And if anyone who is nobly born and of high lineage wants to be included, but he is not a very good knight, take care not to let him be included. For a single person who is not of such great chivalry would shame and degrade the chivalry of the whole company.[19]

Of course acquiring land and wealth is assumed to follow naturally, and is welcomed as an enhancement of honour. Any deep gulf between the acquisition of wealth and the practice of chivalry is a modern myth; gold and glory in fact made a fine amalgam in the medieval knightly view. William Marshal was taught that lesson early in his model chivalric career and he was long troubled by the slight reward in terms of land that his great prowess had earned him. In time, of course, it won him fiefs almost beyond his dreams. Moreover,

---

[17] Cable, tr., *Death of King Arthur*, 179–80; Frappier, ed., *La Mort*, 196. The French term, in fact, is *preudomes*. This general sentiment appears repeatedly and again in the Vulgate and Post-Vulgate cycles.

[18] Asher, tr., *Quest*, 137; Bogdanow, *Folie Lancelot*, 119–20. Kay and Gawain soon second this sentiment. Hector later receives a similar blow from Galahad, and comes to the same conclusion, as does the watching Sagramore: Asher, ibid., 189; Bogdanow, ibid., 356–7.

[19] Asher, tr., *Merlin Continuation*, 223; Roussineau, ed., *Merlin*, I, 201.

prowess is the quality hymned without cease in his biography, and in every other piece of chivalric literature. Lancelot's grandfather, as we learn in the *Lancelot*, was not a king's son, but he was chosen as king 'because of his prowess'.[20] Lancelot himself later declares, when he sees Bors in battle, that this young knight should be given lands—he would defend them so well.[21]

In fact, in chivalric literature prowess can come close to conveying the meaning of a man's life, or even of life itself. In the *Perlesvaus* God stops the fight between Perceval and Gawain because he did not want those good knights to kill one another; his wish was that each '*should know the other's worth*'.[22] The Lady of the Lake tells Guinevere she raised the young Lancelot 'because of the great prowess that was to manifest itself in this knight'.[24] Hearing of a great deed of prowess after a period of captivity, the mature Lancelot hopes to God that the valiant knight who is talked of will appear, 'Because, sir,' he tells Galehaut, 'we have been imprisoned here for a very long while, and it has been a long time since we saw jousting or knightly deeds, and we are wasting our time and our lives. As God is my true witness, if he comes, I shall fight with him.'[24] In the *Chevalier de Papegau*, a work of very different tone and quality, the same sentiment appears; the parrot (an enthusiastic and frequently heard voice for prowess) explains that to be lacking in valour is the worst prison for a knight.[25] Gawain is reluctant to kill Nascien who will not surrender although defeated (in a tournament turned deadly): ' "I do not want to kill you," said Sir Gawainet. "That would truly be a shame, for you are most worthy." '[26] His worth has, of course, been demonstrated by prowess. Boson, boasting in *Girart de Roussillon* about the prowess of the men on Girart's side in his war with the king, proudly declares that none of their fathers died in their beds.[27] King Arthur, holding the severed head of Lamorat in his hands, laments the knight in the classic formula: 'Indeed, it's too bad that he is dead so soon, for had he lived a long time he would have surpassed in chivalry all those of his lineage.'[28] In Malory's 'Tale of Arthur and Accolon', the Damsel of the Lake saves Arthur in his fight with Accolon because she saw 'how full of

[20] Carroll, tr., *Lancelot Part VI*, 239; Micha, ed., *Lancelot*, V, 123.
[21] Asher, tr., *Merlin Continuation* 306; Micha, *Lancelot*, VI, 111.
[22] Bryant, tr., *Perlesvaus*, 129; Nitze and Jenkins, eds, *Perlesvaus*, 197, emphasis supplied. Equating prowess with worth is common. A wise dwarf tells a questing Tor he need not fear delay by accepting a joust: 'a valiant man cannot lose by delay,' he assures Tor, 'and here you can find out if you are worth anything'. Asher, *Merlin Continuation*, 234; Paris and Ulrich, eds., *Merlin*, II, 102.
[23] Carroll, tr., *Lancelot Part II*, 232; Elspeth Kennedy, ed., *Lancelot do Lac*, I, 556.
[24] Corley, tr., *Lancelot of the Lake*, 359; Elspeth Kennedy, *Lancelot do Lac*, I, 531.
[25] Vesce, tr., *Knight of the Parrot*, 33; Heuckenkamp, ed., *Chevalier du Papegau*, 32.
[26] Pickens, tr., *Story of Merlin*, 336; Sommer, ed., *Vulgate Version*, II, 304.
[27] Meyer, ed., tr., *Girart de Roussillon*, 401.
[28] Asher, *Merlin Continuation*, 82; Bogdanow, 'Folie Lancelot', 80.

prouesse his body was' and has pity lest 'so good a knyght and such a man of worship sholde so be destroyed'. The view of Sir Outlake is similar: 'that is grete pyté that ever so noble a man as ye ar of your dedis and prouesse, that ony man or woman myght fynde in their hertes to worche ony treson aghenst you'.[29]

Great prowess so expresses the meaning of life that after an unsurpassed day of battle the sated, triumphant knight may yearn for death to close his career on such a high point. In the war to recover Lancelot's inheritance from Claudas, young Claudin, his son, knows that he has fought so magnificently, that he tells a companion, 'Truly, dear friend, were it not for my father's great loss, I wouldn't care if I died in this battle, for I believe I'll never again accomplish what we've done today, you and I.'[30] Near the end of the *Lancelot do Lac*, King Yder, wonderfully successful on the battlefield, hopes that God will 'give him death, for he would never again have such an excellent day'.[31]

Certainly, prowess is the prominent virtue, and sometimes nearly the exclusive virtue, in the summing-up of a great man's life at its close. Mourning her dead husband, King Bors, early in the *Lancelot*, Queen Elaine twice laments 'the great acts of prowess of her lord (*les granz proesces son seignor*)'. Only his prowess and his (unspecified) kindnesses merit mention in the queen's lament.[32] When Gawain is shown a badly wounded knight in a castle hall, he comments on how unfortunate his condition is, since the man is so handsome. 'You would truly say it was a misfortune', says the lady caring for the knight, 'if you knew how great his prowess was.'[33] When later in this text Lancelot goes mad because of his imprisonment in Saxon Rock, Queen Guinevere laments the apparent end of 'his feats of arms, his jousting, his swordsmanship'.[34] The maiden, whose knowledge of herbs saves the poisoned Lancelot later in this cycle, tells her worried brother, 'I can assure you that if God grants that he come through strong and healthy, he'll yet deliver many fine blows with sword and lance.'[35] The queen, fearing that she has lost Lancelot's love, in the *Stanzaic Morte Arthur*, hopes that she will still hear of his deeds of prowess.[36] An untrue report of Arthur's death, when he is under the power of

[29] Vinaver, ed., *Malory. Works*, 87, 89.

[30] Carroll, tr., *Lancelot Part VI*, 304; Micha, ed., *Lancelot*, VI, 103–4.

[31] Corley, tr., *Lancelot of the Lake*, 385; Elspeth Kennedy, ed., *Lancelot do Lac*, I, 550.

[32] Rosenberg, tr., *Lancelot Part I*, 8; Elspeth Kennedy, *Lancelot do Lac*, I, 14–15; Sommer, ed., *Vulgate Version*, III, 14.

[33] Elspeth Kennedy, *Lancelot do Lac*, I, 414; Sommer, *Vulgate Version*, III, 313; Carroll, tr., *Lancelot Part II*, 172–3.

[34] Carroll, *Lancelot Part II*, 231; Micha, *Lancelot*, VIII, 455.

[35] Kibler, tr., *Lancelot Part V*, 147; Micha, *Lancelot*, IV, 137.

[36] Benson, ed., *Morte Arthur*, ll. 752–9. Even after his conversion to the religious life as a hermit, his death elicits from Bors this lament and summation: 'The beste knight his life hath lorn / That ever in stour [battle] bestrode steed!' ll. 3892–3.

the False Guinevere, causes the queen to cry out, 'Dear Lord God, now all prowess is gone and all joy turned to sorrow.'[37] A knight, who has heard a similar rumour about Lancelot, cries out for his own death: 'I have no desire to live any longer now, when the knight who was supposed to surpass all earthly prowess has died.' As he carries Galehaut's dead body to burial at the Dolorous Guard, a weeping Lancelot laments his great friend's 'prowess and valour'.[38] A lady falsely informed by Sir Gawain that her lover, Sir Pelleas, has been slain, intones the formula: 'that is grete pyté for he was a passynge good knyght of his body'. She adds that any lady should love Gawain, since he is well born and of such prowess.[39]

Perhaps the most striking instance appears, however, late in Malory's *Morte Darthur*. The king, learning finally beyond doubt of the liaison between Lancelot and the queen, is told how they were taken together, how Lancelot escaped by fighting his way out against numerous would-be captors:

'Jesu mercy!' seyde the kynge, 'he ys a mervaylous knyght of proues. And alas,' seyde the kynge, 'me sore repentith that ever sir Launcelot sholde be ayenste me, for now I am sure the noble felyshyp of the Rounde Table ys brokyn for ever, for wyth hym woll many a noble knyght holde. An now hit ys fallen so,' seyde the kynge, 'that I may nat with my worshyp but my quene muste suffir dethe,' and was sore amoved.

Without diminishing our sense of the king's feelings, or of the deeply moving prose with which Malory sets forth this crisis in the story of Arthurian knighthood, we can only note that Arthur comments here first on Lancelot's great prowess, second on the impending collapse of the great fellowship of knights, and third on his ineluctable judgement on his queen. As he says shortly after, it is the loss of the knights, not the loss of the queen, that makes him sorry.[40]

Identification of Chivalry with Prowess

Only after reading scores of works of chivalric literature can we fully appreciate the utterly tireless, almost obsessional emphasis placed on personal prowess as the key chivalric trait.[41] Not simply one quality among others in a list of virtues, prowess often stands as a one-word definition of chivalry in these texts.[42]

---

[37] Rosenberg, tr., *Lancelot Part III*, 266; Micha, ed., *Lancelot*, VII, 114.

[38] Krueger, tr., *Lancelot Part IV*, 61, 83; Micha, *Lancelot*, II, 218, 309.

[39] Vinaver, ed., *Malory. Works*, 102.   [40] Ibid., 682, 685.

[41] My impression is reinforced by the careful study of Burgess, 'The Term *"chevalerie"* '. Burgess finds the term is specific, rather than abstract, and generally refers to deeds of prowess and the *mentalité* which produces them. I owe thanks to Alan Lupak for this reference.

[42] Emphasized even when a knight's other qualities are disreputable. Blioblieris, in *Le Bel Inconnu*, is described as harsh, cruel, proud, and wicked, 'but no one ever saw a better knight':

This identification appears regularly in *chansons de geste*. Folchers rides out into battle 'seeking great chivalry' in *Girart de Roussillon*. He achieves it, putting his lance through the heart of 'the valiant Count Routrou'.[43] Characters in the *Chanson de Roland* link chivalry with deeds of prowess, as, for instance, does Ganelon (a great knight, even if a traitor) when speaking with Marsilion. If the pagan leader can kill Roland, he assures him, 'then you will have done a noble feat of arms [literally a noble act of chivalry, *gente chevalerie*]'.[44] William, in the *Chanson de Guillaume*, observes Rainouart smash a Saracen's head into four fragments: 'You should be a knight', he shouts approvingly.[45]

Statements linking chivalry with prowess in the vast Vulgate and Post Vulgate cycles almost defy sampling.[46] In a tournament at Pomeglai,

[Lancelot] drew out his sword like an expert swordsman and delivered heavy blows to the right and to the left, felling knights and horses with blows of the sword blade and by the hilt. He grabbed men by the hoods of mail and by the edge of their shields; he pulled helmets from heads; and he hit and shoved and pounded and struck with his limbs and his horse, *for he was very skilled in doing all that a great knight must do.*

Those who witness Lancelot's work with edged weapons regularly pronounce him 'the flower of chivalry'. Arthur, for example, declares that Lancelot has earned the status of best knight after a tournament at Camelot, and a defeated Gawain agrees; the stump of Lancelot's spear has just been extracted from his side, and he is beginning a month of recuperation.[47]

A knight who has seen Lancelot perform in a tournament (in the *Lancelot*) can scarcely find words sufficient to praise his prowess:

[I]t takes a lot more to be a worthy man than I thought it did this morning. I've learned so much today that I believe there's only one truly worthy man in the whole world. I saw the one I'm talking about prove himself so well against knights today that I don't

---

Fresco, ed., and Donagher, tr., *Renaut de Bâgé*, ll. 36–41. At the opening of the *Lancelot do Lac* we meet Claudas, 'a king, and an excellent knight' who was 'very clever and very treacherous': Elspeth Kennedy, ed., *Lancelot do Lac*, I, 1; Corley, tr., *Lancelot of the Lake*, 3. Of many cases in Malory, note Helyus and Helake who 'were men of grete prouess; howbehit that they were falsse and full of treson, and were poore men born, yet were they noble knyghtes of theire hondys': Vinaver, ed., *Malory. Works*, 437. For examples from a *chanson*, *Girart de Roussillon*, see Mary Hackett, 'Knights and Knighthood'.

[43] Meyer, ed., tr., *Girart de Roussillon*, laisse 159, particularly ll. 2744–5.
[44] Brault, ed., tr., *Chanson de Roland*, 38–9.
[45] Muir, tr., *The Song of William*, 193; Suard, ed., *Chanson de Guillaume*, 197–8.
[46] In addition to the passages quoted below, see, e.g., Krueger, tr., *Lancelot Part IV*, 34; Kibler, tr., *Lancelot Part V*, 180, 203, 204, 215; Carroll, tr., *Lancelot Part VI*, 280, 312; the corresponding passages in Micha, ed., *Lancelot* are II, 115, IV, 273–4, 385, 387; V, 36; and VI, 8, 138.
[47] Krueger, *Lancelot Part IV*, 30, 32, 38; *Part V*, 204–5; Micha, *Lancelot*, II, 99 (emphasis supplied), 107, 129–30; IV, 389–91.

believe any mortal man since chivalry was first established has done such marvellous deeds as he did today.

He explains explicitly what these marvels were:

I could recount more than a thousand fine blows, for I followed that knight every step to witness the marvellous deeds he did; I saw him kill five knights and five men-at-arms with five blows so swift that he nearly cut horses and knights in two. As for my own experience, I can tell you he split my shield in two, cleaved my saddle and cut my horse in half at the shoulders, all with a single blow. . . . I saw him kill four knights with one thrust of his lance . . . if it were up to me, he'd never leave me. I'd keep him with me always, because I couldn't hold a richer treasure.[48]

In a tournament at Camelot (fighting, by Guinevere's wish, against the proud knights of the Round Table), Lancelot again displays his prowess:

Lancelot put his hand upon his good sword, striking left and right like a man to whom it was more natural than a raptor pursuing its prey. He began killing knights and horses and striking down whatever he met in his way. . . .

Then were the great marvels of his prowess, which had been testified to in many places, shown to be true, for he split knights and horses and heads and arms and lances and shields, and beat down knights to the right and left; he did so much in so little time that all those who had been pursuing others stopped on his account . . . to watch him and see the marvels he performed.[49]

Other heroes perform wonders of prowess, highly praised as the essence of chivalry. The *Mort Artu* refers repeatedly to acts of prowess as 'deeds of chivalry' or 'feats of chivalry'; the link between the two is often apparent.[50] Once he has seen Morholt defeat Yvain, in the *Merlin Continuation*, Gawain almost foams with praise: 'Oh, God! what greatness there is in a valiant man! God, how powerful this man is; how effective he is, and how much he can do! God! what a fool and how guilty of excess would he be who pressed such a man to battle, unless he had a good reason!'[51]

Hector does so well in the war against Claudas that Gawain looks on with rapt admiration:

Hector threw down his shield, took his sword with both hands and began to slay knights and horses and clear the space around him so wondrously that there was no one so bold as to dare to put out a hand to stop him. Looking at him Sir Gawain said to himself, 'My God, what a knight we have here! Who would have thought that such a young man had such prowess in him?'[52]

---

[48] Kibler, tr., *Lancelot Part V*, 161–2; Micha, ed., *Lancelot*, IV, 198–9.
[49] Kibler, *Lancelot Part V*, 197; Micha, *Lancelot*, IV, 359–60.
[50] Cable, tr., *Death of King Arthur*, 36, 139; Frappier, ed., *La Mort*, 17, 144.
[51] Asher, tr., *Merlin Continuation*, 272; Roussineau, ed., *Merlin*, II, 374–5.
[52] Carroll, tr., *Lancelot Part VI*, 303; Micha, *Lancelot*, VI, 96–97.

In the seemingly endless battles with the Saxons the Round Table knights' prowess is constantly praised: 'open displays of knightly prowess could be seen by all', we learn; Arthur's men 'slaughtered knights and horses, they sent shields flying from necks and helmets from heads, they chopped off feet and hands and they did such wonders that scarcely anyone could believe the great slaughter of the Saxons they did'. Merlin enthusiastically promises them more of the same, in words that almost define prowess: 'Today we'll see who has prowess in him. Today we'll see who can fight boldly with sword and lance. Today the great and worthy knighthood of the Kingdom of Logres [literally, 'the great acts of prowess of the Kingdom of Logres', *'les grans proesces del roialme de Logres'*] will be displayed.'[53]

Even Galahad, for all his spiritual qualities, attracts similar eulogies. Arthur the Less, wonders at the 'great prodigies' performed by Galahad in battle against King Mark's knights, for, the text says, 'he reached no knight, no matter how well armed, whom he did not lay on the ground dead or mortally wounded or crippled'. Such work elicits fulsome praise from Arthur the Less:

Oh God! What can I say of this man? By my faith, no mortal man could do what he's doing. Truly, all the other knights in the world are nothing compared to him, for if everyone else in the world were a knight and he faced them all in one place, I think he would defeat them all, for it doesn't seem to me, from what I've seen, that he could grow weary from striking during the lifetime of one man. Now may I have ill fortune if I don't from now on call him the best of all those who now bear arms, for I see well that he deserves it.[54]

Prowess was thought to bring other qualities in its train (as we will see), and these qualities may have more appeal for most modern readers than prowess itself;[55] but we will radically misunderstand the medieval view and the

---

[53] Pickens, tr., *Story of Merlin*, 386, 387, Sommer, ed. *Vulgate Version*, II, 397–8. The phrase about open displays of knightly prowess, reads, 'si peust on ueoir apertes cheualeries faire darmes'. Even the voluble Parrot in the *Knight of the Parrot* sings praises for the 'chivalries' Arthur has 'done'. Vesce, *Knight of the Parrot*, 54; Heuckenkamp, ed., *Chevalier du Papegau*, 52. Physical strength may take forms modern readers (incorrectly) suspect are parodic. William of Orange struts with such vigour in the royal hall (in the *Charroi de Nîmes*) that he bursts the uppers of his Cordovan leather boots. He similarly leans on his bow with such vigour that it shatters. Price, tr., *The Waggon Train*, 62–3; McMillan, ed., *Charroi de Nîmes*, 61, 64. In the *Chanson de Guillaume* even his vigour in eating shows he is a man of prowess; the Saracens eat men like ripe apples: Muir, tr., *Song of William*, 152, 159, 165, 193; Suard, ed., *Chanson de Guillaume*, 72, 94, 113, 198.

[54] Asher, tr., 'Quest', 246. A few pages earlier Galahad has 'struck to the left and right and killed all those he reached, and he performed so many marvels among them that no one who saw him would have thought him mortal man but some strange marvel': p. 237.

[55] The 'worthy man' tells Arthur: 'no one recognizes a man of worth so well as a man rooted in great prowess': Corley, tr., *Lancelot of the Lake*, 242; Elspeth Kennedy, *Lancelot do Lac*, I, 287. Hervi of Rivel, attending at Arthur's table when a monk comes with messages from the queens of Gaunes and Benoic, tells Arthur that the man is trustworthy, as a former knight of prowess:

medieval reality if we push the bloody, sweaty, muscular work done with lance and sword swiftly and antiseptically to the side and hasten on to speak of more abstract, more appealing qualities. What is at issue is less a set of idealized abstractions than what Malory called 'dedys full actuall'. Such deeds leave combatants 'waggyng, staggerynge, pantyng, blowyng, and bledyng'.[56]

But is this all merely literary artifice? Did knights actually hack so heroically and endure so resolutely? Historical accounts, it is true, do not generally follow lance thrusts and sword strokes in anatomical detail; in the confusion of most battles it could scarcely have been possible. Usually they praise heroes more simply by enumerating foes slain.[57]

Yet time and again a chronicler or biographer assures us he wants to record the great deeds of his subjects, just as a writer of *chanson* or romance might. No less than imaginative literary texts, historical sources show us single great men turning the tide of battle by their prowess, cutting paths through their enemies, who fall back in stunned fear. Perhaps this is not merely flattery and topos; given relatively small numbers, close fighting with edged weapons, and the sudden surges or panics so often described, one unusual man might well tilt the balance.

In the pages of the biography of William Marshal chivalry often becomes prowess pure and simple. At the siege of Winchester, for example, we are told that groups of knights sallied forth each day 'to *do* chivalry (por *faire* chevalerie)'.[58] The knight can *do* chivalry just as he can *make* love: it has this

My lord, believe whatever this man tells you, for kings and princes should heed his words. Be assured that with his great courage and prowess he so far outshone any other knight in God's creation that in dire need I would confidently have turned to him to defend my honour and preserve my head.

Rosenberg, tr., *Lancelot Part I*, 25; Elspeth Kennedy, ed., *Lancelot do Lac*, 55; Sommer, ed., *Vulgate Version*, III, 46.

[56] Vinaver, ed., *Malory.Works*, 23, 198. John Barbour's chronicle has men at least 'stabbing, stocking and striking': McDiarmid and Stevenson, eds., *Barbour's Bruce*, bk. XVII, l. 785. Malory's characters describe fierce fighting as 'noble knyghthode': Vinaver, *Malory.Works*, 277. Sir Kay cites prowess as the quality that earns Gawain a seat at the Round Table: 'He is beste worthy to be a knyght of the Rounde Table of ony that is rehersed yet and he had done no more prouesse his lyve dayes': ibid., 80. Tristram thinks himself unworthy to be a knight of the Round Table until his 'dedys' win him a place: ibid., 300. Unhorsing Kay and matching Lancelot allows the young Gareth similarly to believe he can 'stonde a preved knyght': ibid., 181. Blamour fears Tristram 'May happyn to smyte me downe with his grete myght of chevalry': ibid., 253. Sir Darras, whose three sons Tristan did 'smyte downe', agrees Tristan acted 'by fors of knyghthode': ibid., 338. Lionel defeats and kills Calogrenant who tries to intervene in his fight with Bors, 'for thys sir Lyonell was of grete chevalry and passing hardy': ibid., 575.

[57] The chronicler of Richard the Lion-Heart's crusade praises Geoffrey of Lusignan as a successor to Roland and Oliver for despatching ten Muslims with an axe at the siege of Acre: Hubert tr., and La Monte, *Crusade of Richard Lion-Heart*; Gaston Paris, *L'Histoire de la guerre sainte*, ll. 4662–70.

[58] Meyer, ed., *Histoire*, I, l. 176; my italics. As Burgess points out, this phrase appears frequently in twelfth-century Old French imaginative literature with just the meaning suggested here: 'The Term "*Chevalerie*" '.

dimension as a physical process. At the battle of Lincoln, writes the biographer, the French did not have to look far to 'find chivalry', the quality here again clearly equated with prowess on the battlefield. Knighting the young king, the eldest son of Henry II, William asks God to grant him prowess and to keep him in honour and high dignity. We are also told that it was right for William to be the 'master' of the young king while he prepared for this day because William increased his pupil's prowess.[59]

Most readers of Marshal's biography, however, will better remember the vivid visual evidence of prowess. In the classic instance William receives the news that he has won a tournament with his head on the blacksmith's anvil where the deep dents in his helmet are being sufficiently hammered out to allow him finally to pull the battered iron off his head.[60]

If Geoffroi de Charny knew this story (more than a century later), he must have laughed in hearty approval. In his *Livre de chevalerie* this renowned knight lauds prowess unceasingly and urges his contemporaries to invest their lives and their bodies in the honourable following of arms, in individual jousts, in tournaments, and above all in war. 'For I maintain', Charny writes, 'that there are no small feats of arms, but only good and great ones, although some feats of arms are of greater worth than others.'[61]

Describing the battle of Methven (1306), John Barbour says Bruce's men 'Schewyt thar gret chewalry (showed their great chivalry)'; they 'swappyt owt swerdis sturdyly / And swa fell strakys gave and tuk / Yat all ye rank about yaim quouk (They whipped out swords boldly and gave and took such grievous strokes that all the ground around them shook.'[62]

Such sword blows are highly prized. Gerald of Wales obviously esteems the knight Meiler Fitz Henry's fighting against the Irish:

[S]urrounded by the enemy on every side, [he] drew his sword and charging the band, boldly cut his way through them, chopping here a hand and there an arm, besides hewing through heads and shoulders and thus rejoined his friends on the plain unhurt, though he brought away three Irish spears stuck in his horse, and two in his shield.

He states explicitly the value he finds in John de Courcy: 'He who had seen how John of Courcy wielded his sword, with one stroke lopping off heads, and with another arms, must needs have commended him for a most valiant soldier.'[63]

---

[59] Meyer, ed., *Histoire*, II, ll. 16830–3, I, 2088–9, 2635–6.   [60] Ibid., I, ll. 3101–44.

[61] Kaeuper and Kennedy, *Book of Chivalry*, 86–7; Charny's ideas are explored in detail in this work. cf. Chapter 13, below.

[62] McDiarmid and Stevenson, *Barbour's Bruce*, bk. II, 366–8.

[63] Wright, ed., tr., *Historical Works*, 256, 279. In Welsh border fighting, a recipient of such a blow, Ranulf Poer, sheriff of Herefordshire, is cut through the windpipe and veins of the neck and only manages by signs to summon a priest before he dies: p. 369.

Richard the Lion-Heart regularly chops his enemies' skulls down to the teeth.[64] Richard Marshal (second son of the famous William) with one mighty stroke cut off both hands of the man reaching for his helmet in a close encounter. With an even mightier blow he cut a knight down to the navel.[65] Finding a young clerk who has taken revenge on three royal serjeants who robbed him—piercing one with a crossbow bolt, with a sword cutting the leg off the second, and splitting the head of the third to the teeth—Louis IX takes the young man into his service 'pour vostre proesce', though he tells him such prowess has closed off the road to the priesthood.[66] Joinville, who tells the story, later admires three fine blows delivered by a Genoese knight in an expedition to Jaffa: one enemy is run through with a lance, one's turbaned head is sent flying off into the field, one lance-wielding enemy arm is cut off with a swift back-handed sword stroke, after dodging the foe's lance.[67] Lancelot could scarcely have done better. Robert Bruce, we learn, could hack off an arm, or arm and shoulder, or ear, cheek, and shoulder at a single sword stroke.[68]

If Robert Bruce's most noted feat of prowess was to split the head of Henry de Bohun at the opening of the battle of Bannockburn, he also defended a narrow river ford alone, against a large body of English knights who could only come at him singly.[69] 'Strang wtrageous curage he had', Barbour proclaims proudly, as the number of bodies in the water mounts; after Bruce has killed six men, the English hesitate, until exhorted by one of their knights who shouts that they must redeem their honour and that Bruce cannot last. Yet he does. When his own men finally appear, they count fourteen slain. Barbour breaks into fulsome praise:

> A der God quha had yen bene by
> & sene hove he sa hardyly
> Adressyt hym agane yaim all
> I wate weile yat yai suld him call
> Ye best yat levyt in his day.[69]

---

[64] Many examples in Hubert tr., and La Monte, *Crusade of Richard Lion-Heart*; Gaston Paris, *L'Histoire de la guerre sainte*.

[65] Described in Prestwich, *Armies and Warfare*, 1–2. The chronicle of the crusade of Richard the Lion-Heart tells of a knight whose right hand is cut off in battle; he is praised for shifting his sword to his left hand and fighting on: Hubert and La Monte, *Crusade of Richard Lion-Heart*, ll. 5777–86; Gaston Paris, *L'Histoire de la guerre sainte*.

[66] Wailly, ed., *Joinville*, 50–2. The good king has a second motive, as he explains: he will never support royal officials in evildoing.

[67] Ibid., 230–1.

[68] McDiarmid and Stevenson, eds., *Barbour's Bruce*, bk. III, ll. 114–5; bk. VI, 625–31, 644.

[69] Ibid., bk. XII, ll. 51–61. The blow was delivered by axe rather than sword.

(Dear God! Whoever had been there and seen how he stoutly set himself against them all, I know well he would call him the best alive in his day.)[70]

Here, two centuries earlier, is Richard the Lion-Heart in action while on crusade:

> Never did man such mighty deeds;
> He charged among the miscreant breed
> So deep that he was hid from sight . . .
> Forward and back he hewed a swath
> About him, cutting deadly path
> With his good sword, whose might was such
> That everything that it could touch,
> Or man or horse, was overthrown
> And to the earth was battered down.
> I think 'twas there he severed
> At one stroke both the arm and head
> Of an emir, an infidel
> Steel-clad, whom he sent straight to hell,
> And when the Turks perceived this blow,
> They made broad path before him.[71]

Froissart gives us Sir Robert Salle, confronted outside Norwich by English rebels in 1381, who want to force him to be their military leader. His refusal leads to mortal combat:

[Sir Robert] drew a long Bordeaux sword which he carried, and began cutting and thrusting all around him, a lovely sight to see. Few dared to come near him, and of those who did he cut off a foot or a head or an arm or a leg with every stroke he made. Even the boldest of them grew afraid of him. On that spot Sir Robert gave a marvellous display of swordsmanship. He was himself overwhelmed soon, however, and dismembered.[72]

The biographer of Don Pero Niño records his hero's fight with a famous opponent named Gomez Domao, who used his shield so well that no disabling blow could reach him, and who returned such blows that Pero reported

---

[70] McDiarmid and Stevenson, eds., *Barbour's Bruce*, bk. VI, ll. 67–180; l. 315 notes that fourteen were slain 'with his hand'.

[71] Hubert tr., and La Monte, *Crusade of Richard Lion-Heart*, ll. 605–26; Gaston Paris, ed., *L'Histoire de la guerre sainte*. Cf. ll. 6478–530, or ll. 7349–61, where Richard 'cut and smote and smashed / Through them, then turned about, and slashed / And sheared off arm and hand and head. / Like animals they turned and fled. / But many could not flee.' The author (ll. 10453–66) assures his readers he is not flattering; an entire throng witnessed Richard's blows, splitting his enemies to their teeth with his brand of steel. In ll. 10494–8 we learn the crusading knights 'lopped off hands and heads and feet, / Split eyes and mouths with many a wound.'

[72] Brereton, tr., *Froissart*, 222–4.

later that sparks flew from his eyes when they struck his helmet. Finally, the great Castilian knight 'struck Gomez so hard above the shield, that he split it for a hands-breadth and his head down to the eyes; and that was the end of Gomez Domao'. Pero went forward later in that fight with lance stubs in his shield, an arrow binding his neck to his armour, and a crossbow bolt lodged in his nostrils (driven deeper by sword blows that struck it in the close fight-ing). His shield was cut to bits, his sword blade was notched like a saw and dyed with blood. 'And well do I think that until that day Pero Niño never had been able to glut himself in an hour with the toil he craved.'[73]

In fact, both imaginative literature and the historical accounts of their lives picture knights enjoying a privileged practice of violence; it suggests that they found in their exhilarating and fulfilling fighting the key to identity.[74] It would otherwise be hard to explain the thousands of individual combats and mass engagements that fill page after page in each major category of chivalric litera-ture: *chanson de geste*, romance, vernacular manual, chivalric biography, chron-icle. Marc Bloch called these interminable combats 'eloquent psychological documents'.[75] Clearly, the personal capacity to beat another man through the accepted method of knightly battle—in fact the actual physical process of knocking another knight off his horse and, if required, hacking him down to the point of submission or death—appears time and again as something like the ultimate human quality; it operates in men as a gift of God, it gives mean-ing to life, reveals the presence of the other desired qualities, wins the love of the most desirable women, determines status and worth, and binds the best males together in a fellowship of the elect. Many writers also recognized it as a power akin to fire: if noble, necessary, and useful, such violence requires much care and control.

The ideal chivalric figure is not, of course, a latter-day Viking berserker, dri-ven by what modern evaluation might call overactive glands or psychopathic personality. Granted, Arthurian society might well have recognized such a comparison in Sagremore the Unruly, but he surely stands at the rough end of the scale. When he is imprisoned, in the *Lancelot*, his captor, the lord of the Castle of the Narrow March, admits that he released him lest Sagremore 'go

---

[73] Evans, tr., *The Unconquered Knight*, 36–8. In a later battle he splits the iron cap and skull of a knight who grabs his horse's reins. From this battle he sent his notched sword, 'twisted by dint of striking mighty blows, and all dyed in blood' to his ladylove: pp. 195, 196.

[74] Chivalry regularly means either deeds of prowess or the body of knights on some field in both Barbour's chronicle and Sir Thomas Gray's chronicle: Maxwell, tr., *Scalacronica*; McDiarmid and Stevenson, *Barbour's Bruce*. Pope and Lodge, eds, *Life of the Black Prince*, note that the empha-sis of the work is on prowess and piety. Keen notes that to the combatant in the Hundred Years War '[t]he *ius militare* meant . . . the law of chivalry . . . the law of a certain privileged class, whose hereditary occupation was fighting': *Laws of War*, 19.

[75] Bloch, *Société Féodale*, II, 294.

mad because he is in an enclosed place, and he wanted to engage in battle and fight with my knights'. Sagremore is justly called the Unruly, this lord says, 'for he showed no trace of reason in what he did, and never in all my life have I seen a single knight perform as many feats of arms as he did'. He was, the text announces, 'never much of a knight nor very confident until he was thoroughly worked up. Then he feared nothing and gave no thought to himself.'[76] In *Merlin Continuation* he is characterized as 'a very good knight and so unruly when he was upset that his chivalry was highly esteemed'.[77]

Yet even if we grant that the knights are so much more than berserkers, there is, nevertheless, behind great prowess an element of rage and sheer battle fury. It is hard to imagine the one without the other. We can, of course, see this not only in such ambivalent figures as Raoul de Cambrai, but in great idols such as Lancelot and the other Round Table knights. To read much chivalric literature is to find admired knights regularly feeling rage as they fight; their blood boils; when honour is challenged, they nearly lose their minds.[78] As the tournament held to celebrate Arthur's wedding becomes more heated, Gawain can scarcely be stopped, 'for he was hot with anger and bent on inflicting pain'.[79] In battle against the Irish and Saxons, 'Lancelot's prowess was demonstrated, for he cut through Saxons and Irishmen, horses and heads, shields and legs and arms'. The author tells us '[h]e resembled an angry lion that plunges among the does, not because of any great hunger it might have, but in order to show off its ferocity and its power.' Lionel tries to restrain him, asking, the most pragmatic questions about prowess: 'Do you wish to get yourself killed in a spot where you can perform no act of prowess? And even if you did perform some act of prowess, it would never be known. Haven't you done enough?' At this suggestion of restraint Lancelot threatens Lionel with 'some harm', and is finally stopped only by an admonition in the name of the queen.[80]

---

[76] Carroll, tr., *Lancelot Part II*, 187, 210; Elspeth Kennedy, ed., *Lancelot do Lac*, 448–9, 506.

[77] Asher, tr., *Merlin Continuation*, 51; Sommer, ed., *Zeitschrift*, 131–2: 'moult a prisier de cheualerie'.

[78] E.g. William of Orange and his opponents in Hoggan, tr., 'Crowning of Louis', 39, 40, 43, 53; Langlois, ed., *Couronnement de Louis*, 86, 87, 94, 113. Raoul feels 'all his blood boil', is 'unbridled in his wrath', goes 'mad with anger', and burns nuns in a 'rage', etc. (examples in Kay, ed., tr., *Raoul de Cambrai*, laisses 32, 62, 68). Lancelot feels rage in his first tournament: Rosenberg, tr., *Lancelot Part I*, 95; Elspeth Kennedy, *Lancelot do Lac*, 231. Lancelot and even Galahad feel rage as they fight each other, incognito, just to test prowess: Bryant, tr., *Perlesvaus*, 92–3; Nitze and Jenkins, eds, *Perlesvaus*, 140–1.

[79] Pickens, tr., *Story of Merlin*, 336; Sommer, ed., *Vulgate Version*, II, 307.

[80] Carrol, *Lancelot Part II*, 234–5; Micha, ed., *Lancelot*, VIII, 469–474. Yvain tells him he should not have gone on: 'doing so would not have been boldness, but rather folly'. Yvain similarly holds back the impetuous Lancelot, at the time of Gawain's capture by Caradoc, swearing, 'By the Holy Cross, my lord! You can't go ahead like that! You mustn't rush in so wildly to show your prowess! It would be a lost cause. . . . Prowess should be shown only where it can work!' Rosenberg, *Lancelot, Part III*, 281; Micha, *Lancelot* I, 178–9.

Rage in battle is not limited to imaginative literature. Joinville describes the Comte d'Anjou as mad with rage during a fight along the Nile on St Louis's crusade.[81] The Chandos Herald's *Life of the Black Prince* tells of Sir William Felton charging into action 'come home sanz sens et sanz avis, a chevall la lance baissie'.[82] John Barbour reports that at Bannockburn the Scots fought as if in a rage, 'as men out of wit'. He describes Sir Thomas Murray, a Bruce supporter, fighting in Ireland 'as he war in a rage'. Robert Bruce, to the contrary, managed to use reason to control such impulses, inherent in chivalry: 'And with wyt his chewelry / He gouernyt . . . worthily.'[83] Froissart says that when Philip VI saw the English in battle formation at Crécy, 'his blood boiled, for he hated them'.[84] Saladin, in Richard the Lion-Heart's crusade chronicle, is pictured admiring his opponent, but exclaiming,

> With what rashness doth he fling
> Himself! Howe'er great prince I be,
> I should prefer to have in me
> Reason and measure and largesse
> Than courage carried to excess.[85]

The frequent praise of *mesure*, restraint, balance, and reason in all forms of chivalric literature can surely be read as countering a tendency that was real, and dangerous. At a minimum, we know that knights in historical combat frequently found it hard to restrain themselves and sought release in impetuous charges, disregarding some commander's plan and strict orders.[86]

---

[81] Wailly, *Joinville*, 88. Joinville was grateful that the man was 'hors dou sens' and 'courouciez', because his actions spared Joinville and others.

[82] Pope and Lodge, *The Black Prince*, 84–5.

[83] McDiarmid and Stevenson, *Barbour's Bruce*, III, bk. XIII, l. 143; bk. XVI, l. 199; bk. IX, ll. 373–6. The association of chivalry with a mental state requiring governance is notable. McKim, 'Ideal of Knighthood', emphasizes Barbour's deliberate contrast between the *mesure* of James Douglas as ideal knight and the foolhardiness that cost Edward Bruce victories and, finally, his life.

[84] Brereton, tr., *Froissart*, 88.

[85] Hubert tr., and La Monte, *Crusade of Richard Lion-Heart*, ll. 12146–52; Gaston Paris, ed., *L'Histoire de la guerre sainte*.

[86] On Richard I's crusade two knights, despite his careful plan for counterattack, cannot take the ignominy of enduring provocative attacks from the Muslims; they charge the enemy and bring about a general assault, joined by the Bishop of Beauvais. The resulting fight, with lances through bodies, could almost come from the *Song of Roland*: see ll. 6421–60 in Hubert tr., and La Monte, *Crusade of Richard Lion-Heart*; Gaston Paris, *L'Histoire de la guerre sainte*. A Templar similarly breaks ranks and puts his lance through an enemy's body. The author says his chivalry made him do this: ll. 9906–46. Miles de Cogan, who cannot stand the delay during a parley over the fate of Dublin, leads an attack which takes the city, along with much loot: Orpen, ed., tr., *Song of Dermot*, ll. 1674–711. Joinville tells a number of such stories of impetuosity from the crusade of Louis IX, including one in which the Master of the Temple cries out, 'For God's sake, let's get at them! I can't stand it any longer!' His charge provokes a general action unintended by the French king: Wailly, ed., *Joinville*, 78. Froissart says the royal plan of battle at Crécy could not be carried out because French lords wanted no restraint and pressed forward to show their power: Brereton, *Froissart*, 86.

All this violence was effected by a knight's own skilled hands; chivalry was not simply a species of officership more distanced from the bloody work with swords and spears. This is no argument that the medievals knew no generalship; we have been taught how skilfully medieval knights could carry out impressive tactical and strategic plans.[87] But we must also note that chivalric literature emphasizes personal might, courage, and skill in hand-to-hand fighting.[88]

Summing up hundreds of years of this tradition, Malory refers time and again to the wondrous work done by his knights' hands, firmly gripping their weapons.[89] We are assured that Lancelot has won Joyeuse Garde, his refuge, 'with his owne hondis', that Arthur 'was emperor himself through dignity of his hands', that he awaits a tournament where '[the knights] shall . . . preve whoo shall be beste of his hondis'. We hear Outelake of Wentelonde proudly stating his claim to a lady: 'thys lady I gate be my prouesse of hondis and armys thys day at Arthurs court'. Such hands wield a lance or sword well. Seeing King Pellinore cut Outelake down to the chin with a single sword stroke, Meliot de Logurs declines to fight 'with such a knyght of proues'.[90]

Chronicle and biography speak the same language and show the same emphasis. John Barbour praises Edward Bruce as 'off [of] his hand a nobill knycht', and assures us that Robert Bruce slew all the fourteen Englishmen at the ford, noted above, 'vif [with] his hand'.[91] In his first fight Don Pero Niño, as his biographer tells us, 'accomplished so many fair feats with his hands that

---

[87] See Gillingham: 'Richard I'; 'War and Chivalry'; and 'William the Bastard'.

[88] Gerald of Wales is capable of clearly distinguishing between personal, knightly valour and generalship. For his description of these qualities in John de Courcy, see Wright, tr., *Historical Works*, 281, 318.

[89] Many other writers could be cited widely. In the Post-Vulgate *Merlin Continuation* a poor knight asking a lady's hand of her father, promises that 'If in one day I can't bring . . . ten knights to defeat *with my own hands*, and you afterwards—all knights renowned for prowess—I don't want you to consider me a knight.' Asher, tr., *Merlin Continuation (end)*, 64; Bogdanow, ed., 'Folie Lancelot', 33; emphasis supplied. Inverse cases—fears of the work done by knights' hands— likewise appear in this work; see Asher, ibid., 100; Bogdanow, ibid., 127.

[90] The examples in Malory almost defy citation. Vinaver, ed., *Malory, Works*, 415–16, 111, 72–3. Malory draws on long-held belief. The vast Vulgate cycle, written more than two centuries earlier, repeatedly emphasizes hands-on prowess. Lancelot, learning of the defeat of so many Arthurian knights at the Forbidden Hill, declares, 'he who defeated them can truly say that there is great prowess in him, if he defeated them with his own hands.' Carroll, tr., *Lancelot Part VI*, 232; Micha. ed., *Lancelot*, V, 96. There is a similar statement from Lambegue in Krueger, tr., *Lancelot Part IV*, 71; Micha, *Lancelot*, I, 260. In a later crisis Guerrehet's valour saved the day, 'for he killed four of them with his own hands and wounded six, including the first whose arm he had severed': Kibler, tr., *Lancelot Part V*, 118; Micha, *Lancelot*, IV, 21. In the Middle English *William of Palerne*, the hero in his first battle does wonders 'wiþ his owne hond', killing six prominent enemies and overcoming the enemy leader: Bunt, ed., *William of Palerne*, ll. 1195, 1230–54. In the *Alliterative Morte Arthure* (Benson, ed., tr., 52), Arthur greets Cador after a battle with the words, 'You have done well, Sir duke, with your two hands.'

[91] McDiarmid and Stevenson, eds., *Barbour's Bruce*, II, bk. IX, l. 486; bk. VI, l. 313.

all spoke well of him'. The biographer is proud that 'none did so much with their hands as he'.[92]

This hands-on work of chivalry was very bloody. The young Arthurian heroes in *The Story of Merlin* (Sagremore, Galescalin, Agravain, Gaheriet, Guerrehet) have fought so well in a battle against the Saxons 'that their arms and legs and the heads and manes of their horses were dripping with blood and gore'. They are described as having done 'many a beautiful deed of knighthood [*mainte bele cheualier*] and struck many a handsome blow, for which everyone should hold them in high esteem'.[93]

Similarly, in his biographical chronicle John Barbour stresses the bloody character of such fighting: grass red with blood, swords bloody to the hilt, heraldic devices on armour so smeared with blood they cannot be read.[94] Gerald of Wales unforgettably characterized Richard I of England as not only 'fierce in his encounters in arms', but 'only happy when he marked his steps with blood'.[95] The historian of the Lion-Heart's crusade more than once records Richard hewing off enemy heads and displaying them as trophies, or riding into camp after a night of skirmishing with more Muslim heads hanging from his saddle.[96] Such trophies were not limited to crusading; after the bloody battle of Evesham in the English civil war of Henry III's reign, the head and testicles of the defeated Simon de Montfort were sent as a gift to Lady Wigmore.[97]

The incident might not be too gruesome for romance. A maiden whose rights Bors defends in *Lancelot* has given him a white banner to attach to his lance. After combat with her enemy, Bors 'saw that the banner which had been white before, was scarlet with blood, and he was overjoyed'. A little later in the same text an opponent evaluates Sagremore in revealing terms:

He noticed that his shield had been completely destroyed by lances and swords, and he saw that his hauberk was broken in several spots; he looked at Sagremore himself, bloodied with his own blood and with the blood of others. He had great respect for him, for he thought no knight deserving of greater esteem.[98]

---

[92] Evans, tr., *The Unconquered Knight*, 30.

[93] Pickens, tr., *Story of Merlin*, 268; Sommer, ed., *Vulgate Version*, II, 185. Heroes are so covered by gore that their heraldic devices can scarcely be recognized.

[94] McDiarmid and Stevenson, *Barbour's Bruce*, bk. II, 366–70; bk. X, l. 687; bk. XIII, ll. 183–5.

[95] Wright, ed., *Historical Works*, 160.

[96] Ll. 7439–40, 8964–79 in Hubert tr., and La Monte, *Crusade of Richard Lion-Heart*; Gaston Paris, *L'Histoire de la guerre sainte*.

[97] Maddicott, *Simon de Montfort*, 344.

[98] Krueger, tr., *Lancelot Part IV*, 42–3, 78; Micha, ed., *Lancelot*, II, 148–9, 291. For a parallel case to the bloody banner in a Middle English text (*Blanchardyn and Eglentine*), see Gist, *Love and War*, 148.

An old hermit who is a former knight tells Yvain (in the *Lancelot*) that the custom at Uther Pendragon's court was that no knight could be seated unless he had been wounded.[99]

Even Lancelot's great work—often powered by his love for the queen—necessarily involves hacking and chopping, great bloodshed, frequent decapitations, and regular eviscerations. He was filled with rage as he rescues a maiden from other knights:

[Lancelot] struck the head off one, who fell dead to the ground; he took aim at another and struck him dead. When the others saw this they were afraid of being killed themselves and scattered this way and that to save their lives. Lancelot pursued them, hacking and eviscerating and slaying them as if they were dumb animals; behind him were the somber traces of more than twenty slaughtered men.[100]

Hector and Perceval, who meet and (as is so often true of knights in chivalric literature) fail to recognize each other, fall at once to combat:

At every moment they were so quick and so aggressive that it was a wonder to behold; in great anguish they endured great and terrible wounds that each inflicted on the other in quick succession, like knights of great prowess, hacking apart their shields and helmets with their swords and making the blood gush forth on every side.[101]

It is worth remembering that no great cause, no great love, is at stake in this fight; the knights meet in the woods; they fight. So near to death are they both brought that only the appearance of the Grail preserves their lives.

Given its centrality, such prowess must get an early start in the young knight's career.[102] Accounts of youthful origins of heroes stress just this precocious display of commendable violence, a harbinger of things to come. In the *Chanson de Aspremont* the young Roland and his companions, kept from battle by an overly solicitous Charlemagne, severely beat the porter guarding the door of their chamber, and escape. They acquire the horses they need by beating up the keepers who conduct them to the battlefield. Roland encourages the others: 'Young Roland says: "We'll have these four—come on! / Nor

---

[99] Kibler, tr., *Lancelot Part V*, 174; Micha, ed., *Lancelot*, IV, 248. Here, one of the occasional notes of ambiguity can be heard, for he adds that the custom was ended in Arthur's day, but replaced by one equally 'unpleasant'—that no knight be seated at a high feast who has not sworn on relics that he has defeated a knight 'by deeds of arms' within the past week.

[100] Kibler, *Lancelot Part V*, 191; Micha, *Lancelot*, IV, 328.

[101] Carroll, tr., *Lancelot Part VI*, 327; Micha, *Lancelot*, VI, 200–1.

[102] For overviews of education in arms, see Orme, *From Childhood to Chivalry*, 181–91; Chris Given-Wilson, *English Nobility*, 2–7. Patterson notes that 'The biographers of both du Guesclin and Boucicaut stress the violence of their heroes' *enfances* as evidence of their single-mindedness': *Chaucer*, 176. On the other hand, the education proposed for the knight by Christine de Pisan in *L'Epître d'Othéa à Hector*, as Willard notes, was 'moral rather than military': 'Christine de Pisan', 512.

shall we ask them first for what we want!" / His friends reply: "With the blessing of God!" ' When the news comes to King Salemon, the owner of the horses, that the lads have 'killed' the porter, stolen the horses, and beaten his men, he laughs in warm appreciation of their valour.[103]

Rainouart, another hero of *chanson*, was angered as a boy by a beating from his tutor; he responded by hitting the man so hard that his heart burst.[104] A tutor who fails to appreciate noble largesse and 'who wished to dominate him' likewise causes the young Lancelot trouble in the *Lancelot do Lac*. Lancelot endures his slap in brave silence, but when the tutor strikes a greyhound he has just received, he breaks his bow into pieces over the man's head. Angered at the man for his broken bow, he then beats him soundly and tries to kill the tutor's helpers; they all run for safety. When he tells his patroness, the Lady of the Lake, that he will kill the tutor anywhere but in her household, 'she was delighted, for she saw that he could not fail to be a man of valour, with God's help and her own'.[105] But the most striking case of early promise of prowess comes from Tristram, in Malory's tale. Tristram's mother, dying as he is born, says he is a young murderer and thus is likely to be a manly adult.[106]

Competition

This obsession with prowess stands behind the seemingly numberless tests the chivalrous undergo in this literature to determine who is the best knight in the world. Marvellous swords can be grasped, or pulled from a stone, or drawn from a wondrous scabbard only by the best knight in the world. Shields may only be borne by, beds may only serve the finest knight in the world. We even learn of a magical chess board which defeats all but Lancelot.[107]

But the supreme honour of being the best is determined primarily by fighting everyone else who wants that same honour. Anthropologists and historians regularly conclude that any society animated by a code of honour will be highly competitive; it will much value the defence of cherished rights and the correction of perceived wrongs through showy acts of physical violence. In a classic formulation, the anthropologist Julian Pitt-Rivers argued:

[103] Newth, ed., tr., *Song of Aspremont*, 34–5; Brandin, ed., *Chanson d'Aspremont*, 42–3.

[104] Ferrante, ed., tr., *Guillaume d'Orange*, 272; Wienbeck *et al.*, eds, *Aliscans*, 496–7.

[105] Corley, tr., *Lancelot of the Lake*, 36–7; Elspeth Kennedy, ed., *Lancelot do Lac*, I, 45–7; cf. p. 98; also see Rosenberg, tr., *Lancelot Part I*, 29; Sommer, ed., *Vulgate Version*, III, 55.

[106] Vinaver, ed., *Malory. Works*, 230: 'A, my lytyll son, thou haste murtherd thy modir! And therefore I suppose thou that arte a murtherer so yonge, thow arte full lykly to be a manly man in thyne ayge.'

[107] Kibler, tr., *Lancelot Part V*, 205; Micha, ed., *Lancelot*, IV, 393.

Respect and precedence are paid to those who claim it and are sufficiently powerful to enforce their claim. Just as possession is said to be nine-tenths of the law, so the *de facto* achievement of honour depends upon the ability to silence anyone who would dispute the title.[108]

Writing about the problem of violence in early modern England, the historian Mervyn James similarly points to 'the root of the matter' in the concept of honour, 'emerging out of a long-established military and chivalric tradition . . . characterized above all by a stress on competitive assertiveness'. As he notes concisely, 'Honour could both legitimize and provide moral reinforcement for a politics of violence.'[109]

We will find ample evidence for investigating the politics of violence; the fierce physical competitiveness so characteristic of what anthropologists have called honour cultures could scarcely be better illustrated than by extensive reading in chivalric literature.[110] As a code of honour, chivalry had as much investment in knightly autonomy and heroic violence as in any forms of restraint, either internal or external. Asked why there is strife between the queen's knights and the knights of the Round Table, Merlin answers in plain terms: 'You should know . . . that their jealousy has done that, and they want to test their prowess against one another.' In the tournament held to celebrate the wedding of Arthur and Guinevere, the knights 'began hitting roughly, although they were playing, because they were good knights".[111] The tournament turns into a virtual battle, as do so many tournaments in chivalric literature.

Seeing unknown knights appearing prominently on another battlefield earlier in this same work, Yvonet the Great and Yvonet the Bastard wonder who they can be. Aces of Beaumont gives them answer in hard, stirring words: 'If you want to know who they are, ride over to them and fight so well that they ask *you* who *you* are! For it is by their valiant feats of arms that people know who the worthies are.[112]

---

[108] Pitt-Rivers, 'Honour and Social Status', 24.

[109] Mervyn James, 'English politics', 308–9.

[110] Hostility is assumed when an unknown knight appears. E.g. Rosenberg, tr., *Lancelot Part I*, 93; Carrol, tr., *Lancelot Part II*, 153; Micha, ed., *Lancelot*, VII, 383; VIII, 145.

[111] Pickens, tr., *Story of Merlin*, 379, 335; Sommer, ed., *Vulgate Version*, II, 382, 302. When Arthur rebukes the knights they say that 'they could not resist it, and they did not know where the urge came from'. Similarly, Arthur the Less defends his competitiveness in the *Post Vulgate Quest*; chastised by Palamedes for going about, attacking knights and considering that courtesy, Arthur replies,

You shouldn't blame me if I go around attacking you and the other good knights, for I'm a young man and a new knight who needs to win praise and acclaim, and if I don't win them now, when will I win them?

Asher, tr., 242; Magne, ed., *Santa Graal* II, 221.

[112] Pickens, *Story of Merlin*, 273; Sommer, *Vulgate Version*, II, 194. Cf. Pickens, ibid., 232, 259, 287, 317, 359; Sommer, ibid., 119, 168, 220, 272, 347.

Intense competition is sometimes shown, only to be criticized. Milun, in Marie de France's lay by that name, is so jealous of the much-praised prowess of a young knight sweeping the tournament circuit that he searches him out and engages in a fight 'in order to do some harm to him and his reputation'; though he thinks he will afterwards look for his long-lost son, he is, of course, defeated in the joust by that very son.[113] Knightly competition has edged out affection and nearly brought tragic results. Chivalric competition in Marie's lay 'Le Chaitivel' does end tragically. When four knights in love with a lady fight in a tournament, three are killed and one is castrated by a lance thrust.[114]

Yet competition and its results are usually accepted or even highly regarded. A real man of prowess will bear the marks of other men's weapons on his body for life. Running nearly naked in the woods, mad, when he thinks he has lost the queen's love, Lancelot is recognized as a man of worship by those who see him simply in terms of the scars left on his body from his ceaseless combat.[115]

Almost from the beginning of the classic Arthurian story, as told and retold in the Vulgate Cycle, the Post-Vulgate Cycle and Malory's *Morte Darthur*, the rivalries and jealousies among the knights foreshadow the break-up of the Round Table. Much of this strife originates, of course, in the fierce hatreds caused by so much killing (and a certain amount of sex) within a restricted group of warriors and their ladies. Here, in Malory's words, is Gawain's view, at one point:

Fayre bretherne, here may ye se: whom that we hate kynge Arthure lovyth, and whom that we love he hatyth. And wyte you well, my fayre bretherne, that this sir Lamerok woll nevyr love us, because we slew his fadir, kynge Pellynor, for we demed that he slew oure fadir, kynge Lotte of Orkenay; and for the deth of kynge Pellynor sir Lamerok ded us a shame to our modir. Therefore I woll be revenged.[116]

Of course, Gawain and his brothers are revenged and the destructive feud between the houses of Lot and Pellinore rolls on.

But the factionalism and competition in Arthurian stories often result from simple and immediate jealousy, from resentment that someone else has won worship. Gawain, while on the quest of the white hart, encounters two brothers fighting, as one of them explains, 'to preff which of us was the bygger knyght'.[117] Tristram, or Lancelot, both of whom invariably ends up being 'the

---

[113] Hanning and Ferrante, trs, *Marie de France*, 171–4; for their comments, see pp. 177–80, and Rychner, ed., *Marie de France*, 136–40.

[114] Hanning and Ferrante, *Marie de France*, 183–4; Rychner, *Marie de France*, 145–7.

[115] Vinaver, ed., *Malory. Works*, 499.   [116] Ibid., 375.

[117] Ibid., 64. In the *Merlin Continuation* (Asher, tr., 228–9, Paris and Ulrich, eds., *Merlin*, II, 81–3) Gawain strongly denounces their fight as foolish and gets them, as a favour, to promise peace in the future. Malory has Gawain more simply say that brother should not fight brother and then threaten them with force if they disagree.

bygger knyght', provoke endless jealousy, which is openly discussed.[118] On the queen's urging, Lancelot is anxious to fight the Round Table in tournament: 'he was filled with joy, for he had often wanted to test himself against those knights who had tested their own prowess against all comers'.[119] Having just witnessed Lancelot kill Tarquin, in the *Morte Darthur*, Gaheris pronounces Lancelot the best knight in the world: he has just eliminated the second best.[120] After Lancelot decapitates the wicked Meleagant with a great sword stroke in the *Lancelot*, Kay similarly proclaims Lancelot's well-earned status: 'Ah, my lord, we welcome you above all the other knights in the world as the flower of earthly chivalry! You have proved your valour here and elsewhere.'[121]

In the *Lancelot* Bors meets a knight (who turns out to be Agravain) who stoutly asserts Lancelot is not the knight Gawain is. Their argument over who is best fighter is, of course, settled by fighting. Bors unhorses his opponent, and hacks him into a disabled state on the ground. When he refuses to surrender ('you will take nothing more of mine away'), Bors hammers his head with his sword pommel until blood spurts, pulls away the armour protecting the knight's throat, and prepares to deliver the fatal blow. Agravain, with an ugly grimace, agrees Lancelot is the better knight.[122]

Bademagu leaves court in a huff when Tor gets a seat at the Round Table before he does. Balin, during his brief perch on the top rung on the ladder of prowess, wins so much worship that it generates reaction; after he alone can pull the wondrous sword from its scabbard, Launceor, for example, 'had grete despite at Balin for the enchevynge of the swerde, that any sholde be accompted more hardy or more of prouesse'. Balin and his brother Balaan, when setting out to fight King Rion, intend to 'preve oure worship and prouesse upon hym'. Worship is won by prowess which is of necessity done unto others.[123]

Danger, mounted and armed, lance at the ready, thus lurks along every forest path, in every glade, at every river ford. Knights must ride encased in their metal as soon as they venture forth from the castles or hermitages in which they shelter for the night; they must assume hostility from any other knights whom they may meet. In the prose (Didot) version of the *Perceval*, the hero's sister describes this environment plainly:

Dear brother, I have great fear for you who go thus, for you are very young and the

[118] See, for example, Vinaver, ed., *Malory. Works*, 411.

[119] Kibler, tr., *Lancelot Part V*, 196; Micha, ed., *Lancelot*, IV, 352–3.

[120] Vinaver, *Malory. Works*, 159. Numerous statements of this sort appear in the pages of Malory.

[121] Krueger, tr., *Lancelot Part IV*, 32; Sommer, ed., *Vulgate Version*, IV, 225.

[122] Krueger, *Lancelot Part IV*, 51; Micha, *Lancelot*, 179–82.

[123] Vinaver, *Malory. Works*, 81, 42, 44.

knights who go through the land are so very cruel and wicked, and be sure that if they can they will kill you in order to win your horse; but if you trust me, dear brother, you will leave this endeavour upon which you are entered and will dwell with me, for it is a great sin to kill a knight, and also you are each day in great danger of being killed.[124]

The author of the *Perlesvaus* suggests that after Perceval's failure to ask the right questions in his moment of trial, 'all lands are now rent by war; no knight meets another in a forest but he attacks him and kills him, if he can'.[125]

But is winning all? Is not fighting well just as honourable? The medieval response to such questions seems somewhat unstable. Sometimes a text specifies that the honour of the loser has not been sullied. Palomides tells Gareth, beaten in a joust in the tournament at Lonezep, that he has lost no honour: 'And worshypfully ye mette with hym, and neyther of you ar dishonoured.' No less an authority than Queen Guinevere declares flatly, in Malory's words, that 'all men of worshyp hate an envyous man and woll shewe hym no favoure'.[126]

In fact, chivalric literature may declare it an honour to die from the blows of a man of great prowess. Owein, dying in the *Quest for the Holy Grail* after Gawain (not recognizing him) has put a spear into his chest, regards his death as fitting: ' "Then I set my death at naught," said he, "if it comes at the hand of so fine a knight as you." '[127] Yvain the Bastard, similarly skewered by Gawain in the Post-Vulgate *Quest*, dies with the same sentiment on his lips. An unidentified knight in this text demands a gift of Galahad: he wants Galahad to kill him so that he can die by the hands of the greatest knight in the world.[128] In the *Lancelot*, one of the opponents Lancelot defeats in the judicial combat concerning the False Guinevere tells him, 'I want to die by your hand, because I couldn't die by a better one.' Lancelot obliges him with a powerful sword stroke cutting through helmet and skull, and down into the man's spine.[129]

Yet winning is undoubtedly better, for all the fair words given to trying one's best and losing like a gentleman. As Malory observes, 'for oftetymes thorow envy grete hardynes is shewed that hath bene the deth of many kyd knyghtes; for thoughe they speke fayre many one unto other, yet whan they be in batayle eyther wolde beste be praysed.'[130] Experienced knights such as

---

[124] Skells, tr., *Perceval in Prose*, 28–9. When (p. 30) her hermit uncle sees her coming with Perceval, he assumes that this knight has seized and robbed her.

[125] Bryant, tr., *Perlesvaus*, 27; Nitze and Jenkins, eds., *Perlesvaus*, 38.

[126] Vinaver, ed., *Malory. Works*, 444, 466.

[127] Matarasso, tr., *Quest*, 168; Pauphilet, *Queste*, 153–4. Gawain is, of course, practising the wrong kind of chivalry in the view of this text. But the sentiment expressed by Owein (in Pauphilet, he is called Yvain the Bastard) retains its interest.

[128] Asher, tr., *Quest*, 155, 125; Magne, ed., *Demanda*, I, 211, 57.

[129] Rosenberg, tr., *Lancelot Part III*, 272; Micha, ed., *Lancelot*, I, 140.

Charny and Malory know that even the most capable must expect to suffer defeat in some fights.[131] If all bruises can thus be poulticed in defeat with the knowledge of having fought well, however, winning decisively eliminates the need. So many knights must have agreed with Malory's Palomides, who frequently appears weeping and lamenting that when a great hero such as Lancelot or Tristram is on the field he can never win 'worshyppe'.[132]

Characters who have been defeated in the initial, mounted fight with lances, often declare that they have been 'shamed', and want a chance to win worship on foot with sword and shield.[133] At one point in the *Lancelot* no fewer than sixty-four knights of the Round Table are forced by Arthur to admit that they have been defeated by Lancelot in a tournament; equally bad, put on oath, none can claim to have defeated him. Having been beaten by the best does not soften their feelings, heightened by Arthur's praise of Lancelot. The author tells us: 'These words of King Arthur so embarrassed the knights of the Round Table that ever afterwards they hated Lancelot with a mortal hatred.'[134] The hatred of the defeated is similarly directed against Bors, who has overcome fourteen of Arthur's court at the Forbidden Hill:

they were much more dismayed than before by the fact that they had been defeated by Bors, who was but a youth, whereas some of them were old, experienced knights of great strength; every one of them felt great sorrow and resentment in his heart because they had been defeated by him, and that was one of the things for which they bore the greatest rancour against Lancelot's kindred.[135]

It is true that many knights in chivalric literature find the choice between honourable defeat and death an easy decision; one after another saves his life at the last moment as the victor stands over his prostrate body, sword ready for the final, decapitating stroke. Yet the truly heroic prefer to die without ever yielding, without ever once having said 'the loath word' of surrender. Blamour speaks in just these terms to the triumphant Tristram, who has just defeated him:

Sir Trystrames de Lyones, I requyre the, as thou art a noble knyght and the beste knyght that ever I founde, that thou wolt sle me oute, for I wolde nat lyve to be made lorde of all the erthe; for I had lever dye here with worshyp than lyve here with shame. And nedis, sir Trystrames, thou muste sle me, other ellys thou shalt never wynne the fylde, for I woll never sey the lothe worde.

[130] Vinaver, ed., *Malory. Works*, 133–4.
[131] For Charny, see Kaeuper and Kennedy, *Book of Chivalry*, 130–3; Vinaver, *Malory. Works*, 318. Malory's Sir Dynadan gives the maxim, 'he rydyth well that never felle'.
[132] E.g. Vinaver, *Malory. Works*, 325, 419.
[133] E.g. ibid., 355. Mark says to Lamerok, 'I woll fyght wyth a swerde, for ye have shamed me with a speare.'
[134] Kibler, tr., *Lancelot Part V*, 206; Micha, ed., *Lancelot*, IV, 397.
[135] Carroll, tr., *Lancelot Part VI*, 236; Micha, *Lancelot*, V, 112.

Blamour's brother, Bleoberis, agrees that 'though sir Trystrames hath beatyn his body, he hath nat beatyn his harte, and thanke God he is nat shamed this day'.[136] In this view defeat rests in the fallible body, but shame is locked out of an infallible heart.

A knight whom Tor defeats in the *Merlin Continuation* takes just this line: 'Certainly, I'd rather die a hundred times, if that were possible,' he declares, 'than one single time to say or do something that looked like cowardice.' He repeats his stand even after Tor flattens him, driving the links of mail into his head, even after Tor beats his head with the pommel of the sword, so that 'he made the blood flow all down his face'.[137]

Conclusion

A conversation between the Lady of the Lake and the young Lancelot (in the *Lancelot do Lac* and *Lancelot* of the Vulgate Cycle) may well be, as Elspeth Kennedy has suggested, the fountainhead for all later discussions about balance between prowess and other qualities in chivalry. Responding to his lady's Socratic questions, Lancelot says:

It seems to me that a man can have the qualities of the heart even if he cannot have those of the body, for a man can be courteous and wise and gracious and loyal and valorous and generous and courageous—all these are virtues of the heart—though he cannot be big and robust and agile and handsome and attractive; all these things, it seems to me, are qualities of the body, and I believe that a man brings them with him out of his mother's womb when he is born.[138]

Here the ideal qualities of the chivalrous are pressed to the fore, and prowess—competitive, bloody work with edged weapons—is veiled in softening and restraining virtues, as it is, again, when the Lady of the Lake tells Lancelot about the origins of chivalry. Each of the first knights, she says, knew:

[that he] should be courteous without baseness, gracious without cruelty, compassionate towards the needy, generous and prepared to help those in need, and ready and prepared to confound robbers and killers; he should be a fair judge, without love or hate, without love to help wrong against right, without hate to hinder right in order to further wrong.

---

[136] Vinaver, ed., *Malory. Works*, 256.

[137] Asher, tr., *Merlin Continuation*, 236–7; Roussineau, ed., *Merlin*, I, 247–8. The sentiment is bold, but the defeated knight suddenly loses resolve. A maiden appears to whom Tor grants a favour: she wants the knight's head; Tor (though the knight now pleads for his life from the maiden) swings so stoutly that the man's head flies six feet from his body.

[138] Quotation from Corin Corley, tr., *Lancelot of the Lake*, 51; Elspeth Kennedy, ed., *Lancelot do Lac*, I, 141. Cf. Rosenberg, tr., *Lancelot Part I*, 59; Micha, ed., *Lancelot*, VII, 248.

'A knight', she says, summing up, 'should not, for fear of death, do anything which can be seen as shameful; rather he should be more afraid of shame than of suffering death.' She then proceeds elaborately to explain the significance of knightly arms and armour in terms of desirable qualities, especially protecting the Holy Church.[139]

All of the great issues, all of the tensions and paradoxes, lie just out of sight in this splendid discourse—just beneath the surface here and echoed in famous books by Geoffroi de Charny and Ramon Llull.[140] Knights are presented as the righteous armed force of Christendom, the practitioners of licit force, the fair judges in society, wise men motivated and restrained by high ideals, bravely avoiding shame. Courtesy, generosity, the strong helping the weak against robbers and killers—such ideals resonate as much today as they did eight centuries ago.

Yet we need to remember how much these are reform ideas, prescriptive rather than descriptive. We know they do not describe how knights actually behaved. The evidence as a whole shows a core ideal of prowess, belief in sheer aptitude with arms, animated by courage, mildly, ideally, tempered by reason, wise restraint, and strategic pragmatism.

After he has seen Lancelot perform on the battlefield, Galehaut finally manages to meet him for the first time, and to ask him who he is. Lancelot replies: 'Good sir, I am a knight, as you can see.' ' "Indeed", said Galehaut, "a knight you are, the best there is, and the man I would most wish to honour in all the world." '[141] Galehaut has seen prowess personified. It has manifested itself in almost miraculous work with ashen lance and sharp-edged sword. The battlefield is strewn with slashed and mangled bodies lying in bloody proof. The vast body of literature about Lancelot regularly takes just such work as its focus—not all of the other fine qualities so praised by the Lady of the Lake. We are tirelessly shown Lancelot thrusting lance and swinging sword, not Lancelot defending the personnel and tithes of Mother Church or playing the fair judge. What other characters in the romances praise repeatedly is his awe-inspiring fighting, not abstract ideals.[142]

We have already considered evidence showing the fear inspired by the estate of medieval warriors, often expressed with prudent indirection. Open devalu-

---

[139] Corley, tr., *Lancelot of the Lake*, 52–6; Elspeth Kennedy, ed., *Lancelot do Lac*, I, 142–5; Rosenberg, tr., *Lancelot Part I*, 59–61; Micha, ed., *Lancelot*, 248–58.

[140] See discussion in Kaeuper and Kennedy, *Book of Chivalry*, 67, 69–74.

[141] Carroll, tr., *Lancelot Part II*, 135; Elspeth Kennedy, ed., *Lancelot do Lac*, I, 320. This formula is repeated in the Post-Vulgate Quest of the Holy Grail. Tristan, who has seen Galahad's prowess in a tournament, asks him to identify himself. 'I'm a knight', Galahad says simply. 'I know quite well that you're a knight', Tristan responds, 'and you're the best in the world': Asher, tr., *Quest*, 217; Bogdanow, ed., *Version Post-Vulgate*, 484.

ations of prowess are rare, indeed, but a writer like Walter Map is capable of at least declaring it morally neutral. 'Goodness only makes a man good', he writes; 'prowess makes him either.'[143] An intensely religious knight such as Sir John Clanvowe could stand traditional chivalric values on end:

ffor byfore God alle vertue is worsshipe and alle synne is shame. And in þis world it is euene þe reuers, ffor þe world holt hem worsshipful þat been greete werreyours and fighteres and þat distroyen and wynnen manye loondis.

(for in God's sight all virtue is worship and all sin is shame. But the world always reverses this, for the world holds as worshipful those who have been great warriors and fighters who destroy and win many lands.)[144]

The tension between sheer prowess and the restraint of reason or wisdom animates major texts, most famously in the *Song of Roland*. 'Roland is full of prowess, Oliver of wisdom', sings the author of that text, as he unfolds for his audience the complex consequences.[145] *Raoul de Cambrai* more than once warns that 'an unbridled man passes his days in sorrow'.[146] Near its end *The Story of Merlin* pointedly praises a Roman leader as 'a very good knight, worthy and bold', who 'knew how to fall back and turn about, and . . . knew how to storm in among foes'.[147] Malory, through Sir Tristram, says that 'manhode is nat worthe but yf hit be medled with wysdome'.[148] The wise Pharian tells his nephew, Lambegue, in *Lancelot*, 'almost never do we see great intelligence and great prowess lodged together in a youth. And it is true that for your age you have unusual prowess, enough, in fact, to dim your view of wisdom.'[149] Yet we should note that he goes on to urge unbridled prowess in the right situations, matched by quiet restraint in council:

---

[142] The household of two hermits term Lancelot 'the valiant man, who by his chivalry made all the world tremble before him': Asher, tr., *Merlin Continuation*, 69; Bogdanow, ed., 'Folie Lancelot', 45. Earlier, the ladies on the Island of Joy witnessed Lancelot unhorse a good challenger so forcefully that the man's neck is nearly broken and he faints in agony. Their response is to bow, sing, and dance before his shield, and proclaim him the best knight of the world. Asher, 78; Bogdanow, 70. A maiden late in the *Perlesvaus* tells her lady he is 'the violent Lancelot who killed your brother. It is no lie that he is one of the finest knights in the world, but because of the vigour and worth of his chivalry he has committed many an outrage.' Bryant, tr., *Perlesvaus*, 201; Nitze and Jenkins, eds., *Perlesvaus*, 312.

[143] M. R. James, ed., tr., *Walter Map*, 416–17.

[144] Scattergood, ed., *Sir John Clanvowe*, 69.

[145] 'Rollant est proz e Oliver est sage', the opening line of laisse 87, in Brault, ed., tr., *Chanson de Roland*.

[146] Kay, ed., tr., *Raoul de Cambrai*, laisses, 24, 104; and see the related sentiment in laisse 90.

[147] Pickens, tr., *Story of Merlin*, I, 406; Sommer, ed., *Vulgate Version*, II, 434.

[148] Vinaver, ed., *Malory. Works*, 428.

[149] Rosenberg, tr., *Lancelot Part I*, 36; Micha, ed., *Lancelot*, VII, 151–2. Cf. Meyer, ed., *Girart de Rousillon*, 94ff: Girart says to his nephew, 'Beau neveu, vous êtes preux; votre ardeur juvénile serait bonne, si vous aviez la sagesse.'

in battle or combat or in lists where the finest knights are gathered, take care to stand aside for no one, whether younger than yourself or older, but spur your horse on before all the others and strike the best blow you can. When it comes to arms, you see, no man need yield to young or old to gain fame and honor; but in important deliberations young men should attend to their elders. The truth is that there is great honor in dying boldly and bravely in combat, but only shame and reproach can come from foolish speech and thoughtless counsel.[150]

King Bademagu takes another corrective line on prowess as he tells his evil son Meleagant, jealous of Lancelot and anxious to fight, that 'size of body and limbs is not what makes a good knight, but greatness of heart'.[151]

Even in those passages that praise some hero's prowess interesting elements of doubt, or at least cautionary lines of thought, put in an appearance. Gawain twice fails to have a transforming experience (in the *Lancelot*) when the Grail comes into his presence: once he cannot keep his eyes off the beautiful maiden carrying it and, in recompense, is not served; the second time he is so worn out with fighting a mysterious knight in the hall of the Grail castle that he is lying, wounded and almost in a stupor on the floor. Through the very presence of the Grail heals his wounds, he fails to recognize it. A hermit tells him later that his failure was '[b]ecause you were not humble and simple'.[152]

In the *Lancelot* five sons of a duke, fighting their father, convince Lancelot by lies to join their side. He characteristically goes to work 'killing whatever he hit', and wins the day, even sending the duke's head flying with one of his great sword strokes. He is greeted with the usual effusive celebration in the winner's castle as 'the best knight in the world'. Yet, the text tells us, this victory was a pity, for Lancelot has been fighting on the wrong side, against members of the Round Table who were aiding the duke.[153]

We can only wonder at the way in which, with or without conscious intent, authors give us curiously shaded descriptions of Lancelot and other heroes in full battle fury. Lancelot is not only compared to a raptor, a wolf, or lion, but more than once to an 'evil demon', 'the Devil himself', 'Death itself'. Bors and even Perceval can likewise be termed 'demon'.[154] William of Palerne is described by enemies who feel the force of his chivalry as 'sum devel degised þat doþ al þis harm (some disguised devil who does all this harm)!'[155]

Balain's great prowess likewise produces deep ambivalence. The *Merlin Continuation* asserts that Balain was the most praised knight on a battlefield, for 'he practised a chivalry so expert, wherever he went, that everybody

[150] Carroll, tr., *Lancelot Part II*, 36; Micha, ed., *Lancelot*, VII, 151–2.
[151] Rosenberg, tr., *Lancelot Part III*, 260; Micha, *Lancelot*, I, 87.
[152] Krueger, tr., *Lancelot Part IV*, 100–2; Micha, *Lancelot*, II, 376–88.
[153] Kibler, tr., *Lancelot Part V*, 152–3; Micha, *Lancelot*, IV, 159–64.

watched him marvelling'. Wondering observers, however, say he is no mortal, but a 'monster' or 'devil'. Even King Arthur said that 'he was not a knight like other mortal knights, but a man born on earth for human destruction'.[156]

Those who would reform chivalry knew that they had to come to terms with prowess. They all hoped to channel or change the force and energy of this great virtue. Some even harboured futile hopes of substituting another quality in the uppermost slot. But prowess holds centre stage; it is essential to the chivalry with which the reformer must deal, however he or she wants to channel or change it. A layman lacking prowess might show other qualities in the textbook chivalric list; but at least in the realm of chivalric literature no one would particularly notice, because no one would particularly care. The chief virtue must come first. It is probable that complex figures in chivalric literature, such as Roland himself, or even darker figures, such as Raoul in *Raoul de Cambrai*, Claudas in the *Lancelot do Lac*, or Caradoc in *Lancelot*, were so interesting to their contemporaries in medieval society because of the tension between their admirable prowess and other qualities warped or missing in them.[157]

We must recognize how strongly chivalric literature acknowledges the impulse to settle any issue—especially any perceived affront to honour—by couching the lance for the charge or swiftly drawing the sword from the scabbard. Force is regularly presented as the means of getting whatever is wanted, of settling whatever is at issue.[158] Accusations of a more or less judicial nature, of course, lead to a fight, as does assertion of better lineage. But so does assertion that one's lady is fairer than another knight's lady, a request for a knight's name or even an answer to the question, 'Why are you so sad?' Of course, as often as not the fight is over no stated question at all, but simply seems a part of the natural order of the imagined world of chivalry: two knights meet in the

---

[154] Kibler, tr., *Lancelot Part V*, 160, 198, 204; Micha, ed., *Lancelot*, IV, 193, 359–61, 388; VI, 150, 160, 195–6; Carroll, tr., *Lancelot Part VI*, 315, 317, 326; Asher, tr., *Merlin Continuation*, 104; Bogdanow, ed., 'Folie Lancelot', 139.

[155] Bunt, ed., *William of Palerne*, l. 3888.

[156] Asher, *Merlin Continuation*, 197; Roussineau, ed., *Merlin*, I, 107–8.

[157] Claudas, has, for example, given up love and shows no interest in largesse; his loyalty clearly leaves something to be desired. Yet he is elaborately praised by Pharian as the finest knight in the world. Rosenberg, tr. *Lancelot Part I*, 34; Elspeth Kennedy, ed., *Lancelot do Lac*, 78. Caradoc is described as 'the cruelest and most disloyal of all men who had ever borne arms'. Yet he is also 'of great prowess and strength beyond measure': Rosenberg, tr., *Lancelot Part III*, 282. Micha, *Lancelot*, I, 182–3. *Raoul de Cambrai* will be discussed in Chapter 11.

[158] Honoré Bonet provides an instructive list of foolish reasons why knights fight: over which country has the best wine or the most beautiful women, which country has the best soldiers, which man has the better horse, the more loving wife, the greater success in love, more skill in dancing or fighting: see Coupland, ed., tr., *Tree of Battles*, 207.

8

KNIGHTHOOD IN ACTION

✦✦✦

SINCE the greatest opportunity for exercising prowess was war, a delight in war becomes an important corollary to the worship of prowess at the centre of chivalric ideology. Such an emphasis raises fascinating if difficult questions. Did knights love war so fully they could engage in it without fear? Does chivalric literature accurately portray their conduct of war? Did their chivalric ideas and ideals modify warfare, making it a somewhat kinder, gentler enterprise? Does chivalric literature accommodate any countercurrent voices for peace? If chivalric literature praises loyalty, to what were knights loyal?

A Delight in War and Tournament

If Geoffroi de Charny, the renowned warrior and theoretician of chivalry in mid-fourteenth-century France, praised war as the ultimate chivalric enterprise, he echoed an even more enthusiastic and unrestrained voice sounded nearly two centuries earlier in the poetry of Bertran de Born. Bertran's glowing account of the coming of spring quickly modulates into praise for the joys of displaying prowess in war:

The gay time of spring pleases me well, when leaves and flowers come; it pleases me when I hear the merriment of the birds making their song ring through the wood; it pleases me when I see tents and pavilions pitched on the meadows; and I feel great happiness, when I see ranged on the fields knights and horses in armour.

And it pleases me too when a lord is first to the attack on his horse, armed, without fear; for thus he inspires his men with valiant courage. When the battle is joined, each man must be ready to follow him with pleasure, for no one is respected until he has taken and given many blows.

I tell you, eating or drinking or sleeping hasn't such savour for me as the moment I hear both sides shouting 'Get 'em!' and I hear riderless horses crashing through the shadows, and I hear men shouting 'Help! Help!' and I see the small and the great falling in the grassy ditches, and I see the dead with splintered lances, decked with pennons, through their sides.[1]

---

[1] Paden *et al.*, eds, *Poems of the Troubadour*, 338–43.

In abbreviated form, this sentiment appears again in the thirteenth-century *Story of Merlin*:

Mild weather had come back with the pleasant season when the orchards and woodlands are in leaf, when the birds sing sweetly and softly and the blossoming, leafy forests ring with their singing, when the meadows are thick with grass and the gentle waters go back into their beds—and when it is better to make war than any other time of the year.[2]

'Peace', as Maurice Keen notes concisely, 'was not regarded in the middle ages as the natural condition of states.'[3] Writing to the French king Charles VI in 1387, Honoré Bonet observed that 'it is no great marvel if in this world there arise wars and battles, since they existed first in heaven'.[4] Explicit assertions that the coming of peace saddened the knights, that they preferred war, appear throughout chivalric literature. When peace is made between Arthur and Galehaut in the *Lancelot do Lac* and the *Lancelot*, '[m]any, who preferred war, were saddened by this'.[5] Of course, some of the motives of actual knights may have been purely economic, stemming from their need for booty; but usually it is the delight in prowess that is openly praised.[6] In the First Continuation of the *Perceval*, a knight announces, 'my name is Disnadaret: I'm much more fond of war than peace, and never tire of doing battle.'[7] Boson in *Girart de Roussillon* is described as a man whose 'taste for war' is 'always new'.[8] The author of the Middle English romance *William of Palerne* relates of the young hero William, newly knighted, that there 'was no glader gom þat ever God made' when he learned of an impending war between the Roman Emperor and the Duke of Saxony.[9] When Claudas announces that war with Arthur is coming, 'The good and bold knights were happy and joyful at this, for they felt

[2] Rosenberg, tr., *Lancelot Part I*, 309; Sommer, ed., *Vulgate Version*, II, 256

[3] Keen, *Laws of War*, 23.

[4] Coupland, ed., tr., *Tree of Battles*, 81. Bonet refers, of course, to Satan's rebellion and soon also discusses the wars chronicled in the Old Testament. He is, in fact, deeply troubled by the issue of war and divine will. He argues (pp. 118–19) that peace is all but impossible, that war is built into the stars, men, and animals, though he admits God might be able to bring about peace and that good men can be lords over the power of heavenly bodies. Yet he soon declares that God, as lord and governor of battles, has instituted war, that it is in accord with all law, human and divine, and that soldiers are the flails of God's righteous (if hidden) justice (pp. 125–6, 157).

[5] Carroll, tr., *Lancelot Part II*, 138; Kennedy, ed., *Lancelot do Lac*, 328; Sommer, *Vulgate Version*, III, 250.

[6] In *Girart de Roussillon* (Meyer, ed., tr.) the problem with ending the war is seen in the plight of poor knights. How will they live without war? The answer is easily found in a new war, not of Christian versus Christian, but against the pagans. See laisse 633. Again, in laisse 672, the solution for knights who want to prove their worth is clear: let them fight pagans.

[7] Bryant, tr., *Perceval*, 114. Cf. Paden *et al.*, eds., *Poems of the Troubadour*, 116–17, 244–5, 262–3, 298–9, 364–5 ('A peace such as this does not enhance prowess, nor any other peace'), 372–3, 398–9, 460–1; Elspeth Kennedy, ed., *Lancelot do Lac*, I, 296.

[8] Meyer, *Girart de Roussillon*, laisse 474.   [9] Bunt, ed., *William of Palerne*, l. 1092.

they had been at peace too long. But it grieved the mean-spirited and the cowardly, who preferred peace to war.'[10]

The sentiment is often repeated. Knights in the twelfth-century *Chanson Gaydon* 'have no desire to make peace, they have always heard the war-cry, and they love war more than Nones or Compline. They would rather one town burned than two cities surrendered without a struggle.'[11] Classic warrior speeches urging immediate and vigorous war against the Romans are given to the notables of Arthur's court by Geoffrey of Monmouth (in his *History of the Kings of Britain*), and by Lawman (in the *Brut*).[12] The theme of warriors lauding war was venerable on this side of the Channel, as on the other.[13]

If knights liked piling up honour and the material rewards of battle, at least some of them also sensed an aesthetic element in war. The author of *The Story of Merlin*, shortly after he had declared spring as being the best time for war, pictured Arthur and his knights after they had rampaged in near darkness through the encampment of their enemies, in the campaign to relieve the siege of Trebes: 'Then it was broad daylight and the sun began to rise. The sun shone on the armour, which flashed in the light, and it was so beautiful and pleasing to look at that it was a delight and a melody to watch.'[14] In this text, as in many others, the author wants his readers to see colourful banners, rich pavilions and costly armour. The biographer of Robert Bruce similarly pauses to admire the massed English chivalry at the outset of the battle of Loudon Hill in 1307; the morning sunlight gleamed on shields and polished helmets:

their spears, pennons and shields illuminated the entire field with light, their best and embroidered bright banners and various horse trappings and varied coat armour and hauberks that were white as flour made them glisten as if they were angels from heaven's realm.[15]

Yet the text may bring such trappings into view just as sword strokes and lance thrusts destroy them.[16] Peter Haidu has made the interesting suggestion that we are observing a celebration of conspicuous consumption in the wanton

[10] Carroll, tr., *Lancelot Part VI*, 288; Micha, ed., *Lancelot*, VI, 42. Later in this same work Mordred, in a conversation with Kay, denounces the young Perceval: 'He looks like a simple knight . . . who prefers peace to war.' Kay agrees, noting that Perceval's shield bears no signs of fighting: Carroll, ibid., 325; Micha, ibid., 192.

[11] Ll. 4802 ff, quoted in Daniel, *Heroes and Saracens*, 26.

[12] Thorpe, tr., *Geoffrey of Monmouth*, 231–5; Allen, tr., *Lawman, Brut*, ll. 12426–50.

[13] For a survey of views in Middle English literature, see Gist, *Love and War*, 113–46, 194.

[14] Pickens, tr., *Story of Merlin*, 311; Sommer, ed., *Vulgate Version*, II, 261.

[15] McDiarmid and Stevenson, eds., *Barbour's Bruce*, II, ll. 220–34.

[16] *The Song of Roland* and the poetry of Bertran de Born provide splendid examples. In 'Lo coms m'a mandat e mogut', for example, Bertran writes, 'And nothing will keep splinters from flying to the sky, or taffeta and brocade and samite from ripping, and ropes and tents and stakes and shelters and high-pitched pavilions': in Paden *et al.*, eds., *Poems of the Troubadour*, 108–9.

destruction of so much finery; in a society in which few could even imagine such extravagance, the knights can not only wear and use fine and costly clothing and equipment, they can destroy it in the great game of war.[17]

If the great game was not always and everywhere available for knights to hone and demonstrate their prowess, tournament was available, even in the absence of war, as scholars regularly point out; it became the great sport and, in time, the great social event of chivalry.[18]

Early tournaments made good substitutes for war, and in both literature and life the tournament which quickly warmed up to the temperature of battle appears prominently.[19] Tournaments were at first distinguished from war only in the prearranged nature of the combat, an absence of deliberate destruction visited on non-combatants, and the provision of some safe zones from the fighting in which knights could rest and recover. Otherwise, the knights—and accompanying bodies of footmen—ranged over the countryside, and sometimes through narrow urban streets, manoeuvring, ambushing, attacking at will. Even though tournaments gradually restricted their scope and functioned by ever clearer forms and rules, there can be little wonder that they were known as 'schools of prowess'.[20]

The place of tournament in knightly ideology will likewise be evident to any reader of chivalric literature. From the time of Chrétien de Troyes in the last quarter of the twelfth century, descriptions of magnificent tournaments fill page after page of chivalric romance; they have become settings around which plots turned, events in refined literature demanded by refined audiences. Those who heard or read these works evidently could not have enough of colourful display and valorous action. In a splendid instance of art and life playing leapfrog, the imagined becomes the actual; the actual outdoes even the imagined.[21] Each great occasion must be decorated with its magnificent tournament; each peerless knight errant wandering on some erratic orbit out of touch with the solar centre of the court can only be brought home by his admirers spreading news of a great and tempting tournament. 'No knight should avoid a tournament if he can get there in time', is the straightforward advice of an honourable vavasour in the *Lancelot*.[22]

---

[17] Haidu, *Subject of Violence*, 46–9.

[18] For general discussions, see Barber and Barker, *Tournaments* and Keen, *Chivalry*, 83–102.

[19] For dangers associated with historical tournaments, see Barker and Barker, *Tournaments*, 139–49. A tournament of 1273 became known as the 'Little war of Chalons': Prestwich, *Edward I*, 84–5. Classic literary examples in Sommer, ed., *Vulgate Version*, II, 302–7; Pickens, tr., *Story of Merlin*, 335–54. Literature sees dangers to the knightly caste and courtly society, rather than to the sub-knightly.

[20] See citations in Keen, *Chivalry*, 99.

[21] See the discussion in Benson, 'The Tournament'.

[22] Carroll, tr., *Lancelot Part VI*, 259; Micha, ed., *Lancelot*, V, 216.

For nearly half a millennium (and increasingly before an audience featuring women as well as men), tournaments become a stock feature of chivalric life both as lived and as portrayed in literature: horse hoofs pound, lances splinter, shields crack, swords bite into helmets—in a continuum of tourneying that blurs chivalric ideology and practice. Passionate belief in tournament as the ideal sport unquestionably figures as one line in the creed spoken by those who worshipped at the high altar of prowess.

Any real disparity between historical events and literary portrayals appears when literary texts ignore the gradual safeguards that knights actually used, especially blunted weapons for combats *à plaisir*, instead of the sharp lance heads of combats *à outrance*. Literary tournaments are potentially deadly affairs, with no hint of rebated weapons, perhaps to emphasize the sense of danger and the vigour of the combatants.

The Fact of Fear? Voices for Peace?

Did they ever play the game, whether in war or tournament, with sweaty palms and shaking hands? In any sane person the prospect of being wounded, maimed, or killed with edged weapons in fierce combat would surely produce to some degree the phenomenon of fear. That warriors in all ages have experienced and more or less mastered these fears we can take as given. Replacing fear with gritty endurance and courage or even converting it into steel-edged battle fury must be a prime goal of any successful warrior culture.[23] High praise for honour secured through prowess and larded with visions of loot is the ideological path usually taken. Yet the tensions are obvious. If knights seldom left any record of their intimate thoughts, chivalric literature allows us occasionally to hear amidst the trumpet-calls the small but insistent voice of fear.[24] As a battle waxes fierce, we learn that 'even the bravest were afraid (*li plus hardis ot paör*)'.[25] The *Chanson de Guillaume* shows a warrior so fearful that his loose bowels have soiled his saddle blanket.[26] More traditional historical sources make the same point. The *Song of Dermot and the Earl*, written at about the turn of the thirteenth century, tells a chilling tale of two armies encamped at night near Wexford in Ireland, expecting battle on the morrow. Suddenly a

---

[23] His biographer tells us the late fourteenth-century Castilian knight Don Pero Niño was instructed as a youth to emulate St James, whose body was chopped bit by bit, but who steadfastly refused to renounce his faith: see Evans, tr., *The Unconquered Knight*, 20–1. Geoffroi de Charny regularly praises steady endurance: see Kaeuper and Kennedy, *Book of Chivalry*. With an eye to German chivalric literature and to the distinction between the world and the court, Stephen Jaeger discusses fear in 'Sociology of Fear'.

[24] See the discussion in Verbruggen, *Art of Warfare*, 43 ff.

[25] Roche-Mahdi, ed., tr., *Silence*, l. 5464.

[26] Muir, tr., *The Song of William*, Ernest Langlois, ed., *La Chanson de Guillaume*, laisse 28.

'phantasm (*un enfantesme*)' comes upon the English camp and the watch is sure they are beset by an armed enemy. 'St David! Barons, Knights!' calls out Randolf FitzRalph; men come tumbling out of the huts and Randolf (thinking him one of the enemy) strikes the first man he sees, bringing the fellow to his knees. The phantom soon passes to the Irish camp, causing them, in turn, to think that they are entrapped by their enemies. Yet in the morning the two sides formed up and got to their martial work.[27] Such phantasms of fear must often have stalked camps and battlelines; Froissart tells a similar story of the Flemish camp in the early morning hours before the battle of Roosebeke in 1382.[28]

Parodies of knightly ways, of course, speak more openly of fear.[29] But in his *Livre Charny*, even Geoffroi de Charny, the very soul of courage, admits plainly that a knight thinks of fleeing as arrows and lances rain down upon him, as he sees his friends lying dead on the ground around him: 'Is this not a great martyrdom?' he asks.[30] Yet he knows martyrdom is the cost of honour and he knows the rewards if fear is mastered. In his *Livre de chevalerie* he pragmatically urges knights not to think what the enemy will do to them, but what they will do to the enemy.[31]

Against the profound commitment to war reiterated in chivalric literature could any reforming voices praise peace? The question touches one of the deep paradoxes of chivalric ideology, of course, for the ideal goals of spiritual and social peace, which the critics and reformers pressed and which some knights must have accepted, were, finally, incompatible with the widespread worship of prowess.[32] Obviously, if war is the highest expression of prowess, the best opportunity for prowess, knights need war. When in romance a knight brings peace to some castle, region, or kingdom, that martial achievement usually spells the end of prowess there and thus the end of interest; the romance

---

[27] Orpen, ed., tr., *Song of Dermot*, 72–7.

[28] Brereton, tr., *Froissart*, 243–5. Froissart reports that some thought the disturbance was the revelling of devils delighted at the souls they would win for hell that day.

[29] See Whiting, 'Vows of the Heron', 263–4.

[30] Taylor, 'Critical Edition', 18–19, quotation at ll. 457–8: 'N'est ce grant martire / Qui a tel ouvrage s'atire?'

[31] Kaeuper and Kennedy, *Book of Chivalry*, 194–5. William of Palerne, in a fourteenth-century English romance, calls out to his men not to flee, even if they are afraid of the enemy: see Bunt. ed., *William of Palerne*, l. 3343. He wants them to think of their lovers instead: l. 3370.

[32] Burns, in Lacy, ed., *Lancelot-Grail*, I, xvi, says the prose romances 'attempted to combine the irreconcilable interests of earthly chivalry and military conquest with the spiritual quest for peace'. One example of the paradox: near the end of *The Death of King Arthur* Arthur laments unthinkable losses in battle with Mordred: 'Ah! day, why did you ever dawn, if you were to reduce the kingdom of Great Britain to such great poverty when its heirs, who are lying here dead and destroyed in such suffering, were so renowned for prowess?' If these losses are unusually great, the prowess praised at the end of his statement, of course, requires battles. Cable, tr., *Death of King Arthur*, 221; Frappier, ed., *La Mort*, 245–6.

moves on to the next adventure, the next setting for prowess, the next battle zone. 'That day they rode in peace,' says the author of the *Merlin Continuation*, 'finding nothing that one should record in a story'.[33] Fighting for peace is acceptable to these professional warriors only so long as there is no real danger of a surfeit of peace; they could scarcely cheer any smothering of chances for displays of prowess that so well repay their hard efforts in the bright coinage of honour (and in other coinages as well).

Yet reforming voices raised in the interests of peace can also be heard in chivalric literature, at least as a brake on enthusiasm. They never draw on fear, nor on the reluctance we know prudent commanders felt about risking all in open battle. The ideals usually come, instead, from the world of *clergie*.

When Chrétien de Troyes presents a world weighed down by the hero's failure to ask the Fisher King questions which would have cured him and restored his pacific rule, he reveals a cursed land that seems to be afflicted by war:

> Do you know what we must withstand,
> if the king cannot hold his land
> and for his wounds obtains no cure:
> The married women will endure
> their husband's deaths, lands will be wrecked,
> and orphaned maids will live abject,
> with many deaths among the knights,
> calamities and other plights.[34]

In the anonymous *Perlesvaus* which picks up Chrétien's unfinished story, the link is explicit: because Perceval failed in his moment of trial, 'all lands are now rent by war; no knight meets another in a forest but he attacks him and kills him if he can'.[35] As if to ensure that his point has registered, the author repeats the link of grail curse, war, and universal violence shortly thereafter: the curse means that 'all lands were engulfed by war; whenever a knight met another in a forest or glade they would do battle without any real cause'.[36]

A hermit in the continuation of the *Perceval* by Gerbert says that 'God did not make knights to kill and to make war on people, but to uphold justice and defend Holy Church'. How knights are to achieve these high professional goals in an imperfect and violent world without killing and making war is, of course, not specified. Yet peace is praised. Perceval's last secular act in this romance, before retiring from the world as a hermit, himself, is to give an

[33] Asher, tr., *Merlin Continuation*, 249; Roussineau, ed., *Merlin*, I, 292.
[34] Cline, tr., *Perceval*, ll. 4675–87.
[35] Bryant, tr., *Perlesvaus*, 27; Nitze and Jenkins, eds., *Perlesvaus*, 38.
[36] Bryant, *Perlesvaus*, 35; Nitze and Jenkins, *Perlesvaus*, 50.

extended peace to the land: 'Perceval remained in his own land and for seven years he held it in peace, free of war, untroubled by any man.'[37]

Sometimes the wickedness and sheer lack of wisdom in fighting Christian against Christian is stressed. Girart's war with King Charles in *Girart de Roussillon*, is stopped by divine intervention: God sends a great storm and the banners of both sides are symbolically destroyed by fire.[38] Several characters in this *chanson* get the message and speak out for the peace God obviously wants; Galeran de Senlis advises the king that one who fights a long and unjust war must pay for it. The former enemies are soon, however, hard at work fighting side by side against pagan foes, Slavs, Saxons, and Frisians.[39] In *The Story of Merlin*, Queen Guinevere argues the same line, after a tournament at her wedding has got out of hand: the knights, she says, should save their prowess for the Saxons and not waste it in destroying one another.[40] This same advice was given to the kings of England and France in the closing years of the fourteenth century by Philippe de Mézières: they must think whether they want to appear before the throne of divine judgement with blood dripping from their fingers 'through following the advice of your knights, nurtured in bloodshed'.[41]

Could the fears have been even more comprehensive? R. Howard Bloch's argument for a general, brooding fear about the social cost of warfare in early chivalric literature can be extended throughout the literature of the entire chivalric era.[42] This persistent countercurrent, however thin and infrequent, suggests either that at some subliminal level the fear of violence gave knights themselves some second thoughts, or that some authors were speaking their own minds to the necessary but dangerous warriors. Whoever wrote the *Vows of the Heron* (likely to have been someone interested in the peace and prosperity needed by the commercial society of the Low Countries) produced a 'grimly satirical' text early in the Hundred Years War. This biting parody of chivalric vows of wartime prowess links the knights with 'unsuccessful, mean or revolting acts' by an author 'who realized that only peace could bring prosperity'.[43]

Less savage but equally interesting critiques appear in better-known texts. If Cador speaks out powerfully against the softening effects of peace in Geoffrey of Monmouth's *History of the Kings of Britain*, his successors Wace and

---

[37] Bryant, tr., *Perceval*, 266, 301.   [38] Meyer, ed., tr., *Girart de Roussillon*, laisse 166.

[39] See ibid., laisses 184, 186, 190. In fact, a leitmotif of this poem is the cost of starting and continuing wrongful war.

[40] Pickens, tr., *Story of Merlin*, 352; Sommer, ed., *Vulgate Version*, II, 333.

[41] Coupland, ed., tr., *Letter to King Richard II*, 90. He at one point calls the warriors sharp-toothed locusts, at another leeches who so greedily suck the lifeblood of the poor that they burst: pp. 132–3.

[42] Bloch, *Medieval French Literature and Law*.

[43] Analysed, with full textual citations, in Whiting, 'Vows of the Heron'.

Lawman give a short but powerful answering speech in praise of peace to no less a figure than Gawain.[44] The *Mort Artu*, written a century later, regularly cautions against the danger of 'a war which will never come to an end', the war which in fact destroys the Round Table by the end of this romance.[45] Nearly two centuries later, Malory carried the theme forward in the monumental closing section of his *Morte Darthur*. He pictures Arthur reduced to tears as he mutters, 'Alas, alas, that ever yet thys warre began!'[46] The knights who support Lancelot in this struggle know the cost: 'in thys realme woll be no quyett, but ever debate and stryff, now the felyshyp of the Rounde Table ys brokyn.' And Lancelot himself, undergoing the transformation that marks his character both in the *Mort Artu* and here, declares that 'better ys pees than allwayes warre'.[47]

Warning statements may be more indirect, and partial, yet even more dramatic. In an unforgettable scene in the *Perlesvaus*, Perceval drowns his mother's enemy, the Lord of the Fens, by suspending him upside-down in a vat of his own knights' blood, to allow the man finally to get enough of the blood of knights for which he has seemingly longed. The result is a land with untroubled joy. Yet Perceval has, just before this, responded to his mother's pleas for a more peaceful solution with a firm dictum: ' "My Lady," he said, "it is thus: you must make war on the warlike and peace with the peaceful." '[48]

Conduct of War

Could one not argue, however, that in the inevitable warfare of early European history chivalry functioned as a restraining force, that war on its sliding medieval scale of possibilities—from the dispute of two lords over a mill to the dispute of two kings over a province—was less horrific because its key practitioners were knights? As John Gillingham and Matthew Strickland have shown, chivalric ideals may indeed have made fighting less barbaric for the knights themselves. Gillingham has argued strenuously that a reduction in torture and killing of prisoners came with the advent of chivalry. Strickland suggests even more broadly a lessening of the horrors of war for the knights;

---

[44] Thorpe, tr., *Geoffrey of Monmouth*, 231–2; Arnold, ed., *Brut de Wace*, 562–4; Allen, tr., *Lawman, Brut*, 318.

[45] Cable, tr., *Death of King Arthur*, 114, 117, 123; Frappier, ed., *La Mort*, 114, 118, 125.

[46] Vinaver, ed., *Malory.Works*, 691. The line also appears more than once in the *Stanzaic Morte Arthur*, on which Malory drew. See Benson, ed., *King Arthur's Death*, e.g., ll. 2204–5, 2442–3. Lancelot often expresses a desire for peace late in this romance, e.g. ll. 2498–9, 2596–603. Even the lords of England are said to complain that 'Arthur loved nought but warring': l. 2975. In her last conversation with Lancelot, Guinevere urges that he 'keep thy reme from war and wrake' and decries a world with 'nought, / But war and strife and batail sore': ll. 3666, 3720–1.

[47] Benson, *Morte Arthur*, 699, 701.

[48] Bryant, tr., *Perlesvaus*, 151–2, 150; Nitze and Jenkins, eds, *Perlesvaus*. 234–5, 232.

despite their martial culture, medieval warriors tried to limit the occurrence and mortality of serious combat, granted truces and respites, treated prisoners well, and ransomed rather than massacred them.[49]

Chivalric literature, especially from the thirteenth century, supports the idea of a lively concern about the proper way knights should treat each other when they fight. Since single combats or small group encounters are pictured in romance, the writer may have tournament in mind as much as the chaos of battle.[50] The focus is on taking unfair advantage of another; the use of horses in combat is a topic of special importance. Can one fight an unarmed or inadequately armed opponent? Is an opponent's horse a legitimate target? Should a mounted man attack one already unhorsed? Should a mounted man ride his great warhorse over an enemy knocked flat on the ground?[51]

Chrétien de Troyes, near the end of the twelfth century, tells his readers that Yvain and the Storm Knight 'fought most honourably' because neither strikes his opponent's horse.[52] Early in the next century, the biography of William Marshal tells the vivid story of William, fully armed and acting as rear-guard for Henry II, confronting Richard the Lion-Heart, unarmed and in active pursuit of his father. When Richard pointed out the disparity to William, the Marshal simply disabled Richard's horse with his lance.[53] The courtesy here, certainly the prudence, lay in not striking at Richard himself. In *The Marvels of Rigomer* (written about the same time), important characters—and sometimes the author himself—speak out against the idea of several fighting against one, claiming that knights in their day simply fight to win, but that in the good old days such practice was considered felony.[54] Gawain, the hero of this text, is said to want to defeat an opponent using nothing but 'strict chivalry (*droit chevalerie*)'.[55] *Le Bel Inconnu* takes the same line, declaring that in the good old days knights fought one-to-one, but now twenty-five will attack a solitary opponent.[56]

Over the next several decades the vast cycle of romances based on Lancelot and the Grail provides repeated discussions of ideal martial behaviour. When, in the *Merlin Continuation*, Gawain fights a knight at a ford, and knocks him

---

[49] John Gillingham, 'Introduction of Chivalry'; Strickland, *War and Chivalry*.

[50] A point of view in agreement with Ayton, *Knights and Warhorses*, 20.

[51] The examples that follow are largely drawn from Old French literature. For many examples drawn from Middle English texts, see Gist, *Love and War*, 155–90.

[52] Kibler, ed., tr., *Yvain*, ll. 855–8.   [53] Meyer, ed., *Histoire*, ll. 8803–49.

[54] Vesce, tr., *Marvels of Rigomer*, 45, 84–5, 184; Foerster, ed., *Mervelles de Rigomer*, ll. 1995–2007, 3619–798, 8511–38.

[55] Foerster, *Mervelles de Rigomer*, ll. 11501–3.

[56] Fresco, ed., and Donagher, tr., *Renaut de Bâgé*, ll. 1011–24, 1066–82, 5818–21. The editor and translator suggest a date 'from 1191 into the first quarter of the thirteenth century' (p. xii). The elusive nature of any 'golden age' of chivalry is once again evident in these passages.

from his saddle, he is taught proper manners: 'Either come down on foot,' shouts the dismounted man, gripping his lance, 'or you will cause your horse to be killed; then you will be completely humiliated.' Though Gawain with one blow splits the man's head like a melon, he has accepted the dictum.[57] Having learned, he teaches. Not long after, when Morholt, who had unhorsed him, charges him on horseback, he cries out, 'Morholt, if you don't dismount, you'll make me kill your horse, for which the blame will be mine and the shame yours.' Morholt accepts the admonition at once, exclaiming, 'You have just taught me a courtesy so great that I will observe it all my life, provided I am not in too bad a situation.'[58] The reform quality of the passage is as clear as the prudent qualifier, which clings to it like a burr.

This same romance pictures Arthur, having unhorsed Pellinor, voluntarily dismounting to fight on foot, 'something no one had yet done in the kingdom of Logres, although later many a valiant man would do it'.[59] Such basic lessons are preached repeatedly: not only do good men disdain mounted advantage, they refuse to fight several against one, and (as Lancelot instructs Mordred) they will not fight, armed, against an unarmed man.[60]

Yet all these romances show somewhat more ambiguity on the question of riding over prostrate opponents. The valiant Bors rides his horse over a flattened opponent, for example, until the trampled man yields. Even Lancelot can appear graciously dismounting to fight an unhorsed enemy in one passage and then shortly thereafter ride over another's body 'until he had completely broken it' so that 'the knight fainted in his great agony'.[61] Debate and ambiguity continue through the texts of the post-vulgate cycle of romances.[62] A similar tension can be found in Malory's *Morte Darthur*.[63]

On one aspect of knightly fighting chivalric literature is quite unambiguous: the standard display of all-important prowess takes the form of combat on horseback, at least as long as the knights could keep their saddles. Malory has Sir Lamerok say to his brothers, unhorsed on the sixth day of the great tournament at Surluse:

Bretherne, ye ought to be ashamed to fall so of your horsis! What is a knyght but whan

---

[57] Asher, tr., *Merlin Continuation*, 231; Paris and Ulrich, eds, *Merlin*, II, 84–5.

[58] Asher, *Merlin Continuation*, 272; Roussineau, ed., *Merlin*, II, 375.

[59] Asher, *Merlin Continuation*, 179–80; Paris and Ulrich, *Merlin*, II, 191. These 'later' displays of courtesy have, of course, actually already appeared in romances that preceeded this one in date of composition.

[60] E.g. Krueger, tr., *Lancelot Part IV*, 44, 61, 93; Micha, ed., *Lancelot*, II, 152, 221, 347; IV, 69; V, 207–8; Kibler, tr., *Lancelot Part V*, 130; Carroll, tr., *Lancelot Part VI*, 257.

[61] Krueger, *Lancelot Part IV*, 44, 34–5; Micha, *Lancelot*, II, 152–3, 116–17.

[62] See, e.g., Asher, *Merlin Continuation*, 13, 17, 27–8; *Quest*, 190, 275; Sommer, ed., *Zeitschrift*, 42, 53, 76; Bogdanow, ed., *Version Post-Vulgate*, 361; Piel, ed., *Demanda*, 396.

[63] Examples can be found in Stroud, 'Malory and the Chivalric Ethos', 336.

he is on horseback? For I sette nat by a knyght whan he is on foote, for all batayles on foote ar but pyllours in batayles, for there sholde no knyght fyghte on foote but yf hit were for treson or ellys he were dryvyn by forse to fyght on foote. Therefore, bretherne, sytte fast in your sadyls, or ellys fyght never more afore me![64]

This link between a focus on mounted prowess in all ideological statements and the changing role of heavy cavalry in actual combat provides us with a fact of considerable importance. Many scholars have argued that chivalry began to take on recognizable form at roughly the time a basic set of changes appeared in the favoured mode of fighting. Mounted shock combat had arrived.[65] With feet planted in sturdy platform stirrups and lance firmly tucked under the arm, an individual knight or a thundering line of knights could be expected to deliver the decisive blow on the tournament field or the battlefield. In fact, such a charge delivered at lance point all the combined force of man and mount. Two lines of such units clashing produced a roar of battle so deafening that, as one medieval writer after another swears, 'you could not hear God's thunder'.[66]

We now know that the dominance of heavy cavalry on medieval battlefields was much less total than was once thought.[67] Moreover, war typically took the form of the less-than-heroic raid, or the grind of siege operations, and even set-piece battles might depend on dismounted knights rather than the sweeping cavalry charge, pennons snapping in the wind. The knights themselves, most famously the English in the course of the Hundred Years War, could fight with much success on foot. Some of the most famous engagements of even the twelfth century had been won by dismounted knights.[68] Moreover, specialist footmen with crossbows and eventually with longbows, engineers with increasingly powerful forms of counterweight artillery, throwing 'stinking Greek fire'[69] or sizeable projectiles, sappers with humble picks and shovels— all actually formed essential elements of military victory.[70]

---

[64] Vinaver, ed., *Malory. Works*, 408. This same knight is surprised when Palomides wants to fight him on foot: 'hit wolde beseme a knyght to juste and to fyght on horsebacke' (p. 367).

[65] A discussion of the classic thesis of Heinrich Brunner, with an emphasis on the significance of the stirrup, appears in White, *Medieval Technology*, 1–38.

[66] See comments in D. J. A. Ross, 'Pleine sa hanste', and *idem*, 'L'originalité de "Turoldus" '.

[67] See especially DeVries, *Infantry Warfare*.

[68] Strickland, *War and Chivalry*, 23; Ayton, *Knights and Warhorses*, 19–20.

[69] Muir, tr., *Capture of Orange*, 113; Régnier, ed., *Prise d'Orange*, l. 1118.

[70] For the most recent and thorough overviews, see Prestwich, *Armies and Warfare*; Strickland, *War and Chivalry*; Bachrach, 'Caballus and Caballarius'. The actual breeding of suitable horses is explored in R. H. C. Davis, *Medieval Warhorse*; the relationship between military technology and military service in Ayton, *Knights and Warhorses*.

Yet the powerful strata of medieval society maintained and projected in the literature they patronized a belief in the superiority of the mounted warriors who *were* chivalry.[71] The *Lancelot do Lac*, playing with *cheval* and *chevalier*, states that when knighthood originated 'as the Scriptures reveal, no one was so bold as to mount a horse, if he was not a knight; and that is why they were called knights'.[72] In his equally mythical account of the origins of chivalry, Ramon Llull places the choosing of the horse as the knight's characteristic beast immediately after his account of the selection of the knight for his characteristic role.[73]

One literary passage after another links chivalric ideology with mounted shock combat. Boson, in *Girart de Roussillon*, we learn, is ready to fight anyone, once he was on his horse.[74] Having discovered the liaison between his queen and Lancelot, Arthur, in the *Stanzaic Morte Arthur*, pragmatically doubts if Lancelot can be taken 'Yif he were armed upon his steed'.[75] The author of the *Perlesvaus* tells us that Lancelot, besieged by robber knights in a hall, 'would have cared little for their threats if he had had his horse with him, but in combat he was not so sure of himself on foot as on horseback, nor has any good knight ever been'.[76] Being Lancelot, he, of course, accounts for himself well, breaking out of the hall, cutting off the leg of one of his mounted opponents at the thigh, and getting the essential horse, 'and at once he felt more assured'.[77] If we want a real-life parallel—though with a less successful conclusion—we need only consider Richard Maluvel, a twelfth-century Scottish knight, who did marvellous feats of arms in a battle at Alnwick: 'As long as he was on his horse he feared nothing; he had a splendid horse and he was splendidly accoutred; but once his horse was slain, he promptly surrendered'.[78]

Horses are, of course, significant characters in early chivalric literature; those ridden by heroes are often named and may be as individualized as any other character. *Aliscans*, for example, features Vivien's horse which even

[71] The same mounted self-image appears in manuscript illuminations and on seals. As Ayton points out, the illustrations in the Ellesmere manuscript shows the knight and squire mounted not on the palfreys they would have routinely ridden, but on their status horses, the great beasts they would ideally ride into battle: *Knights and Warhorses*, 31–2. Rezak surveys chivalric use of seals in 'Medieval Seals'.

[72] Corley, tr., *Lancelot of the Lake*, 53; Elspeth Kennedy, ed., *Lancelot do Lac*, I, 143. This text mentions in passing a significant bit of imagined chivalric history, the first appearance of a warhorse covered in protective iron. Corley, ibid., 384; Kennedy, ibid., 550.

[73] Byles, ed., *Book of the Ordre of Chyvalry*, 15. He later feels compelled, significantly, to remind his reader that chivalry lies not in horse and arms, but in the knight himself: p. 114.

[74] Meyer, ed., tr., *Girart de Roussillon*, ll. 6289–90.

[75] Benson, ed., *Morte Arthur*, l. 1751.

[76] Bryant, tr., *Perlesvaus*, 135; Nitze and Jenkins, eds, *Perlesvaus*, 206.

[77] Bryant, *Perlesvaus*, 139; Nitze and Jenkins, *Perlesvaus*, 213.

[78] Prestwich, *Armies and Warfare*, 328. Michel, ed., tr., *Chronicle*, ll. 1878–86.

understand's the hero's conversation.[79] In more than one story about William of Orange, the great hero fights with an interesting mixture of motives: the desire to defeat pagans threatening Christendom and the desire to possess his opponent's marvellous horse.[80] Two centuries later the register of the Black Prince provides the proud names of some of his destriers: Grisel de Cologne, Morel de Burghersh, Bayard de Brucell, Bayard Dieu.[81] Such horses possess equine prowess. In *Yder* we hear warhorses captured by the hero making a terrible racket as they neigh and try to injure one another.[82] In the alliterative romance *William of Palerne*, the warhorse that had served the hero's father recognizes the returning son, bows down on its forelegs before him, and carries him proudly into battle, conscious of the knight's valour.[83]

French knights seem to have prided themselves on a particular act of knightly horsemanship, quick turns for a second charge against a surprised foe. Turning 'in the French style' is mentioned admiringly in more than one *chanson de geste*.[84]

The author of the *Mort Artu* (a man much interested in tactical details) informs his readers that King Arthur, on his way to the climactic battle against the traitor Mordred, wisely went at a pace that would not tire the warhorses for the critical moment of battle.[85] Whoever wrote *The Story of Merlin* was likewise fascinated with horses and comments closely on the details of mounted formations.[86]

The staple of all combat in all chivalric literature, of course, is the encounter of two mounted knights, lances 'straight out' in the words of the *Chanson de Roland*.[87] Many thousands of these combats appear in works that were listened

---

[79] Ferrante, tr., *Guillaume d'Orange*, 201; Wienbeck *et al.*, eds, *Aliscans*, 35. Don Pero Niño's biographer asserts that 'horses [have] been found that in the thick of battle have shewn themselves as loyal to their masters as if they had been men'. They are so 'strong, fiery, swift and faithful, that a brave man, mounted on a good horse, may do more in an hour of fighting than ten or mayhap a hundred could have done afoot': Evans, tr., *The Unconquered Knight*, 11. He later describes such a horse, ridden by his hero against the Moors. Hit by many stones, the horse half-wheeled, causing Pero Niño to feel shame at turning from his foe. But the horse, 'which was gallant and loyal, returned to the charge, feeling the will of its rider, amd thrust itself into the midst of the Moors': p. 194.

[80] Wienbeck *et al.*, eds, *Aliscans*, 77. In the *Crowning of Louis*, William likewise covets his pagan opponent's great horse: see Hoggan, tr., *Crowning of Louis*, 15; Langlois, *Couronnement de Louis*, 22.

[81] Prestwich, *Armies and Warfare*, 30–1.   [82] Adams, ed., tr., *Romance of Yder*, 76–7.

[83] Bunt, ed., *William of Palerne*, ll. 3282–95.

[84] Kay, ed., tr., *Raoul de Cambrai*, laisses 199, 206. Muir, tr., *Song of William*, 195; Suard, ed., *Chanson de Guillaume*, 204.

[85] Cable, tr., *Death of King Arthur*, 205; Frappier, ed., *La Mort*, 226.

[86] E.g. Pickens, tr., *Story of Merlin*, 240; Sommer, ed., *Vulgate Version*, II, 135: 'Right away the squires ran to put their armour on. They got on their horses and lined up by rows and then squeezed right together, just as the knights showed them to do.' This text and others provide numerous battlefield scenes which turn on procuring horses for unhorsed comrades.

[87] Brault, ed., tr., *Chanson de Roland*, l. 1204.

to or read for centuries. Audiences seemingly never tired of the details: one lance pierces shield, hauberk, and body; or both lances splinter spectacularly, perhaps leaving the two knights unhorsed and temporarily dazed, soon to rise and go at each other with their sharp swords. Tens of thousands of lines of poetry and later of prose are devoted to the variations on this pattern. The rare comic scenes only make the same point more obliquely: the huge pre-knightly Rainouart in the William of Orange cycle mounted on a charger for the first time—backwards—or learning the economical use of the sword as opposed to his beloved but rather undiscriminating club (which crushes both the enemy and his valuable horse).[88] In literature, chivalry fights its battles with lance, shield, and sword astride a *cheval*. Virtually every problem that arises in the great bulk of chivalric literature is solved by the outcome of such encounters.

The yawning gap between ideal and practice seems significant. If knights often—and by the later Middle Ages increasingly—fought on foot, but appear without fail as mounted fighters in chivalric literature, is this not a good case for discounting the evidence of imaginative literature? In fact, though the literary portrayal is not a guide to battlefield practice in this regard, it is assuredly an important window into chivalric *mentalité*. The evidence of romance is, we should note, redoubled by that of historical writing (Froissart, the Chandos Herald) and of manuscript illumination (Sir Geoffrey Luttrell in the Luttrell Psalter): in all representations of themselves knights want to be seen mounted on great chargers, a noble man atop a noble beast, literally above commoners.[89] Purveying this image must have been considerably more important than getting the particulars of battle right.

Moreover, the image was less far off than might seem, if we think of the entire range of deeds in a life of prowess and not just moments of full-scale battle. Tournaments filled more days than such battles and usually meant a classic mounted encounter. Even during campaigns jousts *à outrance* were fought before or in place of battle, as individual knights or small groups challenged each other to these 'jousts of war', lovingly described by chroniclers and biographers. Hunting, too, meant horsemanship, another species of prowess, another active display of lordship. Even funerals make the final point, as one or more caparisoned warhorses preceded the warrior's body in procession.[90]

The literary accounts may also reveal a congruence in timing between romance writing and military technique. Michael Prestwich suggests that after some significant experience of fighting on foot in the twelfth century, English

---

[88] Muir, tr., *Song of William*, 196; Suard, ed., *Chanson de Guillaume*, 206; Wienbeck *et al.*, eds, *Aliscans*, 251, 261.

[89] Prestwich, *Armies and Warfare*, 13, provides the scene from the Luttrell Psalter.

[90] Ayton provides a good discussion in *Knights and Warhorses*, 20–39.

knights became reluctant to dismount on thirteenth-century battlefields. They had to relearn a willingness to fight on foot in warfare with the Scots in the early fourteenth century.[91] The flourishing of chivalric literature and the setting of its conventions would fit nicely into this chronology. The physical, social, and military superiority of the knight atop his huge warhorse could easily have become a fixed theme in the heyday of the writing of chivalric works.

Looting and Destruction

If chivalry made warfare better for knights, what of everyone else? Historians have long been tempted to believe that knights tried to limit damage to non-combatants; some have attributed the horrors of medieval warfare to common soldiers who could simply not be regulated by their social superiors in brighter armour.[92] What does the 'historical' and 'literary' evidence show?

In the second half of the twelfth century the poetry of Bertran de Born glories in the very opportunities for looting non-combatants that war brings the knightly. Hoping that strained relations between Richard the Lion-Heart and Alfonso de Castile will bring war in the late twelfth century, he writes, in words that have become well known:

Trumpets, drums, standards and pennons and ensigns and horses white and black we soon shall see, and the world will be good. We'll take the usurers' money, and never a mule-driver will travel the roads in safety, nor a burgher without fear, nor a merchant coming from France. He who gladly takes will be rich.[93]

His poetry joins other works that show the knight's hand holding the torch that fires peasant homes, bourgeois shops, even churches. Bertrand declared that 'War is no noble word when it's waged without fire and blood'.[94] The English king Henry V agreed; speaking three centuries later he declared that 'War without fire is like sausages without mustard.'[95] This sentiment was far from theoretical: accounts of one fourteenth-century English *chevauchée* after another show that English commanders seldom denied themselves their mustard while campaigning in the French countryside. We also know that the royal fleet which carried Edward III and his army to Brabant in 1338 indis-

---

[91] Prestwich, *Armies and Warfare*, 317–19.

[92] Idealist writers of the time could hope the same; Philippe de Mézières wrote in 1395 that 'countless ills and cruelties . . . occur in war, against and outside the laws of chivalry': see Coupland, *Letter to King Richard II*, 52–3, 126.

[93] Paden *et al.*, eds., *Poems of the Troubadour*, 398–9.

[94] Ibid., 358–9. He says in another poem; 'War wants you to shed blood and set fire and never avoid giving, or tire of it' (pp. 454–5).

[95] Quoted in Gillingham, 'Richard I', 85.

criminately plundered merchant shipping in the Channel.[96] Private wars in all ages regularly caused widespread arson.[97]

This association of warfare with destruction by fire appears as a commonplace in many *chansons*. Near the end of the twelfth-century *Coronation of Louis*, William of Orange hopes that his seemingly endless fighting for king and Christendom may be over: 'But that was not to be for as long as he lived, for the Frenchmen took to rebelling again, making war against each other and acting like madmen, burning down towns and laying waste the countryside. They would not restrain themselves at all on Louis's account.'[98] In the *Chanson d'Aspremont*, Girart, Duke of Burgundy, refers to such local warfare almost casually in a speech to his knights:

> If my neighbor starts a quarrel with me,
> With fire burns my land to cinders;
> And I, his, on all sides;
> If he steals my castles or keeps,
> Then so it goes until we come to terms,
> Or he puts me or I put him in prison;[99]

'Then so it goes.' Girart is simply recalling the facts of raid, arson, and counter-raid at home, as a contrast to the great battle to the death they are facing now, against a pagan host.

The language of *Raoul de Cambrai* speaks to the same subject with characteristically brutal clarity: 'Then they cross the boundary of Vermandois; they seize the herds and take the herdsmen prisoners; they burn the crops and set fire to the farms.'[100]

Girart de Roussillon, another *chanson*, presents the same picture, although with greater epic exaggeration. When Fouque, speaking for Girart, warns King Charles that his baronial style of war is to burn every town, hang every knight, and devastate every land taken, the royal response is to promise even worse by way of revenge. When the sage Fouque stays in an abbey while on a mission to the king, he is so pleased with their hospitality that he gives the monks a revealing promise: the bourg where the monastic house is located will not be destroyed or ruined in the coming war.[101] As warfare goes on for years in this *chanson*, the knights cut down vines and trees, destroy wells, and turn

---

[96] See Kaeuper, *War, Justice, and Public Order*, 98, and the sources cited there. Though only one example from among hundreds, this case is interesting because ships of all nationalities suffered—not simply those of the enemy.

[97] E.g. the raid discussed in ibid., 82–3.

[98] Hoggan, tr., *Crowning of Louis*, 56; Langlois, ed., *Couronnement de Louis*, 83.

[99] ll. 5012–17; my translation.   [100] Kay, ed., tr., *Raoul*, laisse 59.

[101] Meyer, ed., tr., *Girart de Roussillon*, 113, 121–2.

the land into a desert; they pillage and destroy even churches and monasteries. One monastery goes up in flames with a thousand royalist refugees inside. Those captured in the war, the poet tells us, are hanged or mutilated. Charles later claims that Girart has killed or wounded 100,000 of his men and that he has ravaged and devastated his realm: 'His great valour is only wickedness (*mauvaistez*).' Merchants who hear a false report of Girart's death respond with joy, since his war always heaped evils upon them. Fleeing from the victorious king at the nadir of his fortunes, Girart and his wife must endure similar maledictions from a widow and daughter in a household which lost knightly father and son in Girart's war. Even Girart's wife tells him that he has killed and despoiled more men than he can reckon, earning the rebuke of God. King Charles is not spared criticism himself, however; the Bishop of Saint-Sauveur rebukes the king for having burned 10,000 churches on his own, causing monks and priests to flee. In his sermon denouncing the war, late in the poem, the pope tells the warriors that God is angry; they have burned churches and their clergy; they have caused great suffering among simple folk; they have destroyed towns and caused great sorrows. They must make restitution for their own souls and those of their ancestors. At the end of his life, Girart, thinking about making final amends, proposes grants to support 500 poor people and 1,000 monks; but he hears that it is not enough, for he has driven 100,000 people from their homes and his father's earlier warfare has actually killed no fewer.[102]

Epic exaggeration, of course. Yet the knightly role in warfare appears much the same in works traditionally classified as romance. Despite its fashionably classical setting, the *Eneas* attributes knightly warfare to imagined Trojans and Latins. The Trojan knights 'dispersed the peasantry, who were not trained for battle,' sacked a nearby castle, and 'set out for home, gathering booty from the countryside. They plundered and seized everything and they burdened a thousand sumpter horses with wheat.'[103]

Two knights in *William of England* enthusiastically conduct war against the lady whose lands border those of their lord, not knowing that this lady is their mother. Confronting them before she learns of their identity, the mother curses the two knights, damning the day they were born. They have, she claims, killed her men or held them for ransom, harassed her to the point of death, ravaged her land so that nothing worth six pennies remains standing outside fortified spots. 'They waged the entire war. They are the most evil on earth.' Of course, once she learns the two are her sons, all is forgiven. William,

---

[102] Meyer, ed., tr., *Girart de Roussillon*, laisses 113, 121, 283, 320, 356 (especially ll. 5528–31), 413–15, 521, 525, 633 (the pope's sermon, especially from l. 9384), 606.
[103] Yunck, tr., *Eneas*, 125–31: Grave, ed., *Eneas*.

her husband, has already told them that their warfare has been at once treacherous (to their mother) and loyal (to their lord). The contradictions in knightly warfare could scarcely be presented more starkly.[104]

Such estimates of the warfare conducted by knights are common. In the *Didot Perceval* Arthur's men land in France 'and ran through the land and took men and women and booty and you may be sure that never before had a land been so dolorous.'[105] In the *Chevalier du Papegau* we encounter 'a great cry and noise made by people fleeing before a knight who was laying waste to all the district'.[106]

The language itself can be instructive. In more than one romance, war appears in the telling guise of a great and destructive storm. Early in Chrétien's *Yvain, or the Knight with the Lion*, a frightening storm descends whenever any knight pours water over a stone at a magic spring. When the Storm Knight, defender of the spring, chastises Calogrenant for causing the storm, he speaks the language of knightly war:

> Vassal, greatly have you
> shamed and injured me, without proper challenge.
> You ought first to have challenged me.
> if you had just cause,
> or at least sought amends,
> before you brought war against me. . . .
> He who is injured has the right to complain;
> and I complain and with justice,
> that you have driven me from my house
> with lightning and rain;
> you have wronged me
> and cursed be he who finds it good,
> for against my woods and my castle
> you have levelled such an attack
> that great towers and high walls
> would have been of no avail to me. . . .
> But know from now on
> you will have no truce or peace from me.[107]

After Yvain has killed the Storm Knight, Lunete counsels her widowed lady, Laudine, to seek advice on how to defend the spring, for failure will bring

---

[104] Staines, tr., *Romances of Chrétien de Troyes*, 486, 488; Holden, ed. *Guillaume d'Angleterre*, ll. 2934–6, 3041–58.

[105] Skells, tr., *Perceval in Prose*, 71–2.

[106] Vesce, tr., *Knight of the Parrot*, 14; Heuckenkamp, ed., *Chevalier du papegau*, 14.

[107] Kibler, tr., *Knight with the Lion*, ll. 491–516. The Old French crackles with legal terminology of defiance, plaint, etc.

utterly destructive war.[108] Laudine presents this view to her court through her seneschal, in justification of her decision to marry her husband's conqueror:

> My lords, war is upon us:
> not a day passes that the king isn't
> making preparations as fast as he can
> to come lay waste to our lands.
> Before these two weeks are over
> everything will be laid waste
> unless a good defender be found.[109]

Near the end of the romance, Yvain's own words again explicitly link the storm and war. He decides that to win back his lady's affection he will return

> and wage war at her spring;
> and there he'd cause so much
> thunder and wind and rain
> that she would be compelled
> to make her peace with him.[110]

William of England identifies war with storm in even more explicit fashion. During a terrifying storm at sea, the author says the four winds are at war, acting 'as do lords of the land who burn and ravage castles for their pleasure'. This comparison is possible, says the poet, because the lords 'devastate the world, just as the winds devastate the waves'.[111]

This impressionistic linkage of knightly violence with at least quasi-natural forces also appears in the pedestrian *Chevalier du Papegau*. Arthur, here a young hero, confronts a hideous fish-knight who grows his own armour as a monstrous hide. This creature's approach causes a commotion 'as great as any storm', and in the course of the fight he whirls like a tornado through fields and meadows. After defeating him, Arthur and his friends trace the monster's trail to the sea where a fierce storm batters the search party so severely they fear for their lives.[112]

In the continuation of Chrétien's *Perceval* by Gerbert de Montreuil, and in the *Perlesvaus*, the dread Knight of the Dragon besieges his enemies, 'destroying castles and cities and knights and whatever he can attack', not only with a mortal army, but with a shield which features a fire-spewing dragon's head as a boss; he consumes his opponents with this sulphurous medieval forerunner

---

[108] Kibler, tr., *Knight with the Lion*, ll. 1627–9, 1640–1.
[109] Ibid., ll. 2085–91.   [110] Ibid., ll. 6524–9: the verb is *guerroier*.
[111] Staines, tr., *Romances of Chrétien de Troyes*, 478–9; Holden, ed., *Guillaume d'Angleterre*, ll. 2302–12.
[112] Vesce, tr., *Knight of the Parrot*, 14–25; Heuckenkamp, ed., *Chevalier du papegau*, 14–24.

of a flamethrower, supplied, we find it no surprise to learn, from the arsenal of Hell.[113]

This popular Perceval legend connects war to a haunting and socially comprehensive image—the *terre gaste*, the land laid waste.[114] In his *Perceval*, Chrétien pictures entire regions desolated by knightly warfare. The beautiful Blancheflor tells Perceval, who seeks lodging in her castle, that she has been besieged 'one winter and one whole summer'. Her garrison of 310 knights has been cut down by violent death and capture to 50. This terror is the work of 'one knight: Clamadeu of the Isles' cruel seneschal Anguingueron'. His siege has produced a veritable wasteland in this region:

> For if, without, the youth had found
> the fields were barren, empty ground,
> within there was impoverishment;
> he found, no matter where he went,
> the streets were empty in the town.
> He saw the houses tumbled down
> without a man or woman there.
>
> . . .
>
> The town was wholly desolate.[115]

The initial setting of the poem lies in the *forest soutaine*, the 'lone and wild forest', to which Perceval's mother has fled from the chaos and warfare that swept the land following the death of Uther Pendragon, the future King Arthur's father. With her husband badly wounded and Perceval's two elder brothers both slain on the very day they were made knights, Perceval's mother hopes to keep him from the world of knightly combat. The first time he utters the word knight she falls in a faint.[116]

Chivalric biography is even less reticent about the realities of knightly warfare. The Chandos Herald, writing the life of the Black Prince late in the fourteenth century, tells his readers how his master's host behaved between the Seine and the Somme during their invasion: 'the English to disport themselves

---

[113] Bryant, tr., *Perceval*, 245–55; idem, tr., *Perlesvaus*, 153, 162–4; Williams and Oswald, eds, *Gerbert de Montreuil*, ll. 8906–10153; Nitze and Jenkins, eds., *Perlesvaus*, 237, 250–4. Such texts remind us that in many minds strong, intuitive bonds linked war—on any scale—and fire, its inevitable accompaniment, with hellfire and demons.

[114] Bloch, *Medieval French Literature*.

[115] Cline, tr., *Perceval*, 51–2, ll. 1749–55, 1773; Roach, ed., *Roman de Perceval*. The continuator Gerbert of Montreuil thought that the devastation of a siege would be so complete that Gorneman, Blancheflor's kinsman, could scarcely recognize her land when he saw it restored to prosperity: 'Gorneman was bewildered, for he had not been there since Clamadeus had laid waste the land and the country all around; but now it was as splendid a sight as you have heard from my description': Bryant, *Perceval*, 229.

[116] Bryant, *Perceval*, 1–7; Roach, *Roman de Perceval*, ll. 69–634.

put everything to fire and flame. There they made many a widowed lady and many a poor child orphan'.[117] It is helpful to remember that this passage appears in a laudatory life, setting forth the prowess and piety of Edward, the Black Prince, son of Edward III.

Nearly two centuries earlier, the biographer of William Marshal, it is true, pictured William, during the burning of Le Mans, helping a woman drag her possessions from her flaming home; William nearly suffocated on the smoke which entered his helmet. But the action was scarcely typical of the times or even of the hero's life. The biography tells us that the mature William advised Henry II to delude the French king into thinking he had disbanded his army, but then to carry devastation into French territory. Of warfare between Henry II and his sons, the biographer observed that many places in his day still showed the scars of that war. These scars, in other words, had yet to heal after forty years.[118]

Chronicles, less concerned with the mix of prescription and description than imaginative literature, point specifically and repeatedly to knights as the bane of their author's hopes for a more orderly life. The historian Matthew Paris tells a striking story of Hubert de Burgh leading a troop harrying the lands belonging to King John's enemies in England; looting as thoroughly as they could and destroying what they could not carry off, even churches seemed fair game. But then Christ himself appeared to Hubert in a dream, admonishing him to spare and worship the crucifix when next he saw it. The very next day a priest whose church was being looted ran up to Hubert carrying a large crucifix. Remembering the warning, Hubert fell to his knees, adored the cross, and restored the looted goods to the priest.[119] Such worthy restraint led to the telling of the story; the common practice, of course, looms in the background.

Orderic Vitalis tells an even more striking story in Book XII of his *Ecclesiastical History*. His account deserves quotation in full, for the unforgetable picture it paints is worth many words of more abstract analysis. On a raiding expedition which yielded an important prisoner and much booty, Richer de Laigle 'did something that deserves to be remembered for ever':

While country people from Grace and the villages around were following the raiders and were planning to buy back their stock or recover it somehow, the spirited knights (*animosi milites*) wheeled round and charged them, and when they turned tail and fled continued in pursuit. The peasants had no means of defending themselves against a

---

[117] 'Mais les Englois poier iaux esbatre / Misent tout en feu et a flame. La firent mainte veve dame / Et maint povrae enfant orfayn': Pope and Lodge, eds., *The Black Prince*, ll. 236–9.

[118] Meyer, ed., *Histoire*, ll. 2193–2222. Unvarnished accounts of devastation also appear prominently in the fifteenth-century biography of Don Pero Niño: see Evans, tr., *The Unconquered Knight*.

[119] Paris, *Chronica Majora*, III, 290–1, cited and discussed in Cazel, 'Religious Motivation', 109–10.

mailed squadron and were not near any stronghold where they could fly for refuge, but they saw a wooden crucifix by the side of the road and all flung themselves down together on the ground in front of it. At the sight Richer was moved by the fear of God, and for sweet love of his Saviour dutifully respected his cross. He commanded his men to spare all the terrified peasants and to turn back . . . for fear of being hindered in some way. So the honourable man, in awe of his Creator, spared about a hundred villagers, from whom he might have extorted a great price if he had been so irreverent as to capture them.[120]

Not seizing the bodies of the peasants whose homes he has already looted (out of respect for the potent symbol of the cross) earns him the adjective honourable or noble (*nobilis*); indirectly, Orderic speaks volumes about ordinary practice.[121] Not that he is reluctant to speak his mind directly. Often he describes casual brutality outright. In the course of feudal warfare carried on right through the holy season of Lent, Count Waleran, 'raging like a mad boar, entered the forest of Bretonne, took prisoner many of the peasants he found cutting wood in the thickets, and crippled them by cutting off their feet. In this way he desecrated the celebration of the holy festival rashly, but not with impunity.'[122] Orderic describes the followers of Robert, the future Duke of Normandy, as 'of noble birth and knightly prowess, men of diabolical pride and ferocity terrible to their neighbours, always far too ready to plunge into acts of lawlessness'.[123] Of lords such as Robert of Bellême and William of Mortain, he writes, 'It is impossible to describe the destruction wrought by vicious men of the region; they scarred the whole province with slaughter and rapine and, after carrying off booty and butchering men, they burnt down houses everywhere. Peasants fled to France with their wives and children.'[124] When this same Robert fought with a neighbour, Rotrou, over the boundaries of their lands, Orderic says:

they fought each other ferociously, looting and burning in each other's territories and adding crime to crime. They plundered poor and helpless people, constantly made

---

[120] Chibnall, ed., tr., *Ecclesiastical History*, VI, 250–1.

[121] The author of *Girart de Roussillon* tells us, with disapproval, that Girart and Boson slaughtered a hundred knights gathered around a wayside cross in search of sanctuary during battle. Meyer, ed., tr., *Girart de Roussillon*, laisse 413. The poet says God turned the war against Girart's side after this.

[122] Chibnall, *Ecclesiastical History*, VI, 348–9.   [123] Ibid., III, 102–3.

[124] Ibid., VI, 58–9. This description might be compared with the actions of the giant knight Malduit who ravages the land because Yvain has insulted his shield: 'He rode wherever he thought he might find people, knocking down tents and pavilions and shelters, destroying whatever he encountered, killing knights and ladies and maidens, sparing only the dogs': Kibler, tr., *Lancelot Part V*, 175–7; Micha, ed., *Lancelot*, IV, 250–61. Malduit appears to be a symbol of knightly war; the victims, however, are here made exclusively knights and ladies, rather than villagers and townspeople.

them suffer losses or live in fear of losses, and brought distress to their dependants, knights and peasants alike, who endured many disasters.[125]

Knightly ferocity and brutal acquisitiveness likewise appear when we cross the Channel. Outright private war was less likely in England, where it was formally forbidden by law, but some English knights took every opportunity that crown weakness presented and did what they could at other times. William Marshal's father, to take a well-known example, was during the civil war as thoroughgoing a robber baron as any lord denounced by Orderic. William's *Histoire* praises John Marshal as 'a worthy man, courtly, wise, loyal, full of prowess (*preudome corteis e sage . . . proz e loials*)'; it also shows him collaborating with a Flemish mercenary, dividing up regions of southern England for exploitation like any Mafioso; it further tells us that at this time England knew great sadness, great war, great strife, because there was no truce, no agreement, no justice while the warfare lasted.[126]

The Anglo-Saxon chronicle similarly evaluated conditions in another part of the country, East Anglia:

For every man built him castles and held them against the king; and they filled the land with these castles. They sorely burdened the unhappy people of the country with forced labour on these castles; and when the castles were built they filled them with devils and wicked men. By night and day they seized those whom they believed to have any wealth, whether they were men or women; and in order to get their gold and silver they put them into prison and tortured them with unspeakable tortures. . . . When the wretched people had no more to give, they plundered and burnt all the villages, so that you could easily go a day's journey without ever finding a village inhabited or field cultivated . . . and men said openly that Christ and his saints slept.[127]

At the end of the fourteenth century even Froissart was still inserting into his narratives admonitory tales of what happened to church violators. An English squire who seized a chalice from a priest's hands at the altar in a raid on the village of Ronay (and then gave the celebrant a backhanded blow to the face) soon whirled out of control on the road and, screaming madly, fell with broken neck and was reduced to ashes. His fearful companions swore never to rob or violate a church again. 'I do not know whether they kept their promise', comments Froissart.[128]

---

[125] Chibnall, ed., tr., *Ecclesiastical History*, VI, 396–7.

[126] Meyer, ed., *Histoire*, ll. 27, 31–8, 63 on John Marshal, 125–30 on the state of England. Crouch says John and his men 'issued regularly from the defiles of those grey hills [of north-east Wiltshire], demanding tribute and obedience from all those lowlanders who had no protection of their own': *William Marshal*, 12.

[127] Quoted in Davis, *King Stephen*, 83–4.   [128] Brereton, tr., *Froissart*, 162–3.

His contemporary, Honoré Bonet, knew. In his famous *Tree of Battles* he tells the French king that 'nowadays . . . the man who does not know how to set places on fire, to rob churches and usurp their rights and to imprison the priests, is not fit to carry on war'.[129] Far from protecting the helpless, the warriors loot them without mercy, 'for in these days all wars are directed against the poor labouring people and against their goods and chattels. I do not call that war, but it seems to me to be pillage and robbery.'[130] One is reminded of Merigold Marches, the *routier* leader executed in Paris in 1391. He had seized people for ransom, burned and looted in wartime France; his claim that he had acted as one should in a just war was brushed aside; his crime was not the activities themselves, however, but simply that he, a mere mercenary, had lacked proper status and authority.[131]

Chivalry brought no radical transformation in medieval warfare, as it touched the population as a whole; above all, it imposed no serious check on the looting, widespread destruction, and loss of non-combatant lives that seem to have been the constant companions of warfare. Recent historical scholarship suggests that we have no reason to think that chivalry should have transformed war in this broad sense, nor that knights were somehow unchivalrous cads for not attempting it. As a code, chivalry had next to nothing to do with ordinary people at all.[132]

Loyalty

Yet knighthood needed to emphasize its own internal cohesion, its own management of the highly competitive force of prowess. From its origins, chivalry had shown a collective dimension; it placed the particular knight within the entire group or class of knights, all—in idealistic plan—living by something like a common ethos. If chivalry was to be more than a purely individualistic, even radically anarchic force, a corresponding military virtue was needed to bind the individual to the collective ethos. That virtue was loyalty and it was attached as firmly as possible to prowess in chivalric ideology. Loyalty functioned as the rudder which steered the great vessel of prowess into acceptable channels.

---

[129] Coupland, ed., tr., *Tree of Battles*, 189.

[130] Ibid. A few years later Philippe de Mézières called contemporary warriors leeches who sucked the blood of the poor until they burst, though he piously hoped that the victims would be better off, having less distracting wealth: Coupland, *Letter to King Richard II*, 58–9, 132.

[131] Discussed in Keen, *Laws of War*, 97–100.

[132] See, e.g., Strickland, *War and Chivalry*, passim; Prestwich, *Armies and Warfare*, 1–12, 231–43; Hewitt, *Organisation of War*, 93–140; Kaeuper, *War, Justice, and Public Order*, 184–269; Keen, 'Chivalry, Nobility'; Gillingham, 'War and Chivalry'; idem, 'William the Bastard'.

As this practical, working corollary to prowess, however, loyalty is easily misunderstood as essentially political and highly idealistic. Beginning students often mistake it for nothing short of steadfast devotion to king and country, or to the church as a holy abstraction. We might better attach it to the broadest conception of law, intending by that term what it so often means in literature: the entire body of beliefs that guide practice and provide self-definition.[133] In the Vulgate Cycle of romances, loyalty often means adherence to the oath taken by all Round Table knights.[134]

We could almost say the focus of a knight's loyalty was chivalry itself, since chivalry provided such guides, such an identity. 'A knight who is treasonous and disloyal', announces a knight in the *Lancelot do Lac*, 'is one who has renounced knighthood.'[135] A guilty knight brought to the point of death by Lancelot, in the *Lancelot*, in effect begs for mercy by arguing that the hero would be disloyal to chivalry to refuse: 'Noble knight, have mercy on me! Indeed, it would be disloyal and brutal to kill me after I'd admitted defeat and begged for mercy.'[136] The danger lurking here, as so often, is a distorting romanticization in which knights appear in pastel hues, fervently believing in all the ideals, in each of the reform plans that emanated from the worlds of *clergie* and *royauté*. Of course, knights were not unfailingly loyal to kings, not endlessly obedient sons of Holy Mother Church, and seldom appeared in life in pastel hues.

But they could show behaviour consistent with ideals of their own group and thus behave predictably; they could be loyal, then, in the sense of being held trustworthy both by their social and political superiors and inferiors (at least down through the ranks of knights, that is). Adherence to the sworn word, to obligation, is crucial to the reliability and predictability that stand at the heart of loyalty. 'Sir knight,' says an old woman to Yvain in one of his adventures, 'if there's any loyalty in you, keep your promise to me. . . . Truly, if you were a knight, you wouldn't break your oath, even if it meant your life.'[137] The statement could almost stand as a definition of loyalty, but it scarcely stands alone. 'God help me,' Hector says to Marganor (who has arranged a fight between one of his knights and Hector in the *Lancelot*), 'I

---

[133] Roland, for example, speaks out 'following the law of chivalry (*Dunc ed parled a lei de chevalerie*)': Brault, ed., *Chanson de Roland*, l. 752.

[134] As noted by Asher, tr., *Merlin Continuation*, 9, n. 2. Examples appear in this text and in other works in this cycle.

[135] Elspeth Kennedy, ed., *Lancelot do Lac*, I, 222; see the same sentiment in Rosenberg, tr., *Lancelot Part I*, 91, Sommer, ed., *Vulgate Version*, III, 172. In the romance of Yder, Kei is said to have no chivalric virtue because he lost it through disloyalty: Adams, ed., tr., *Romance of Yder*, 14–15.

[136] Kibler, tr., *Lancelot Part V*, 190; Micha, ed., *Lancelot*, IV, 322.

[137] Kibler, *Lancelot Part V*, 173; Micha, *Lancelot*, IV, 244.

consider you a loyal knight because you made the knight respect the compact you had with me.'[138] Lancelot is, of course, the great exemplar: returning from the tournament at Pomeglai to hateful captivity, as he had promised, Lancelot is greeted by Meleagant's worried seneschal as 'the most loyal knight in the world'.[139] Lancelot even denounces Fortune as 'traitorous and disloyal', for being so fickle, 'ever changing like the wind!'[140]

'Loyal' is not surprisingly one of the most common terms of virtue applied to knights in chivalric literature. The prowess of the loyal was exercised in the proper manner and for the right causes; their violence was predictable as well as praiseworthy. Pharian's nephew, early in the *Lancelot*, makes the link of loyalty and prowess explicit: 'disloyalty turns a good knight into a bad one, and a knight who is true fights well and confidently even if he has never done so before.'[141] A worthy opponent of Lancelot later in this romance echoes this point of view clearly in the exact words we have already noted from the *Lancelot*: 'A knight who is treacherous and disloyal is one who has renounced knighthood.'[142] Gawain expresses surprise that a treacherous heart can show great prowess.[143] He heroically bears being bound and whipped by the evil Caradoc in *Lancelot*, but 'almost went out of his mind' when he was called a traitor, that is, when accused of disloyalty. Kay of Estral announces in this same text, 'I have always feared being disloyal more than dying.' And Pharian, in *Lancelot*, cautions Claudas against 'some act of disloyalty or treachery that would lose him the honour of this world, towards which all prowess struggles, and the honour of the other, everlasting one, which is the great joy of Heaven'.[144] The author of the *Lancelot* even states that Meleagant's disloyal nature spoiled his commendable prowess: 'he would have been quite valiant if he had not been so disloyal.'[145]

A great show of prowess is taken, conversely, to mean corresponding loyalty. Bors tells the model knights Claudin and Canart (captured in the war against Claudas): 'in God's name . . . you will not be placed in chains or irons, but keep your word on your honour as worthy knights, for the great prowess

---

[138] Carroll, tr., *Lancelot Part II*, 190; Micha, ed., *Lancelot VIII*, 294 (a section of the romance much concerned with issues of oaths and loyalty to obligations).

[139] Krueger, tr., *Lancelot Part IV*, 29; Sommer, *Vulgate Version*, IV, 221.

[140] Kibler, tr., *Lancelot Part V*, 187; Micha, *Lancelot*, IV, 302–3.

[141] Rosenberg, tr., *Lancelot Part I*, 14. I have substituted the term 'knight' for the 'warrior' in the translation, since this is what the text says.

[142] Ibid., 91.

[143] Carroll, *Lancelot Part II*, 205.

[144] Rosenberg, *Lancelot Part III*, 288; 314; *Part I*, 39.

[145] Krueger, *Lancelot Part IV*, 5 (using her footnote to alter the translation); Micha, *Lancelot*, II, 8–9: 'kar preus estoil il assés, s'il ne fust si desloials'.

God has given you would be put to ill use indeed if you committed any act of disloyalty or treachery.'[146]

In all these texts prowess and loyalty are bonded as solidly as prowess and honour. This important fusion helped to create chivalry and give it great strength. Yet chivalry itself was an ambivalent force where a peaceful life and public order were concerned. Its strengthening did not radically transform the general conduct of war as Europeans of all social ranks experienced it so bountifully in these centuries.

---

[146] Krueger, tr., *Lancelot Part IV*, 314; Micha, ed., *Lancelot*, VI, 147.

9

SOCIAL DOMINANCE OF KNIGHTS

✦✦✦

MEN who possessed and exercised the right to fight and who enjoyed the blessing of God on their hard way of life easily came to believe that they were, or deserved to join, the social elite; they readily demanded recognition of their rising status. Assertion of a right to social dominance thus provides another crucial component for the fusion that made chivalry and gave it such power in medieval society. Over time, knights rose in status and even the nobility decided to wear the chivalric mantle.[1]

Chivalry and Nobility

The knights initially had to separate themselves from anything suggesting cultivation of the soil and the smell of manure, for many of those who became the knights were at first not fully and not always differentiated from villagers, tillers of the soil, even the unfree.[2] At the opening of our period, when a fighting man was termed *miles* (plural *milites*) — the word which will come to designate knight — the meaning often carried a distinct sense of subservience and could be used of warriors of rather low social status. Many owned no land and few could have claimed to be possessors of political power.[3] In fact, the term *miles* in this early period had no clear connotation of status and referred simply to function. Yet over time knighthood fused with nobility as a result of common military function, the decline of effective royal power over much of

---

[1] The frame for current historical discussion was set by Duby, 'Origines de la chevalerie', *Chivalrous Society*. General discussions in Keen, *Chivalry*, especially 18–43, 143–61; Coss, *The Knight*; Crouch, *Image of Aristocracy*; Barber, *Knight and Chivalry*, 3–46; Jackson, *Chivalry*, 37–84; Strickland, *War and Chivalry*, 19–30, 143–9; Flori, *Essor de la chevalerie*; Hunt, 'Emergence of the Knight'; Poly and Bournazel, *Feudal Transformation*; Barbero, *L'aristocrazia*. Useful essays on particular subjects appear in Contamine, ed., *La Noblesse au Moyen Age*; Keen, *Nobles, Knights*; and Duby, *Chivalrous Society*.

[2] In a document from the decade before the Norman Conquest, William the Conqueror thought it necessary to specify that he was referring to 'free knights': Marie Fauroux, ed., *Recueil des actes des ducs de Normandie*, cited in Strayer, *Medieval Statecraft*, 67. Many *chansons de geste* carefully specify that the knights are free men.

[3] Strayer, *Medieval Statecraft*, 655–9.

continental Europe, the increasing valorization of knighthood via ecclesiastical efforts for peace and crusade, and the influence of romance literature.[4]

Though the process was far from uniform, in most regions of France knighthood and noble status began to fuse in the course of the twelfth century; knighthood became the 'common denominator of the aristocracy'.[5] The rise of knights was slower in German lands and took a different turn in England, where a distinct legal nobility never emerged; in Italy it gradually accommodated with swiftly reviving urbanism.[6] But everywhere the right to commit warlike violence whenever honour was at stake became a sign of superior status; in time, it hardened into noble right over much of Europe.

By the early thirteenth century, *The Romance of the Wings*, a popular vernacular manual for knights (*c.* 1210), says 'their name, rightly speaking, is the true name of nobility'.[7] This century, as Maurice Keen notes, shifted emphasis away from entry into knighthood via the ceremony of dubbing towards eligibility via noble lineage.[8]

Works of literature show the conviction that chivalric qualities are rooted in genetic inheritance. Ceremonies welcoming back Lancelot to the Arthurian court (in the *Lancelot*) include a procession which orders the great men 'according to their valour and lineage'.[9] The assumption, of course, is that these two scales exactly coincide. In fact, knights in chivalric literature who fail to show the highest qualities may turn out to have a bad genetic line or other ignoble formation. Antor assures Arthur in *The Story of Merlin* that Kay's unpleasant ways must have come from the peasant girl who nursed him.[10] In *The History of the Holy Grail* from the same cycle, a bad knight, we learn, was born 'the son of a vile peasant, descended from a bad line and bad seed'. He was not the king's son he had been thought to be.[11] Inversely, Tor's prowess, in the *Merlin Continuation*, proves his nobility; he was not the son of the peasant who had raised him; his mother had been raped by Pellinor, a great chivalric figure. Arthur has sensed the lineage from the start, as he tells Tor: 'I believe that if nobility had not come to you from somewhere, your heart would never have drawn you to something as exalted as knighthood.'[12]

---

[4] Flori, *L'Idéologie du glaive*; Hunt, 'Emergence of the Knight'.
[5] The phrase used by both Bur and Chédeville, quoted in Contamine, *La Noblesse au Moyen Age*, 26.
[6] Barber, *Knight and Chivalry*, 41; Larner, 'Chivalric Culture'.
[7] Busby, ed., *Ordene de chevalerie*, l. 39.   [8] Keen, *Chivalry*, 143.
[9] Carroll, tr., *Lancelot Part VI*, 283; Micha, ed., *Lancelot*, VI, 20. See Elspeth Kennedy, 'Quest for Identity'.
[10] Pickins, tr., *Story of Merlin*, 214; Sommer, ed., *Vulgate Version*, II, 84.
[11] Chase, tr., *History of the Holy Grail*, I, 113; Sommer, *Vulgate Version*, I, 197.
[12] Asher, tr., *Merlin Continuation*, 225; Roussineau, ed., *Merlin*, I, 208. Once Arthur has evidence of Tor's prowess, he argues that 'the son of a cowherd and a peasant could not have had such a noble start . . . heredity and true nobility have led and taught him in a short time': Asher, ibid.,

The young Gawain, at the tender age of eleven, likewise shows heroic genes at work. Standing by his father's graveside, he vows revenge on the killer, King Pellinor, in terms that elicit much admiration: 'Please God, my lord, may I never earn praise for knightly deeds until I have taken appropriate vengeance and killed a king for a king.' Those within hearing marvel at his words, 'for they were noble, especially for a child'.[13]

Nobility was likewise proved by physical beauty. In their literature knights portrayed themselves tirelessly as more beautiful than other mortals. A well-proportioned body and a comely face identify the truly chivalrous, even if the young man is unknown, in disguise, or in rags.

When the Lady of the Lake brings the young Lancelot to be knighted by Arthur, the king at first resists her request to knight him wearing the armour and robes she has provided; he only knights men dressed in his own robes, he explains. Yvain, however, urges Arthur to make an exception: 'you mustn't just let him go, not a fine fellow like this! I don't remember ever seeing such a good-looking young man.' His advice is accepted and the Lady of the Lake leaves Lancelot at court. Her parting advice to him links moral and physical beauty with prowess: 'Take care to be as beautiful in your heart as you are in body and limb, for you have as much beauty as God could bestow on any child and it would be a great wrong if your prowess did not prove its equal.'[14]

Some reality may even have supported the idea of superior physical form among the chivalrous. Surely not every villager or townsperson was unattractive, but better diet, better living conditions, and the catalyst of confidence might have produced distinct physical improvements in appearance. In their literature they are the beautiful people, the perfection of their bodies enhanced by contrast with the dwarves who so regularly appear in their menial service and who are usually as uncourtly in speech and manners as they are unlovely in body.

As knighthood continued its social rise, the term knight even took on a more restrictive meaning than the term noble. Knighthood, in the close sense of those who had actually been dubbed and become active, strenuous knights, became a minority, a subset, even among the nobility.

The case is clear from England. The number of men called knights in the England of William the Conqueror stood at about 6,000; by the mid-thirteenth century actual or potential knights numbered only about 3,000,

237; Roussineau, ibid., 251. Merlin reinforces the sentiment soon: 'if you were of peasant stock,' he tells Tor, 'the desire to be a knight would not have seized you, but nobility must show itself, be it ever so deeply hidden.' Asher, ibid., 243; Roussineau, ibid., 272.

[13] Asher, tr., *Merlin Continuation*, 199; Paris and Ulrich, eds., *Merlin*, I, 263.

[14] Rosenberg, tr., *Lancelot Part I*, 63; Elspeth Kennedy, ed., *Lancelot do Lac*, I, 154; Micha, ed., *Lancelot*, VII, 269.

with about 1,250 actually having been dubbed.[15] Perhaps three-quarters of a typical fourteenth-century English army was composed of men below the rank of knight.[16] The cost of the ceremony of dubbing, of horses, and more elaborate armour restricted the group. Obligations to participate in local activities of royal governance supply another reason, adding to the economic costs of taking up knighthood the investment of time and the sheer bother of serving on the judicial and administrative inquests so characteristic a feature of medieval England.

In France, also, the cost of active participation in chivalric life rose, and the number of dubbed knights fell accordingly; knighthood as a specific status ceased to encompass all those who were recognized as noble. Fewer than half the French nobles had actually been dubbed in the early fourteenth century.[17] To read any documents relating to this nobility is to encounter many esquires (*damoiseaux*) alongside the knights and great lords.[18] Strenuous knights were only a core of the medieval French nobility, as they were only a core of a medieval French army. Such an army meant a small body of belted knights accompanied by a much larger company of men-at-arms.[19]

Does this trend mean a waning of the influence of chivalric ideas? On the contrary, the chivalric ethos in fact generalized to all who lived by arms, whether of noble family or not; chivalry served as a source of inspiration even beyond the ranks of lords and active, strenuous knights; it touched all men-at-arms. In theory, chivalry might best be exemplified in the conduct of those formally noble or the practising *milites*, but several social rings beyond this inner circle aspired to the status and benefits it conferred.[20]

Christine de Pisan wanted the ideal of chivalry extended to all warriors. Geoffroi de Charny endorsed the aspirations of those below the social level of knights; the key to the honoured and honourable life inherent in chivalry, he thought, ought to guide all who lived by the honest practice of arms.[21] He would have been less happy with the aspirations of those bourgeois families that kept arms and armour and showed devotion to tournament and romance

---

[15] Denholm-Young, 'Feudal Society'. Prestwich suggests stability in numbers for a century after the 1270s, followed by rapid decline: *Armies and Warfare*, 52.

[16] Ayton, *Knights and Warhorses*, 5, 228–9.   [17] Cazelles, *Société politique*, 66.

[18] Examples appear plentifully in *Actes du Parlement*.

[19] Contamine, *Warfare in the Middle Ages*, 80–6.

[20] Keen, *Chivalry*, 145. He notes: 'The shift of emphasis away from the taking of knighthood towards nobility of blood . . . clearly did not, in any significant degree, undermine the conception of the essential role of the secular aristocracy as being a martial one' (pp. 152–3). Cf. Ayton, *Knights and Warhorses*, 3–6, and Ayton and Price, eds, *Medieval Military Revolution*, 81–103.

[21] On Christine, see the comment of Willard, 'Christine de Pisan', 511, and the passages quoted at length from Christine's *Le Livre des fais et bonnes meurs du sage roy Charles V*, in ibid., 518–19. On Charny, see Kaeuper and Kennedy, *Book of Chivalry*: in his text Charny regularly praises and gives advice to both knights and men at arms.

literature.[22] Yet their interest, too, makes the point, valuable for our enquiry, that to all who wanted any share of power and influence, any recognition of high status, showing signs of a chivalrous life was crucially important.

This fact would not be lost on those wearing mitres, tonsures, or cloth hats rather than iron helms. A powerful show of prowess could add an accepted, perhaps necessary layer of respectability to high status grounded in ecclesiastical office or the unheroic possession of moneyed wealth. A town facing a formal declaration of war by the lord of the nearby castle, a religious house threatened or attacked by a knight who contested some monastic rights, a bishop defending his rights as a great lord—all would quickly appreciate the power of chivalry as prowess, the valorization of vigorous action taken with arms in defence of honour.

Public order was a problem of such urgency in high medieval society precisely, that is, because the capacity to use arms in this manner and a belief in its efficacy, even in its nobility, were such characteristic features at the top of society. The Abbot of Saint-Nicholas-au-Bois presumably had such thoughts in mind as he led an armed troop against the town of Crespy in Laonnais in the early fourteenth century; as his troop attacked the outskirts of the town, crying 'Kill, kill! Death to the louts from Crespy!', the abbot wounded one man with his own hand and then rode his horse over another.[23] For their part, French townspeople claimed the characteristic chivalric right to private war; French knights indirectly recognized such rights by issuing formal challenges of war against these collective lordships.[24] The number of men who claimed the social status of knighthood and who went to the wars as practising warriors undoubtedly declined during the Middle Ages; yet the code of knights, with its strong focus on prowess as the key to honour, cast its mantle over a widening circle of believers.

The Role of Largesse

Even as the knights soared far beyond any fear of identification with mere rustics, they still had to close ranks and watch another flank as well. Significant social and economic change, as always, created problems with an existing hierarchy: noble or knightly rank did not always equate with wealth.[25] Given the

---

[22] See, for example, the evidence provided by Juliet Vale, *Edward III*, 40.
[23] *Actes du Parlement*, 6147.
[24] Kaeuper, *War, Justice, and Public Order*, 190, and sources there.
[25] Honoré Bonet thinks it necessary in 1387 to insist, in his famous treatise, that 'a knight must not till the soil, or tend vines, or keep beasts, that is to say, be a shepherd, or be a matchmaker, or be a lawyer; otherwise, he must loose knighthood and the privileges of a knight': see Coupland, ed., tr., *Tree of Battles*, 131.

commercial and urban boom that so marked the High Middle Ages, knights became more keenly aware of the need to establish distance between themselves and the elite townsmen. For the bourgeois were most anxious to join them on the social summits and would take on identifying characteristics of chivalry as swiftly as they were able. It proved impossible to keep them from holding tournaments of their own, from showing coats of arms, from marriage alliances with proud but impecunious knights. What could prevent them from reading chivalric literature and imitating fine manners? Perhaps it was all the more necessary to stress chivalric distance from such folk, as knights actually broke the code themselves, mingled with the middling classes, relied on their loans, their commercial expertise and management, and married their daughters.[26] The great chivalric exemplar William Marshal worked at profitable urban development on his estates and was no stranger to London moneylenders.[27] The family of Ramon Llull, author of the most popular vernacular treatise on chivalry—which emphasized the link between nobility and chivalry—was only a few decades away from bourgeois origins in Barcelona.[28]

Of course the knights raised as many barriers as they could. The distance between their exclusive, chivalrous life and the lives of the sub-chivalric bourgeoisie could be clearly established by a quality tirelessly praised in all chivalric literature: only they could truly display the magnificent, great-hearted generosity known as *largesse*. This great virtue could then, especially in France, appear in sharpest contrast to the mean-spirited acquisitiveness of the merchants.

On this line, moreover, *chevalerie* and *clergie* could join forces. Images of the bourgeoisie tainted by disgusting avarice and sinful usury appear frequently in medieval art, as Lester Little has shown. All those with noble bloodlines could agree, whether clerics or knights: Avarice looks like a merchant; he counts and hoards his coins (when he is not depicted defecating them); he has assuredly not learned to broadcast his wealth to the deserving with grand gesture, confident that valour can always replenish the supply.[29]

The southern French poet Bertran de Born sings the praises of largesse and links it with prowess and love. All these traits necessarily connect; they all separate the one who possesses them in his eternal youthfulness from ordinary folk:

---

[26] As noted by Keen, *Chivalry*, 147. Cf. Stanesco, 'Le chevalier dans la ville', and the numerous sources cited there.

[27] Crouch, *William Marshal*, 168–70.   [28] Cardona, 'Chevaliers et chevalerie', 142.

[29] Little, 'Pride Goes before Avarice'. The more fluid social hierarchy in England and developed urbanism in Italy made for differences, of course.

Young is a man who pawns his property, and he's young when he's really poor. He stays young while hospitality costs him a lot, and he's young when he makes extravagant gifts. He stays young when he burns his chest and coffer, and holds combats and tourneys and ambushes. He stays young when he likes to flirt, and he's young when minstrels like him well.[30]

No miserly merchant need apply. In fact, townsmen are often pictured in chivalric literature as fair game for the knightly lions, who will put the booty to nobler use. The biography of the great William Marshal passes over his father's career as a robber baron, it is true, and paints no scene of William looting merchants in glad war; but it does picture him taking money from a priest who is running off with a lady of good family. The money which the priest intended to put to usury William spends more nobly, as his biographer proudly tells us, on a feast for a circle of knightly friends. His friends' only dissatisfaction with William is that he failed to take the horses as well.[31]

Largesse pointedly reinforces high social status in the early life of Lancelot.[32] Out of innate nobility he gives his own horse to a young man of noble birth who has been ambushed, his horse incapacitated: without Lancelot's gift he would miss a chance to confront a traitor in court. Lancelot's generosity preserves him from shame.

Meeting an aged vavasour shortly after, Lancelot politely offers him some of the meat of a roebuck he has shot. The man, who has had poorer luck in his own hunting, had been trying to put food on the wedding table of his daughter. Lancelot, learning that he is talking to a knight, tells him that the meat 'could not [be] put to better use than to let it be eaten at the wedding of a knight's daughter'. He graciously accepts the gift of one of the vavasour's greyhounds in return. But Lancelot's tutor—one of the sub-knightly, insensible to such fine points of generosity—refuses to believe Lancelot's truthful account; he slaps the lad, and whips the greyhound. In a rage, Lancelot drives off the man (and his three subordinates), promising to kill him, if he can catch him outside the household of his patroness, the Lady of the Lake.[33]

The young Arthur gives another case in point. As claimant to the throne (having pulled the sword from the stone), Arthur is shown 'all kingly things and things that a man might lust after or love, to test whether his heart was greedy or grasping'. But he treats all these things nobly, giving them all away appropriately. His actions win him regard and support: 'They all whispered

---

[30] Paden *et al.*, eds, *Poems of the Troubadour*, 298–9.

[31] Meyer, ed., *Histoire*, ll. 6689–864.

[32] See the discussion in Elspeth Kennedy, *Lancelot and the Grail*, 15.

[33] Corley, tr., *Lancelot of the Lake*, 30–7; Elspeth Kennedy, ed., *Lancelot do Lac*, I, 41–7. Cf. Rosenberg, tr., *Lancelot Part I*, 20–1; Sommer, ed., *Vulgate Version*, III, 35–40.

behind their hands that he was surely of high birth, for they found no greed in him: as soon as anything of worth came his way, he put it to good uses, and all his gifts were fair according to what each one deserved.'[34]

Clearly, this virtue sets men like Arthur apart from the grasping, retentive, bourgeois, or—God forbid—from any among the nobles who might stoop to such base behaviour. It is interesting to note that the scruffy townsmen and their money appear only faintly and in the background in this literature, almost as part of the scenery. They now and then put up knights for a tournament or house the overflow crowd gathered for a colourful royal occasions; they are called forth by the author to cheer when a hero frees a town from some evil custom through his magnificent prowess.

Of course largesse not only keeps the ambitious townsmen out of the club, in the hands of a great lord or king it becomes a crucial buttress to dominance, a tool of governance. Repeatedly in *The Story of Merlin* Arthur's largesse to poor, young knights secures their loyalty and provides him with armed force. Early in his career, '[h]e sought out fighting men everywhere he knew them to be and bestowed on them clothing, money, and horses, and the poor knights throughout the country took him in such love that they swore never to fail him even in the face of death.' After his forces have been joined by those of King Ban and King Bors, 'King Arthur bestowed gifts of great worth on those in the two kings' households according to their rank, and he gave them warhorses, saddle horses, and beautiful, costly arms . . . and they swore that never, ever in their lives, would they let him down.[35]

Ideally, it was warfare, not simply the income from one's own vast estates, that produced the wherewithal for such lavish generosity. After a great battle with the Saxons, Arthur hands out all of the wealth garnered from them, and

he let it be known throughout the army that if there were any young knights who wanted to win booty and would go with him wherever he would lead them, he would give them so much when they came back that they would never be poor another day in their lives. And so many of them came forward from here and there that it was nothing short of a wonder, for many wished always to be in his company because of his open-handedness.[36]

In his great encounter with Galehaut, an alarmed Arthur finds his knights deserting him.[37] The Wise Man explains the causes of this crisis and presents a list of reforms which features a return to generosity: Arthur is to ride a splen-

[34] Pickens, tr., *Story of Merlin*, 215; Sommer, ed., *Vulgate Version*, II, 87.

[35] Pickens, *Story of Merlin*, 220, 223; Sommer, *Vulgate Version*, II, 96, 102.

[36] Pickens, *Story of Merlin*, 300; Sommer, *Vulgate Version*, II, 242–3.

[37] When Arthur's largesse lags early in the *Perlesvaus*, the knights similarly begin to drift away from his court: see Nitze and Jenkins, eds, *Perlesvaus*, 26.

did horse up to the poor knight and 'give him the horse in consideration of his prowess and the money so that he may spend freely'; the social hierarchy must be reaffirmed by a downward flow of largesse producing an upward flow of loyalty; the queen and her ladies and maidens must likewise cheerfully show largesse; all are to remember that 'none was ever destroyed by generosity, but many have been destroyed by avarice. Always give generously and you will always have enough.'[38] This advice in romance reappeared in a bold motto on the wall of the Painted Chamber in Westminster Hall during the reign of Henry III: 'He who does not give what he has will not get what he wants.'[39]

In romance the goods were given out according to two scales, which, we are not surprised to find, always smoothly merged: high status and exemplary prowess. Asked to distribute the loot taken from the Saxons at one point in *The Story of Merlin*, Gawain defers to Doon of Carduel, explaining that 'he can divide it up and distribute it better than I can, for he knows better than I do who the leading men are and the worthiest'.[40]

Sometimes the pious fiction of funding knighthood with booty snatched from the unworthy hands of pagans slips a bit. In the *Lancelot do Lac* Claudas's son Dorin looks remarkably like one of the disruptive 'youths' whose role in French society Georges Duby analysed so tellingly.[41] Like these young men, Dorin admits no check on his vigour and will, and spends with even less restraint:

The only child [Claudas] had was a very handsome, fair boy almost fifteen years old, named Dorin. He was so arrogant and strong that his father did not yet dare make him a knight, lest he rebel against him as soon as he was able; and the boy spent so freely that no one would fail to rally to him.[42]

Claudas, moreover, learns from his own brother by what means Dorin has acquired the wealth he dispenses so grandly: 'Dorin had caused great harm in the land, damaging towns, seizing livestock, and killing and wounding men.' Yet Claudas plays the great chivalric lord even more than the indulgent father in his response: 'I am not troubled by all that. . . . He has the right, for a king's son must not be prevented from being as generous as he may like, and royalty cannot allow itself to be impoverished by giving.'[43] The attitude was, of

---

[38] Carroll, tr., *Lancelot Part II*, 122; Elspeth Kennedy, ed. *Lancelot do Lac*, I, 288–9.

[39] Colvin, gen. ed., *History of the King's Works*, I, *The Middle Ages*, 497: 'Ke ne dune ke ne tine ne prent ke desire.'

[40] Pickens, tr., *Story of Merlin*, 243; Sommer ed., *Vulgate Version*, II, 140.

[41] Duby, 'Dans la France du Nord-Ouest'.

[42] Corley, tr., *Lancelot of the Lake*; Rosenberg, tr., *Lancelot Part I*, 15.

[43] Elspeth Kennedy, *Lancelot do Lac*, I, 38; Rosenberg, *Lancelot Part I*, 18. Claudas is a morally complex figure in this romance; yet his advice here does not seem to contradict common practice and attitude.

course, not limited to royalty, as many villagers and merchants in many centuries of medieval European history could testify. Knightly prowess and largesse went hand in hand throughout the countryside. Some feud, skirmish, or war could regularly be counted on to provide opportunity for despoiling the wealth available in fields or villages, or hoarded in merchants' town houses. One of the five villages attacked in a private war by Gilles de Busigny in 1298 lost (Robert Fossier estimated) the equivalent of 40,000 man hours of work by a labourer such as a mason, roofer, or harvester.[44] Loot from such raids could be distributed grandly, and according to well-established rules, as Maurice Keen has shown.[45]

Thus the great virtue of largesse is enabled by the great virtue of prowess. Knights know how to get money and how to spend it. 'Lords, pawn your castles and towns and cities before you stop making war!' Bertran de Born cries out in one of his poems.[46] Largesse falls like ripe fruit from the tree of prowess into the strong hands of the worthy.

Might these two great chivalric qualities prove rivals? Competition usually turns thin and unconvincing on close inspection. Largesse wins high formal praise, for example, early in Chrétien's *Cligés* where it appears as the queen of virtues enhancing all others; largesse by itself can make a man worthy, the old Emperor of Constantinople tells the young hero Alexander, though nothing else can (rank, courtesy, knowledge, strength, chivalry, valour, lordship).[47] Yet in this romance, as in so many others, the glittering prizes are won by prowess. Not by largesse does Alexander win the battle outside Windsor, seize the castle itself, and earn the love of Soredamor; nor does his son Cligés by largesse defeat the nephew of the Duke of Saxony (and kill him in a later encounter), unhorse and behead the Duke's most vigorous knight, foil the Saxon ambush of the Greeks, rescue Fenice from her captors, defeat the Duke of Saxony in single combat, carry off the prize in King Arthur's great four-day tournament (fighting even Gawain to a draw), and range all over Britain doing feats of chivalry, before returning to the Eastern Empire and a final triumph. In the reception that Arthur's knights give Cligés after he has won the great tournament at Oxford, near the end of the story, they crowd around him in great joy, telling him how much they value him, declaring that his prowess outshines theirs as the sun outshines little stars.[48]

---

[44] Fossier, 'Fortunes et infortunes'.   [45] Keen, *Laws of War*.

[46] Paden *et al.*, eds., *Poems of the Troubadour*, 344–5.

[47] Luttrell and Gregory, eds., *Chrétien de Troyes*, ll. 192–217,

[48] Ibid., ll. 4983–95. Chrétien is more willing than most writers of chivalric romance to allow his characters to solve important issues by means other than sheer prowess. Cleverness, rather than prowess, alone, effects the bond of Cligés and Fenice at the end of Chrétien's *Cligés*; yet prowess retains its importance.

The Role of Chivalric Mythology (Revisited)

If the knights first strode swiftly away from the rustics and then at least kept the bourgeois at arm's length (while funding loyalty among fellow knights), they always had the clerics to contend with as social rivals. The issue was complicated, as we have already noted, by the clerics' sacerdotal role and by the close link they claimed with their supernatural chief. Yet thinking in pragmatic and worldly terms, knights could never forget that the clerks often came from the same social levels, even from the same families as they themselves; some clerics, of course, could claim little or no status by birth.

Prudently and piously recognizing the essential clerical role in the economy of salvation, the significant voices of both Ramon Llull and Geoffroi de Charny grant that the clerks merit high status in the world; both state outright that the clerics form the highest order in Christian society. Each wants, however, to give chivalry a secure place, to yoke *clergie* and *chevalerie* as the twin motive forces of their society. And Charny's statement of clerical superiority has a somewhat formal ring; he soon betrays his sense that the great role chivalry must play in the world gives it a special status. Like William Marshal a century before, he is happiest when religion comes heavily blended with chivalry; again in company with the Marshal, he most heartily endorses clerics who perform all the needed rites and then stand aside for the magnificent work with sword and lance.

In fact, as Maurice Keen has emphasized, the knightly demonstrated their autonomy vis-à-vis clerics by elaborating a chivalric mythology.[49] It came complete with stories of origins, lists of men worthy of reverence, and great texts produced in language that was sometimes sonorous and solemn, sometimes wonderfully witty and sophisticated. We have seen that all this distinctly lay culture functioned not so much as a form of anticlericalism as a complex and autonomous borrowing and parallel process of creation, using clerical symbolism to draw the veil of accepted piety over the rigours of knightly life.

Chapter 3 examined this mythology as evidence for the complexities of knightly lay piety in the face of clerical claims to directive power. This mythology also allows us to see related, knightly efforts to secure their social status in the face of clerical claims as primary *ordo* in Christendom.

Valorizing ideas are important even if propaganda often is intended as much to reinforce the morale of the group as to win over outsiders in debate. In effect, the knights imagined a mirror version of the world as conceived by *clergie*—that is, themselves in control and the priests reduced to specialist

[49] Keen, *Chivalry*, 102–24.

(though necessary) functionaries. They posited an independent chivalric mythology and learning (cast always in the most pious hues) standing alongside if not actually in place of the clerical learning of the schools, with manly violence ensuring all that is sound and sacred. This line of thought justified their self-assurance that the role of knights matched or even overshadowed that of the less than heroic clerics, for all their claims. The task was not onerous; they simply created an origin for chivalry as old or even older than that claimed by the ecclesiastics for their own order.

Chrétien de Troyes imagined a genealogy of chivalry (virtually equated with civilization) that reached back into classical Greek and Roman history.[50] Anonymous works, like the *Romance of Eneas*, the *Romance of Alexander*, the *Romance of Troyes*, pictured figures and events from ancient history and legend in chivalric dress and spirit. The glory of the classical world stemmed in no small measure from its fine chivalry.[51] Knights contemporary to Chrétien could trace their functional if not their biological lineage back to great heroes.

Precise definition (characteristic of high medieval Europe) came with the famous Nine Worthies, unexcelled champions, extending chivalric roots beyond the classical past into ancient Israel. Using sacred threes, writers presented three sets of three heroic knights: medieval (Arthur, Charlemagne, and the crusader Godfrey de Bouillon); classical (Hector, Alexander, and Julius Caesar); and Jewish (Joshua, David, and Judas Maccabaeus). This fusion of Judaeo–Christian and classical history gave chivalry the most ancient and most venerable lineage possible.[52]

Sometimes the same effect was achieved not by anchoring accounts of origins in historical time and personage, but by moving them outside of time. In his vastly influential book on chivalry, Ramon Llull (who had been a knight before he became a quasi-cleric) presented a human fall from virtue redeemed by the creation of chivalry in just such a distant, misty past. To ensure order and virtue, the human race was divided into thousands and the knight was chosen as literally one out of a thousand as the most noble and most fit to rule and fight.[53]

The author of the *Lancelot do Lac* presents a similar account (probably the model for Llull) in the form of advice given by the Lady of the Lake to the

---

[50] Luttrell and Gregory, eds., *Chrétien de Troyes*, ll. 30–9.

[51] Grave, ed., *Eneas*; James, ed., *Romance of Alexander*, a facsimile of the French manuscript; Constans and Faral, eds, *Roman de Troie*, an abridged prose version of the original metrical French text.

[52] There were local variants. Writing the life of Don Pero Niño in the late fourteenth century, Gutierre Diaz de Gamez lists nine worthies with the classical trio omitted, Charles Martel substituted for Arthur, and three Castilian heroes added: see Evans, tr., *The Unconquered Knight*, 8–9.

[53] Byles, ed., *Book of the Ordre of Chyvalry*, 14 ff.

young Lancelot, though here the myth is loosely attached to more standard Christian chronology and to a somewhat surprising populism.[54] Originally, all men were equal, being offspring of one set of parents:

but when envy and greed began to grow in the world, and force began to overcome justice . . . [and] the weak could no longer withstand or hold out against the strong, they established protectors and defenders over themselves, to protect the weak and the peaceful and to maintain their rights and to deter the strong from their wrongdoing and outrageous behaviour.

Thus, knighthood was given to those who, 'in the opinion of the common people', were most worthy; that is, to 'the big and the strong and the handsome and the nimble and the loyal and the valorous and the courageous, those who were full of the qualities of the heart and of the body.'[55]

Similar qualities set apart noble knights in Christine de Pisan's myth, laid out in her account of the deeds of the French king Charles V. Once evil and disorder entered the world, laws and various professional groups were formed to provide structure and order. The knights came into being 'pour garder et deffendre le prince, la contrée et le bien commun' (to guard and uphold the prince, the country, and the common good).[56]

The life of the great fourteenth-century Castilian knight Don Pero Niño simply concentrates on how good fighting men (functionally equated with nobles) were first found. The 'Gentiles' and 'the People of the Law' followed different courses. The Gentiles first relied on carpenters and stonemasons who could give great blows in battle; but their courage and resolve failed, as did that of the next group, the butchers, chosen because they were inured to blood and slaughter. So a third group was chosen: those who were observed to be resolute and strong in battle became the knights, their sons following them in an hereditary and privileged concentration on fighting.[57] Among the Jews, nobility/knighthood originated differently, as the Old Testament shows. With divine direction, Gideon chose an elite set of warriors: rejecting those who drank with mouths in the water like animals, without shame, he chose the good men who drank with their hands, guided by reason. As he assures his readers, 'noble renown is a matter befitting knights and those who pursue the calling of War and the art of Chivalry, and not any others whatsoever'. They are only a little lower than the angels, for God 'has set three orders of

---

[54] Corley, tr., *Lancelot of the Lake*, 52; Elspeth Kennedy, ed., *Lancelot do Lac*, I, 142–3.
[55] Corley, *Lancelot*, 52; Kennedy, *Lancelot do Lac*, I, 142.
[56] Solente, ed., *Livre des fais*, I, 111–16, quotation at 116.
[57] A little classical patina is added, as knights lead their thousands (a *miles* in charge of a *mille*) and a duke, called a legionary, commands a legion of six thousand, six hundred and sixty men.

knighthood': the angels who warred with Lucifer in heaven, the martyrs who fought the good fight on earth and gave their lives for faith, and the good kings and knights, for whom heaven will be the reward.[58]

More commonly, an author simply tells readers that God's will is manifest in knightly origins. In the famous Sword in the stone episode (in *The Story of Merlin*), the worthy archbishop explains to all who have seen the marvel of Arthur drawing out the sword:

[W]hen our Lord established law and order on the earth, He set them in the sword. The rule that was over the laity must come from a layman, and must be by the sword, and the sword was, at the beginning of the three orders, entrusted to knighthood to safeguard Holy Church and uphold true law and order.[59]

As we have seen, the Grail stories bring the knightly and priestly mythologies into much closer conjunction, integrating the account of chivalric origins more fully into salvation history, in the process creating unmistakable and significant parallels. *The History of the Holy Grail*, for example, provided knights with a non-ecclesiastical story of the coming of Christianity to their own region, with much emphasis on the need for knightly virtues in fighting for the Grail and the new faith.

In this and other prose romances which tell the Grail story, a powerful trinitarian formulation appears. Three fellowships, gathered round three tables, have marked the history of the world, which means, of course, the history of chivalry: the table of Christ and his disciples; the table of 'that worthy man and perfect knight, Joseph of Arimathea' (to whom the Grail was given); and, finally, the Round Table of King Arthur. However tenuous this linkage may seem to modern sensibilities, more than one romance draws this line from Christ, through the first Grail-keeper and the later Round Table fellowship to the flesh and blood knighthood of the High and Late Middle Ages.[60]

Perhaps fourteenth-century founders of chivalric orders such as the English king Edward III or his cousin of France, John the Good, thought of the fellowships they created as latter-day additions to this glorious tradition, although it meant adding to the sacred three. In many minds another addition seemed sure. Certainly, many of those who wrote about chivalry, Geoffroi de Charny prominent among them, looked forward to joining a

---

[58] Evans, tr., *The Unconquered Knight*, 4–7.

[59] Pickens, tr., *Story of Merlin*, 213; Micha, ed. *Merlin*, 271. The divergence from the usual clerical theory of two swords is noteworthy here.

[60] Matarasso, tr., *Quest*, 97–9; Pauphilet, *Queste*, 74–7; Skells, tr., *Perceval in Prose*, 4–5; Hucher, ed., *Le Saint-Graal*, I, 417; Pickens, *Story of Merlin*, 196–7; Sommer, ed., *Vulgate Version*, II, 54. The quotation about Joseph comes from Matarasso, *Quest*, 151.

final chivalric fellowship at God's table in paradise, and spoke of heaven in just such terms.[61]

Genealogies created for heroes of the Grail stories make a final link between myths of knighthood and the standard sacred history. Joseph of Arimathea, as loyal burier of Christ's body in the New Testament accounts and first keeper of the Holy Grail in chivalric accounts, plays a crucial bridging role. The links in the chain of Grail knights are formed by his successors as keepers of the Grail or their close associates. Perceval, though his father is not named in Chrétien's Grail romance, becomes the son of Alain, a Grail-keeper, by the early thirteenth century (in the *Didot Perceval* and the *Perlesvaus*). For Galahad, who enters the tradition at about the same time, a more oblique attachment to the main line had to be found. According to *The Quest of the Holy Grail*, after divine commandment sent him away from Jerusalem, Joseph of Arimathea met and converted a pagan king (who took the baptismal name Mordrain) by helping him obtain God's aid in beating his enemy in battle. Mordrain becomes one of the standard figures in the Grail stories and an important agent in the mythical conversion of Britain. One splendid and pious knight begets the next until Lancelot enters the world and, finally, through his union with the daughter of the Fisher King (a Grail-keeper), the Good Knight Galahad appears.

Chivalric literature, then, shows us in how many ways *chevalerie* both aped and rivalled the pretensions of *clergie*. Moreover, this literature was in itself a significant body of learning, a key element in the collection of texts which knighthood came gradually to set alongside the sacred texts controlled by the priesthood. The tales of chivalric literature, after all, present themselves as history and claim the venerable authority owed to ancient accounts penned by eyewitnesses; repeatedly, chivalric authors assure us such manuscripts stand behind the thoroughly stylish, modern, versified, or prose texts written in the vernacular which they now presented to an appreciative audience in the form of *chanson* or *romanz*.

Sometimes, the bridging, literate cleric responsible for the text is Turpin, knight and archbishop. The *Chanson d'Aspremont* relates that Turpin witnessed the important meeting between Girart and Charlemagne, and recorded it, in Latin, while on horseback.[62]

But clerics—even when simultaneously knights—are not always needed. Pauline Matarasso describes the anonymous author of *The Quest of the Holy*

---

[61] Kaeuper and Kennedy, *Book of Chivalry*, 196–9. After one of his escapes from temptation in the *Quest*, Perceval prays that he may never 'forfeit the company of His knights above': Matarasso, tr., *Quest*, 113; Pauphilet, *Queste*, 92.

[62] Newth, tr., *Song of Aspremont* and Brandin, ed., *Chanson d'Aspremont*, laisse 232.

Grail as 'most likely . . . one of that great army of clerks who wandered anonymously in that no-man's land between the lay and ecclesiastical worlds'.[63] Occasionally, authors of chivalrous learning are straightforward laymen, as Geoffroi de Charny was. The heralds who rose with the institution of the tournament and gradually won a secure place for themselves in chivalrous society by the later thirteenth century were certainly laymen; Maurice Keen has termed them 'a lay priesthood' for the cult of chivalry 'and an educated, literate lay priesthood to boot'.[64]

And we should note that from the early years of the thirteenth century this historical mythology of chivalry was written, significantly, in prose. This, as E. Jane Burns has noted, 'carried for many medieval writers a truth-telling value absent from the rhetorical artifice of purely literary verse accounts'.[65] The medieval translator of the *Chronique de Pseudo-Turpin*, rendering that work into French prose, declared flatly, 'No rhymed story is true.'[66]

The authors of Arthurian and Grail stories, in other words, claimed historical authenticity and buttressed such claims time and again with careful descriptions of the sure and certain manner in which their story got from actual events to the written page. The knights themselves become authors in a sense, for we are told more than once how they swore to recall all their adventures on their return from the quest; Arthur had clerks to set them down in detail in a book.[67] Merlin is author of other parts of the tale, and is frequently shown dictating the story to his clerk, Blaise.[68] At some points 'the story' even asserts that it has been written by God or Christ himself.[69] Merely human authors include Walter Map, a figure at the court of the great king Henry II, who was himself, of course, linked with the Arthurian legend.[70]

Perhaps the most powerful combination of authority, however, appears in *The History of the Holy Grail*, whose author tells us not only that he has been given his book from God, but that he has divinely learned of his own descent from 'so many valorous men that I hardly dare say or acknowledge that I am descended from them'. This ideal combination, of course, unites divinity with the demi-god prowess.[71]

---

[63] Matarasso, tr., *Quest*, 27.

[64] Keen, *Chivalry*, 142. For the importance of heraldry in general as a species of knightly learning see, pp. 125–42.

[65] In Lacy, ed., *Lancelot-Grail*, I, xvi.   [66] Quoted in Kelly, *Perlesvaus*, 18.

[67] See, for example, Elspeth Kennedy, ed., *Lancelot do Lac*, 298, 406, 571; Pickens, tr., *Story of Merlin*, 345; Sommer, ed., *Vulgate Version*, II, 321; III, 227, 307, 429; Carroll, tr., *Lancelot Part II*, 126, 169, 238.

[68] Pickens, *Story of Merlin*, passim; Sommer, *Vulgate Version*, II, passim.

[69] E.g. Chase, tr., *History of the Holy Grail*, 4, 76; Hucher, ed., *Le Saint-Graal*, II, 13, 438.

[70] See the comments of Burns, in Lacy, ed., *Lancelot-Grail*, I, Introduction.

[71] Chase, *History of the Holy Grail*, 4; Hucher, *Le Saint Graal*, II, 12–13.

The Role of Formal Manners

As natural lay leaders in society, knights display the ideal behaviour to be expected of them. They know just how to speak to each person in the elaborate social hierarchy; they know when to speak, and when to fall politely silent. They know how to receive orders as graciously as they accept hospitality or fine gifts. They are now unmovably resolute, now overcome and swooning as their fine emotions take hold. As if seated in an opera house, we may feel that the measured gestures should be accompanied by music, the monologues and choruses being sung to tunes we simply no longer hear.

Agreement on the importance of fine manners among medieval contemporaries is impressive. Non-fictional works of instruction for knights provide the same point of view as that of so many works of imaginative literature. Yet so much seeming agreement raises interesting questions.

We might especially ask about the origin and intent of all this tireless emphasis on proper behaviour in various social settings and in dealings with various social levels. Was this instruction an attempt by those outside the caste to remake knights, to change their thinking and, in time, their behaviour? Did knights themselves resist, only reluctantly accepting a somewhat cramped framework for behaviour, or did they think that following such behaviour was important to their social dominance? Did the concern for manners and courtly behaviour actually civilize the knights in the exact sense of reducing their violence and integrating them into a more ordered society?

These are large questions that have attracted the attention of distinguished scholars. In the early decades of the twentieth century, Johan Huizinga and Norbert Elias pictured the rough warrior being slowly civilized as the early modern gentleman.[72] More recently, Stephen Jaeger has convincingly located the origins of courtliness—which would become so important in French romance and in all the vernaculars it touched—in the German court tradition beginning in the tenth century.[73] No one, moreover, would deny that basic changes in aristocratic behaviour and aristocratic violence took place between (say) the later tenth and the later seventeenth century.

Recognizing the force and attractiveness of all this work, it is possible to consider chivalry at best as an unsteady ally of the complex forces at work producing these great changes. The evidence brought into play in this book reinforces a view that chivalry was no simple force for restraint.[74] The worship of prowess makes chivalry a poor buttress to a unilinear progressive view of

---

[72] Huizinga, *Autumn of the Middle Ages*, Elias, *The Civilizing Process*.
[73] Jaeger, *Origins of Courtliness*.
[74] I am developing this theme in a forthcoming article.

civilization. In fact, the formally polite modes of behaviour seem less an intrusive check on knighthood than an expression of the knights' own high sense of worth, of rightful dominance in society; good manners were less a restraint on knightly behaviour than they were its characteristic social expression. These forms of good behaviour, after all, informed the entire span of knightly life and set it apart from anything common. Much knightly violence itself was enthroned in good manners, not prohibited by them. As the anthropologist Julian Pitt-Rivers wrote so succinctly, 'the ultimate vindication of honour lies in physical violence'.[75] The range of this good behaviour, as we have seen, extended from bloody deeds of prowess on the field of battle or in the tournament, through a piety which never lost its degree of lay independence, to polite behaviour and correct speech among mixed company whether in a great court or humble vavasour's hall.

We need only think of the scene repeated hundreds if not thousands of times in chivalric literature. A wandering knight comes conveniently to some castle or fortified house at the end of a hard day of riding and fighting. The knight meets with a gracious reception from the good man in charge, who welcomes him into his home with open-handed hospitality; the host inevitably has a beautiful daughter who removes the knight's armour, and dresses him in a soft robe of fine stuff; they converse most politely while the tables are set and the roast finishes. The next morning, after mass in the chapel, the knight is again on his way to adventure, which quite often means freeing his hosts from some dread peril which has become evident during his brief stay. In gratitude the host offers the victorious knight his beautiful daughter, an offer which is acknowledged with many thanks, but must be turned down with apologies because of a pressing quest or an earlier claim on the knight's heart.[76]

This scene celebrates the formal and superior chivalric manners under discussion. The knight is most polite in speech and action with everyone in this setting, male and female, even the enemy whose defeat will free the gracious host from an evil custom or a siege. Having unhorsed this enemy and hacked him into submission, the knight rips off his foe's helmet and turns down the mail ventail (protecting the vulnerable throat), perhaps pounds the fellow's face a bit with the pommel of his sword; then, bloody sword blade at the ready, he politely offers a choice of surrender or decapitation. If the foe yields, the victor cuts not.

What scholars traditionally term *courtoisie* is much in evidence here, and in all the knight's social relations. The scene likewise indirectly praises the *largesse*

---

[75] Pitt-Rivers, 'Honour and Social Status', 29.

[76] For a discussion of hospitality and good manners as aristocratic rites of unification, see Chênerie, *Le Chevalier errant*, 503–91.

of the host who freely gives what is his to the worthy knight. All show an interest in *amors*. If the knight makes no sexual advances to the daughter (or resists hers, if she is more forward) he has demonstrated *loiauté* by not repaying his host's good with ill. The mass heard in the castle chapel shows the hero is *pius*. Even if no mortal combat is actually portrayed, from either wing of this domestic stage set, like summer thunder, come the echoes of the knight's *prouesse*.[77]

Sometimes courtliness and fine manners even seem subsumed within prowess, despite our sense (rooted in etymology) that they represent gentler virtues that internalize restraints.[78] As Norman Daniel observes, 'the sense of *cortois* seems to extend to any expedient favourable to a knight. Giving freely is aristocratic, and it is taking such an expedient brutally that makes it possible.'[79] William Marshal's tactical advice that King Henry should pretend to disband his forces but then secretly reassemble them and suddenly ravage French territory elicits from the king a telling compliment: 'By God's eyes, Marshal, you are most courteous [*molt corteis*] and have given me good advice. I shall do exactly as you suggest.'[80] In the opening of his *Yvain*, Chrétien refers to Arthur 'whose prowess taught us to be brave and courteous'.[81] When Perceval converts the Coward Knight to prowess in the *Perlesvaus*, he gives him the new name of Bold Knight, 'for that is a more courtly name than the other'.[82] At one point in the *Lancelot do Lac* Arthur rebukes Gawain for interrupting his reverie at a meal; his thoughts were courtly because they were about a man of great prowess: 'Gawain, Gawain, you have shaken me out of the most courtly thoughts I ever had . . . for I was thinking about the best knight of all men of valour. That is the knight who was the victor at the encounter between Galehot and me.'[83]

Certainly any denial or neglect of the accepted forms will quickly acquaint the miscreant with the cutting edge of prowess. Chivalric texts invariably note that two honourable people meeting each other exchange greetings; any failure is a significant event. Thus a squire riding disconsolate in the *Lancelot* (troubled by the news that his brother has been slain) commits a serious

---

[77] Burgess, *Contribution*, discusses several of these key terms, their interconnections, and shifts in their meanings towards the mid-twelfth century.

[78] See the discussions in Frappier, 'Vues'; Burgess, *Contribution*, 22–34. As noted above, the most recent study, with a different emphasis, is that of Jaeger, *Origins of Courtliness*.

[79] Daniel, *Heroes and Saracens*, 27. He notes that in the *chansons*, 'Cortois is most often used as an indeterminate epithet in praise of someone, with no meaning more specific than "civilised" (in an aristocratic way).'

[80] Meyer, ed., *Histoire*, ll. 7738–69, discussed in Gillingham, 'War and Chivalry', 6.

[81] Kibler, ed., tr., *Yvain*, ll. 1–3.

[82] Bryant, tr., *Perlesvaus*, 157; Nitze and Jenkins, eds, *Perlesvaus*, 243.

[83] Corley, tr., *Lancelot of the Lake*, 255–6; Elspeth Kennedy, ed., *Lancelot do Lac*, I, 296–7.

offence when he neglects to greet another squire waiting before some tents he passes; the offended squire attacks and mortally wounds him. A lapse of courtesy has cost him his life.[84]

Denial of hospitality can easily be fatal if it touches Lancelot. Near the end of the *Lancelot*, the hero seeks lodging in a pavilion, but is refused by the maiden within, who tells him her knight will return and will object. He announces he is staying regardless, for he has no other lodging. Her knight does return, denies Lancelot hospitality, and orders him out with threats. Lancelot arms and tells the knight he will die for this dishonour. His first sword stroke cuts off the man's arm. Both the mortally wounded knight and his lady faint. When the knight's brother tries to take vengeance, Lancelot stuns him with another great sword stroke, rips off his helmet, and beats him nearly to death with it. He spares the man's life on condition of pardoning him for the death of his brother. It then emerges that there was a hermitage nearby; the battered brother takes Lancelot there.[85] For the audience of this romance, was the point not that hospitality must not be denied?

Chivalric largesse, mythology, and refined manners certainly purveyed social power. They created an image of knights as naturally superior to all other laymen and on a par with the clerics; pious and appropriately violent, they are splendidly refined in life and love.

These chivalric ideas, even if they sometimes seem rather abstract in their details, flowed into daily life through a thousand channels to became a force in social relationships. If the process is complex and can only be seen indirectly from our six or seven centuries of distance, the broad social result is by no means in doubt.

---

[84] Krueger, tr., *Lancelot Part IV*, 64; Micha, ed., *Lancelot*, II, 232.
[85] Carroll, tr., *Lancelot Part VI*, 272–3; Micha, *Lancelot*, V, 274–9.

IO

KNIGHTS, LADIES, AND LOVE

✦✦✦

A LONGSIDE prowess, piety, and status, a fourth major element consti-
tuting the great fusion of chivalry comes from its role as a framework for
love and the relationship between the sexes. Thoughtful men and women
pondered much about love in all of its manifestations in high medieval
Europe, but we are concerned here with romantic love, *eros* rather than *agape*
or *caritas*. Many modern scholars have focused on romantic love since it is this
wonderfully complex and compelling human emotion, seen here in something
like the springtime of its life in Western culture, which interests and attracts
them.

The result has been enthusiastic and even heated scholarly debate. Since the
nineteenth century scholars have argued in particular over 'courtly love', dis-
puting whether it is simply a modern scholarly construct, or whether it had an
existence outside of literary texts; more recent scholarship has argued over
whether it brought an advance or a regression in the status of women, and
whether the question has meaning in such sweepingly general terms.[1]

The discussions have produced much interesting work, but we need not
enter the prickly thickets of controversy in order to register the power invested
in chivalry by its connections with ideas about love and, in a broader sense,
about relations between the sexes. It will serve the purposes of this book to
attempt simpler goals in this chapter: first, to show through all the evidence
presented in the sections that follow that in one of its essential dimensions
chivalry formed the frame for the important issue of gender relations; second,
to document the variety of medieval views on this subject, in the process showing that chivalric literature is—in this area as in so many—a literature of criticism and reform as much as a mirror to society; third, to establish the close link

---

[1] See the extensive bibliography in Burns and Krueger, eds, *Courtly Ideology*, 375–90, which lists
earlier bibliographies as well as selected works. A general discussion on knights, ladies, and love,
published just after the foregoing bibliography, appears in Chênerie, *Le Chevalier errant*, 411–501.
On the opening page of this section, she notes that warrior societies are usually characterized by
'l'attitude de gynopnobie'. Cf. Krueger, *Women Readers*.

between love and gender relations on the one hand, and the key chivalric virtue of prowess on the other; and, finally, to discover in a new form the continuing concern over the problem of violence as it relates to chivalry.

The Variety of Voices

Near the end of the thirteenth-century prose romance *The Story of Merlin*, Agravain, Gaheriet, and Guerrehet—three brothers, all prominent Arthurian knights—ride through a deep forest, enjoying a respite from their bloody battles with the invading Saxons. Since the weather is fine and birds are singing sweetly 'in their language', first Gaheriet and then all three brothers begin to sing, 'and the woodlands resounded with it'. The talk soon turns to the two daughters of Minoras the Forester of Northumberland with whom they have just stayed. Guerrehet asks his brothers to tell him 'if you had one of our host's two daughters with you now, what would you do with her?'

The answer of Agravain, the eldest, is straightforward: 'God help me . . . if I felt like it, I would make love to her right now.' By the same oath, Gaheriet says, 'I wouldn't do that, but I'd take her to safety.' Guerrehet answers his own question more carefully: 'I would . . . make her my lady love, if she liked, and I would not do anything to her by force. For the game of love would not be sweet unless it pleased her as much as me.'[2]

Since their father, King Lot, and their eldest brother, Gawain, have joined them in time to hear the question and their answers, the three brothers ask for a judgment. Who has spoken best? When his father assigns him the task, Gawain evaluates the answers without hesitation, recognizing Guerrehet's position as ideal, but endorsing Gaheriet's view as that of his own choosing:

Gaheriet spoke best and Agravain worst. For if Agravain saw anyone hurting the women, he ought to help them, protect and defend them with all his strength. It seems to me that there need be no one other than he! Guerrehet spoke better still, for he said that he would not have wanted to do anything to them by force, and that can have come to him only from love and courtliness. But Gaheriet spoke like a worthy gentleman, and I would do what he said if it were up to me.

Despite the smiles and laughter with which the debate has proceeded, the serious undertone soon emerges. King Lot registers his disappointed surprise by asking Agravain, 'Would you shame your host's daughter to satisfy your mad cravings?' His son's response is revealing: 'Sir . . . the daughters would lose neither life nor limb.' To his father's reply that the daughters would lose their honour, Agravain counters that to deny himself sexual pleasure, given the

---

[2] For a general discussion of this idea in medieval thought, see McCash, 'Mutual Love'.

opportunity, would be an intolerable loss to his own honour. Such a man 'would just be the butt of jokes, and people would esteem him less because of it'. When his father continues to denounce such views as vile, Agravain ends his side of the argument: 'Then there is no other way out . . . than for my brother and me to become monks in a place where we do not see women.'[3]

The range of views on knightly relationships with women could scarcely be made clearer: the scale begins with rape, with a determination to have sex whatever the woman's wishes, and moves on through protection, to mutual affection. The element of reform likewise appears prominently. Willingness to use force is denounced by two of the three debating knights and by both judging knights. Just after the passages quoted the author even alerts his readers to Agravain's deserved suffering for his attitudes to women, to be detailed later in the story. Yet we should also note that the reform position is carefully tempered; the high ideal of mutuality in love is acknowledged as best in theory, but the goal of simple protection and maintenance of the knight's own honour—by avoiding giving shame either to the woman or perhaps especially to another male protector—is stressed in Gawain's judgement and in King Lot's subsequent angry conversation with Agravain. In later romances, even Guerrehet's record is far from a perfect match with his announced standards. When a lady he has rescued resists his pleas for sex, he respects her wishes. Shortly after this he climbs into bed with a sleeping lady in a tent and enjoys sex with her, she sleepily thinking he is her husband. When this man appears, Guerrehet kills him, forces the lady to ride off with him, kills a knight who tries to stop him, and defeats the lady's four brothers. When they stop in a nunnery, she joins the order to escape him.[4]

Chivalric literature, then, does not establish a single ideological position, some uniform and elaborated code, but, rather, shows intense concern with the issue of relations between males and females. It seems impossible to press all of these views into a single ideology and attach a label such as 'courtly love' or even *fin'amors* in confidence that we have captured the essence of 'the medieval view'. The texts show us not a single view, but a running debate.[5]

Idealization of women in many chivalric texts, of course, stands as one of their significant features, generally noted and examined in great detail by scholars. Scenes of Lancelot trembling and barely able to speak or to look up when he is first in Queen Guinevere's presence, of Lancelot genuflecting at the

---

[3] Pickens, tr., *Story of Merlin*, 361–2; Sommer, ed., *Vulgate Version*, II, 350–1.
[4] Kibler, tr., *Lancelot Part V*, 120–7; Micha, ed., *Lancelot*, IV, 30–52.
[5] Interesting arguments in support of this view appear in Leclercq, 'L'amour et le mariage'; Gold, *The Lady and the Virgin*; Calin, 'Contre la *fin'amor*?'; Krueger, 'Misogyny, Manipulation'; idem, *Women Readers*; Keen, *Nobles, Knights*, 20–42.

foot of Queen Guinevere's bed as if it were an altar, before joining her in it for a night of bliss, provide unforgettable emblems of this worship.[6] Even Geoffroi de Charny, that scarred and experienced knight of the very real world, urged his readers to 'indeed honour, serve and truly love these noble ladies . . . who inspire men to great achievement, and it is thanks to such ladies that men become good knights and men-at-arms'.[7]

This point of view was not entirely theoretical. An English knight died outside Douglas Castle in Scotland, trying to live up to such a belief. His enemies found he carried a letter from his lady saying he must hold the castle a year to win her love.[8] Sir Thomas Gray tells the better-known story from this part of the world. A page whose lady-love gave him a helmet with a gilt crest, telling him to make it famous in the most dangerous part of Britain, charged headlong into the besieging Scots outside Norham Castle. After they 'struck him down, wounded him in the face, and dragged him out of the saddle to the ground', the garrison, on foot, rescued him as they had pledged to do.[9]

If love exercises great power in this literature and in this society, some writers place women on a pedestal; others spit sour misogyny. Negative views of women can be found most readily in texts with particularly strong monastic influence, *The History of the Holy Grail*, or *The Quest of the Holy Grail*, for example.[10] But the *chansons de geste* can provide an abundant supply of evidence and even the romances of Chrétien have similar passages. If women are protected, idealized, sometimes even worshipped, they may also be denounced as wily, unstable, controlled by appetite, the very impediments to real male concerns in the most timeless manner of anti-feminist diatribes. The classic case appears early in *Raoul de Cambrai*. Raoul scornfully denounces the advice of his mother when he decides on a course of action that will unleash feud between powerful families for generations:

Devil take the nobleman — what a coward he must be — who runs to a woman for advice when he ought to go off fighting! Go and loll about in bedrooms and drink drinks to fatten your belly, and think about eating and drinking, for you're not fit to meddle with anything else.[11]

[6] Rosenberg, tr., *Lancelot Part I*, 65; Elspeth Kennedy, *Lancelot do Lac*, I, 157–8; Kibler, ed., tr., Chrétien de Troyes, *Lancelot*, ll. 4583–684.

[7] Kaeuper and Kennedy, *Book of Chivalry*, 95. We might note, of course, how much his view is characteristically focused on women as the inspiration for the great virtue, prowess.

[8] McDiarmid and Stevenson, eds., *Barbour's Bruce*, bk. VIII, ll. 490–9.

[9] Maxwell, tr., *Scalacronica*, 61–2.

[10] See the 'Legend of the Tree of Life' section of *The Quest of the Holy Grail*, for example.

[11] Kay, ed., tr., *Raoul de Cambrai*, laisse LIV. As Gold notes, Raoul is showing the *demesure* that will cause so much trouble in this story. *The Lady and the Virgin*, 12–18.

Chrétien de Troyes would never give his characters such crude language, yet he can tell us that changeable women have a hundred hearts, and says of the lady Laudine:

> but she had in her the same folly
> that other women have:
> nearly all of them are obstinate
> and refuse to accept what they really want.[12]

The constant goal across the entire spectrum of views is to establish for males the right way to understand and to relate to these creatures who seem so different from themselves, standing outside the code of practising prowess in the quest for honour. Pero Niño's biographer, praising his hero's temperance, quickly slides into characterizing male/female differences: 'he said that sharp words should be left to women, whose vice and custom they were, and that men would do better to come to blows, which are their virtue and calling; but no man ever cared about coming to blows with him.'[13]

The honour involved is usually focused on the male. In the 'Tale of Balain', when Balain suddenly decapitates the lady who has come to ask a favour of the king, Arthur's response is directed to his own honour: his complaint is that Balain's act has shamed *him*, tarnished *his* honour, violated the protection offered by *his* court.[14] In the *Perlesvaus* Lancelot enforces a marriage promise on a knight who is trying to renege on his agreement; Lancelot threatens the man with death, but specifically states that he acts,

> not so much for the maiden's sake as to overcome the wickedness in you, lest it be an object of reproach to other knights; for knights must keep a vow made to a lady or a maiden and you claim to be a knight; and no knight should knowingly act wickedly. And this is a greater wickedness than most, and whatever the maiden may say I will not permit it; if you do not do as you promised, I will kill you lest it bring reproach upon chivalry.[15]

Modern scholars reading such evidence can observe not only the reform ideal of knights keeping their word to ladies, but also the clear and exclusive focus of concern on knighthood itself.

Perceval later encounters the unhappy couple, sees this knight reviling his lady, and is told he can have lodging with them if he makes no criticisms. He responds that 'since she is yours you may do as you please with her, but in all

---

[12] Kibler, ed., tr., *Yvain*, ll. 1644–8.   [13] Evans, tr., *The Unconquered Knight*, 203.

[14] Asher, tr., *Merlin Continuation*, chs 8, 10–13, 16–23; Paris and Uhlric, eds, *Merlin*, I, 212–25, 233–61, 276–80; II, 1–60 tell the story of Balain. Campbell has also translated these passages: see *Tale of Balain*. Of course, honour is focused on the leading male even when another male is killed in his presence, as Balain is when the invisible knight slays those under his protection.

[15] Bryant, tr., *Perlesvaus*, 113; Nitze and Jenkins, eds, *Perlesvaus*, 172–3.

things one should keep one's honour.' This knight, who now forces his wife to eat with the squires, away from high table, has become a leper. In a tournament Perceval wins the gold cup that is coveted by this knight and sends it to the patient, long-suffering wife, whose views on knighthood we do not learn.[16]

In *Raoul II*, Bernier, who has been presumed dead, returns to find that his wife Beatrice has—with the aid of a wondrous herb—prevented Erchambaut, the new husband forced upon her, from consummating the marriage. 'I have managed him like this for a whole year', Beatrice informs Bernier proudly. 'When Bernier hears this he gives a heartfelt sigh and says in a whisper so that no one can hear, "All honour to you Father of glory, that my wife has not brought shame on me." '[17]

Geoffroi de Charny asks rhetorically:

Which one of two ladies should have the greater joy in her lover when they are both at a feast in a great company and they are aware of each other's situation? . . . Is it the one who loves the good knight and she sees her lover come into the hall where all are at table and she sees him honoured, saluted and celebrated by all manner of people and brought to favourable attention before ladies and damsels, knights and squires, and she observes the great renown and the glory attributed to him by everyone?

The second lady has nothing, Charny thinks, because her lover lacks the essential deeds of arms:

Ah God! what small comfort and solace is there for those ladies who see their lovers held in such little honour, with no excuse except lack of will! How do such people dare to love when they do not know nor do they want to know about the worthy deeds that they should know about and ought to perform. . . .[18]

Sometimes, readers of chivalric literature will even encounter the view, implicitly or explicitly, that knights are the only humans who truly count, worth much more than any women. The Lord of the Fens says just this to Hector in the *Lancelot*, as Hector is about to fight on behalf of the man's niece: ' "She is my niece," said the lord of the Fens, "but don't do it for that reason, for God help me if I did not prefer her death to yours; more is lost in the death of one worthy knight than in the death of all the maidens in a land." '[19]

Better known, but stating the same view, is King Arthur's assessment of the loss of Guinevere compared with the loss of the Round Table fellowship of

[16] Bryant, tr., *Perlesvaus*, 258–62; Nitze and Jenkins, eds, *Perlesvaus*, 398–404.

[17] Kay, ed., tr., *Raoul de Cambrai*, laisse 304.

[18] Kaeuper and Kennedy, *Book of Chivalry*, 121.

[19] Rosenberg, tr., *Lancelot Part III*, 215; Elspeth Kennedy, ed., *Lancelot do Lac*, I, 517; Sommer, ed., *Vulgate Version*, III, 389.

knights near the end of the *Morte Darthur*: 'And much more I am soryar for my good knyghtes losse than for the losse of my fayre quene; for quenys I myght have inow, but such a felyship of good knyghtes shall never be togydirs in no company.'[20] A maiden whom Eric meets in the *Merlin Continuation* makes a similar assessment; she is carrying a badly wounded knight over whom she utters grieving words: 'Oh, noble knight, how much better it would have been if I, who am worth nothing and can do nothing, had been killed in this misadventure, rather than you, who were so worthy and valiant and true [*preux et vaillans et loyaux*].'[21] Only a few pages earlier in this same text Gaheriet, who has found his mother in bed with Lamorat, commits matricide, but spares the adulterous knight, 'because he seemed too handsome and valiant, and he was disarmed, and if he laid a hand on an unarmed knight, people would think him the worst and most cowardly knight'.[22]

Even clearer is the statement of the Grail companions (Galahad, Perceval, and Bors) who find the tombs of at least sixty maidens who died giving the basin of blood required by harsh custom to save the lady of a castle. Especially upset to find stones marking tombs of twelve daughters of kings, 'they said that the people of this castle had upheld an evil custom and that the people of the land had done great evil by enduring it so long, for many good men could have sprung from these maidens'.[23]

Many texts thus try to convince knights that women really do count, that a good knight will not abuse them and will keep his word sworn to them. *Le Bel Inconnu*, for example, recognizes that many make a habit of deceiving women and say this is no sin. The author assures his audience it is a great sin and more than once warns that those who ill-use ladies will suffer for it.[24]

Male Bonding

Some scholars have even argued that the attraction between males in important chivalric romances is more powerful than that between knight and lady.[25] Those interested in psychological analyses might well think that some form of special bond is created between knights by the common element of violence in

[20] Vinaver, ed., *Malory. Works*, 685.

[21] Asher, tr., *Merlin Continuation (end.)*, 61; Bogdanow, ed., 'Folie Lancelot', 25.

[22] Asher, ibid., 53; Bogdanow, ibid., 3. Though condemned by many others, Gaheriet's weighing of the merits of his action remains of interest. Arthur and many worthy men soon decide that they do not want Gaheriet to die for his deed since he is 'a good and worthy knight [*bon chevalier et preux*]'. Asher, ibid., 54; Bogdanow, ibid., 6.

[23] Asher, tr., 'Quest', 239; Piel, ed., *Demando*, 306–7.

[24] Fresco, ed., and Donagher, tr., *Renaut de Bâgé*, ll. 1243–64, 4927–8, 4848–50.

[25] Frappier, 'La mort Galehot'; Marcello-Nizia, 'Amour courtois'. Duby makes the same case for the biography of William Marshal: *Guillaume le Maréchal*, 52–4.

their lives, perhaps especially by their violence against each other.[26] In Marie de France's 'Milun', a father unhorsed by his son (neither recognizing his opponent) declares:

> I never once fell from my war-horse
> because of a blow from another knight.
> You knocked me down in a joust—
> I could love you a great deal.[27]

Certainly the pattern of truly savage fighting, respect, reconciliation, and great affection between two knights is repeated often enough at least to raise questions about a process of bonding that would be a powerful element in understanding the primacy of prowess in chivalry.

Chrétien provides an excellent case in point in the combat between Guivret the Short and Erec in his *Erec et Enide*.[28] When from his tower Guivret sees any passing knight he rushes into armour and into combat; to him Erec represented someone 'with whom he wished to exhaust himself in combat, / or the other would wear himself out / and declare himself defeated'. He rides full tilt at Erec, his horse's hoofs grinding pebbles like a mill working wheat and shooting so many sparks the four feet seem to be on fire. Enide's last-minute warning heard, Erec meets his challenger in a classic encounter: broken shields, hauberks ripped, spears lodged in entrails, horses and riders on the ground. Then the sword play keeps them active from mid-morning to mid-afternoon, blades biting through chain armour to vulnerable flesh. One would have killed the other, Chrétien tells us, but for an accident; Guivret's sword snaps on the rim of Erec's shield and he flings away the useless remnant in disgust. He calls for mercy, but hesitates to say he is defeated and must be threatened into the admission. As soon as they exchange names, however, Guivret is delighted to learn how noble Erec is, and '[e]ach of them kissed and embraced the other':

> Never from such a fierce battle
> was there such a sweet parting,
> for, moved by love and generosity,
> each of them cut long, broad bands
> from the tail of his shirt,
> and they bound up each other's wounds.

[26] Lorenz writes of 'the ingenious feat of transforming, by the comparatively simple means of redirection and ritualization, a behavior pattern which not only in its prototype but even in its present form is partly motivated by aggression, into a means of appeasement and further into a love ceremony which forms a strong tie between those that participate in it. This means neither more nor less than converting the mutually repelling effect of aggression into its opposite': *On Aggression*, 167. I owe this reference to Michelle Dowd.

[27] Hanning and Ferrante, trs., *Marie de France*, 174; Rychner, ed., *Marie de France*, 140.

[28] The following quotations all come from Carroll, ed., tr., *Erec*, ll. 3629–889.

Since the shirt-tail could carry phallic meaning in medieval literature, a determined Freudian might read this scene as a symbolic end of the phallic aggression so evident in the previous several hundred lines of verse, and note its
conversion into mutual respect and love. The latter phenomenon is striking,
even if one hesitates over the former.

Other cases could make a similar point. The bond between Lancelot and
Galehot in the *Lancelot do Lac*, again based on prowess, represents an unusually high peak in the mountain ranges of knightly friendships. Indeed, in this
romance the tension emerges not out of the competing claims of prowess and
love, but rather, as Corin Corley writes, 'between friendship with a companion in arms and love of a man for a woman'.[29] Gretchen Mieszkowski has even
made an argument that, at least from Galehot's perspective, this is a homo-
erotic relationship.[30]

Having seen Lancelot, in disguise, perform on the battlefield, Galehot,
Arthur, Guinevere, and Gawain discuss what each would give up 'to have his
companionship forever'.[31] Arthur would offer half his possessions. Gawain, in
turn, declares, 'If God gives me the health I desire, I should wish there and
then to be the most beautiful damsel in the world, fit and well, on condition
that he loved me more than anything, as much as I loved him.' ' "Indeed," said
Galehot, "you have offered a good deal." ' The queen skilfully sidesteps the
issue, observing, 'By the Lord, Sir Gawain has made every offer that a lady can
make, and no lady can offer more.' Following a round of polite laughter,
Gawain tells Galehot that he must answer his own question. He swears, 'As
God is my witness, I should change my great honour to shame, provided that
I could always be as sure of him as I should wish him to be of me.' Gawain
praises this answer—stunning in the context of an honour society—as the
most generous, but he later warns Arthur that Galehot will take Lancelot
away, 'for he is more jealous of him than a knight who has a beautiful young
lady'. When Arthur wants to keep Lancelot as his companion, Galehot issues
a passionate objection: 'Ah! my lord . . . I came in your hour of need with all
my might, for I could not do more. And may God never be my witness, if I
could live without him: how could you take away my life?' In order to be with
Lancelot, Galehot, a king who could have conquered Arthur, offers his own
services to Arthur as a simple retainer, 'for I would rather be poor and content',
he states, 'than rich and unhappy'. He begs Arthur to accept his offer: 'And

[29] Corley, tr., *Lancelot of the Lake*, xii.
[30] Mieszkowski, '*Lancelot's* Galehot, Malory's Lavain'; I am indebted to Professor Mieszkowski
for a copy of this article.
[31] What follows comes from Corley, tr., *Lancelot of the Lake*, 303–4; Elspeth Kennedy, ed.,
Lancelot do Lac, I, 333–4.

you certainly ought to do so, both for his sake and for mine, for you should know that all the love I have for you, I have because of him.' Arthur takes him into his entourage as companion, not as retainer, but at the end of the romance Galehot sickens, fearing Lancelot will be taken away by love for Guinevere, and dies of grief, upon hearing a false report of Lancelot's death. We learn in the *Post-Vulgate Death of Arthur* that Lancelot is finally buried, by his own instructions, in the same tomb with Galehot.[32]

The case is extreme, but the sentiment is scarcely unique. After a strenuous fight that seems to last most of the day, Gawain and Morholt (in the *Merlin Continuation*) engage in a classic act of bonding: '[T]hey went to kiss each other at once and swore to each other that from that time on they would be friends and loyal companions and that there would be no rancour between them for anything that might have been.'[33] A few days later Morholt says to Gawain, as he is about to depart, healed of his wounds: 'I never met a young man I admired as much as I do you. Don't think I say this idly. Because I love you with such great love, I want to be a knight errant from now on, so that I may better have your company and see you more often.' When their adventures part them, another scene of tears and declarations of love follows:

Morholt said to Sir Gawain, 'Sir Gawain, remember the spring at the end of a year. so that you come there on the day, for certainly I'll be very impatient to see that day and to be able to be in your company again. For know that I have never loved or admired a knight as much as I do you.[34]

Though a romance of far lower aesthetic merit, the *Chevalier du Papegau* once again supplements ideas found in greater works.[35] Arthur, the Knight of the Parrot, is attacked by a huge baron, the Knight-Giant; they fight until exhaustion and darkness force a halt (the bright, illuminating jewel on the baron's helmet having been cut away). The warriors try to get some rest leaning against each other in the dark, but each is wary and they continually give each other blows throughout the night. Daylight allows the full fighting to resume and to continue well into the day. Arthur finally lands the decisive blow which cuts off his opponent's leg.

The sequel is fascinating. The Knight-Giant calls out, 'My good lord, for God's sake, mercy! For you are surely one of the best knights in the world. For

---

[32] Asher, tr., *Death of Arthur*, 310; Magne, ed., *Demanda*, II, 484.

[33] Vinaver, ed., *Malory. Works*, 96, gives the same scene: 'And therewith they toke of her helmys and eyther kyssed other and there they swore togedyrs eythir to love other as brethirne. And sir Marhaus prayde sir Gawayne to lodge with hym that nyght.'

[34] Asher, tr., *Merlin Continuation*, 273–5; Roussineau, ed., *Merlin*, I, 378–85.

[35] For what follows, see Vesce, tr., *Knight of the Parrot*, 46–53; Heuckenkamp, ed., *Chevalier du Papegau*, 44–50.

this reason, I pray you to please take the hauberk I am wearing.' The hauberk, unusually fine, possibly even magical, must go to the man who had shown such prowess. Near death, he gives Arthur a second gift, his store of wisdom embodied in three unexceptional maxims his father had taught him. Finally, he asks a willing Arthur to hear his confession, which he makes 'and died right there on the spot'. Once again, we are shown ferocious fighting followed by rapid reconciliation and the creation of a bond (however foreshortened in this case) by the giving of the most precious gifts.

The Link with Prowess

However one reacts to issues of male bonding, so strong is the focus on knighthood and knightly prowess that in some chivalric writing women can only be defined as those who are not knights, who do not win honour through prowess. A striking case in point comes in *Raoul de Cambrai*, as Raoul is about to burn the town of Origny. A procession of nuns comes out to dissuade him, each one with her psalter in her hand, their leader, Marsent, carrying 'an ancient book held in reverence since the days of Solomon'. Clearly, we have here a confrontation of *clergie* with *chevalerie*. Yet it is also a male and female confrontation, for it is the female embodiment of *clergie* that we see. The self-characterization attributed to these women is fascinating: 'My lord Raoul, would prayer persuade you to withdraw a little? We are nuns, by the saints of Bavaria, and will never hold lance or standard, or cause anyone ever be laid to rest through force of ours.'[36] Though Marsent says they are nuns, would not the description work equally well if she said simply that they were women? The point is reinforced by repetition. Marsent speaks again to Raoul: ' "Sir Raoul," said Bernier's mother, "we are not able to handle weapons. You can easily slaughter and destroy us. I tell you truly, you will not see us wield lance or shield in our defence." '[37] The defining fact about these women is that they are non-knights. In a world in which knighthood was so significant, in a literature obsessed with knighthood, women must somehow be fitted into the general scheme of things.

Given the importance of prowess in the defence of honour, prowess the demi-god is likely to play a major role in most formulations of the ideal relationship between the sexes. Could the relationship be other than troublesome? Would not considerable tension strain lives caught between the demands of prowess and the demands of love? Many scholarly analyses have explored these tensions, noting how hard it is for major figures like Lancelot or Tristram to

---

[36] Kay, ed., tr., *Raoul de Cambrai*, laisses 63, 65.   [37] Ibid., laisses 65–6.

find a viable balance, how readily such tensions lead to tragic endings in romances.

If tension arises when the desired woman is already married to one's feudal lord (as in the case of Lancelot), it even arises after the desired woman has been won and the characteristic knightly freedom to wander and fight, to play the tournament circuit, is suddenly curtailed by the needed stability of married life. Could a life of prowess be continued by the knight who settled into married life? Chrétien wrestles with the problem in more than one of his romances. In *Erec and Enide* he states the problem concisely. After his marriage to Enide,

> Erec was so in love with her
> that he cared no more for arms,
> nor did he go to tournaments.
> He no longer cared for tourneying;
> he wanted to enjoy his wife's company,
> and he made her his lady and his mistress.[38]

Here Chrétien answers the question enthusiastically and in positive terms. Erec amply demonstrates his prowess, with Enide's active support. Yvain, in Chrétien's slightly later romance by that name, likewise proves his prowess after marriage, against Gawain's expressed doubts, and finally against Gawain in person. Married love must be saved from denigration, since it can be so important a medium for love. The significance of prowess to love, of course, remains fully evident in Chrétien's works.

Yet for many heroes of chivalry no marriage, no feudal complication intrudes; the link between love and prowess is not presented as a wrenching problem. As R. W. Hanning has concisely observed, a cycle is at work: prowess inspires love and love inspires prowess.[39] This cycle rolls through nearly all of the chivalric literature traditionally classed as romance, and appears in many *chansons* as well.[40] Scholars have understandably found the subject of romantic love more fascinating than prowess and have filled substantial library shelves with books and articles in intricate witness. But we must not forget the prowess; a two-cycle engine does not run on one cylinder.

Even the love of Guinevere for the young King Arthur begins, of course, as she sees him fighting splendidly. Merlin, ever helpful, arranges for her to kiss the shy Arthur, but then reminds Arthur of that kiss in battle, in the midst of

---

[38] Carroll, ed., tr., *Erec*, ll. 2396–401.   [39] Hanning, *The Individual*, 4, 54.

[40] There are, of course, exceptions. Gawain is at one point said to be so courteous that it causes 'many ladies to love him less for his chivalry than for his courtesy': see Krueger, tr., *Lancelot Part IV*, 108; Micha, ed., *Lancelot*, III, 409. He is also said to love poor people and to be kind and generous to them.

'a very great slaughter', resounding with 'the dreadful screams and wailing when men were being killed or wounded'. Merlin now expects the kiss to be paid for in enemy blood: 'Arthur, now we'll see what you can do here today. See to it that the kiss that your lady gave you is dearly paid for, so that it will be talked about all the days of your life.' The fighting goes on and on, and Merlin returns to his theme:

Then he said to King Arthur that he must have forgotten the kiss his ladylove had given him, for he had done poorly in the first fighting. And when Arthur heard this, he blushed all over from shame, and he hung his helmeted head and said not a word; but he stood so hard on his stirrups that the iron bent. And King Ban began to smile within his helmet and pointed him out to King Bors, his brother; then all the knights of the Round Table looked at him, and they found him very worthy and held him in high esteem because they saw his look of noble pride.[41]

Fuelled by the potent mixture of equal parts sensual excitement and aroused pride, Arthur returns to the fight and performs prodigies of prowess.[42] He will do similar feats on another battlefield later, while he is being watched by a lover, the pagan maiden of Saxon Rock. 'In fact,' we learn, 'he did . . . better than ever before, and this was more for the maiden who was watching him from the Rock than for himself.'[43]

If love inspires prowess, prowess inspires love. Guinevere has enjoyed a tryst with Lancelot while Arthur dallied with his Saxon lady. This text, however, will not accept sauce for the goose serving as sauce for the gander. She is later denounced by the all-wise Master Elias as standing 'accused of the basest wrongdoing that a woman can be charged with . . . for she was so untrue as to dishonour the most honourable man in the world'. No mention is made of Arthur's dishonouring of his queen.[44]

She defends herself later by saying that her love, stirred by Lancelot's prowess, was simply irresistible: 'But the power of the love that led me to do it was so great that I could not resist it; and besides, what was calling me was the valour [*la proesce*] of the finest of knights.' Her self-defence is the same when speaking later to Lancelot himself; she ends with a fascinating rhetorical question, puzzling over the ragged border where the world of *chevalerie* marches with that of *clergie*:

---

[41] Pickens, tr., *Story of Merlin*, 288, 292; Sommer, ed. *Vulgate Version*, II, 220, 227–8.

[42] The same combination moves the young Erec; see Carroll, ed., tr., *Erec*, ll. 911–94.

[43] Carroll, tr., *Lancelot Part II*, 226; Elspeth Kennedy, ed., *Lancelot do Lac*, I, 542; Sommer, *Vulgate Version*, III, 407.

[44] Rosenberg, tr., *Lancelot Part III*, 254; Micha, ed., *Lancelot*, I, 58. Arthur later collapses and confesses to a hermit, in fear of death. He is told how evil he is for, among other sins, disloyally deserting his lawful wife; but this woman is the False Guinevere. Carroll, *Lancelot Part II*, 276; Sommer, *Vulgate Version*, IV, 76.

. . . I have been hurt by the sin of going to bed with a man other than my husband.

. . . Still, there is no upstanding lady in the world who would not feel impelled to sacrifice something to make an upstanding knight like you happy. Too bad Our Lord pays no heed to our courtly ways, and a person whom the world sees as good is wicked to God.[45]

They return to this troubling subject in the *Lancelot*, when Guinevere realizes that a vision of the future experienced by Gawain refers to Lancelot's failure to achieve the Grail because of their illicit love:

I am very distressed that the flames of passion have caused you to fail to achieve the adventure for which all earthly knighthood must strive; you can rightly say that you have paid dearly for my love, since on my account you have lost something you can never recover. Understand that I am no less sad about this than you, and perhaps even sadder, for it is a great sin in that God made you the best and most handsome and most gracious of all knights. . . . It seems it would have been better for me never to have been born.

The lament is powerful: God is the source of prowess and their adulterous love has spoiled the fruits of Lancelot's knighthood. But he will have none of it:

'My lady,' said Lancelot, 'what you say is wrong. You must understand that without you I would not have achieved as much glory as I have. . . . For I was well aware that if my valor did not bring me through the adventures, then I would never be able to win you, and I had to win you or die.'

This is not simply a classic statement of the link between love and prowess, for Lancelot is countering the queen's assertion that God is the source of his deeds with the statement that she is herself that source. He could have noted that the queen not only inspired prowess, but sometimes specifically demanded it. As she says to Lancelot before a great tournament at Camelot: 'see to it that you do so well on that day that there is not a knight who dares await your blow. Pursue them until they flee for their lives back to Camelot, and don't be weak or scared, for if I thought that my love sapped your strength, then I would never love you again.'[46]

Other texts simply state outright that the knight's prowess is the great spur to a woman's love; the link seems obvious and independent of any moral qualms. In a classic statement, a lady tells Hector that though she has not seen Lancelot since he was two months old, she has 'loved him more than anyone

---

[45] Rosenberg, tr., *Lancelot Part III*, 267, 275; Micha, ed., *Lancelot*, I, 118, 152; Sommer, ed., *Vulgate Version*, IV, 28, 53–4.

[46] Kibler, tr., *Lancelot Part V*, 207, 202; Sommer, *Vulgate Version*, V, 193; Micha, *Lancelot*, IV, 380.

in the world, because of the great prowess they've described to me'.[47] Beatrice, in the continuation of *Raoul de Cambrai* known as *Raoul II*, explains her sudden love for Bernier in an even more revealing monologue:

Then she whispered so no one could hear: 'Lucky the lady whom this man were to choose, for he has a tremendous reputation for knighthood [*molt a los de grant chevalerie*]; anyone who could hold him naked beneath her bed hangings would find him worth more than any living thing.'[48]

She tells Bernier frankly about her feelings, and is even more explicit about the causative force his prowess represents:

'My lord Bernier,' said the wise lady, 'if I love you, I ought not to be blamed for it, for your reputation stood so high that when my father was in his flagged hall, everyone used to say within his trusted household that whoever you struck with your smooth lance could not remain in his gilded saddle. I was filled with desire for you; I would rather be burned or cut limb from limb than be married to anyone else.'[49]

Claudas, one of the major and most fascinating characters in the early chapters of the *Lancelot do Lac* and the *Lancelot*, will have none of this linking of men and women, prowess and love in his own life. Yet his very denial speaks to the force of the bond. He has, we learn, been in love only once and ended it deliberately. When asked why, 'he would answer that his desire was to have a long life'. As he saw matters:

a knight who has true love in his heart can desire only one thing: to surpass everyone else; but no man, however valiant, has a body that can survive all the trials his heart is rash enough to undertake . . . for there is no great achievement at arms without true love behind it.

We are assured that Claudas spoke truthfully, 'for when in love he had shown remarkable prowess and in many a land had gained great renown for his knightly valor'.[50] Though Claudas is not a devotee of love, even his reasons for avoiding it speak to its power and to its link with prowess.

Sometimes the admiration for prowess simply overwhelms ideas of love altogether. Morholt, in the *Merlin Continuation*, is a notorious hater of ladies. On their adventures Yvain and Gawain even come upon a group of ladies executing a dance in which the key manoeuvre is spitting on Morholt's shield. Gawain quickly distances himself from a knight who 'hates the maidens of this

---

[47] Krueger, tr., *Lancelot Part IV*, Micha, ed., *Lancelot*, II, 399–400: 'por la grant proesce qe l'en m'avoit dite de lui'.

[48] Kay, ed., tr., *Raoul de Cambrai*, 332–3.   [49] Ibid., 340–1.

[50] Rosenberg, tr., *Lancelot Part I*, 15; Sommer, ed., *Vulgate Version*, III, 26–7; Elspeth Kennedy, ed., *Lancelot do Lac*, 30–1.

country so mortally that he does them all the dishonour and insult he can.' He adds: 'I couldn't love Morholt for anything, because he hates young ladies with all his heart.' Yet Gawain's evaluation changes significantly as he sees Morholt's vast prowess demonstrated against Yvain, and then as he experiences it himself in classic combat. With the triumph over Yvain achieved before his eyes, Gawain exudes these fulsome words of praise: 'Oh, God! what greatness there is in a valiant man! God, how powerful this man is; how effective he is, and how much he can do!' After he has fought with him personally, Gawain is happy to exchange kisses, pledges of mutual friendship, agreements never to be parted except by death.[51]

More often and more famously, ideas about ladies and about prowess work in harness. The lesson is taught over and over in chivalric literature: knights must use their prowess in the defence of gentle ladies. In the start of his knightly career, narrated in the *Merlin Continuation*, for example, Gawain himself must absorb the painful lesson by carrying to court, slung over his horse, the body of a lady he has slain, there to have his penance adjudged by the ladies of the court. They announce that he must swear on relics that, saving his death or dishonour, he will never harm maidens but will always protect them when they request his help. Gawain becomes ever after the loyal Knight of Maidens. The entire process at court, we might note, is carried out under the aegis of Arthur's authority, regal and male.[52]

Of course, in one work after another Lancelot's entire career provides the classic tribute to the power of love realized in prowess. In the terrible test of Escalon the Dark, in the *Lancelot* (to note one case out of scores) he piously calls upon God and the Virgin, but then, 'looking as directly toward London as he could and mindful of the woman whom he loved more than himself, he said, "My lady, I entrust myself to you; and whatever peril I face, may I always bear you in mind!" '[53] No reader can be surprised that he triumphs where others have failed. The source for his successes has been made especially clear, as Elspeth Kennedy has noted, by the messenger sent to him by his patroness, the Lady of the Lake, at the time his magnificent career is only just getting under way. The message is:

[Y]ou should give your heart to a love that will turn you not into an idle knight but a finer one, for a heart that becomes idle through love loses its daring and therefore can-

---

[51] Asher, tr., *Merlin Continuation*, 270–4; Roussineau, ed., *Merlin*, II, 370–85.

[52] Asher, *Merlin Continuation*, 230–3; Roussineau, *Merlin*, I, 225–38. This portion of this text is much concerned with founding incidents in the history of chivalry; at this same time Gawain learns that it is courteous not to kill a knight who has yielded.

[53] Rosenberg, tr., *Lancelot Part III*, 302; Sommer, ed., *Vulgate Version*, IV, 110–11.

not attain high things. But he who always strives to better himself and dares to be challenged can attain all high things.[54]

The pattern shown time and again in chivalric literature—love stirring a knight on to deeds of arms—need not entail as elevated a view as this. In *The Story of Merlin*, Gaheriet reminds his brother Agravain of his hot desire for the daughters of the Forester of Northumberland (the maidens who had sparked their debate noted above). As they go into battle, he says: 'Keep in mind those maidens you knew so well what to do with this morning and see to it that you are as good a knight with your arms when you fight against those Saxons!'[55] The mental—perhaps the glandular—link of sex and violence is here writ large.[56]

Sexual Violence

The prevalence of prescriptive as well as descriptive statements and an emphasis on prowess help to connect chivalry as a focus of gender relations to chivalry in its other dimensions. What, then, of the concern about violence which we have found so inescapable a feature of these other dimensions of chivalry? Does this concern likewise appear when medieval writers use chivalry to talk of love and relationships between men and women?

As a number of scholars—Kathryn Gravdal in particular—have argued, the sexual violence of rape was a serious issue in medieval society, particularly from the twelfth century. The topic was regularly discussed by medieval jurists and canonists and by authors of the entire range of literary works that involved knights as characters (that is, saints' lives and pastorals as well as more traditional chivalric forms).[57] Sexual violence, in other words, fits into a broader pattern of concern over societal peace.

That women themselves should be concerned about forced sex seems to require little discussion. Yet Gravdal argues that the issue was in fact discussed

---

[54] Rosenberg, tr., *Lancelot Part I*, 84; Sommer, ed., *Vulgate Version*, III, 160–61; Elspeth Kennedy, ed., *Lancelot do Lac*, 205–6.

[55] Pickens, tr., *Story of Merlin*, 362; Sommer, *Vulgate Version*, II, 352.

[56] Any reader will encounter many examples. In the *Song of Aspremont*, for example, the young Roland calls out to the companions he leads onto the battlefield:

> 'Let your aggression loose henceforth, my barons!
> Let each lay claim to knighthood by his valor!'
>
> . . .
>
> He cries 'Mountjoy! Lay on, lusty companions,
> And Charles will give each man a girl to marry!'

Newth, tr., *Song of Aspremont*; Brandin, ed., *Chanson d'Aspremont*, ll. 5558–9, 5572–3.

[57] Gravdal, *Ravishing Maidens*; Robertson, 'Comprehending Rape'; Hawkes, 'Bibliography of Legal Records'. I am grateful to Roberta Krueger for providing these sources.

in medieval literature and law from the point of view of males, that sexual violence was a problem in this society because they saw it as a problem. We might, building on her argument, suggest that the issues involving rape which so engaged male attention were closely linked with the prowess and honour so much at the heart of chivalry. Even when idealized or adored, women seem to have been considered property in much chivalric literature, prizes to be won by knightly prowess or to be defended against the prowess of others.[58] The chronicle of Richard the Lion-Heart says plainly that in the attack on Messina 'there were women taken, fair / And excellent and debonair'. When some of the king's ships have wrecked on the coast of Cyprus and Richard's sister is endangered he, of course, rushes to the defence.[59]

Honour is the real prize, as Agravain, quoted at the opening of this chapter, understood. Geoffroi de Charny also understood, even though he strongly disagreed; he complained, in effect, that many followed Agravain's view:

And there are many who say that they would not want to love Queen Guinevere if they did not declare it openly or if it were not known. Such men would prefer it to be said by everyone that they were the accepted lovers of ladies, even if this were not true, than to love and meet with a favourable response, were this to be kept secret.[60]

This game of males winning renown by fighting over prized ladies is surely as old as the story of the *Iliad*, and as widespread as the furthest reaches of anthropological field study.

The game is played endlessly in chivalric literature, reinforcing on each round the reformist ideal that it is the duty and right of knights to protect ladies. In theory, in the world of Arthurian romance, every maiden or lady is protected within Arthur's realm. In *The Story of Merlin*, Gawain, seeing two knights preparing to rape a young lady, shouts at them, 'that they were already dead, because they were assaulting a lady in King Arthur's land. "For you know very well," he went on, "that ladies are guaranteed their safety." '[61] In the practice presented in literature, every maiden or lady might be considered at risk in this forested Hobbesian world. Sometimes the threat comes from robbers or assorted ruffians who would not make the social register; more often the threat comes (as it does in this case) in armour, from unreformed knights.

---

[58] Vesce, tr., *Marvels of Rigomer*, 103; Foerster, ed., *Mervelles de Rigomer*, ll. 4581–6, casually mentions that a maiden whom Lancelot has saved from rape is pregnant with her deliverer's child after he stayed in her household for a week.

[59] Hubert and La Monte, tr., *Crusade of Richard Lion-Heart* and Paris, ed., *L'Histoire de la guerre sainte*, ll. 819–20, 1435 ff.

[60] Kaeuper and Kennedy, *Book of Chivalry*, 119.

[61] Gawain has been reduced to the physical size of a dwarf because of his discourtesy to a lady. His prowess is undiminished, of course, and his rescue in this case restores him. Pickens, tr., *Story of Merlin*, 422–3; Sommer, ed., *Vulgate Version*, II, 462.

In this same text, Hector must defeat Marigart the Red, a knight of great prowess, who rapes a virgin a month.[62] Perceval and his sister, setting off to visit their mother's grave, in the first continuation of Chrétien's *Perceval*, find that 'even though they were in their own land, they were not, it seems, free and clear of war. Perceval glanced to one side and saw an armed knight come riding.' The challenging knight wants Perceval's sister and can be dissuaded only by being beaten in combat. When Perceval and his sister set off together to continue his grail quest, later in this romance, the same sort of attack recurs, for the same motive.[63]

The threat of knights is so often portrayed as a specifically sexual threat. In Chrétien's *Erec and Enide*, the heroine must, as a test, ride through the forest ahead of her lord, fetchingly attired, to attract the knights who want to 'win' her by defeating Erec. When the Lord of the Fens learns (in *The Story of Merlin*) that his young daughter cannot marry his powerful neighbour Leriador because she is already pregnant by King Ban, he is confronted by an irate Leriador, who

swore that, since he could not have the lady by love, he would take her by force; and after him, all others who wanted her could have her. So this is how he left, and he went into his country and called his men together until there were a good eight hundred knights.[64]

In the *Lancelot*, a maiden who wants to accompany Hector on a quest is told she is foolish, ' "for if it happened," said the queen, "that another knight defeated Hector, he would take you and do with you as he wished." '[65] In Chrétien's *Lancelot*, this possibility is even formulated as a custom:

The custom and policy at that time were as follows: any knight meeting a damsel who is alone should slit his own throat rather than fail to treat her honourably, if he cares about his reputation. For if he takes her by force, he will be shamed forever in all the courts of all lands. But if she is led by another, and if some knight desires her, is willing to take up his weapons and fight for her in battle, and conquers her, he can without shame or blame do with her as he will.[66]

In some corners of the world of Arthurian literature even the first part of this custom is not observed. Sagremore rapes a beautiful and noble maiden who

[62] Krueger, tr., *Lancelot Part IV*, 103–4; Micha, ed., *Lancelot*, II, 393–5.
[63] Bryant, tr., *Perceval*, 151, 214; Roach, ed., *Continuations*, IV, ll. 23770–809. Perceval's lance skewers the man, two feet of it protruding on the other side of his body.
[64] Pickens, tr., *Story of Merlin*, 413; Sommer, ed., *Vulgate Version*, II, 446.
[65] Carroll, tr., *Lancelot Part II*, 169; Sommer, *Vulgate Version*, III, 307.
[66] Quoting Gravdal's translation, *Ravishing Maidens*, 66. The *Lancelot Part IV* likewise states that an unaccompanied lady could travel unmolested, but if she had an escorting knight, 'and another knight can win her in battle, the winner can take the lady or maiden in any way he desires without incurring shame or blame': Krueger, *Lancelot Part IV*, 10; Micha, *Lancelot*, II, 24.

fails to greet him courteously in *The Marvels of Rigomer*; he leaves her the bag of coins he carries for charitable gifts; he also leaves her pregnant.[67] Of course women of no status are simply targets outside the debate. King Pellinor fathered Tor on 'a shepherdess, whom the king found in a field watching her beasts, but her beauty was so great that the king took a fancy to her, and lay by her and fathered Tor'.[68]

Even ladies of position might be troubled. Guinevere's father, King Leodagan, seeing his chance to have his seneschal's wife, crawls into bed with the fearful lady:

and he told her to keep quiet; if she shouted a single word, he would kill her with his sharp sword, or if she thrashed about in the least. The lady defended herself with words as much as she could, but she did not dare speak out loud, so her arguments availed her very little.[69]

Round Table knights swore to do no rape. Malory's *Morte Darthur* gives the famous oath knights of the Round Table must swear each year; it includes a clause never to 'enforce' any 'ladyes, damesels, and jantilwomen and wydowes'.[70] The sentiment is as noble as the evident need for its regular swearing is instructive. Even Round Table knights appear in chivalric literature in the very role they formally renounce. In the *Merlin Continuation*, for example, Perceval must stop the combat of Sagremore and the Ugly Hero, fighting over who shall have a desirable maiden. Freed and offered Perceval's protection, the maiden declines: 'I've no need of an escort, for I won't meet anyone in these parts who will make any demands on me, since I'm safe from these two.'[71]

Even King Arthur is a rapist in the Post-Vulgate *Quest for the Holy Grail*. Lost while hunting, he comes upon a beautiful maiden and 'was so pleased with her that he lay with her by force. She was a young girl and still knew nothing of such matters, and she began to cry out while he was lying with her, but

---

[67] Vesce, tr., *Marvels of Rigomer*, 169–73; Foerster, ed., *Mervelles de Rigomer*, ll. 7759–982. Though the author terms the rape 'grant folie', (noting that the son engendered will take vengeance on Sagremore), he pauses to admire the beauty of Sagremore's body and arms as he rides away, and pictures the lady thinking so handsome a man must surely be of high status; none of the locals is as handsome as he. Casual sex is the reward of the heroes of this text; see, e.g., Vesce, ibid., 25, 103; Foerster, ibid., ll. 1056–68, 4581–6.

[68] Asher, tr., *Merlin Continuation*, 238; Paris and Ulrich, eds., *Merlin*, II, 114–15.

[69] Pickens, tr., *Story of Merlin*, 248; Sommer, ed., *Vulgate Version*, II, 148–9. A little later, this same text (Pickens, ibid., 257; Sommer, ibid., 165) presents Yvain the Bastard, son of King Urien who kept his seneschal's wife in his castle, by force, for five years.

[70] Vinaver, ed., *Malory. Works*, 75. Cf. Kibler, tr., *Lancelot Part V*, 208; Micha, ed., *Lancelot*, V, 7.

[71] Asher, tr., *Merlin Continuation (end)*, 108–9; Bogdanow, ed., 'Folie Lancelot', 150–511: Perceval tellingly lectures the other Round Table knights on the ideal: 'A knight who is courteous should never think of taking a maiden away by force, for truly it's the most ignoble thing a valiant man can do, to lay a hand on a maiden against her will.'

it did her no good, for the king did what he wanted anyway.'[72] Under threat of decapitation by her father, the weeping maid tells all. Her wrathful father charges Arthur with dishonouring him; yet he well knows he cannot take standard revenge against his sovereign so he merely rejects the king's offer of a rich marriage and keeps his daughter under watch, to see if she has been impregnated by Arthur. Yet the knight's show of outrage is quickly compromised, for he soon rapes his own daughter-in-law, kills his son, and kills his daughter as well, when she protests his actions.[73]

Sometimes the ladies are only too happy to give their bodies to the knights.[74] Not a few times a desirable lady offers herself as the prize to be awarded the winner of a much-advertised tournament or some *pas d'armes*. But the general attitude seems to be that valiant knights should not be denied, whatever the lady's personal inclinations. Watching Sagremore fight in a rough tournament, the ladies in the window of the great hall state this creed: 'he is a handsome knight in body and limb, he is yet a better knight in spirit. And she who has him can well boast that she has one of the best knights in the court; likewise, she would be uncourtly and unwise who refused the love of such a knight.'[75] For the truly reluctant women in chivalric literature, unless Merlin is conveniently at hand to cast a spell dissolving resistance,[76] the threat of sexual violence looms large. It seems more than symbolic that the verb *esforcer* is used in this literature, even within the same literary work, both in the military sense of 'to strive, to make a great effort', and in the sense of 'to rape'.[77]

This is no argument, obviously, that most knights were rapists.[78] Yet is it not likewise unlikely that knights simply protected ladies who were endlessly grateful? to imagine that this medieval world was (unlike all other worlds of which we have any knowledge) blissfully happy and without conflict in the arena of relations between the sexes? Surely we might guess that in life as in lit-

---

[72] Asher, tr., *Quest*, 215; Bogdanow, ed., *Version Post-Vulgate*, 473. For Mordred's desire to rape a passing maid, and the disastrous consequences, see Asher, ibid., 192–4; Bogdanow, ibid., 370–6.

[73] Arthur the Less has already been born from Arthur's sexual union with this maid.

[74] E.g. the lady who yields to the urgings of Girflet, or the daughter of the King of North Wales, who says, when Gawain finally manages to get into her bed, 'now I have what I have always desired': Carroll, tr., *Lancelot*, 202, 212; Sommer, ed., *Vulgate Version*, III, 365–6; Elspeth Kennedy, ed., *Lancelot do Lac*, 485, 509.

[75] Pickens, tr., *Story of Merlin*, 347; Sommer, *Vulgate Version*, II, 324.

[76] As he was, famously, in the sexual union of Uther Pendragon and Ygraine, which produces Arthur (Pickens, *Story of Merlin*, 204; Sommer, *Vulgate Version*, II, 67–8) and, less famously, in the union of Arthur and Lisanor, which produces Loholt (Pickens, ibid., 235; Sommer, ibid., 124).

[77] Tobler and Lommatzsch, *Altfranzösisches Wörterbuch*, 3: ll. 1045–6.

[78] It would even be difficult to establish any exact sense of the incidence of rape in society generally, let alone that committed by knights, even in England, with its miles of surviving court rolls. As Hanawalt asks rhetorically, 'Who can say how many masters raped servants or lords raped peasant women?' *Crime and Conflict*, 106.

erature knights played more complex and more ambiguous roles, that troubling problems cried out for solutions as a warrior aristocracy fitted itself into a framework of social and public order; if this order was largely acceptable and somewhat of their own making, sometimes it crimped a bit. Their literature stands in clear witness to such problems and to the ideal solutions that were eagerly put forward for the knights' education and edification.[79]

We can, in short, recognize in such ideals new attempts to fit the relationships between males and females—at least those who ranked within the privileged, lay, social strata—into the knightly frame of life based especially on prowess and honour. The point of view was congenial to most males in this privileged group, though they must have been aware of an undercurrent of reform ideas aimed at modifying aspects of their behaviour.

Thus we can recognize that this literature not only heaped upon chivalry a great measure of idealized responsibility for the protection of women and for the elimination of the most coarse and brutal forms of subjection; it also endowed knights with an even greater valorization of their powerful place in society in general, and especially with regard to women. These works offered the knights a more refined form of male dominance as one powerful element of their chivalry. Knighthood was here, as always, both challenged and buttressed by reform ideas.

---

[79] Examples are plentiful in Middle English literature, no less than in the Old French texts largely cited above. See Gist, *Love and War*, 75–84, 111.

II

CHANSON DE GESTE AND REFORM

✦✦✦

MEDIEVAL France was the veritable home of chivalry and the birth-place of the *chanson de geste*, a body of texts especially concerned with emerging institutions of governance.[1] How this literature portrayed the relationship of chivalry to Capetian royalty and to the reformed Church is thus worth a close look.[2]

To sample this vast body of literature we can turn to a well-known division suggested in a thirteenth-century poem.[3] The entire corpus of *chansons*, this text suggests, can be divided into three broad cycles, today generally known as the Cycle of the King, the Cycle of William of Orange (or of Garin de Monglane, his ancestor), and the Cycle of the Barons in Revolt.[4] We will look briefly at one example from each.

Though written in the twelfth century, each is set in the Carolingian era, the monarch in each case being Charlemagne or his son Louis. Scholars have long recognized that these twelfth-century poems reflect society and issues of their time of composition, not those of the eighth- or ninth-century setting in which the action takes place.[5]

---

[1] See Chapter 2, footnote 3.

[2] See Kay, *Chansons de Geste*; Calin, *Old French Epic*; Kaeuper, *War, Justice, and Public Order*, 315–25, and sources cited there; Flori, 'L'Historien'; Boutet, 'Chansons de geste'; Boutet and Strubel, *Littérature, politique et société*, 39–68; Rossi, 'Le duel judiciaire'; Hackett, 'Girart de Roussillon'.

[3] As Rossi notes, in research on the role of kingship, family quarrels, and private wars, 'le corpus français des chansons de geste [est] en définitive peu exploité': *Essor et fortune*, I, 264.

[4] Yeandle, ed., *Girard de Viane*, ll. 11–80.

[5] Writing of the *Couronnement de Louis*, Frappier notes that 'La cérémonie dans la chapelle d'Aix évoke le sacre de Louis VII à Reims en 1131 autant ou plus que l'événement de 813': *Chansons de geste*, II, 141. He suggests (p. 158) that the text creates a double reference, uniting the Capetian present with memories of the Carolingian past. As Rossi says, 'les personnages carolingiens et tout un arsenal de stéréotypes narratifs sont utilisés pour narrer des événements pseudo-historiques qui, en fait, renvoient à la réalité et aux problèmes du royaume capétien des XIIe et XIIIe siècles': *Essor et fortune*, I, 264.

The Song of Aspremont

The *Song of Aspremont* (*Chanson d'Aspremont*), an anonymous poem from the Cycle of the King, probably written late in the twelfth century,[6] tells the story of an imagined pagan invasion of Italy in the time of Charlemagne. These invaders are overcome only after horrific battles won by the Christian host under Charlemagne, aided by Duke Girart of Burgundy.

The author constantly buttresses the justification, even the sacralization, of the knightly role. In his mind, only one standard measures human conduct and achievement. The young Roland and his friends, for example, embody the noble urge to demonstrate their prowess on the battlefield. Though only boys, they nearly kill the man set to keep them safely away from the combat, soundly beat another set of men in order to obtain the warhorses they need, and cause appreciative laughter when their tale is heard by seasoned warriors.[7]

Even the clerics, specialists in mediatory piety though they may be, must show as much participation in chivalry as is possible, if they are truly to rank in the author's estimation. Archbishop Turpin, we learn, is not only a well-bred man, and a dispenser of largesse, he also personally commands a large host. He boasts proudly of being both a priest and a knight, and shows his knightly qualities in the most accepted manner on the battlefield. When Pope Milon wants a man to carry a piece of the true cross into battle, and encounters refusals from two knights who think they serve better with hands free to use their own knightly weapons, Turpin accepts the mission—on condition that the pope bless his dual role.[8] So much for Gregorianism.[9]

The pope himself leads a large contingent of knights in Charlemagne's host, sermonizes all in that host to fight mightily as penance for their sins, and promises absolution without confession. In the crisis of the fight he pledges his own willingness to die alongside the knights.[10]

The sacralization of knighthood, however, works most clearly because of their role as proto-crusaders; through the hard strokes the knights give and receive in action against the pagan foe, they merit the welcome that God prepares for them in paradise. Adroitly avoiding the anachronism of crusaders before there were crusades, the author pictures his Christian warriors placing

---

[6] Unless otherwise stated, all quotations in this section are from Newth, ed., tr., *Song of Aspremont*; Brandin, ed., *Chanson d'Aspremont*.

[7] Laisse 77.

[8] Laisses 420–3. Turpin later gives up the relic to use his own arms.

[9] See Noble, 'Anti-Clericalism'. He notes, p. 149, that 'In these poems the clergy are of little importance, particularly as an organized force. The church seems to have little authority as such, although individual churchmen may be able to exercise some influence.'

[10] Ll. 1614, 1700, 4271–311.

red crosses on their hauberks, ostensibly so that they can recognize each other in the confusion of combat.[11]

The clerics cannot praise the knights too highly or give to them too generously from their spiritual treasury or from ecclesiastical coffers. As the Archbishop tells the Pope,

> It is our duty to cherish all brave knights;
> For when we clerics sit down to eat at night,
> Or in God's service sing matins at first light,
> These men are fighting for our lands with their lives;
> So Abbot Fromer here and you and I
> Should empty all our coffers for their supplies;
> Each one of us should give so much alike
> They'll honor us and serve us all the time.[12]

The pope is in full agreement. He pours forth assurances that the knights' hard service merits paradise, and guarantees the truth of his assertion with his own hope of salvation:

> Brave Christian knights, God keep you in his strength!
> Well might you say that you are lucky men,
> That in your lifetime you can your faith defend;
> You who are born in sin and wickedness,
> For which you all are damned and your souls dead,
> By striking blows with blades of steel unchecked
> Your sins will be absolved and your souls blessed;
> There is no doubt of this—you have my pledge;
> Rise up at once sweet Jesus to avenge!
> You will be saved—or may I go to Hell![13]

Some variant of this speech encourages the warriors time and again, whether from the sermons and speeches of the pope on the battlefield,[14] or from the lay leaders, Charlemagne[15] and Girart.[16] The ghostly presence of famous military saints on the battlefield drives the point home.[17] Those who have already earned paradise with their swords join in the work of those still fighting the good fight.

The knights accept the explicit exchange stated outright more than once: Christ died for them; they must be willing to die for him.[18] They know the reward. Richer, a knight asked to take a message seeking Charlemagne's help,

---

[11] See especially laisses 213, 236, 244, 288.
[13] Laisse 46.
[15] E.g. laisse 244.
[17] Laisse 425.

[12] Laisse 5.
[14] E.g. laisses 244, 288, 455.
[16] E.g. laisses 213, 276.
[18] See, for example, ll. 9380-1.

refuses. To leave the fighting, he objects, would be 'to lose my soul for my body's protection'.[19]

Wearing the crusading cross, then, the knights can apparently do no wrong. Yet the author knows the realities of the knightly life as lived day by day at home. Negative tones intrude insistently and discordantly into his hymning of 'Onward Christian Soldiers'.

Girart provides much of the negative evidence in his attitudes and actions. At first, he plans to attack France while Charlemagne is warring with the pagans. His wife thinks he should rather do penance with his sword and aid the great king.[20] Her view of his motivation, acquired in long years of married observation, is telling:

> You never were happy or felt any real mirth
> If you weren't killing people or causing hurt;
> . . .
>
> A century back you took me for your wife
> And each day since you've spent committing crimes;
> You've robbed and burned and plundered all the time.[21]

Though he accepts his wife's advice to aid in the holy war, his own view of the common, everyday fighting at home remains positive; it is just business as usual, he says in a later speech to his men:

> If my neighbour starts a quarrel with me,
> With fire burns my land to cinders;
> And I, his, on all sides;
> If he steals my castles or keeps,
> Then so it goes until we come to terms,
> Or he puts me or I put him in prison.[22]

Girart never denies clerics their essential function, despite all their trouble-some strictures. He simply thumbs his nose at the high claims of Gregorianism and lives in the old mental world of lay domination.

Sometimes his opposition is a bit more active, as when he tries to knife Archbishop Turpin who has been sent, early in the story, to enlist his help in the coming campaign. Turpin, no slouch at action with blades himself, avoids the blow skilfully and warns Girart that Charlemagne will take vengeance and that the pope will place all Burgundy under interdict. The duke's reply is a clas-

---

[19] 'Se je pert l'ame por le cors espargnier': l. 3949.   [20] Laisse 81
[21] Ll. 1478–80, 1483–5. Kay, *Chansons de Geste*, 46–8, 60–76, notes the role of women especially in speaking a 'counternarrative' against some dominant ideals in the text.
[22] Ll. 5012–17; my translation.

sic speech of lay independence: anti-Gregorianism combined with feudal defiance of kingship:

> Now if my memory's clear,
> There are three thrones chosen and set apart:
> One is called Constantinople,
> Rome is another, and this city makes three—
> The fourth is Toulouse which is part of my heritage;
> Across my own realm I have my own priests;
> Never for baptisms or any Christian service
> do we need the pope's authority;
> I'll make a Pope myself, should I so please!
> In all my possessions whatsoever
> I hold not the value of one shelled egg
> from any earthly man, but from the Lord God alone.
> Your king will never be loved by me
> Unless he is kneeling down at my feet![23]

Although Turpin and Girart easily agree that all power comes from God, the archbishop quickly stresses a different conception of the hierarchical mediation of that power. In what we might safely take as the theme of reform in this text, Turpin announces to Girart an inescapable fact: 'You won't be without a lord for long.' The importance of the announcement is underscored by Girart's reaction; 'full of hate', he threatens to break the archbishop's neck if he does not flee at once.[24]

In the programme of this text, then, a primary valorization of knightly violence as idealized warfare against the enemies of the faith is in some measure balanced by a message that urges restraint and a need for subjection to more than local authority. The authority steadily praised is an ideal kingship, sanctified (though not controlled) by ecclesiastics.

The point is clearly made in Girart's first meeting with Charlemagne. The duke realizes at once that the great king really is deserving of his loyalty and respect; *royauté* and *chevalerie* meet in amity. As they converse, Turpin, here representing the world of *clergie*, in need of knightly services, skilfully records the scene with black ink on white parchment—while on horseback, no less.[25]

Several speeches on good kingship which appear later in the text seem designed as much to advertise the merits of sound rule to the knightly audience as to sermonize kings about their duties. Greeting Girart 'in love and in faith', Charlemagne asks him why he is not a king. Girart answers that he had

---

[23] Ll. 1164–77; my translation.
[24] For Turpin's warning, see ll. 1187–8; for Girart's reaction, ll. 1189–94; my translations.
[25] Laisses 230–5.

not the worth nor the power ('*ne val tant ne n'en ai le pouoir*'), and then delivers a classic speech on good kingship:

> The type of man who seeks a crown on earth,
> Should look to God and in his faith be firm;
> He should both honour and serve the Holy Church;
> He should cast out bad laws and break their curse,
> And champion good ones, and try to make them work;
> He should help orphans and feed them from his purse,
> Look after widows and their safety preserve.
> The wicked man he should try to convert,
> But none the less destroy if he grows worse;
> He should keep by his side men of good birth,
> For from their counsel he may find out and learn
> The way to govern his own soul and self first;
> To promise little and give much in return
> Will move the heart of everyone he serves;
> A wicked man who seeks his fellows' hurt,
> He who would try to steal another's serf,
> Who would rob churches, then violate and burn,
> Oppress the poor and tread them in the dirt,
> That sort of man should not for kingship yearn.

Once again, such sentiments are quickly covered with the highest ecclesiastical blessing: 'The Pontiff speaks: "You deserve to be heard; / He who seeks wisdom may find it in your words;" '[26] Girart seems to have moved some distance from his earlier casual view of quotidian violence and counterviolence at home, coupled with a fierce determination not to yield so much as 'one shelled egg' to anyone else claiming power and authority over him.

As if to underscore his reform, Girart repeats this speech almost verbatim near the close of the *chanson*, as part of a longer speech of advice to his father-in-law, Florent, whom Charlemagne has named king of Apulia. To the earlier list of wrongdoing to be punished by kings he now adds an explicit warning about those who would usurp a neighbour's fief to add to their own domain; such men the king should banish for seven years as an example for the others.[27]

In a curious way the message delivered by Girart's conversion to reformed practice is heightened by his apostasy at the very end of the text. Suddenly, he announces his adherence to his old views of utter independence of the clerical hierarchy headed by the pope, and the emerging power of the state headed by

---

[26] Ll. 7159–82.
[27] The entire speech comes in ll. 11178–268; ll. 11229–54 largely reproduce the previous speech. The author also strongly advises against putting peasants' sons in high position.

the king; he explains that his cooperation and submission to any authority beyond himself and short of God was only temporary. First, he denies the claims of the Gregorian papacy:

> I have my own clerks, wise enough and wealthy;
> Never do they need nor seek the pope
> for belief or authority
> for baptisms or any Christian rite.

The claims of kingship are next denied:

> Whatever's mine, my wealth, my land, my might,
> I'll hold from no one except Lord God on High;
> Ah, Charlemayn, the truth I will not hide;
> In this campaign we have both won this time;
> Your leadership therein I've recognized
> And my own lips have called you Lord and Sire;
> My name, at court, should never be reviled;
> But all I've done I did for love of Christ;
> I'm not your man nor faith to you do plight
> Or ever shall all the days of my life.

As Girart proudly swings into his saddle and rides off, the French stare at each other in bewilderment. Charlemagne indulges in one of his reveries, and then 'between his teeth' mutters a most royalist reflection: 'If I may live a long life ere I die, / The pride of one of us shall not survive.'[28] Except for a closing summary of the grand events he has recounted, and a prayer for God's mercy, the poet ends his *chanson* here.

He has spoken repeatedly, if somewhat ambivalently to the topics that have shaped our enquiry. He has clearly shown the lively and continuing need for the reform of *chevalerie* vis-à-vis *clergie* and *royauté*. Girart's sudden affirmation of old beliefs at the end of the story would surely have opened the way for spirited discussion of these basic, thoroughly current questions in any audience.

The Crowning of Louis

The *Crowning of Louis* (*Le Couronnement de Louis*),[29] probably written between 1131 and 1137, tells the story of the great work of William of Orange in saving Rome from pagan invasion, in saving Louis, son of Charlemagne, from

---

[28] For all of these speeches, see ll. 11333–55; the translation of the anti-Gregorian passage is my own; the others come from Newth, ed., tr., *Song of Aspremont*.
[29] Unless otherwise stated, all quotations in this section are from Hoggan, tr., 'Crowning of Louis'; Langlois, ed., *Couronnement de Louis*.

rebellion, and finally in saving Rome again, this time from Guy of Germany. As will be apparent, this text, too, speaks with great force to the issues that concern us; it, too, bears witness to the shadows as well as to the light.[30] The reality of knightly motivation and action appears clearly, if indirectly, within the interstices of the ideal portraits drawn. The author, we will see, has mixed feelings about actual knightly behaviour as experienced in the world.

He can, for example, describe deeds of prowess with as loving a hand as ever scratched pen on parchment. All serious issues in the story are solved by knightly violence: the initial challenger to Louis's kingly right is smashed by a single blow of the fist (William remembering just in time to sheath his sword and not spill blood in a church); the pagan threat to Rome is stopped in its tracks when William takes on Corsolt, the unbelieving champion, and with a great sword stroke sends the offender's head, still encased in its helmet, flying off his body; only his ceaseless warfare (and another personal combat, this time with the traitor Acelin, son of Richard of Rouen) rescues Louis and props up his kingship; yet another single combat signals the end of the German attack on Rome near the poem's end. These personal encounters are jewels of prowess set within a gilded narrative of general warfare. No sense of inappropriateness intrudes when William calls on God or the Virgin as sources for his great prowess.

Yet there is worry, or at least an unblinkered realism, intertwined with the praise. The glandular urge to violence surging just below the surface in the warriors appears in both hero and villain; more than once they appear 'mad with rage' when challenged or insulted.[31] The author also knows that knightly motivation included booty and revenge as well as pure faith and loyalty. At the start of his combat with Corsolt, William not only prays one of his famous prayers, filled with theological verities;[32] he also eyes his enemy's horse with frank covetousness: ' "Holy Mary!" he exclaimed, "what a fine charger that is! He would serve a worthy man so well that I must take care to spare him with my weapons. May God who governs all things protect him and prevent me from harming him with my sword!" ' The poet adds approvingly, 'Those were not the words of a coward.'[33] He likewise frankly describes William's army living by looting the countryside around Rome while they are on campaign against Guy of Germany: 'Count William led out the foragers into the sur-

---

[30] For dating and general discussion, see Frappier, *Chansons de geste*, II, 51–186. On the uses of violence in this violent text, see Combarieu, 'La violence', I, 126–52.

[31] See, for example, laisses 44, 51.

[32] Discussed by Frappier, *Chansons de geste*, 137–8, and Maddox and Sara Sturm-Maddox, 'Le chevalier à oraison'.

[33] Laisse 21.

rounding district to spoil the countryside. They plundered the whole region, so that the men of the army were well-off and well provided for.'[34]

Going beyond realism to message, the poet notes that in the course of his warfare for King Louis, William attacked the town of Saint-Gilles one morning. Winning an easy victory, he nevertheless 'acted in a way pleasing to Jesus', the audience is told pointedly, 'when he spared the church there from being laid waste'.[35]

Even more pointed is a critical description of the knighthood of France with whom William had to contend: 'as long as he lived . . . the Frenchmen took to rebelling again, making war against each other and acting like madmen, burning down towns and laying waste the countryside. They would not restrain themselves at all on Louis' account.'[36] When the acts of prowess leave the realm of the mythic and come closer to home and to contemporary politics, the tone clearly changes: trumpet-calls fade and talk of reform surges.

Much knightly independence with regard to the sphere of *clergie*, however, receives at least tacit approval. Of course, there is the usual everyday anticlericalism.[37] Seeing no sign of vigour in his son Louis when he first offers him the crown, Charlemagne exclaims, 'Let us cut off all his hair and put him into this monastery; he can pull the bell ropes and be the sacristan, so he will have a pittance to keep him from beggary.'[38] But more interesting is the ideal of religion and the clerical role.

The most revealing scene comes early in the story, when the pope is trying to persuade William to fight Corsolt. The pope must present both the most powerful relic (the armbone of St Peter, plainly revealed without its usual gold and silver casing) and the most powerfully attractive concessions before he finally convinces William:

Look, here is St Peter, the guardian of souls; if you undertake this feat of arms today on his account, my lord, then you may eat meat every single day for the rest of your life and take as many wives as you have a mind to. You will never commit any sin however wicked (so long as you avoid any act of treason) that will not be discounted, all the days of your life, and you shall have your lodging in paradise, the place Our Lord keeps for His best friends; St Gabriel himself will show you the way.

William can only gasp out his willingness to fight, and his thankfulness for such terms: 'Ah! God help us! . . . never was there a more generous-hearted cleric! Now I will not fail, for any man alive or for any pagan however foul or wicked, to go out and fight against these scoundrels'.[39] In the fight that follows, when William appears to be in danger of defeat, the pope actually

---

[34] Laisse 56. [35] Laisse 50. [36] Laisse 63.
[37] See, in general, Noble, 'Anti-Clericalism', 149–58. [38] Laisse 8. [39] Laisse 18.

threatens St Peter: 'What are you doing, then, St Peter? If he dies out there, it will be unlucky for you: as long as I live and draw breath, there will never be any mass sung in your church!'[40]

Saints' relics were threatened and abused, especially in the earlier Middle Ages, in order to secure some desired result.[41] Yet in these remarkable passages we can also see the clergy and the religion they more or less controlled in life refashioned in chivalric literature to conform to an ideal knightly image. The warrior champions of the more powerful God and his powerful saints will overcome his enemies, the knights' enemies, with sword and lance. The sacrality of religion, protected by knighthood, blesses such chivalry and bends the troublesome rules in payment for the knights' hard service. The only unforgivable sin set in a separate category by the pope, we should note, is treason.[42]

One other example of the knightly beau ideal of a cleric appears later in the person of Walter, Abbot of St Martins, who has hidden away King Louis from eighty traitorous canons and clerics. He gives William an account of their plot and he suggests an unambiguous response: 'Louis is to be disinherited this very day unless God and you yourself are prepared to protect him. Take all their heads, I beg you in God's name! I take all the sin of desecrating a church upon myself, for they are all traitors and renegades.' Hearing this bold plea, William laughs and utters a benediction: 'Blessed be the hour that such a cleric was nurtured!'[43]

Abbot Walter's offer points to an important fact: he presumes that this desecration is both necessary and sinful, requiring his heroic offer to take the sin upon himself. In a similar way, William spends years fighting constantly for his king, even on holy days:

for three whole years there was not a single day, however high and holy, that William did not have his burnished helm laced on and his sword girt at his side, riding fully armed on his charger. There was not a feastday when men should go to worship, not even Christmas Day which should be set above all others, that he was not dressed in his hauberk and armed. The knight suffered a great penance to support and to aid his lord.[44]

---

[40] Laisse 27.

[41] On humiliation and coercion of saints' relics, see Geary, 'L'Humiliation des saints'; *idem*, *Living with the Dead*, 95–124; and Little, *Benedictine Maledictions*. By the thirteenth century the practices described were under criticism and regulation.

[42] 'Se tant puez faire de traison te gardes': l. 393.

[43] Laisse 40. The idea of a cleric taking on a knight's necessary sin is not limited to imaginative literature. Joinville records the offer made to Louis IX (while both were in Muslim captivity). The aged Patriarch of Jerusalem advises Louis to swear whatever his captors require and he will take upon himself any sin involved. Wailly, ed., *Joinville*, 151–2.

[44] Laisse 46.

This hard service, at once loyal and sinful, is undertaken as a penance.[45] Clearly there are duties a knight must rightly assume, even though the rules of *clergie* will formally condemn him for it. In an ideal world, some right-minded cleric would shoulder such sins himself and wipe the slate clean. The *chansons de geste* create such a world.[46]

But they engage in reform of knighthood as well as in imaginative refashioning of the clergy, and in this text one reform theme is stressed above all others. Jean Frappier calls this text, with reason, the most political of the *chansons de geste*.[47] If *chevalerie* is the stalwart and essential defender of both *clergie* and *royauté*, it must shape that role, however uncomfortable the fit, into the sometimes cramping framework of sanctified, legitimate kingship. Chivalry may like to imagine that it can take the clerics on its own terms; it may realize with some degree of grouchiness that royal justice is not always what it should be—'wicked men have made justice a mask for covetousness and because of bribery fair hearings are no longer given', says the author[48]—but whatever the problems, whatever the personal qualities of the current king, the working principle of legitimate kingship is the essential key to an ordered society.

Valorization moves significantly in this direction in *The Crowning of Louis*. William begins as a prototypical crusader, and he and his men receive the usual assurances that the Almighty loves their work, that paradise awaits those killed in it.[49] With this aura of sanctity firmly established, however, William shifts locations and enemies smoothly. He becomes the steady defender of royalty—in France, against domestic enemies—through the next major section of the text (as indeed he has been in one brief incident in its earliest laisses). Legitimate, even holy warfare against the pagans, who are here presented as men literally engaged in feud with God, has given way to legitimate and presumably even holy warfare (or at least atoneable warfare) against Christians in France. The glow of crusading sanctity remains, in other words, as William shifts enemies to fight against the misguided men who have failed to see the need for legitimate kingship. Later in the text William turns to sanctified war against analogously misguided Germans who think they can capture Rome and its bishop, before he returns to the necessary, if endless and even thankless, task of defending French royalty.

Of course Louis himself launched William in this role by turning to him as soon as he has been crowned. On that occasion he appealed to knighthood as

---

[45] Laisse 63.

[46] In the *Chanson d'Aspremont* the pope says he will carry all the knights' sins on his own back as they travel to heaven, having been killed fighting for God: see Brandin, ed., *Chanson d'Aspremont*, l. 5469.

[47] Frappier, *Chansons de geste*, 51.　　　　[48] Laisse 4.　　　　[49] See, e.g., laisse 18.

the buttress of kingship: 'My father says you are a fine knight, that there is no greater warrior under the vault of heaven. I wish to entrust to you my lands and my fiefs so that you may protect them for me, noble knight, until I can bear arms myself.'[50]

The author also gives plain speeches in praise of this high mission to two humbler truth-tellers, a pilgrim and a porter. The pilgrim brings William news of the plot against King Louis and asks, rhetorically, 'Ah! God help us! . . . where have all the noble knights gone now, and the lineage of the bold Count Aymeri? They are the ones who always supported their lord before.'[51] For his news and his declared willingness to help Louis if only he were able, William rewards the man with ten ounces of gold.

William makes a knight of the second speaker, the porter who shortly after the meeting with the pilgrim delivers almost the same speech. The porter is explaining why he will not admit William and his men to Tours, thinking they have only come to increase the forces of rebellion:

Ah! God help us! . . . where have all the valiant knights gone now and the lineage of the warlike Aymeri who used to support their rightful lord so well? . . . There are too many vile traitors in here already, I do not want to increase their numbers. . . . Would to the glorious King of Heaven that the earth might give way under your feet and that Louis were back in his fief! Then the world would be rid of evil men![52]

Given Louis's character and record, given that he is at this moment in the story hiding timidly in a crypt of the cathedral, such confidence might seem misplaced. It might seem even more misplaced after recalling the stirring lines at the opening of the poem describing the ideal king for France:

The king who wears the golden crown of France must be an upright man and valiant in his body. If there is any man who does him a wrong, he must leave him no peace in plain or in forest until he has overpowered him or killed him. If he does not do this, France loses her glory; then, history says, he was wrongfully crowned.[53]

The contrast with Louis could scarcely be more starkly drawn.

Yet this simple image of king as ideal warlord is only one side of the coin of royalty struck in the text. The necessary role of legitimate kingship in securing public order forms the other side. This power must be preserved and it must be used positively. Charlemagne's advice to his son (who is, like a Capetian, to be crowned in the father's lifetime) begins with the basic need for a moral life, since no one can rule others if he cannot rule himself; but he quickly goes on to a requirement that the king should justly regulate the feudal order of society, acting fairly with regard to the granting of fiefs, and utterly destroying

---

[50] Laisse 13.   [51] Laisse 35.   [52] Laisse 36.   [53] Laisse 3.

proud rebels who will not accept his authority. On the one hand this means justice even for the poor:

a king must strike down wrongs under his feet and trample on them and stamp them out. Towards the poor man, you must humble yourself and, if he has a plea, it should not vex you; rather you should help him and succour him and for love of God restore him to his rights.

On the other hand, a king must stamp out prideful rebelliousness:

Towards the proud man, you must show yourself as fierce as a man-eating leopard and, if he tries to make war on you, summon throughout France all the noble knights until you have up to thirty thousand, have him besieged in his strongest fortress and all his land laid waste and devastated. If you can capture him or have him delivered into your hands, show him neither mercy nor pity but have all his limbs cut off or let him be burnt in a fire or drowned in water.[54]

This advice set in the Carolingian era forms a striking parallel to contemporary Capetian policy, to the ceaseless policing of the Île de France by Louis VI. This historical King Louis would undoubtedly have loved to summon the thirty thousand noble knights of the literary Louis to join him in besieging the strongholds of such local tyrants as Thomas of Marle; he was forced to rely, instead, on a much smaller collection of loyal local vassals and parish militia. The ideological point of the text, however, its reforming message, could scarcely be more plain: whatever the foibles of the current king, the institution of kingship needs the support of 'noble knights' if right order is to be maintained in a perilous world.

The corollary is, of course, that kings will rule with their vassals in mind and with their vassals' advice heeded in their courts. No low-born men need apply. 'And another thing I want to tell you about that will be very important to you', Charlemagne adds to his message to Louis:

not to take a lowborn man as your counsellor, the son of a lord's agent or of a bailiff. These would betray their trust in a minute for money. Choose rather William, the noble warrior, the son of proud Aymeri of Narbonne and brother of Bernard of Brubant, the warrior; if these men are willing to support and aid you, you can completely rely on their service.[55]

The formula is, in theory, straightforward: when the ideal king relies on the ideal knight the kingdom prospers. The poet knows, of course, how the real world turns, as the closing lines of the poem detail:

---

[54] Laisse 13. In a contemporary reference the poet warns that if this is not done the Normans will be contemptuous and encouraged in their hostility.

[55] Laisse 13.

Within a year [William] had dealt out such punishment to the rebels that fifteen counts were forced to present themselves at court and do homage for their inheritance to Louis who held command over France. . . . But when he was fully in power, he showed no gratitude to William.

Raoul de Cambrai

The note of ambiguity echoing in the last line of this text will sound even more discordantly in our third example of *chanson de geste*, *Raoul de Cambrai*, a poem from the Cycle of the Barons in Revolt.[56] Here is a wild story of kingly malfeasance and knightly feud, with no veneer of crusading sanctity[57] and with even larger question marks left hanging in mid-air.

It is a poem with a history and architecture that are complex, even for a *chanson de geste*. The first portion seems to have appeared in writing by the mid-twelfth century; it tells the story of the violent, prideful, heedless warrior Raoul; and it apparently used the poetic technique of assonance rather than rhyme. Somewhere in the early years of the reign of Philip II (1180–1223) this original, assonanced epic was rhymed and expanded by a section with focus on Bernier, Raoul's vassal and eventual killer. This entire rewriting is known as *Raoul I*. Towards the end of Philip's reign, another addition appeared, in assonanced form, carrying the story through more adventures, feuding, and battles until '[t]here being no other male characters left, the story comes to an end'.[58] This early thirteenth-century section is known as *Raoul II*. We can draw on the evidence of both sections, but will focus primarily on *Raoul I*, and specifically on that section concerned with Raoul himself, since this was the most widespread part of the text.

The characteristics of the society portrayed in *Raoul I* could have formed a model for Hobbes's state of nature. 'The poem has a nightmarish quality,' as Sarah Kay, its most recent editor and translator, has observed, 'arising both from the horror of the events portrayed and from the ethical opacity of the narrative as it pursues alternative perspectives through unstable characters and competing narrative strands.'[59] In this world, chivalry by and large means prowess crowned with success, an obsession with honour defended by unbeatable violence. The blood of characters boils regularly; they go mad with rage

---

[56] Unless otherwise stated, all quotations in this section are from Kay, ed., tr., *Raoul de Cambrai*. The brief description of the text which follows is based on her thorough introduction. Cf. Calin, *Old French Epic*, passim; *idem, 'Raoul de Cambrai'*; *idem, Muse for Heroes*, 37–56; Pauline Matarasso, *Recherches historiques*.

[57] The knights fight no pagans in *Raoul I*; in *Raoul II*, since some pagans are good, some bad, the force of crusading valorization is likewise missing.

[58] Kay, *Raoul de Cambrai*, lv.   [59] Ibid., ix.

at intervals; they demand hostages to secure each agreement reached as a temporary triumph over suspicious distrust. The tensions that inevitably arise from the ragged intersections of the great forces of the age—kingship, lordship, vassalage, religion, kin ties, vengeance—repeatedly produce the reciprocal and bloody violence of single combat, feud, and battle.

The almost glandular impulse to violence shows up unforgettably near the end of *Raoul I* when an unwise royal seneschal seats the feuding families side by side at a Pentecost banquet. Guerri, uncle of Raoul (the latter by this time dead and buried) is beside himself with rage and can barely be prevented from carrying out his designs on his enemies with a huge steel knife. When he sees the venison served, the cooked meat acts as a catalyst on his wrath and the hall erupts in a brawl; the general violence is distilled into the standard single combat, between Bernier and Gautier (Raoul's nephew and heir). Even when these heroes have hacked each other into disability, they seem ready to renew the fight by crawling from their blood-stained beds, which have been thoughtlessly placed so that the opponents can see and hear one another.[60]

Raoul himself, however, stands as the great embodiment of these issues, and was in fact renowned in the Middle Ages in just that role. Long deprived of a great fief that was rightfully his, and then wrongfully provided with a fief that should go to another, he wars to recover withheld property and to avenge impugned honour. He scorns a counsel of caution from his companion and vassal Bernier, and from his mother Alice, and he specifically rejects her pointed advice that his war must not destroy chapels and churches and slaughter the poor.[61] He insists 'such war be unleashed on the Vermandois that countless churches will be burned and destroyed'.[62] His men soon put his instructions into practical effect as they 'cross over into the Vermandois, and seize the livestock, reducing countless men to ruin. They set fire to the land—the farms are ablaze.'[63]

In what became the most famous scene in the poem, Raoul attacks the town of Origny, controlled by his enemies, and announces his plans for the church there:

Pitch my tent in the middle of the church and my packhorses will stand in its porches; prepare my food in the crypts, my sparrow-hawk can perch on the gold crosses, and prepare a magnificent bed for me to sleep in front of the altar; I will use the crucifix as a back rest and my squires can make free with the nuns. I want to destroy the place utterly.[64]

---

[60] Laisses CCXXIV–CCXXXIV. [61] Laisse LI.
[62] Laisse LVIII. [63] Laisse LIX. [64] Laisse LX.

His 'noble warriors' are dutifully about to commit these multiple sacrileges when they hear the church bells peal: 'remembering God the Father of justice, even the craziest of them felt compelled to show reverence', and so they simply camp outside the town.[65]

On discovering this disobedience, Raoul at first characteristically loses control (*'fu molt demesurez'*), but comes to see that the holy relics of the church must not be destroyed. His uncle Guerri clinches the case with a frank assessment of power: 'If God takes against you, you won't last long.'[66] Raoul even agrees to a truce with the nuns who serve the church, led by Marsent, Bernier's mother. Their meeting (as noted in Chapter 10) is a striking tableau of *clergie* confronting *chevalerie*. The nuns process beyond the town walls, reciting the holy office and carrying books, the symbols of their Latinate literacy and learning; Marsent even holds 'a book from the time of Solomon'.

Though Raoul agrees to a truce, a chance incident, involving what he takes to be disrespect to three of his men, sparks his successful all-out attack and the firing of the town: 'Rooms are burning here and floors collapsing there, barrels are catching fire, their hoops split, and children are burning to death in horrible agony.' The church, too, goes up in flames and all the nuns die; a distraught Bernier sees Marsent lying in the flames, her priceless book symbolically burning on her breast.[67] His work for the day done, Raoul repairs to his tent, dismounts from his great tawny warhorse, and is disarmed by barons who love him, as the poet relates: 'they unlace his green helmet ornamented with pure gold, then they ungird his good steel sword, and take off his good double hauberk from his back. . . . There was not such a fine knight in the whole of France, nor one so fearless at arms.'[68]

Kay's comment about moral opacity and multiple perspectives comes readily to mind. Medieval writers who commented on Raoul saw in him the very model of violent excess, of *demesure*, allowing modern readers to believe that the poet intended to provoke just such reactions. The text is peppered, in fact, with explicit statements against *demesure*. The author observes early in the action that 'an unbridled man (*hom desreez*) has great difficulty in surviving'.[69] Ybert, giving his son Bernier advice, states the same theme: 'I will be honest with you: I can tell you the story of many men's lives, and an arrogant man will never succeed, whatever anyone may say.'[70] Shortly thereafter, Count Eudes makes the same point: 'Barons . . . noble knights! A man without moderation (*sans mesure*) is not worth a fig.'[71]

The idea of sheer war-weariness, moreover, joins moderation as a close ally near the close of *Raoul I*. Bernier and Gautier, the current champions of the

---

[65] Laisse LX.   [66] Laisse LXII.   [67] Laisses LXX–LXXIV.
[68] Laisse LXXIV.   [69] Laisse XXIV.   [70] Laisse XC.   [71] Laisse CIV.

feuding sides, have fought their single combat and, as we have already noted, lie severely wounded. Though Gautier, blood boiling, is shouting defiance from his bed, Bernier suddenly declares enough is enough; peace is the great need; resistance to it is sin. Wounded, semi-naked, publicly prostrating himself in the form of a cross before his enemy, Bernier offers his sword and a pacific ultimatum: Gautier must either kill him or be reconciled. The blessings of *clergie* descend on the offer as the Abbot of Saint-Germain comes into the scene, loaded with sacred relics. A peace is, for the time, arranged.

Looking at such scenes as this, at the structure of the plot as a whole, and at the explicit statements favouring *mesure*, we might easily decide that the 'message' of the text is clear. Yet we cannot be certain how everyone in the audience heard and interpreted; nagging doubts and a sense of the need for qualification remain. The message can scarcely be pacifism: a realignment of the feuding families against the king and the enthusiastic firing of Paris, for one thing, follow quickly on the heels of the reconciliation.

And in a more general way, fears of *demesure* and violence only slowly and partially drag the heavy anchor of sheer, beloved prowess, the undiminished commitment to honour defended with edged weapons. After Raoul dies on the battlefield next to a slain opponent named John, the biggest knight in all of France, the hearts are removed from the two bodies and laid out on a shield to be examined; the result will be significant, for the heart was the seat of prowess, the point of origin for the arteries which in Galenic theory carried the animal vitality of the body. The giant John, it turns out, had the heart of a child, while that of Raoul 'was very much larger than that of a draught ox at the plough'.[72]

The text thus shows some signs of ambivalence. The author wants *mesure* in knights, wants them to learn not to burn churches, and certainly to avoid burning nuns; he thinks there is a time to end wars, even if there is also a time to initiate them. Yet through it all something of the ancient call to arms stirs him, something of the grandeur in noble revenge seems satisfying, even it if must inevitably, sadly, be achieved at great cost.[73]

This sense of complexity of view is reinforced by the absence of that endorsement of royal power which so often appears as a theme in *chanson de geste*. In this text, far from representing a needed regulator and peacemaker, the king is ultimately at the root of the problems; he gives away Raoul's fief to a favourite and later gives Raoul the fief of the faithful royal vassal Herbert, who has four sons. At the end of *Raoul I* the antagonistic families belatedly

---

[72] Laisse CLX.

[73] Matarasso agrees: see *Recherches historiques*, 163–4. 'Raoul est ce héros épique', she writes. 'Il suit son étoile, l'étoile de grandeur, de la démesure, de la déchéance' (p. 174).

recognize these facts and turn against the king. At that point, far from acting as the divine agent for peace, Louis, the author tells us, was privately sorry that the feuding families had come to an accord.[74]

One might argue, of course, that the problem is not kingship per se, but kingship which is too weak to carry out its essential role. Yet there is here none of the endorsement and knightly defence of kingship right or wrong that appeared so strikingly in *The Crowning of Louis*; in that text Louis, after all, was surely another weak king, another king making mistakes.

A sense of the lingering respect for the most unreformed species of chivalry continues, moreover, when we turn to issues of religious ideas and clerical personnel. Occasional traces of anticlericalism cause no surprise, of course, but clerics generally stand in the background of this text (unless they are passive victims), and religious ideas generally need to fit the framework of a most worldly chivalry if they are to live. Religion works, if it works at all, at the exterior level of power relationships negotiated with God, through formal acts and words, not through interior motive or belief. Alice's hasty curse on her son when he refuses her advice works its terrible effects, despite her instant rush to a church to pray for its nullification in accordance with her true intent. Once the words are out, their effects follow, whatever her inner motivation. Ernaut, desperate with fear as Raoul closes in for the kill on the battlefield, suddenly sighs with relief when he hears the pursuing Raoul declare that even God and his saints cannot stop his revenge: Ernaut knows such blasphemy will cancel Raoul's blows. Lady Alice thanks God heartily for the wounds Gautier has inflicted on Bernier in their duel. Just before the battle in which Raoul dies, the knights, in the absence of priests, commune themselves with three blades of grass. Riding into the fray, 'every good knight weeps for the pity of it and vows to God that if he escapes alive he will never in his life commit a sin again or, if he does, he will do penance for it'.[75] The dying Aliaume makes his confession to Gautier, who raises the prone man's head and turns it to face the east. Oaths are sworn on relics, the participating laymen thinking they require no priestly link with divinity for the transaction.

Religion, in other words, means adding required pieties to an essential warrior code, not changing that code in any significant way beyond what prudence requires because of God's superior power; religious ideas express themselves through exteriorities, not by entering the heart or soul to work basic changes within.

---

[74] Laisse CCXLI. King Louis in this poem seems almost a generic king; as Matarasso says, he is not any one in particular, but a 'roi mannequin', or even 'une merionette': see *Recherches historiques*, 153, 155.
[75] Laisse CXX.

Thus the author of the first extant part of *Raoul de Cambrai* writes with certain reform ideas in mind: he wants more knightly *mesure*, he urges immunity for holy places and for clerics, who are essential at times, despite their inconvenience; he knows that revenge and war can drag on until costs exceed worth. Yet he keeps looking back over his shoulder into the imagined past with what seems almost nostalgia for the great game of honourable violence played by stout warriors largely following their own set of rules.[76] The complex way in which chivalry could simultaneously be problem and cure is writ large in the portion of *Raoul* dating from the mid-to-late twelfth century.

Has the picture changed much by the time the continuation known as *Raoul II* appeared a generation later, in roughly the second decade of the thirteenth century? A study of the vocabulary identifying adult males suggests some movement away from the starkly martial quality of *Raoul I*.[77] Moreover, the author of the continuation gives his characters more outright speeches in favour of peace, conciliation, and forgiveness; these go beyond mere war-weariness to a sense of principle. At the very outset, Beatrice presses her lovesuit by arguing that her marriage to Bernier will truly end the war between their families, a result which comes to pass, at least for a time.[78] The wise Doon of Saint-Denis advises King Louis (who, granted, has just suffered a severe reverse) to make peace with Bernier, to exchange prisoners 'and be good friends'. ' "God!" said the king, "what good advice that is." '[79] In a moment of crisis when one of Erchambaut's men recognizes him, despite his careful disguise, Bernier 'adopts a conciliatory manner' and promises to right an old wrong done by his father.[80] He is even more forgiving when he finally confronts Guerri the Red as the guilty father-in-law who was so swiftly willing to marry off Beatrice after hearing uncertain news of Bernier's capture and possible death.[81] Mortally wounded by Guerri near the end of the continuation, Bernier provides the greatest example of forgiveness: 'Oh God our Father who in his great mercy forgave Longinus his death, for that reason I believe I should forgive him too. I pardon him—may God have mercy on me.'[82]

This sense of waxing piety may even be reinforced by the steady mention of standard religious services; the protagonists are casually seen attending mass and baptisms, going on pilgrimage.

[76] Owen makes a similar assessment of what an audience of a 'live' performance of the *Song of Roland* might have thought: 'glorying in Roland's pursuit of his ideal and untouched by Oliver's more worldly wisdom': 'Aspects of *Demesure*', 149.

[77] *Chevalier* throughout this earlier text is primarily a technical term for a man prepared by a specific military training for a particular mode of fighting; in the later text it appears with greater proportional frequency than such terms as warrior, baron, and vassal; at the same time the adjective *preu* gives some ground to *cortois*. See Kay, *Raoul de Cambrai*, xliii–xlv.

[78] Laisses CCXIII–CCLV.   [79] Laisse CCLXXXII.   [80] Laisse CCCXIII.
[81] Laisse CCCXXXIV.   [82] Laisse CCCXXXVIII.

Yet we would be incautious to think this continuation slackens in its praise of prowess or offers a transformed conception of knighthood.[83] From the outset, chivalry means deeds done on a battlefield; Beatrice loves Bernier because of his prowess as well as his good looks, having heard him praised by Guerri as one 'who has performed so many feats of knighthood (*qi avra faites tantes chevaleries*)'. When Bernier sheds tears over his wife's capture and likely remarriage, Guerri accuses him of womanly behaviour, and then tops off his criticism with a précis of the standard knightly ethos: 'No noble man should repine so long as he is able to bear arms.'[84] Bernier proves his skill at bearing arms tirelessly; after severing the head of the invading pagan champion Auciber (in order to secure his own freedom from the pagan King Corsuble), he marks his victory by tying the head to the flowing tail of the dead man's horse.[85] In his second period of service to the pagan king, Bernier is praised unambiguously by Corsuble for showing his nobility through his great prowess: 'My Christian brother, you are everything a high-born nobleman should be. You and your son can boast of being the best in Christendom at sustaining and surviving the great feats of war.'[86]

Being a pagan is clearly no bar to being a good knight or recognizing high knightly qualities in others. The pagans refer to themselves as knights without objection from the author who himself speaks of them being dubbed knights, and even suggests that in combat they 'wheeled round in the French style'.[87] They are not lacking in any of the warrior qualities, and despite a few pro forma swipes at their gods, are viewed simply as a mixture of worthy and unworthy men all of whom suffer an unfortunate religious identification. The warrior virtues, in other words, seem determinative.[88]

In the continuation, clerics more often step from the periphery to centre stage, yet by and large they remain thoroughly dominated by lay powers. A clear case in point occurs when Louis, who has just ambushed Bernier and Beatrice on the way from the church to their wedding feast, wants to marry off the lady to a favourite. She appeals to the clergy present to do their duty and prevent disgrace to Christianity. But '[g]reat and small all keep silent, for they

---

[83] The poet's constant recognition of the importance of booty to the knights provides a good example of his unblinking view of war. See, for example, laisses CCLXI, CCLXV, CCLXXXII, CCCXXII, CCCXXVIII. Likewise, the final war of *Raoul II* involves the same sort of devastation as that which opened *Raoul I*: 'They start fires, sack the towns, seize the livestock, and have it herded into army quarters; the peasant ploughmen take flight', laisse CCCXL. Serial ambushes set up the early plot in *Raoul II*.

[84] Laisses CCLI, CCLXXIX.					[85] Laisse CCXCVII.					[86] Laisse CCCXXIX.

[87] E.g. laisses CCXCIII, CCXCIV. CCCXXIV.

[88] The same point appears, of course, in the continued description of Guerri as a great knight, despite his eagerness to kill clerics, despite what his daughter recognizes as 'an element of treachery in his nature', laisse CCCXXXV.

are very afraid of strong King Louis'.[89] Louis's domination becomes physical intimidation when he actually orders the marriage: 'By the faith I owe St Denis, if there is in all my land any archbishop, bishop, or consecrated abbot who means to gainsay or prevent me, I'll have him hacked limb from limb.'[90] When Bernier and Guerri attack the open-air remarriage Louis is stage-managing, Guerri enthusiastically calls for death to all the participating clerics: ' "Forward!" said Guerri the Red; "So help me God, woe betide us if a single one escapes alive—clerk or priest or consecrated abbot—rather than being killed and hacked to pieces." ' A modicum of *mesure* appears, though, for the knights simply attack the offending clerics with the shafts, not the blades, of their lances.[91]

What of kingship in the continuation? Louis obviously causes endless problems and shows weakness and villainy in *Raoul II*, as he did in *Raoul I*. He provokes a war by denying Bernier the fief his father held; he is humiliatingly unhorsed in that war, 'for he was in the wrong—justice was not on his side'.[92] He ambushes Bernier and his bride, as just noted; and, until stopped by his wife, he was in process of sending the helpless Beatrice out into a ditch for the sexual amusement of his eager squires.[93]

The formal statements about kingship in this portion of the poem, however, look past the particular man to the office. In the midst of their battle against Louis, Bernier suddenly calls out this principled view to his father:

In God's name, sir, we are behaving foolishly. Can you deny that the king of France is our overlord, whom I see here in mortal anguish? We may make peace again some time, if he sees fit and Jesus grants it. If you take my advice, we should desist at once; only if they attack us should we defend ourselves well.[94]

Beatrice gives the same line of advice to her two sons near the end of the poem:

Children . . . you must love each other, serve and respect your father, and protect the king of France with all your power—for no one should act against him, and to do so is to court disaster—upholding the crown and promoting its prestige. If you do as I tell you, no one on earth can do you harm.[95]

An increased emphasis on kingship is obvious. Coming at the very time Philip II was vigorously advancing the powers of the Capetian crown, it need cause no surprise.[96] Yet it is instructive to see that the ambiguities that made *Raoul I* so fascinating and frustrating a text also remain, only slightly diminished, in this continuation.

---

[89] Laisse CCLXXI.   [90] Laisse CCLXXXI.   [91] Laisse CCLXXXII.
[92] Laisse CCLXIII.   [93] Laisse CCLXXIV.   [94] Ibid.
[95] Laisse CCCXXXIII.   [96] The work of Philip is examined in Baldwin, *Philip Augustus*.

Our three examples of *chansons de geste*, then, praise knighthood to the skies, drawing on the timeless warrior ethos written into epic poetry in more than one age, and fashioned here to the world of twelfth-century Europe. At one level they love to praise noble men defending honour and taking revenge with blood boiling, to picture sword strokes delivered in hot wrath.

But they worry; they urge some minimal restraints. Sometimes a sense that war is endless, that, except for crusade, its cost is too high joins the sentiment, expressed with a tenor of regret, that some diminution of heroism is actually necessary.

Gregorianism is scarcely acknowledged. Of course the sacramental rituals intoned by the clerics are hardly to be denied, and even their rules and restrictions are at least half heard; but the rights and duties of the knightly life make their own claims. The truly fine among the tonsured appear as knights at heart (since there can be but one standard) and will open doors, and finally the door of paradise, to good warriors who have done their hard duty. Meanwhile, the choice of clerics for lucrative and powerful positions on earth ought still to remain, despite all the Church reformers' arguments, safely in lay hands. The proper agency of practical direction and restraint, if one there must be, is legitimate kingship loyally supported by idealized knighthood. However troublesome any particular king might be, the principle of kingship deserves reverence and support. The reiterated insistence on this principle, of course, leads us to doubt that it was universally taken for granted in the world, where some degree of tension between chivalric autonomy and royal authority was equally certain. A text like *Raoul I* can only reinforce such doubts.

12

QUEST AND QUESTIONING IN ROMANCE

✦✦✦

ROMANCE elements have always seemed a quintessential ingredient in the literature of chivalry, especially the portrayal of an individual knight on quest, searching for adventure in the outer world and often refashioning meaning in the world within himself.[1] These questing knights are less likely to seek adventures on a panoramic battlefield strewn with slain pagans, or even in heroic defence of legitimate monarchy as guarantor of order, than in individual acts intended to prove worth and to right wrongs. The quest is thus a splendid medium not only for praising ideal knighthood, but for probing the relationship of chivalric practices to the civilization emerging in high medieval Europe.

Though the quest pattern is common, the direction and destination vary from one work to another. Much questing in the Lancelot–Grail cycle, for example, originates in the need to find Lancelot or some other hero, absent from the court on some quest of his own.[2] These quests for the great heroes, for identity, or simply for adventure, allow multiple thematic lines and raise hard questions.

Some texts, however, give the quest motif particular focus, with adventures leading to a dramatic transformation in a single hero or a small group. Here, too, the hard questions keep coming to the surface, sometimes allowing for multiple points of view, always emphasizing the difficulty of finding solutions to problems associated with knighthood in the real world. Three examples will allow us to explore the links between quest and chivalry.

The Quest of the Holy Grail

The Quest of the Holy Grail (La Queste del Saint Graal),[3] written about 1225–30 as a part of the vast Lancelot–Grail cycle, has been termed an anti-romance or

---

[1] See footnote 3, Chapter 2, above.
[2] For the importance of Lancelot's own quest for identity in the slightly earlier *Lancelot do Lac*, see Elspeth Kennedy, 'Quest for Identity'.
[3] Pauphilet, ed., *Queste*. I found two translations useful: Matarasso, tr., *Quest* and Burns, tr., *Quest*. For studies of the text, see Frappier, 'Le Graal'; Bogdonow, *Romance of the Grail*; *idem*, 'An

even a spiritual fable. It has also been called the last flowering of monastic culture.[4] The text draws on biblical and patristic thought in ways that seem in particular to represent Cistercian spirituality which had been elaborated in the previous century and preserved its influence in a newer world of mendicants, scholasticism, and universities.[5] Scholars have thus long sought some species of monastic origin for the author, but he was probably not a Cistercian monk, nor even a product of their schools.[6] Cistercian houses at this time contained almost no vernacular works and considered even books on canon law a dangerous diversion into worldly interests; likewise, Cistercian monks wrote almost no vernacular works, and certainly no romances.[7] Pauline Matarasso's conclusion seems balanced:

The Queste is assuredly the product of a monastic mind, but probably not of a strictly monastic milieu. It could, I believe, have been written by a Cistercian seconded from his abbey to some lay or ecclesiastical dignitary. It is more likely to be the work of a younger man still searching for his vocation, if only because this was a commoner situation. It is unquestionably that of a man alert to the problems of his day.'[8]

How, then, does this author bring the ideals of monastic spirituality to bear on knightly violence and disorder, and on the imperatives of sexuality—surely outstanding instances of 'the problems of his day'?

In significant ways the reforming programme of the *Queste* would have drawn a resounding 'amen' from St Bernard, the great voice of Cistercian monasticism of nearly a century earlier. Fanni Bogdanow has convincingly linked Bernard's theology and the programme of this text.[9] At a more obvious level, the link with the Knights Templar (for whom Bernard wrote 'In Praise of the New Knighthood') appears in the first adventure of the quest. Hearing or reading that the marvellous shield securely kept behind the altar in an abbey of White Monks (the shield which King Baudemagus so unwisely carries for

Interpretation'; Matarasso, *Redemption of Chivalry*; Baumgartner, *L'Arbre et le pain*; Shichtman, 'Politicizing the Ineffable'.

[4] Matarasso, *Redemption of Chivalry*, 242–3.

[5] Meaning in this romance has often been derived from an interpretation of the Grail, rather than the reverse. See the discussion, with citations to other scholarly work, in Bogdanow, 'An Interpretation', 23, n. 2.

[6] Citations of important works on this point in Matarasso, *Redemption of Chivalry*, 228–9. One obvious conclusion is that Walter Map, the worldly cleric claimed by the text as its author, did not write the *Queste*. Not only did he die too soon, he truly hated the Cistercians. Matarasso thinks the attribution reflects either ignorance or, equally likely, interest in causing Walter to roll uneasily in his grave: pp. 232–377.

[7] Ibid., 225–8.

[8] Ibid., 240. In the introduction to her translation, Matarasso terms him 'one of that great army of clerks who wandered anonymously in that no-man's land between the lay and ecclesiastical worlds: *Quest*, 27. Cf. Baumgartner, *L'Arbre et le pain*, 42–5.

[9] Bogdanow, 'An Interpretation'.

so brief a time) bears a red cross on a white ground,[10] the audience would need no prompting to recognize Templar insignia; we are once again in the world of 'The Praise of the New Knighthood'. In company with St Bernard, the author of the *Queste* clearly favours an infusion of the monastic virtues into knightly lives needing spiritual discipline.

If the great sin of pride is constantly under correction, as it is here, sexual laxity is unfailingly on the author's mind. Virginity gets top billing, for example, at the important moment when one of the omnipresent hermits explains to Lancelot the virtues by which he might prosper in his quest for the Grail.[11] After praising Lancelot for once knowing that 'there was no prowess to compare with being a virgin, shunning lust and keeping one's body pure', the hermit's list of ideal knightly virtues continues with humility, long-suffering, rectitude, and charity.[12] Such a list might produce nods of sage agreement in a cloister, but it stands at some distance from the virtues that contemporaries regularly heard praised in a courtly hall, on a tournament ground, or within the glow of a campfire. There, the talk would obviously be first of prowess and honour, loyalty, and largesse. Some voices in these lay settings might speak of love, but they would probably talk of *fin amors*, of frankly sensual love, as the spur and reward of prowess; such views could scarcely please the clerics in general, and certainly would offend the regulars.

Ecclesiastics in the early thirteenth century probably thought the scene between Lancelot and the hermit embodied a stunning opportunity. Mere laymen, after all, are being offered the great benefits of monastic Christianity as equals.[13] We can recall the surprise with which some clerics received the news of this startling innovation in the previous century.[14]

Perhaps another concession is being offered as well. The *Queste* carefully walks the line between acceptance and rejection of prowess as a key knightly

---

[10] Matarasso, tr., *Quest*, 54; Burns, tr., *Quest*, ll; Pauphilet, ed., *Queste*, 28.

[11] Matarasso argues forcefully that the hermit's list of virtues cannot be read as a simple rank ordering. Virginity would serve Lancelot as a chief reform, but humility is stressed generally in the text; the great Cistercian virtue of charity comes at the end of the hermit's list, though it can scarcely be thought last in importance: see *Redemption of Chivalry*, 143–61. The insistence on virginity is, however, striking. Perceval nearly maims his own body after his brush with sexual temptation; the Maimed King, upon recovering his potency, immediately joins the Cistercians. Matarasso, *Quest*, 129, 277.

[12] Matarasso, *Quest*, 141–2; Burns, *Quest*, 40–1; Pauphilet, *Queste*, 123–7.

[13] See comment of Matarasso, *Redemption of Chivalry*, 240: 'It may be objected that the ideal it presented to its readers . . . was in fact unsuited to their needs, and incompatible with their duties. But since no theology of the laity had as yet been elaborated, those who entered the pastoral field must needs fall back on the traditional formulae which had proven their worth in the monastic milieu where they had evolved.' Matarasso praises the author of the *Queste* for giving his message to laymen straight: '[H]e has not diluted this ideal, nor tried to temper the wind to the shorn lamb.' Baumgartner, *L'Arbre et le pain*, passim, emphasizes the role of this text as a praise of ideal chivalry; see especially pp. 150–4.

[14] Sources in Chapter 4, footnotes 23 and 24.

virtue.[15] With open arms it accepts tournament (still, in the early thirteenth century, condemned by *clergie*); it more carefully accepts the heroic use of arms in the right causes.

Even Galahad, the perfect spiritual knight, must show the greatest prowess. Arthur worries that Galahad will never return to court once the quest for the Grail begins and that he will thus never witness his prowess; he proclaims a great tournament 'in order to see something of Galahad's exploits'. He and the others are not disappointed:

Galahad, who had ridden out into the meadow with the rest, began to shiver lances with a force and fury that astonished all the onlookers. He accomplished so much in so short a space that there was not a man or woman present but marvelled at his exploits and accounted him victor over all comers. And those who had never seen him before opined that he had made a worthy beginning in the way of chivalry, and that if his feats that day were proof, he would easily surpass all other knights in prowess.[16]

In another of his improving conversations with the hermit, the encounter leading to his repentance, Lancelot agrees, in principle, to sexual abstinence, but asserts the need to continue his life of arms. The hermit agrees. Lancelot knows that, ideally, his adultery with the queen must end, but he holds fast to prowess with the grip of a drowning man:

in all respects I am as you portrayed me. But since you told me that I have not gone so far but I may yet turn back, if by vigilance I keep from mortal sin, I swear to God and secondly to you that I will never return to the life I led so long, but will observe chastity and keep my body as pure as I am able. But while I am fit and hale as I am now I could not forswear chivalry and the life of arms.

To this remarkably open bargain the hermit agrees, 'overjoyed to hear such sentiments'. Through his brother, who is of course a knight, the hermit even promises Lancelot 'a horse and arms and all things needful'.[17] Lancelot's exercise of his great God-given prowess has not been a major problem and is not a necessary target for the hermit's pointed criticism; sexual laxity is, the hermit knows, the great sin in Lancelot's life. A good hermit knows his sinner and prudently focuses his advice.

[15] Matarasso, *Redemption of Chivalry*, 240: ' "If you can't beat them, join them" is a pastoral method that has always had its adherents.'

[16] Unless otherwise stated, all quotations in this setion are from Matarasso, tr., *Quest*, 42–3, 93–4, 71, 260–1, 266, 162, 200–5, 181–7, 192–4, 128–9, 121, 239–41; Burns, tr., *Quest*, 24, 16, 79, 81, 48, 60–1, 54–6, 57–8, 34–6, 33, 73; Pauphilet, ed., *Queste*, 14, 70–1, 45–6, 253, 259–60, 147, 189–93, 171–3, 184–5, 180–1, 104–10, 99–100, 231–3.

[17] A promise of even heightened prowess seems to lie beneath the hermit's assurance to Lancelot, for he tells Lancelot that if he avoids sexual sin God will 'empower you to accomplish many things from which your sin debars you'. If his obvious reference is to greater success on the Grail quest, the promise is couched in general terms.

The *Queste*, of course, is no paean of praise to the quotidian practice of prowess. To the contrary, the consequences of knightly worship of this demigod are shown unrelentingly. On a spiritual level the *Queste* sets the stage for the dramatic downfall of the Round Table found in the *Mort Artu*, a later romance in the same great cycle. The text insists time and again that the ultimate reliance of the ideal knight must focus on God, not even on superhuman prowess. Melias, just after receiving knighthood from Galahad himself, takes the wrong road, illicitly grasps a crown, and learns that the Devil has pierced him with the dart of pride, 'for you thought that your prowess would see you through, but your reason played you false', as a wise monk tells him. The monk says he suffered in order to learn 'to trust . . . in your Saviour's help sooner than in your own right arm'.

Lancelot, always full of goodwill, but generally falling just short of the mark, learns this lesson painfully in the Grail Castle. Ordered by God to enter the castle, he characteristically prepares to fight his way in, past fierce lions guarding the gate. After a flaming hand falls from the sky to disarm him, he hears the voice say: 'Man of little faith and weak belief, why do you put greater trust in your hand than in your Creator? What a wretch you are not to realize that He in whose service you have placed yourself has more strength than your armour.' Even this warning is insufficient. Allowed a distant view of the Grail as the centre of a religious service glowing with light and resplendent with angels, Lancelot fears the celebrant will drop the vessel; he enters the sacred space forbidden him and is blinded and scorched by God's wrath, left hovering somewhere between living and dying for twenty-four days.

As he recovers, a similarly pointed, if less dramatic, rebuke is delivered to Hector who arrives at the Grail Castle 'in all his armour and mounted on a great warhorse' loudly and repeatedly to demand entry. The Grail King himself must call out to Hector from a window, giving him directly the hard message he has failed to learn from his own experience on his quest:

Sir Knight, you shall not enter; no man so proudly mounted as yourself shall enter here so long as the Holy Grail is within. Go back to your own country, for you are surely no companion of the Quest, but rather one of those who have quit the service of Jesus Christ to become the liegemen of the enemy.

The gate is indeed strait.

The deeds of Gawain make the point even more strongly and more negatively, as he marks his sterile quest with the dead and dying bodies of his opponents. Failing to understand the spiritual nature of the quest, he always remains locked within the tunnel vision of '*chevalerie terrienne*', merely earthly chivalry. 'I have slain more than ten knights already, the worst of whom was more than adequate', he boasts to Hector when they meet at one point, but then concludes in foggy puzzlement, 'and still have met with no adventure'.[18]

In his wild quarrel with his brother Bors, Lionel shows again the distortion of the meaning of quest caused by internecine violence. Enraged that Bors has chosen to rescue a maiden when he was simultaneously in danger, Lionel rides his warhorse into the kneeling Bors 'and straight over his body, breaking it under his horse's hooves'. When a hermit tries to save Bors, Lionel splits the good man's skull with a single sword stroke. A similar blow dispatches Calogrenant, a knight of the Round Table who comes upon the scene and tries to intervene. Only a miraculous fireball and a voice from heaven prevent the long-suffering Bors from finally smiting his brother.

Yet shortly before this quarrel, even Bors, one of the three companions who completes the Grail quest, fights what at first seems the fairly standard romance battle, defending a lady against her sister's champion. That conflict won, he goes sturdily to work against the sister's vassals:

Bors approached all those who held land from her and said that he would destroy them unless they gave it up. Many became vassals of the younger sister, but those who chose not to were killed, disinherited, or banished. Thus did Bors' prowess restore the lady to the lofty position that the king had granted her.

Of course Bors later learns from a Cistercian abbot that the lady he has defended represents Holy Church, that her troublesome sister is the Old Law, and that the king is Christ. His fighting has indeed been in a good cause and, more than tolerable, has been laudable. This is *militia*, not *malitia*.

He likewise passes the sexual test, steadfastly maintaining his chastity, even when a beautiful and rich woman tells him how much she longs for him, even when she and twelve high-born ladies threaten to jump off the castle walls if he will not give the great lady his love. Of course they are all revealed as demons once they do jump; the Devil has been testing Bors.

Perceval learns these lessons in more than one setting. He has a close call with sexual temptation: slipping into bed with a demon in alluringly feminine form, he is only saved when his glance falls on the red cross inscribed on his sword pommel. The 'lady' and her silk tent disappear in a flash and a puff of smoke, leaving the tell-tale sulphurous stench of hell. A distraught Perceval stabs himself through the left thigh in penance.

Alone on his island, surrounded by wild beasts, Perceval trusts in God's help, and the text again delivers an important message: 'Thus did he depend more heavily on divine aid than on his sword, for he saw clearly that without

---

[18] Hector notes that he has met more than twenty Round Table companions, all complaining of the lack of adventure.

God's help, earthly prowess and knighthood alone could not save him.' Yet there is always a role for prowess. When the miraculous ship comes to him while he is alone on this island, its passenger, 'a man robed like a priest in surplice and alb and crowned with a band of white silk [which] . . . bore a text which glorified Our Lord's most holy names', proceeds to instruct him about chivalric duty; he speaks specifically about the courage and hard-hearted determination that must inform an ideal knight's prowess:

[God] would try you to determine whether you are indeed his faithful servant and true knight, even as the order of chivalry demands. For since you are come to such a high estate, no earthly fear of peril should cause your heart to quail. For the heart of a knight must be so hard and unrelenting towards his suzerain's foe that nothing in the world can soften it. And if he gives way to fear, he is not of the company of the knights and veritable champions, who would sooner meet death in battle than fail to uphold the quarrel of their lord.[19]

Perceval, Bors, and Galahad put this advice into practice in a telling scene at Castle Carcelois late in the romance. Attacked by hostile knights from this castle who demand that they yield, the three companions exclaim that they would not think of surrender. They attack and kill some of their challengers and follow those who sought survival by flight right into the castle hall. There, the three heroes 'set about cutting them down like so many dumb beasts'.

   Their success, however, leads to expressed feelings of guilt as they survey the bloody detritus of their victory. Bors tries to palliate their sense of guilt by suggesting that they had acted as agents of divine vengeance against men who deserved to die. Galahad will have none of it, at least until he can be sure they truly acted by God's will. The words are scarcely out of his mouth when a white-robed priest, bearing Christ's body in a chalice, comes upon the scene. Though at first 'unnerved by the sight of such a carnage', the holy man soon recovers and provides the explanation Galahad required, and in the most glowing terms:

Believe me, Sir, never did knights labour to better purpose; if you lived until the end of time I do not think you could perform a work of mercy to compare with this. I know for certain it was Our Lord who sent you here to do this work, for nowhere in the world were men who hated Him as much as the three brothers who were masters of this castle. In their great wickedness they had so suborned the inmates of this place that they were grown worse than infidels and did nothing but what affronted God and Holy Church.

---

[19] The lord in question here is clearly God, yet the language is very earthly and knightly, and the emphasis is on serving in arms.

These men, the companions learn, had raped and killed their sister, imprisoned their father, murdered clerics, and razed chapels. God himself had visited the imprisoned father, the priest tells them, bringing the news that three of his servants would appear and take revenge for the shame caused by the evil sons. Despite their commendable concerns, the three successful companions on the quest have thus corrected violence hateful in the sight of God and of his Church with sword strokes blessed by highest heaven.

As an allegory, a spiritual fable, the *Queste* is not, of course, primarily concerned with prowess; but it is addressing and drawing on a way of life that was itself primarily concerned with prowess, in a world that was much troubled by violence. Teaching and encouraging the spiritual life, never a light task, becomes so much more daunting when the principal figures in the story live by the use of edged weapons. The quests of the Grail companions thus deliver significant messages on questions that have concerned us throughout this book.

Of all the knights engaged on the quest, only these three companions, Bors, Perceval, and Galahad, finally come to see God and to be united mystically with him by means of the Grail. All three are model practitioners of controlled and righteous prowess; two are virgins, the third at least chaste; all humbly learn the foundations of their religion from hermits and heavenly messengers who interpret their adventures for them, symbol by symbol. Bors alone, having experienced this Pentecostal apotheosis of chivalry, can actually return to the world, to the Arthurian court.

However much the *Queste* edges clerical ideals closer to the grasp of knights, it is, finally, not very accommodating, not very sanguine about the yield of the harvest. The offer of quasi-monastic chivalry may have been generous from the vantage point of the monks; but it was surely leagues beyond the grasp or, probably even the desire of most knights in the world. Perhaps we would not be wrong to imagine them reading or listening with more attention and appreciation as great sword strokes flash and as God reveals himself directly to his good warriors than when one of the hermits delivers a homily on the merits of virginity.

Whoever wrote the *Queste* may well have understood the likelihood that knights absorbed the text through just such a filter. Certainly, the author himself strays from strict clerical views as he advances ideas of decided importance. He presents a non-Petrine notion of the origins and succession of the clergy, for one thing; he accepts knightly participation in tournaments, for another. Moreover, he is unstinting in his praise for prowess of the right sort, exercised by the right sort. Clearly, reform required the carrot as well as the stick; clearly, even an allegory such as this attempts to build a bridge between *clergie* and *chevalerie*. But the bridge is dauntingly high, all but obscured in idealistic mists, and its pathway is barely wide enough to accommodate a mounted knight.[20]

The Death of King Arthur

In one sense our second example is well named, for *The Death of King Arthur* (*La Mort le roi Artu*), written about 1230–5 as the final part of the original Lancelot–Grail or Vulgate cycle, tells the tragic and compelling story of the collapse of the Arthurian world and the death of the king.[21] The romance could with equal justice, however, be called 'The Ascent of Lancelot', for this is precisely what a central theme of quest in the story reveals.[22] In the process of narrating Lancelot's transformation, it offers another route to ideal knighthood. Though closely related to the text we have just examined from the same cycle, it differs from the *Queste* in important ways.

Above all, the lively spirituality of *The Death of King Arthur* is almost totally free from ecclesiastical dogma, from standard religious forms and practices (even confession and communion), and from the sermonizing voices which tirelessly explain meaning and prescribe knightly behaviour in the *Queste*. Even the extra-Christian force of Fortune plays a powerful role. Jean Frappier captures the character of religion in *The Death of King Arthur* concisely:

The great originality of the author of the *Mort Artu* lies in locating the conquest of the Grail within a man's soul. The Grail is interior, and the adventures that lead to it are psychological adventures. The personal experience of evil, not the sermon of a hermit, turns Lancelot toward holiness.[23]

---

[20] The bridge referred to here is not that which Frappier suggested between earthly and mystical chivalry, which Bogdanow condemns as a misunderstanding of the entire theology of the *Queste*. Rather, it is an attempt to show knights the true, mystical nature of chivalry as the road to salvation. Bogdanow believes that the text is fully negative about the majority of knights, as was St Bernard himself: see Bogdanow, 'An Interpretation'.

[21] Unless otherwise stated, quotations in this section are from Frappier, ed., *La Mort*, 13–19, 140, 151, 152, 185–6, 203, 2, 13, 140, 169, 118; Cable, tr., *Death of King Arthur*, 33–7, 135, 144, 145, 171, 185, 24, 33, 135, 158, 117; Lacy, tr., *Death of Arthur*, 94–6, 127, 130, 139, 143, 91, 94, 127, 135, 121. A useful bibliography of modern scholarship on this romance is provided in Baumgartner, *La Mort*, 16–24, a volume which reprints important segments of this scholarship. See also Dufournet, ed., *La Mort*, which prints twelve essays by French scholars, and also includes a bibliography.

[22] This is the interpretation of Frappier, *La Mort*, and of Cable's introduction to his translation, *Death of King Arthur*. Cf the comment of Chênerie: '[C]e roman, qui semble raconter avec la mort du roi, la fin d'un monde idéal, développe en réalité un véritable panégyrique du héros chevaleresque et courtois que fut Lancelot, un modèle de la *chevalerie terrienne*, après l'impossible réalisation de la *chevalerie celestiele*, figurée dans le mythe du Graal et la disparition de Galaad': 'Preudome', 82.

[23] Frappier, *La Mort*, 235 (my translation).

Here is knightly lay piety in pure form. Even if the author was, as seems likely, a cleric with a good Latinate education, it seems equally likely that he was one of that number of clerics who lived in the world and was comfortable with the details and with the ethos of the tournament and the battlefield. His guiding ideas are thoroughly Christian (and Cistercian): he stresses the need for the great virtue of *caritas* in humans and the saving presence of divine grace in their lives. These ideas show themselves powerfully, if obliquely, in this text; however, they never take on explicitly ecclesiastical formulation or issue from ecclesiastical authority.[24]

The spiritual height to which Lancelot will rise is emphasized by the level to which he has slipped at the start of the tale. He cannot stay away from the queen for even a month, though he had promised a life of celibacy to his hermit-confessor in the *Queste*; he has even become fairly open about it. About the vainglorious joy of tournaments there could be no question; while in full repentance, he had even (as we have seen) frankly told the hermit that he could scarcely give up the life of arms. In *The Death of King Arthur* he fights—splendidly, of course—in the opening tournament held at Winchester.

The issues are, once again, sex and violence, and the consequences of Lancelot's adultery and his fighting quickly set in motion the events that lead to chivalric *Götterdämmerung*. At the same time, Lancelot's experience of anguished suffering, and the outpouring of God's grace for him, begin his spiritual transformation. It comes in the upheaval following the open discovery of his relationship with Queen Guinevere, and his dramatic rescue which saves her from death by burning. The result is war, with Lancelot versus King Arthur, goaded on by Gawain, whose three brothers Lancelot has killed in the dramatic rescue.

As the war goes on, Lancelot banishes pride; he makes kings of Bors and Lionel, giving up his own earthly dominion in clear witness of the transformation at work in him. He soon shows the change even more clearly in his subordination of his own vast prowess.

Seeing Arthur's avenging army encamped against him around the walls of Joyeuse Garde, Lancelot feels only great sadness and great love:

When Lancelot saw how the castle was besieged by King Arthur, the man he had most loved in the world and whom he now knew to be his mortal enemy, he was so saddened that he did not know what to do, not because he feared for himself but because he loved the king.

---

[24] See the discussion of Frappier, ed., *La Mort*, 21–4, for questions of authorship, pp. 219–58 for a thorough discussion of religious ideas.

After his secret efforts to establish peace have come to naught and the battle in the field has begun in earnest, Lancelot proves his love in the eyes of all. Arthur shows wondrous prowess (especially wondrous for a man aged 92), and inspires all his men. When he attacks Lancelot in person, Lancelot only raises his shield to save his own life and will strike not one blow. Hector, however, reacts in the standard knightly fashion and swiftly gives Arthur a blow on the helm that leaves him not knowing whether it is day or night. Thus he thinks he has set up Lancelot for the grand stroke: 'My lord, cut off his head, and our war will be over.' Instead, Lancelot rescues the fallen Arthur and securely remounts him in the saddle, before quitting the field.

He makes an even greater sacrifice shortly thereafter: he subordinates his own mortal love by agreeing to return Queen Guinevere. Though his companions mistakenly ask what fear of Arthur has led to his action, Lancelot is actually placing her honour before his own desires; he fears, in fact, that he may die because of missing her so much. The same concern for her honour apparently leads him to lie to Arthur by denying that any adultery ever took place.

Ever unforgiving, Gawain convinces Arthur that the war must be prosecuted to the end, to the downfall and death of Lancelot. Gawain demands a single combat. Having already spared Arthur, Lancelot now likewise spares his true arch-enemy Gawain, after defeating him decisively.[25] As he explains to Hector, 'I should not kill him for all the world, because I think he is too noble. Moreover, he is the man, out of all those in the world that have meant anything to me, that I have most loved, and still do, excepting only the king.' At this time Gawain himself is still hoping that God will be so 'courteous' as to allow him finally to kill Lancelot and at last taste sweet revenge.[26]

But Lancelot meets Arthur to talk peace again. In fact, he convinces a very reluctant Bors and Lionel to dismount in show of respect for the man they continue to denounce as their mortal foe. The generous peace plan Lancelot proposes, however, is rejected by Gawain, who ignores Arthur's tearful entreaties. Even another single combat fails to generate wrath in Lancelot. Asked why he did not, once again, kill Gawain, as was within his power, he responds tellingly, 'I could not do it because my heart, which directs me, would not allow it for anything.'

[25] On the nature of the term *preudome*, so often applied to Lancelot in this text, see Chênerie, 'Preudome'. For the view this text takes of tournaments as diversions from the highest knightly activity, see Lachet, 'Les tournois d'antan'.

[26] As Boutet suggests, only Lancelot retains *mesure*; Gawain, and even Arthur, show *demesure* and think along the lines of vengeance and private war; the great men of the court, with latent jealousy of Lancelot working in them, want to show their prowess in battle against him: see 'Arthur et son mythe', 50–6.

Invasion by Roman enemies and treason by Mordred at home complete the downfall of Arthur's world playing contrapuntally to the spiritual rise of Lancelot. Gawain is mortally wounded and comes finally to a new vision of the good, asking Lancelot for forgiveness. Lancelot comes to offer help to Arthur, but is too late. On the site of the climactic battle between Arthur and Mordred he finds the principal combatants already slain; he can only finish off Mordred's supporters and, with justice, kill the traitor's two sons.

This work done, Lancelot rides off in a kind of fog, almost aimlessly, it seems. But the transformation that has been working in Lancelot leads him to the logical conclusion of his spiritual odyssey. In a chapel attached to a poor hermitage he finds the Archbishop of Canterbury and his cousin Bleobleeris, robed as hermit-priests before the altar. Lancelot joins them in the fullest sense, becomes an ascetic hermit and priest, lives out a new form of heroism on a diet of bread, water, and roots. After his death, the archbishop dreams of angels carrying off his soul to bliss.

This theme of Lancelot's spiritual journey is, for good reasons, stressed in analyses of the text. But the author continually drives home the superiority of Lancelot's transformed chivalry in another way important for analysis: he shows the problems caused by the accustomed practices and attitudes of most of his knightly contemporaries. Indeed, the tale opens with Arthur angrily establishing the precise scorecard of Gawain's victims while on the Grail quest. Gawain's answer delivers the author's message on this topic explicitly:

I can tell you in truth that I killed eighteen by my own hand, not because I was a better knight than any of the others, but since misfortune affected me more than any of my companions. Indeed, it did not come about through my chivalry, but through my sin. You have made me reveal my shame.[27]

Shortly after that, in the tournament at which the king proclaims to keep up knightly spirit in an age of declining adventures ('because he did not want his companions to cease wearing arms'), Arthur has thought it necessary to prohibit Gawain and Gaheriet from participating; Lancelot will be present and Arthur fears bad feeling and combat which goes beyond even rough sport.

In fact, the danger of the great war that will finally doom the Round Table swirls like a malignant mist throughout even the early action of the poem. Knightly vengeance and the setting of kin against kin is, of course, a theme of the entire text. The author works the theme in miniature as well. When Arthur's knights besiege Lancelot in the Joyeuse Garde, Lancelot cannot bring himself to spring the pincer movement he has skilfully prepared. As a result,

[27] An interesting redefinition of chivalry seems to be intended here; victory through fine prowess is simply sin if it brings about the death of other knights, a result hard to avoid.

'Arthur's men felt more confident than before, and said among themselves that if Lancelot had had large forces, nothing would have stopped him from coming out to attack them and the whole army, because no true knight would willingly suffer injury from his enemy.' Lancelot's love for his enemies is inconceivable to them.

The nobility of pure prowess is hymned time and again by one character after another. Chivalry is repeatedly equated with deeds done with weapons, with feats of arms (*chevaleries*); prowess is equated with nobility, great blows being noted specifically as proof of nobility. Little wonder that Lancelot's men rejoice when they learn that he will lead them out of the city of Gaunes against King Arthur's army the next morning: 'most of them were pleased and happy about this, because they preferred war to peace'. Little wonder that some more thoughtful characters in the romance repeatedly speak their fears—as Bors does when he foresees the collapse of the Round Table—of the 'war that will never end in our lifetimes'.

The author, in other words, not only shows an ideal spiritual path for the regeneration of knighthood, he shows the dangers that quickly accumulate if that path is not taken. To think only in terms of victory on the tourney grounds and the battlefield, to equate chivalry simply with prowess, to give in to sensual love whatever the consequences, to open the gates for vengeance fortified with kin loyalties, is to slide toward endless, destructive war.[28]

Robert the Devil/Sir Gowther

The numerous romances which sprouted from the story of Robert the Devil doubly recommend themselves as the final case study for this chapter. In the first place, these romances show nearly fathomless depths of knightly evil followed by repentance that elevates the reformed sinner to the skies, with the problem of violence a central issue in the double process. Second, the basic story proved to be genuinely popular and spoke its messages repeatedly in one European language after another through the centuries that concern us—and

[28] In the latter half of the fourteenth century this gripping story was rewritten in a north Midlands dialect of Middle English as a work only about a fifth as long as the French original. Benson, ed., *Morte Arthur*. The narrative frame is retained and the focus is once again on Lancelot and on all of the difficult issues raised by his role in Arthur's court and his love for Arthur's queen. But, as in the *Mort Artu* he is not condemned; rather, he appears as an admired hero who gains in self-knowledge and the grace of God, who transcends not only merely earthly chivalry based on war, but merely earthly love as well. He thus stands in marked contrast to Gawain, who falls from his previous reputation as peacemaker into sterile, unrelenting vengeance. As Barron notes, the poet 'does not preach', but conveys his messages more subtly, always showing the impossibility of perfection and the looming danger resulting from merely human forms, even when they are practised in the hope of perfection, even when they are such valued qualities as the prowess of Lancelot or his mutual love with Guinevere. See the discussion in Barron, *English Medieval Romance*, 142–7.

well beyond.[29] There are many texts; to keep our case study manageable, the analysis will draw on three that seem especially useful: *Robert le Diable*, written in Old French in the late twelfth century; *Sir Gowther*, the Middle English rewriting from the latter part of the fourteenth century; and the printed English text of Robert's story produced by Wynkyn de Worde shortly after 1500.[30]

Exactly why Robert/Gowther is so lost in evil at the beginning of his career depends upon the text. In the Old French romance and in Wynkyn de Worde's text, he has been conceived after an anguished appeal to the Devil by the wife of the duke of Normandy, desperate to save her long-childless marriage (ll. 25–73).[31] In *Sir Gowther* (set in Estryke, rather than Normandy), a 'shaggy fiend' who has taken the duke's form is actually the father of the child, impregnating the duke's wife beneath a Chestnut tree in a classic scene familiar to folkloric tradition (ll. 52–81).

The child grows abnormally in every sense—at seven times the rate of physical growth of ordinary children, for example. The Middle English text gives him an inordinate appetite that leads him to suck nine wet-nurses to death (ll. 109–20) and to bite off his own mother's nipple with his premature teeth (ll. 127–32). Yet at fourteen he is a perfect specimen of a young man: 'none is as beautiful as Robert', the French romance says (nien est si biaus comme Roibers'; l. 123).

With appropriate precociousness he is early entering that dangerous age of turbulence and disruptive violence which medieval writers called 'youth' and which Georges Duby studied in a famous article.[32] Physically, if not emotionally, mature, these young men often formed into bands, and wandered, gambled, philandered, and fought in tournaments and in wars. Duby thinks that they 'formed the primary audience for all the literature that is called chivalric'.[33]

---

[29] Breul, ed., *Sir Gowther*, 45–134, traces the widespread telling of this story.

[30] Quotations in this section, unless otherwise stated, are from Löseth, ed., *Robert le Diable*; Laskaya and Salisbury, eds., *Breton Lays*; Wynkyn de Worde's printed text, from Cambridge University Library, 1502?: 'here beginneth the lyf of the moste myschevoust Robert the deuyll whiche was afterwarde called the servaunt of god', published in modern print in Thoms, ed., *Early English Prose Romances*, 169–206. Warm thanks to Anne McKinley whose fine seminar paper studied these texts when I had all but forgotten their existence. Interesting discussions of *Gowther* in relation to the other texts appear in Hopkins, *Sinful Knights*, 144–78; Novelli, 'Sir Gowther'; and Breul, *Sir Gowther*. Vanderlinde, 'Sir Gowther', argues for enough difference between the two surviving manuscripts of *Sir Gowther* to consider them essentially separate poems, sharing the same source. These differences (which will interest many) do not seem sufficiently great for the issues investigated here to require separate analyses of the two texts. These texts are printed in Mills, ed., *Six Middle English Romances*, 148–68; Rumble, ed., *Breton Lays*, 178–204; and Novelli, *Sir Gowther*, 83–157.

[31] Wynkyn de Worde text in Thoms, ed., *Early English Prose Romances*, 171–2.

[32] Duby, 'Dans la France du Nord-Ouest'. Trempler has even used the story of Robert as a case study of adolescent destructive narcissism: see 'Robert der Teufel'. The author is interested in the origins of delinquency and destructive hate.

Gowther seems a parodic exemplar of these turbulent, wandering, violent youths. Having from an alloy of iron and steel fashioned a great falchion (a heavy sword with a single curved cutting edge) that he alone can swing, Gowther sets enthusiastically to work.[34] Robert's band of like-minded fellows (in the French romance) is composed of robbers in the woods near Rouen. Behind him now are the youthful pranks of smashing beautiful church windows or throwing ashes into the mouths of yawning knights (ll. 132–3, 157–9). If he had long 'set by no correccyon', as Wynkyn de Worde says, going on to tell us Robert had eviscerated his 'scole mayster' with a bodkin, he was now 'able to bere armes'—the real weapons of warriors.[35] If neighbouring children have for years feared him as 'Roberte the Deuyll', giving him his name, he now sets about troubling a much wider neighbourhood. The French romance says *plaintes* (legal complaints against his actions), come daily to his father, the duke (ll. 165–6). By the age of twenty, he has been excommunicated by the pope and banished by his father, to no avail. He regularly kills merchants and pilgrims; he has burned twenty abbeys to the ground (ll. 196–7, 199–204, 221–2). Gowther continues his devilish campaign by raping wives and virgins, hanging priests on hooks, and forcing friars to jump off cliffs. In the Middle English romance he has already been knighted, that ceremony changing him not a whit (ll. 189–204).

The Old French romance makes much more of the effort to reform Robert by enrolling him in the ranks of chivalry. When his father swears he will settle all by drowning the lad (ll. 229–34), the mother suggests knighting him instead: 'Make your son a knight. You'll see him give up his wickedness, cruelty and evil deeds when he has been made a knight. Robert has done evil deeds in his youth [*bachelerie*]. He'll do good deeds as soon as he becomes a knight.'[36] It is a classic statement of ideal knightly reform. The intent is highly interesting: so is the failure. Even though the quid pro quo is carefully explained and Robert enthusiastically agrees, dismissing his band of robbers in apparent enthusiasm for a new life (ll. 254–64), he cannot stem the power of evil within. At the inevitable tournament held to celebrate his new state, he begins his 'bad chivalry [*ses chevaleries males*]' (l. 281). Following a wild night of partying—no vigil in a church—Robert fights as if the tourney were war to

---

[33] Duby, 'Dans la France du Nord-Ouest', tr., Cheyette, 205.

[34] Illustrations of falchions from the Douce Apocalypse and a picture of a surviving example appear in Prestwich, *Armies and Warfare*, 28, 30. The illustrations show the Devil's cavalry, riding lion-headed horses, as noted on the dust jacket of John Maddicott's *Simon de Montfort*.

[35] Thoms, ed., *Early English Prose Romances*, 173, 174. Young heroes of romance tradition did not rip out their teacher's entrails, but more than one did beat them severely. See Chapter 7.

[36] Combining Löseth, ed., *Robert* ll. 239–44 from ms. A, with several lines from ms B, given in a note, Ibid., 16.

the death; he wants to decapitate all those whom he has unhorsed. His ferocity disrupts this tournament and his subsequent tour of the tournament circuit
across France spreads terror; back in Normandy, he renews his assaults on clerics (ll. 275–322).[37]

The action comes to a climax as he attacks a nunnery. If Robert plays Raoul
here, re-enacting the infamous scene at Origny from *Raoul de Cambrai*, he
descends even deeper into the pit of sin by personally thrusting his sword into
the breasts of the nuns, killing fifty of the sixty religious with his own hands,
before setting the torch to the structures (ll. 341–52).[38]

At this point, the blood-red tide begins slowly to turn.[39] Robert finds himself alone before the scene of desolation. The loud neighing of his warhorse
reverberates. None of his men will answer his call, even when summoned by
name. Falling into unaccustomed introspection, he wonders about the course
of his life and its relationship to his birth; with the aid of the Holy Spirit, he
dimly realizes he could yet be God's friend, and goes, soaked in blood, to see
his fearful mother; with threats, he finally extracts the painful truth from her
(ll. 353–468). In *Sir Gowther*, recognition that he has been formed in evil by his
fiendish father comes from a wise old duke whose observations send Gowther
to his mother, from whom he gets the truth, told with the dreaded falchion
poised over her heart (ll. 205–33).

Weeping with sorrow and shame, Robert/Gowther experiences conversion.
He will rid himself of devilish influence; he will go to Rome to seek absolution
from the pope himself. In the French romance he symbolically throws away
his sword and cuts his hair before setting off for Rome (ll. 465–8).[40] Yet his sins
are so great, he learns in a hard-won papal audience, that even the pontiff cannot set penance, nor yet can that archetypical figure of chivalric romance, the
holy hermit, to whom the pope sends him.[41] It takes a hand from heaven, bearing a little script, to establish what Robert must do: until released from the
penance, he must play the fool, provoking violence and derision in the streets;
he must play the mute, speaking not a word; he must eat only what he can

---

[37] Thoms, ed., *Early English Prose Romances*, 175–7.

[38] The early sixteenth-century text has Robert violate the sacred bond between knight and hermit: Robert slays seven holy hermits and goes to see his mother, covered in their blood: l. 180.

[39] Ms. B of *Robert le Diable* emphasizes the bloodiness of the slaughter: Löseth, ed., *Robert le
Diable*, 26. In Wynkyn de Worde's version, Robert shows his change of life by killing all his company of robbers before setting off for Rome. He deposits the keys to his forest robber's nest, his
horse, and his sword with the head of an abbey he had 'many tymes robbed': Thoms, *Early English
Prose Romances*, 184–6.

[40] In *Sir Gowther* he retains the falchion, as discussed below.

[41] In the Wynkyn de Worde text the pope tells Robert (whose evil reputation he knows) that
he will 'assoyle' him, but wants a promise 'that ye do no man harme'. Robert promises, 'I will
neuer hurte Crysten creature': Thoms, *Early English Prose Romances*, 187.

wrest from a dog's mouth (ll. 490–885).[42] This heaven-sent burden bears a clear message: Robert must willingly suffer at least a few sparks of the raging flames of violence he had inflicted on others and experience the slow burn of shame; he must resolutely dethrone his heedless pride.[43] The several texts elaborately detail how thoroughly Robert/Gowther embraces and then for years fulfils this penance, in full public view, in the streets of Rome and in the emperor's hall.

Then the Turks invade and all is thrown into confusion. Upon each of three threats to Rome by the Sultan's army, Robert/Gowther receives horse and arms from heaven (either in response to his silent prayer, as in the French and Middle English romances, or by direct divine command, according to Wynkyn de Worde). Only the emperor's mute daughter from her chamber window witnesses the transformation of the fool into the saviour/knight. Dressed in white armour and mounted on a white charger, the hero performs wonders of prowess against the enemy in the field, saving Rome three times in a row by emptying saddles, shearing off arms and legs, and spilling brains.[44] Each time he then returns, divests himself of knightly horse and arms, and becomes again the humble and unknown penitent.[45] All imperial efforts to detain and identify the white knight fail; the effort after the third battle even results in Robert being wounded by Roman knights who would take him to their chief (ll. 3414–500).

Resolution follows swiftly. The emperor's mute daughter miraculously begins to speak and is at last enabled plainly to say the truth about the fool in the hall who is actually the White Knight. She produces as material proof the lance-head which had wounded the knight, and which she had watched him hide after he had painfully removed it. When the holy hermit releases Robert from his penance, he joyfully tells his story openly (ll. 4490–866). In *Sir Gowther*, the princess, who has steadily loved Gowther throughout his stay at court, is given the privilege of pronouncing God's forgiveness on him. Gowther happily marries her and, upon the death of the emperor, takes the crown himself, instituting a reign of peace and justice:

[42] *Sir Gowther* pictures the pope himself absolving Gowther and setting his penance, which is condensed to two elements: silence and eating only what he can take from dogs. The Wynkyn de Worde text is closer to the French romance, but the penance comes to the hermit in a dream.

[43] Wynkyn de Worde draws the moral explicitly: 'Now haue this in your myndes, ye proude hertes and synners, thynke on Roberts grete penaunce and wylfull pouerte and how he so grete a gentylman borne . . . hathe all forsaken for the saluacyon of his soule': Thoms, ed., *Early English Prose Romances*, 191.

[44] Gowther even rescues the emperor himself and decapitates the Sultan: ll. 625–31.

[45] The Middle English text gives him, on successive days of battle, black, red, and white armour. Some scholars have suggested a progressive process of purging. See Marchalonis, '*Sir Gowther*', 20–3.

> What mon so bydus hym for Godys loffe doo
> He was ey redy bown theretoo,
> And stod pore folke in styd,
> And ryche men in hor ryght,
> And halpe holy kyrke in all is myght (ll. 715–19).

(He was always ready for love of God to do what people asked, and supported both the poor, and the rights of the powerful).[46]

The text printed by Wynkyn de Worde similarly ends with worldly as well as spiritual happiness. Robert is even commanded by God to marry the princess. He brings her to Normandy where he secures the peace, hanging a troublesome knight who had bothered his mother after the death of his father. A message from Rome hurries Robert there with an armed force to save the emperor from his wicked seneschal. Though he cannot arrive in time—the seneschal has already slain the emperor in battle—Robert does split the wicked traitor's head down to the teeth with one of his great sword blows and so saves Rome yet again. He rules well over rich and poor alike. As a final boon, Robert and his wife give Christendom a champion in their son who joins Charlemagne in the endless fight against pagan forces.[47]

The French romance ends more starkly. Robert announces he has left the world and will for nothing endanger his soul by re-entering it for even a day. He rejects the appeal of four knights who have come from Normandy to tell him of strife after the death of his parents there; he sets aside the Roman princess and the claim to the imperial crown; and he goes to live with the holy hermit outside Rome. He follows in that saintly man's steps upon the hermit's death. For the rest of his life Robert serves God, who does many miracles for him. At his death the Romans bury him with reverence in the church of St John Lateran. Years later, a Frenchman, who has come to a council held to make peace in many wars, takes Robert's bones to a site near Le Puy and builds an abbey over the new tomb. It is called the Abbey of St Robert (ll. 4490–5078).

For all their variance in detail, all three texts speak forcefully to a fear that knightly prowess and pride, especially when spurred by the heedless energies of youth, will turn to disruptive and destructive violence. The very devil is in it. The best hope, the authors agree, lies in the shaping and restraining force of religious ideals.

---

[46] In the early sixteenth-century text the hermit releases Robert from his penance (as in the French romance) and allows him to marry the princess (as in the Middle English romance): see Thoms, ed., *Early English Prose Romances*, 199–203.

[47] Ibid., 202–6.

Yet, as we have regularly seen in other texts, the authors take a view of knightly prowess which has its twists and turns. Violence in the right causes is enthusiastically endorsed. Wynkyn de Worde's Robert ends his life as a model hero from epic or romance, putting a rope round the neck of a Norman troublemaker, putting his sword into the skull of a Roman traitor, and then ruling well, even engendering a warrior son. The text of *Sir Gowther* valorizes a rough-hewn chivalric atmosphere from the beginning by noting that at the tournament to celebrate his wedding the duke who will be Gowther's supposed father is an expert tourneyer; the text proclaims that he unhorsed ten men in the joust and cracked skulls generally in the mêlée (ll. 40–8). Gowther himself does not throw away his sword, as Robert does, upon going on pilgrimage to Rome. Specifically told to discard his beloved falchion by the pope, he refuses; it is again in his expert hands on the battlefield against the Turks. Though the text condemns Gowther in his wild days for slaying his mother's retainers with this great sword, cutting through both rider and horse with powerful blows, when, later, he cuts through the Sultan's men and mounts, the action is, of course, praised in the manner of any great sword stroke in romance. The falchion seems almost to function as a symbol of the force of his knighthood, which can be turned to good or ill use.[48]

If in the French romance Robert has horribly stained his sword with the blood of nuns early in the text, he then gloriously stains the sword lent from heaven with the blood of the Sultan's men.[49] This text lingers admiringly over Robert's arming and his stunning appearance in the white armour as he prepares to go into action (ll. 1840–58); it can equate chivalry with prowess, noting that the emperor 'saw the beautiful chivalry that Robert *did* in his presence' on the battlefield ('la chevalerie bele / Que Robers devant lui *a faite*'; ll. 1935–7, my emphasis); in standard romance fashion it can likewise praise the hall full of the emperor's 'good knights who never were without war' (ll. 2770–3; they are called 'Li flors de la chevalerie' at l. 2205); and it notes that the final victory feast seated not only seasoned knights but even the 'bachelors with the most prowess' (l. 3602).[50]

Complexities of attitude regarding prowess thus put in their appearance, as always. All three texts, however, begin with a knight whose prowess is

---

[48] Swordblows against mother's retainers, (see n. 30) ll. 166–7; against Turks, 592–4. For comments on symbolism of the falchion, see Hopkins, *Sinful Knights*, 158.

[49] Killing of nuns: see especially B text, p. 26 n. Killing of Turks: ll. 1955–60. In each case he is described as plunging his sword into the victim's breast.

[50] The emperor says of the White Knight at the third banquet that no knight could be as good as he, no living man so filled with prowess: ll. 3797–3800. Even the emperor's daughter is once described as 'prous' (ll. 2380), and his ancient bloodhound is praised as formerly 'prous' (ll. 1089–90). When praise flows, prowess seems naturally to command a space in the encomium.

13

CHIVALRIC SELF-CRITICISM AND REFORM

✦✦✦

PREVIOUS chapters have shown knights absorbing ideas and cooperating with practices from the spheres of *clergie* and *royauté*, while filtering through their own high sense of power, privilege, and calling any ideas and practices that seemed constricting or intrusive. Yet reform was not simply forced upon knighthood from outside, by those who were not knights or not primarily knights. The knights themselves clearly had ideals. Even had clerics and royal career administrators ceased to direct a steady stream of exhortations, some of the chivalrous would have found a continual reform programme necessary and desirable. Many knights knew that the great ideal could be better implemented in the world and, to the extent that it was, that the world would be a better, nobler place. The warriors themselves agreed that there was, in other words, ideal chivalry, though they might have debated the details; they thought that difficult and imperfect men must try to do better. *Clergie* or *royauté*, of course, held that chivalry would still need reform even if it were practised according to the ideals sketched in this chapter.

We can best discover the ideals of the knights themselves in works written by them or by those quite close to them. The vernacular manuals or handbooks written to instruct knights provide a classic source. *The Book of Chivalry* by Geoffroi de Charny and *The Book of the Order of Chivalry* by Ramon Llull are especially important.[1] But before considering these it will be helpful to glance at the programme in an earlier work.

The Romance of the Wings

The Romance of the Wings (*Le Roman des Eles*), written by Raoul de Hodenc in about 1210, shows a clear reforming intent from its opening page, even if this intent is wrapped, as always, in extravagant praise of chivalry as an ideal.[2]

---

[1] As emphasized by Keen, *Chivalry*, 6–17.
[2] Busby, ed., *Ordene de Chevalerie*. Translations of quotations in this section from pp. 161–75.

Raoul says that the very name *chevalerie* is full of 'such loftiness and dignity', that, 'rightly speaking, [it] is the true name of nobility'. Only knights drink from the inexhaustible, divine fountain of courtesy: 'it came from God and knights possess it' (ll. 11–15, 25).

Because of its very loftiness, it stands so far above all other lofty names, that if they were to recognize its lofty nature, they would not dare to do some things they now do.—Why?—Out of shame. But they are not aware of the exigencies of their name, for a man may take himself for a knight though he know not what appertains to the name, save only 'I am a knight'. (ll. 40–9)

He thinks it 'indisputably true that they should be such as their name says'. Yet 'many have no understanding of knighthood'. He is specifically worried that the dominance of prowess in the thinking of knights will drive out two other qualities that he wants to see held in great esteem: liberality and courtesy. He tries to be careful, but his enthusiasm carries him along:

Do I mean to say that there is such a thing as a wicked knight? By no means, but some are at the least worth more than the others, whatever the case; and there are many such who are so superior in prowess that they do not deign to exercise liberality, but rather trust so much to their prowess that pride strikes them at once.' (ll. 27–8, 116–26)

He imaginatively recreates the thinking of such a man: 'Why give? What can they say about me? Am I not he of the great shield? I am he who has conquered all, I am the best of my kind, I have surpassed Gavain in arms' (ll. 128–34). To such prideful knights, obsessed with prowess, Raoul responds:

Ah, lords, whatever anyone may say, it is no part of knighthood for a knight to despise liberality on account of his prowess, for to tell the truth, no-one can rise to lofty esteem by means of prowess unless that prowess has two wings; and I will tell you what the matter and manner of those two wings ought to be. (ll. 135–43)

The treatise does just that, providing detailed explanations of seven feathers on the right wing of liberality, seven on the left wing of courtesy.

Raoul fears that an excessive belief in prowess in his own time will reduce the largesse so important to chivalry; significantly, his great enemy is the miser, where Geoffroi de Charny's is the cowardly and inactive man. From the right wing the knight learns that he must be courageous in liberality, give to rich and poor alike, spend without care for landed wealth (saying, 'A knight, God protect me, will not rise to great heights if he enquires of the value of corn'), give what is promised, promptly and liberally, and provide fine feasts.

The left wing is also composed of seven feathers, each a specific component of courtesy. The knight must honour and guard Holy Church, avoid pride; refrain from boasting (he should 'strike high and talk low'), enjoy good entertainment, avoid envy, avoid slander (since simultaneous physical and verbal feats are an impossibility), and be a lover and love truly for love's sake (ll. 144–end).[3]

As Keith Busby, the editor of the text, has suggested, the message is 'largely social, and it concentrates on telling knights how to behave rather than elaborating on the symbolic significance of knighthood'. Though the poem makes its case in religious and moral terms, it 'could not be called essentially religious'.[4] So close is its link with topics we have discussed that we might safely call the poem reformist.

The Book of the Order of Chivalry

Ramon Llull wrote the most popular handbook, *The Book of the Order of Chivalry*, probably between 1279 and 1283.[5] It reached a wide readership in its original Catalan (*Libre qui es de l'ordre de cavalleria*); in French translation (*Livre de l'ordre de chevalerie*) it reached an even wider audience, before being translated into English and transcribed into print by Caxton (*The Book of the Ordre of Chyvalry*) in the last quarter of the fifteenth century.[6]

Llull was the ideal person to write a handbook for knights. He began his adult life as a knight himself and was thoroughly immersed in chivalric culture and literature before experiencing the great conversion, probably in 1263, that sent him on a radically new course. After recurrent divine visitations he became a mystic, a systematic and prolific philosopher, a missionary for the conversion of Muslims and Jews, and one of the founding figures of Catalan literature. But he apparently never became a cleric, however close he was to the Franciscans in thought and life.[7]

The showy, easily remembered, and often quoted statements in his book are all in praise of knighthood, even of the sort of knighthood that clerical critics might view through narrowed eyes as merely 'earthly chivalry'. Llull likes and praises it all: jousts and tournaments, war in defence of one's lord, the liberal life of hall and hunting.

The thin story frame for his treatise is built around that stock figure the wise old hermit who—we learn with no surprise—turns out to be a former knight. A young seeker after chivalry encounters him by his fountain, asks questions, and receives not only a lecture but also a reading assignment, a little book that

---

[3] Busby speculates that Raoul may have been 'a knight of slender means . . . employed as a minstrel', who might well praise open-handed generosity on the part of the wealthy.

[4] Ibid., 18.   [5] Bonner, *Selected Works*, II, 1262.

[6] *Ramon Llull, Obres essencials*; Byles, ed., *Book of the Ordre of Chyvalry*.

[7] For accounts of Llull's life, see Hillgarth, *Ramon Lull and Lullism*, 1–43; Bonner, *Selected Works*, I, 3–52.

he will take to court for the instruction of all. It is, of course, the very book the reader holds. The hermit, now pale and ascetic, had formerly been the sort of hero with whom any knight could identify: '[He] had long maintained the order of chivalry and done so by the force and nobleness of his high courage and wisdom and in adventuring his body had maintained just wars, jousts and tourneys and in many battles had many noble and glorious victories.'[8]

On such honourable men Llull can scarcely lavish enough praise. They form an *ordo* alongside that of the clerics and rank only a little lower than those whose hands produce God's body on the altar. If only these two high orders could be free of error, Llull says, the world would be all but free from error. The knights, if anything, ought to be advanced in honour. Ideally, each knight should have a kingdom or province to rule, an honour prevented only by the unfortunate shortage of suitable territories. Certainly, knights would make excellent judges, if only they were learned, and chivalry is, in itself, so high a subject that it ought to be taught in schools. There can be no doubt that knights are the natural counsellors for kings and princes; to advance the non-knightly to such positions is an offence against chivalry, which produces the men best qualified for rule, best fit for distributing justice. In his *Ars Brevis*, Llull in fact defines chivalry as 'the disposition with which the knight helps the prince maintain justice'.[9]

Llull introduces his general theme by telling a myth of origins. It is a story of a fall and a redemption through chivalry.[10] At issue are all the basic matters concerned with securing right order in the world. The myth relates that at some point in the swirling mists of the past the great virtues—charity, loyalty, truth, justice, and verity—had fallen, producing injuries, disloyalty, and falseness, with social consequences of error and trouble in the world. Fearing disorder and injustice, the populace divided itself into thousands and from each chose the best man to be a knight; they likewise selected the horse as the best beast to carry him in his work.[11] From that time forward the knight has carried out a high and essential mission: he secures order in the world. For fear of him the common people hesitate to do wrongs to each other; for fear of him they till the soil. Just as the clerks (who are brought into the myth without expla-

---

[8] My translation of Caxton, in Byles, ed., *Book of the Ordre of Chyvalry*, 3–4.

[9] Bonner, *Selected Works*, I, 624. See also his knight's comment (to a hermit questioning him) in the *Arbre de Ciencia*: 'Dix lo cavaller que ell mantenia cavalleria ab l'espasa del rei, qui fa estar comuna la sua corona': *Ramon Llull. Obres Essencials*, I, 903.

[10] The similarity between this account and that in the earlier pre-cyclic prose *Lancelot* is interesting. See Elspeth Kennedy, ed., *Lancelot do Lac*, I, 142.

[11] Any medieval reader familiar with contemporary learning on the *Corpus Juris Civilis* might at this point hear echoes of the Lex Digna Vox, which asserted that at some point in the mythic past the people had given up their natural sovereignty to the Roman emperors. See Byles, *Book of the Ordre of Chyvalry*, 113. for an even more strikingly similar statement by Llull.

nation, since it is not their myth) incline the people to devotion and the good life, the knights ensure the order that makes civilized life possible.[12]

Llull makes this same point in slightly different terms in his *Felix* (though here he reverses the roles of hermit and knight). In response to the hermit's quizzing him about what a knight is, 'the knight replied that a knight was a man chosen to ride on horseback to carry out justice and to protect and safeguard the king and his people so that the king could reign in such a manner that his subjects could love and know God'.[13] Yet such praise is only half the picture. Although Llull nearly worshipped chivalry as an ideal, his first-hand knowledge of knighthood as it worked in the world shaped everything he says about it. In fact, his love for chivalry as it might be never eradicates his deep fear of chivalry as social fact. In the *Book of Contemplation*, for example, he refers to knights as 'the Devil's ministers', and asks pointedly, 'Who is there in the world who does as much harm as knights?'[14] At one point in the *Tree of Science* he pictures a hermit asking a knight if he understands the order of chivalry. The knight explains that in the absence of a book on the subject he does not, in fact, understand chivalry. Were there such a book, the knight adds, 'many knights would be humble who are prideful, and just who are criminal [*injurioses*], and chaste who are licentious, and brave who are cowardly, and rich who are poor, and honourable who are dishonourable'.[15] Llull here, of course, clearly if indirectly announces a rationale for the book on chivalry which he himself wrote; in the process, he explicitly establishes the reforming nature of his book. Knights can and must be made better in basic categories of their lives.

Llull knows that he is in a sense whistling past the graveyard in *The Book of the Order of Chivalry*. It will be difficult to refashion the men who cause so much disorder into effective upholders of order. Each gilded wine goblet that Llull raises to toast knighthood thus contains a bitter residue of criticism. The basic dichotomy appears in advice given by the hermit within the very myth of origins:

Beware, squire, who would enter into the order of chivalry what you shall do. For if you become a knight you receive honour and the servitude due to the friends of

---

[12] The myth is elaborated in Llull's second chapter.

[13] Bonner, *Selected*, II, 668–9. In his *Ars Brevis*, Llull says in the same vein: 'Chivalry is the disposition with which the knight helps the prince maintain justice': in ibid., I, 624.

[14] Quoted in Hillgarth, *The Spanish Kingdoms*, 60. The Catalan, kindly supplied in correspondence from Professor Hillgarth, reads: 'E doncs, Sènyer, qui és lo mon qui tant de mal faça com cavallers?'

[15] *Ramon Llull. Obres Essencials*, 903: 'Dix lo cavaller que ell no sabia l'ordre de cavaleria, e blasmava son pare qui escrit no l'havia; car si era fet un libre de l'art de cavalleria, molts cavallers serien humils qui son ergulloses, e justs qui son injurioses, e casts qui son luxurioses, e ardits qui son volpells, e rics qui son pobres, e honrats qui son deshonrats.'

chivalry. For of so much as you have more noble beginnings and more honour, just so much are you more bound to be good and agreeable to God and also to the people. And if you are wicked you are the enemy of chivalry and contrary to its commandments and honours.[16]

Following this pattern, Llull's discussion of each chivalric virtue so lauded in the book quickly inverts to become a sermonette against the vice it corrects. The virtues of the body (such as jousting, tourneying, hunting) must not be exercised at the expense of the virtues of the soul. A knight must protect women, widows, orphans, and weak men; to force women and widows, to rob and destroy the feeble, to injure the poor, is to stand outside the high order of chivalry. A knight must have castle and horse so that he can patrol the roads, deliver justice in towns and cities, and encourage useful crafts there; to play the highway robber, to destroy castles, cities, towns, to burn houses, cut down trees, slay beasts, is disloyal to chivalry. A knight must seek out and punish robbers and the wicked; to thieve himself or to sustain other robber knights is to miss the basic point that honour is the supreme good, infinitely more valuable than mere silver and gold. The list runs on in this vein, one worry after another balanced on the knife edge of reform which stands between fulsome praise and dark warnings.

Llull does, it is true, move at one point beyond the undifferentiated company of knighthood to stress the importance of hierarchy. He opens his treatise with the familiar parallel between social and political hierarchy in human society and natural hierarchy in the created world. As God rules the planets which in turn control the earth, so beneath God the kings, princes, and great lords rule the knights, who, in their turn, rule the common people.[17]

On the whole, however, the thrust of his book is to reform chivalry by enlightening individual knights, by changing the way they think, rather than by stressing the exterior force of any institutions or by placing them in a distinctly subordinate layer in the hierarchy. In some instances he specifically urges the body of right-thinking knights to act as a policing agency themselves, admonishing them even to be willing to kill those knights who dishonour the order of chivalry, as in the case (which so obviously troubles him) of knights who are thieves and robbers, wicked and traitorous.[18] His formal hope, whatever his private estimate, remains the correction of each knight through education, reason, and exhortation.

---

[16] Byles, *Book of the Ordre of Chyvalry*, 18.   [17] Ibid., 1–2.
[18] Ibid., 48. Judging from the number of references to robber knights in various romances, their authors shared Llull's worries. See, e.g., Nitze and Jenkins, eds, *Perlesvaus*, passim; Vesce, tr., *Marvels of Rigomer*; Foerster, ed., *Mervelles de Rigomer*, passim.

The prominence of clerical ideas will be as striking to the reader as the total absence of any idea of clerical institutional power. Many pages of the treatise are filled with what most modern readers will consider tenuous moral meanings attributed to each piece of the knightly equipment, with summary accounts of the theological and cardinal virtues, with warnings against the seven deadly sins.

Yet the treatise preserves a character that is not, finally, clerical.[19] It accepts too many aspects of the chivalric life that were questioned or even condemned by ecclesiastics. Though it formally sets up the clerical *ordo* as highest, it edges chivalry nearly to the same mark. The hermit who dispenses wisdom is apparently a layman and former knight, not a cleric; and he is found at a forest fountain, not in any church. Llull's reform draws on the ideas of *clergie*, in other words, without compromising the degree of lay independence so essential to the knightly self-conception.

Likewise, although he portrays knights as the chief props and active agents of royal power, his book is not really royalist. If only the earth were big enough, after all, each of his idealized and reformed knights would properly be a king, or something very close to that high rank. He never fully confronts the tension between the formal statement of hierarchy which opens his book and his continued portrayal thereafter of an idealized society of knightly equals— powerful and busy men, carving away evil from the world with their broadswords and even doing away with the rotters who give chivalry a bad name. The earthly social hierarchy which parallels that of the heavens seems quickly to recede and to become almost a backdrop; it certainly does not function as the key mechanism for providing ordered life.

In short, like the men for whom he wrote, Llull was deeply immersed in the contradictions chivalry brought to the complex and difficult issues of public order. He wanted to be a reformer of chivalry, not merely a singer of its praises. Yet he was a pragmatic man; his popular book urged reform that came wrapped in gold leaf and that argued its case along lines that most in his audience could find tolerable. We can take instruction both from the book's popularity and from Llull's mixed hopes and fears.

Useful as Llull's *Book of the Order of Chivalry* and his other works are, we can draw on texts by other authors that seem even closer to the world of knighthood, less altered by a clerical programme. Three works—all written, in effect, by practising knights—can best show us the impulse for reform among the knights themselves. They can remind us of the great investment in an

---

[19] See the useful comments in Keen, *Chivalry*, 11.

enduring ideal in whose service such reform was to work. We will turn first to the biography of William Marshal, the greatest knight of the late twelfth century, then to another of the vernacular manuals, the *Book of Chivalry* written by Geoffroi de Charny, one of the greatest knights of the mid-fourteenth century, and finally to the evidence of the *Morte Darthur*, the splendid summing up and shaping of chivalric ideas from literature by another knight, Sir Thomas Malory, in the late fifteenth century. As we will see, the chivalric ideal held by these knights maintains a programme of its own. The changing settings in which the ideal was to work, however, required adjustments in the particular emphases of reform in order to fit basic ideals to new circumstances.

L'Histoire de Guillaume le Maréchal[20]

William Marshal died in 1219. His biography was completed at least seven years later, after information had been carefully collected, by a man known to us only as John (Jean); the cost was underwritten by his oldest son. This John, Georges Duby suggests, 'might well be one of those heralds-of-arms who arranged the jousts on the tournament grounds, identified the protagonists by their insignia, and by singing their exploits boosted the reputation of the champions'.[21] John tells us that his raw material came from his own knowledge and that of two others: the Marshal's eldest son, and especially his companion John of Earley. Some information may already have been set down in writing, some household documents may have been available; the rest came from living memory. Georges Duby argues that from this evidence we hear William Marshal's own memories, that we read, in essence, an autobiography.[22] David Crouch reminds us that this is the first biography of a layman below the rank of king.[23]

This text shows the ideal of chivalry in its spring colours. Yet it is a very pragmatic, quotidian notion of chivalry that we find in the *Histoire*, not something abstract.[24] Criticism or reform figures in this story only indirectly, by setting out an ideal working model for those who would follow the great exemplar, by embodying an ideal of chivalry in a life lived grandly and with success. The rewards of this good life are implicit: all things are possible to the

---

[20] Text and discussion in Meyer, ed., *Histoire*; unless otherwise stated, all quotations in this section come from this edition. Modern biographies: Painter, *William Marshal*; Crosland, *William the Marshal*; Duby, *Guillaume le Maréchal*; Crouch, *William Marshal*.

[21] Duby, *Guillaume le Maréchal*, 33.   [22] Ibid., 30–7.

[23] Crouch, *William Marshal*, 2.

[24] Chivalry in the *Histoire* is discussed by Gillingham, 'War and Chivalry', and by Crouch, *William Marshal*, 171–84. Both scholars make telling criticisms of the views of Sidney Painter and Georges Duby.

knight who will dare all—a great fief, royal patronage, a good lady, seemingly endless admiration.

The key quality is in no doubt: William's life-story unfolds as a ceaseless hymn to prowess, the demi-god.[25] The reader learns that William never gave in to idleness but followed prowess all his life, and is admonished that 'a long rest is a cause for shame in a young man (*lonc sejor honist giemble homme*)', that men know that you must look among the horses' legs for the brave (who, in their boldness, will sometimes be unhorsed). Like a hero in a romance, William goes off seeking '*pris et aventure*', especially in the tournament circuit available only on the continent (ll. 1883–8, 1894, 2402, 6090–2). Page after page of the text details feats of enviable prowess done primarily in war—the war of raid and counter-raid, of siege and manoeuvre—and secondarily in the tourney.[26] William is given the honour of knighting King Henry's eldest son even though he is landless and 'has nothing but his chivalry'. He becomes what the text calls the 'lord and master' of the young king; this position was appropriate, we learn, since he increased the lad's prowess (ll. 2102, 2634–6).

Loyalty is also praised by the *Histoire* as a defining quality of the Marshal, and thus of the ideal chivalric hero. William appears time and again as the steady, reliable, and stalwart warrior, directing his great prowess in honourable and predictable causes.[27] That one of these causes was his own advancement and that of his family is accepted.[28] If ambition leads William (as it had led his father) away from loyalty sketched out in bold black and white, and into the grey, the text goes murky or silent. Of course, because he is primarily an Anglo-Norman knight, baron, and earl, an account of his loyalty must also be a story of touchy relations with the lord king—of whom it could be said, as of a yet greater ruler, the lord giveth and the lord taketh away. William managed to earn all his rewards with his sword and his loyal counsel, despite the complicated politics dominated by Henry II and his sons Richard and John. If William's masterful negotiations over fiefs on both sides of the Channel add a shaded note of realism, the *Histoire* completely obscures what Crouch terms John Marshal's 'quicksilver loyalties' during the civil war of

[25] We should note Crouch's warning that William's career was more military in focus than many of his contemporaries: *William Marshal*, 3, 22–3. The argument is simply that the emphasis in the *Histoire* is not out of line with that in books by Geoffroi de Charny and Sir Thomas Malory, and that prowess as a key element in the general ethos of chivalry was important even to men who did not devote as much of their time to military enterprises as William did.

[26] See the discussion in Gillingham, 'War and Chivalry'.

[27] Even on behalf of King John, 'because he always loved loyalty': Meyer, ed., *Histoire*, l. 14590.

[28] The emphasis on prowess coincided easily with the idea of courtliness, coming into vogue in an era with new forms of patronage. See Crouch, *William Marshal*, 39–40; Southern, *Medieval Humanism*; and Jaeger, *Origins of Courtliness*.

Stephen's reign.[29] Yet the message of the text is clear: William's prowess and his careful and prudent loyalty, continually proved, earned him essential royal patronage. In the last stage of his active life, blessed by the papal legate, William acted as no less than guardian of the young Henry III and of his realm (*tutor regis et regni*).

Through this young Henry's wonderful largesse to valiant young knights, the poet assures his readers, chivalry will be revived (ll. 2635–86). Much admired by poets and writers who lived on its fruits, the quality of largesse, in fact, frequently appears among the signature qualities of chivalry displayed by the Marshal and the young king, son of King Henry. Gentility, we read, was nourished in the household of largesse (ll. 5060–5). As his prowess and loyalty won him prize after prize on the tournament field, the battlefield, and the council chamber, William did the right thing and gave generously, openly, and with a sense of style.

William's piety is likewise manifest, though it is sketched rather quickly and with broad brush strokes. We see him knighted in a ceremony without ecclesiastical overtones. He goes on pilgrimage to the shrine of the Three Kings of Cologne. He goes on crusade, but we are left without the detail we would expect.[30] On his deathbed he is accepted into the Order of the Temple. A note or two of anticlericalism surfaces: we hear of Saints Silver and Gold who are much honoured at the court of Rome. But William has no doubts about the relationship between God and chivalry: on the tourney field and on the battlefield, his cry was 'On! God help the Marshal (*Ça! Dex aie al Maréchal*).' Piety and prowess merge in the same battlecry.

Even as the great Marshal waited out his final days, the deeply rooted sense of lay independence is apparent. On his deathbed he confidently denied the validity of clerical criticisms of knightly practice—specifically of the profit from tourneying:

Listen to me for a while. The clerks are too hard on us. They shave us too closely. I have captured five hundred knights and have appropriated their arms, horses, and their entire equipment. If for this reason the kingdom of God is closed to me, I can do nothing about it, for I cannot return my booty. I can do no more for God than to give myself to him, repenting all my sins. Unless the clergy desire my damnation, they must ask no more. But their teaching is false—else no one could be saved.[31]

---

[29] Crouch, *William Marshal*, 13; he repeatedly points out the gaps and distortions in the *Histoire*. Regarding sovereign claims and land on either side of the Channel, Crouch is less censorious than Painter: see pp. 86–7.

[30] David Crouch, however, makes a good case for thinking that the experience marked William: *William Marshal*, 51–2.

[31] Quoted in translation by Painter, *William Marshal*, 285–6. For the original French, see Meyer ed., *Histoire*, ll. 18480–96.

With eternity stretching before him from the foot of his deathbed, the greatest knight of his age calmly brushed aside clerical strictures on the career that had given him so pleasing a combination of wealth and honour.

In this same conversation he likewise rejected the pious advice that he sell all the fine robes kept in his household and give alms to secure forgiveness for his sins. First, he ordered, let each member of his household have his robes in the accustomed manner; then those left over could go to the poor (ll. 18725–34).

Women usually appear only on the margins of this masculine story.[32] According to Georges Duby, '[t]he word love, throughout the entire *chanson*, never intervenes except between men.'[33] Rumours circulated, it is true, that William was the lover of Margaret, wife of the young king Henry, son of Henry II. In a confrontation at court, William offered to fight any three accusers in turn, even to cut off a finger from his right hand—his sword hand—and fight any accuser with that handicap. Here in life—or at least in the written *Histoire* patronized by his heirs—the great knight plays Lancelot from the pages of romance. The coincidence is hardly surprising. This biography of the Marshal and the great prose romances spinning out the life of Lancelot may be separated by only a decade and a half. Rival knights in this scene from life are as prudent as those who remained silent in the face of Lancelot's challenges in the imagined courts of romance. Though William knows he must leave the court, since the prince's love has vanished, he is soon recalled in order to get on with the real work of prowess, serving in his master's team for the tournament. The biography of the Marshal does not focus on women; the Marshal himself does not look like a devotee of 'courtly love'.[34]

On the whole this biography takes an optimistic tone with regard to chivalry. There are no problems—at least no problems are openly recognized. The great example of chivalry simply must be followed. Even John Marshal, William's father, who at times played as ruthless and unprincipled a robber baron as ever wore armour, is praised by the author as 'a worthy man, courteous and wise (*preudome corteis e sage*)', who was 'animated by prowess and loyalty (*proz e loials*)' (ll. 27, 63).[35] The work is, of course, what moderns would

---

[32] Discussed in Duby, *Guillaume le Maréchal*, 38–55, and Crouch, *William Marshal*, 99, 172–3. Benson even suggests that the appearance of women at some tournaments in the story is anachronistic, that the author here drew upon his own lifetime rather than on events half a century earlier: see 'The Tournament', 7.

[33] Duby, *Guillaume le Maréchal*, 48. Crouch believes the incident which follows, involving the young king's wife, was made up by the poet in imitation of contemporary romance: see *William Marshal*, 45–6.

[34] Crouch seems justifiably critical of Painter on this point: see *William Marshal*, 172.

[35] John does say that he cannot tell us all of John's deeds: he does not know them all. Crouch, *William Marshal*, 9–23, provides the best discussion of the career and character of John Marshal, and insists he was more of a baron than a robber.

call an authorized biography. The appearance of the standard virtue words may, however, interest us as much as their sometimes problematic attribution to John or even William; showing prowess and courtesy, piety, largesse and loyalty are the ideals. Great successes won by the key quality of prowess covers any gaps in the ideal framework, even if they are wide enough for a mounted knight to ride through. The father did what he had to do; the son did all. Be advised.

Geoffroi de Charny, Livre de chevalerie

Geoffroi de Charny, a practising knight and author of a major vernacular text on chivalry ranked among the most renowned knights of his age. His *Livre de chevalerie (Book of Chivalry)*,[36] written about 1350, upholds the glittering goal of fine chivalry no less eagerly than Marshal's biography, and presents it as embodied no less clearly in and effected by martial deeds. The leitmotif of Charny's book is 'he who does more is of greater worth'. Though he is at pains to emphasize that all feats of arms are honourable, he calibrates an ascending scale of knightly prowess: those who fight in individual jousts deserve great honour; those who fight in the more vigorous mêlée merit yet more praise; but those who engage in warfare win highest praise, since war combines joust and mêlée in the most demanding circumstances. It seems to Charny 'that in the practice of arms in war it is possible to perform in one day all the three different kinds of military art, that is jousting, tourneying and waging war'.[37] William Marshal would surely have loved this scale; he lived by it.

In Marshal's case the all-important pursuit of honour through prowess even subordinated love as a major component in the knightly life. We saw in Chapter 10 that Charny finds romantic love a spur to prowess, stating, for example, that 'men should love secretly, protect, serve and honour all those ladies and damsels who inspire knights, men-at-arms and squires to undertake worthy deeds which bring them honour and increase their renown'. These 'activities of love and of arms' overlap easily in his prose; they 'should be engaged in with the true and pure gaiety of heart which brings the will to achieve honour'.[38]

---

[36] Kaeuper and Kennedy, *Book of Chivalry*; Kennedy's translation of Charny's text will be quoted in the following pages.

[37] Ibid., 84–91. Another of Charny's works, his *Demandes pour les jout, les tournois et la guerre*, a series of questions for debate on intricate issues of chivalric practice, similarly emphasizes actual war; he provides twenty questions on joust, twenty-one on mêlée, but ninety-three on war. See Taylor, 'Critical Edition'.

[38] Kaeuper and Kennedy, *Book of Chivalry* 120–3.

Yet this acceptance and validation of love, joyful and worldly as it is, does not form the centre of Charny's book. As one admired choice, rather than the sole path for the knight, it is not the single great goal for which prowess exists. Romantic love is wonderful because it promotes prowess and striving for honour; yet the prowess and the striving take first rank.

But Charny is willing to qualify his praise of prowess in the best reform manner. The finest laymen will combine the very best of three types not only of prowess, but of worth and intelligence as well. Worth may begin with a kind of innocence, and progress to pious formalities such as giving alms and attending mass, but its peak is loyally serving God and the Virgin. Likewise, intelligence involves only malicious cleverness at the lowest level, progresses to the ingenious but overly subtle, and appears at its best in the truly wise. Prowess is seen initially in those with courage and skill who are, however, thoughtless; it appears to better advantage in those who perform great deeds of arms personally, but do not act as leaders or advisers; and it is best found in those brave men who also command and direct other knights.[39]

Charny's omnipresent piety shows as he gives thumbnail sketches of great men from the past who have missed the highest status because they failed to recognize their debt to God. But he presents 'the excellent knight' Judas Maccabaeus from the Old Testament as the model. Those who want to reach such high honours, 'which they must achieve by force of arms and by good works (*par force d'armes et par bonnes euvres*)', should pattern themselves on him.[40] Thus Charny's book is much more explicitly a work of reform than Marshal's biography. He knows that he must address real problems, however carefully he coats every suggestion for improvement with the gleaming whitewash of generous praise.

Reform is absolutely necessary, Charny knows, because the chief problem is of such central importance: he fears that French knights of his day have lost their vital commitment to prowess; and with this centre weakened the entire arch of chivalry threatens to fall about the heads of all. At the time Charny wrote, the English and their allies had defeated French knights repeatedly, and were threatening further devastating incursions. When they most needed to risk all and bear all hardships, the knights of France, incredible as it seemed to Charny, appeared to prefer the soft life and the safe life, blind to the grand vision of an existence vested in vigorous deeds, come what may, a life of honour blessed by divine favour.

---

[39] Ibid., 146–55.

[40] Ibid., 160, line 143. Charny's phrase can be compared to two statements from Malory, quoted fully in the next section: Malory endorses the knight who is 'a good lyver and a man of prouesse', and he suggests, through a speech given to a hermit, that the goal of a knight is 'knyghtly dedys and vertuous lyvyng'.

For a few pages of his book Charny puts aside the whitewash pot and brush altogether and speaks with curled lip of the timid, cowardly men who call themselves knights, but who really care only for bodily comforts and safety:

As soon as they leave their abode, if they see a stone jutting out of the wall a little further than the others, they will never dare to pass beneath it, for it would always seem to them that it would fall on their heads. If they come to a river which is a little big or too fast flowing, it always seems to them, so great is their fear of dying, that they will fall into it. If they cross a bridge which may seem a little too high or too low, they dismount and are still terrified lest the bridge collapse under them, so great is their fear of dying. . . . If they are threatened by anyone, they fear greatly for their physical safety and dread the loss of the riches they have amassed in such a discreditable way. And if they see anyone with a wound, they dare not look at it because of their feeble spirit. . . . Furthermore, when these feeble wretches are on horseback, they do not dare to use their spurs lest their horses should start to gallop, so afraid are they lest their horses should stumble and they should fall to the ground with them. Now you can see that these wretched people who are so fainthearted will never feel secure from living in greater fear and dread of losing their lives than do those good men-at-arms who have exposed themselves to so many physical dangers and perilous adventures in order to achieve honour.[41]

Later he denounces a second group, those unworthy of the great calling of bearing arms 'because of their very dishonest and disordered behaviour under these arms'. If one set of men utterly lack the foundation of prowess, these men possess that great gift, but misuse it: 'it is these men who want to wage war without good reason, who seize other people without prior warning and without any good cause and rob and steal from them, wound and kill them.'[42] He knows what to call such men: they are 'cowards and traitors'. It does not matter if they maintain formal proprieties by abstaining from such behaviour themselves, only sending their men to do the dirty work. Whether doers or consenters, such men, in Charny's view, 'are not worthy to live or to be in the company of men of worth'. They 'have no regard for themselves', and so, Charny asks rhetorically, 'how could they hold others in regard?'[43] It seems he would agree with the assessment of V. G. Kiernan that 'All military élites face opposite risks: some of their members cannot stop fighting, others—far more, probably—lapse too readily into sloth.'[44]

If a failure or misuse of prowess is the chief issue for Charny, it comes as no surprise to find this critical problem redoubled by the absence of its essential companion, loyalty. As prowess withers or mutates, loyalty likewise declines; faction and treachery seem to flourish in their place. Any sentient observer

---

[41] Kaeuper and Kennedy, *Book of Chivalry*, 124–9.
[42] Ibid., 176–7.   [43] Ibid., 176–81.   [44] Kiernan, *The Duel*, 37.

could already have seen what so troubled Charny: ambition, regionalism, and anti-royal politics were already at work in mid-fourteenth century France; they ensured that the Hundred Years War would become a veritable civil war. Charny's book was apparently a part of a royal campaign for reform of governance in the interest of unity, a campaign in which chivalry in general and the king's new royal chivalric order, the Company of the Star, in particular, were to play a role of obvious importance. In his book Charny dedicated three chapters specifically to outlining the nature of true princely rule.[45] Here were reform ideas modern historians might call 'top down': kings must act for the common profit through vigorous good governance.

Yet the crisis showed with painful clarity how much the chivalric ethos was needed. Charny thus offered a set of ideas we might characterize as 'bottom up', understanding that the flooring here rests under the knights and men-at-arms and is in effect a ceiling for the great mass of Frenchmen. Charny's solution is direct and uncomplicated: the code must simply be followed. The knightly—indeed, all men living by the honourable profession of arms—must do their duty manfully, even joyously, knowing the rewards awaiting them when they next walk into a court to a murmur of praise, followed by the soft eyes of the ladies, as in time they will know the rewards awaiting them as they are welcomed into the court of heaven by the God of battles.

The answer seems so obvious to him: practice prowess, show loyalty. This is what God wants; this is what God will reward. Charny seems almost to exhaust even his immense energy, telling the essentials to his audience time and again, in the hope that even the obvious slackers of his own generation will finally see the plain truth.

In a time of crisis, as disaster threatened the very kingdom of France, Jean II and his great knight saw eye to eye on reform of the chief military force in the realm. But we, for our part, need to see that if *chevalerie* and *royauté* travelled the same path here (as they often could and did), the reform suggested by Charny is, in fact, much more elementary, much slighter than the ideas for reform which *royauté* generally thrust at chivalry. Charny's plan is something different, the standard knightly view, understandably recommending itself powerfully at this moment to the French king. In mid-fourteenth century France a clarion call for an augmented display of prowess and loyalty, buttressed by the certitude of divine favour, could sound like a fine reform programme to a monarch facing a military and political crisis.

---

[45] Kaeuper and Kennedy, *Book of Chivalry*, 138–47, provides the relevant text and translation; pp. 53–5, 59–63, provide historical context.

Charny closes his great effort with (to borrow Maurice Keen's characteriza-tion once again[46]) a combination prayer and war cry: 'Pray to God for him who is the author of this book . . . Charni, Charny.' The statement recalls Marshal's war cry, which likewise sounded his own name and called confidently upon God's aid. Charny's piety is more explicit and certainly more voluble. Yet the basic assumptions are similar. Knights who do their hard duty with loyalty and honesty can be assured of divine favour. God will receive them into an eternity of blissful reward. There can be no question whether or not a man can save his soul by the profession of arms; there can be no danger to the soul in fighting for the right causes—in just wars, to protect one's kin and their estates, to protect helpless maidens, widows, and orphans, to protect one's own land and inheritance, to defend Holy Church. The list is generous, and accepts no cavils or criticisms.[47] The divine blessing on reformed chivalry is clear.

Even Charny's statement of clerical superiority has a somewhat formal ring; he soon betrays his sense that the great role that chivalry must play in the world gives it a special status. Like William Marshal a century before, he is happiest when religion comes heavily blended with chivalry; again in company with the Marshal, he most heartily endorses clerics who perform all the needed rites and then stand aside for the magnificent work with sword and lance.

Thomas Malory, Morte Darthur

How can we add Malory's *Morte Darthur*,[48] a work of imaginative chivalric lit-erature, to the model biography and the treatise composed by a practising knight? This book will, of necessity, be quite different from our first two sources, primarily because it is a highly original reworking of a mass of literary texts, English as well as French. These texts bring with them many currents of thought about chivalry (including some of the most intense efforts to infuse chivalry with monastic values), locked in conflict with developed French ideas about *amors*. In addition, because of these numerous sources drawn into Malory's work, and often given new shape there, his book is vastly larger and more complex than the two we have so far considered in this chapter.[49]

---

[46] Keen, *Chivalry*, 14.   [47] Kaeuper and Kennedy, *Book of Chivalry*, 154–67.
[48] Vinaver, ed., *Malory. Works*. For an introduction to the enormous body of scholarship on this author and work, see Life, *Sir Thomas Malory*.
[49] Useful general approaches appear in Brewer, 'Malory'; *idem*, ed., *Malory*, 'Introduction'; and Benson, *Malory's Morte Darthur*. On Malory and chivalry, see Tucker, 'Chivalry in the *Morte*'; McCarthy, *Morte Darthur*, 76–93; Barber, 'Chivalry'. Beverly Kennedy, *Knighthood*, argues a highly schematic typology of knighthood in Malory.

Yet there are sound reasons for making Malory's book our final text, as we consider reform of chivalry by the knightly. One of the few facts about Sir Thomas Malory that can be advanced without igniting instant controversy is that he was a knight himself, and very probably a practising or strenuous knight. He clearly tells us in the pages of the *Morte Darthur* that he is a knight; the favourite scholarly candidate among the several Thomas Malorys advanced as the author of this great book appears to have had an active career in armour.[50]

Moreover, he shows concern for the themes that we have already encountered in the life of William Marshal and in the manual of Geoffroi de Charny. In company with the other knight-authors, that is, Malory shows a vast admiration for prowess (the key to honour, if practised properly), a concern for the crucial role of loyalty, a somewhat subordinate interest in romantic love, and an unswerving belief that God blesses the entire chivalric enterprise. We will examine each of these points.[51]

Could any reader of *Morte Darthur* doubt that Malory admires prowess? The only danger seems to be the modern tendency to hurry past this virtue in an effort to infuse it with deeper and less physical meanings, or quickly to qualify it with checks and softening qualities more to our modern taste. But Malory likes prowess. He vastly admires men who can beat other men in armour, on horseback, with lance and sword.[52]

His admiration stands forth most clearly and without competing distractions in the early tales of his book, full of the 'noble chere of chevalry' equated with 'the hardyeste fyghters that ever they herde other sawe'. Malory says Arthur, fighting with Accolon, has lost so much blood that he can barely stand, 'but he was so full of knighthood that he endured the pain'. Kay is contemptuous of Gareth's first, simple request of Arthur, a request for sustenance, 'for an he had be come of jantyllmen, he wolde have axed [i.e. asked for] horse and armour'.[53]

This admiration for prowess, so evident in Malory's accounts of Arthur's wars to establish and expand his realm, scarcely disappears or lessens throughout the rest of the book, even though other themes (the Grail, the love of

---

[50] Vinaver, ed., *Malory. Works*, 110, 726. For a recent extended defence of the Thomas Malory of Newbold Revel as the author, see Field, *The Life and Times of Sir Thomas Malory*. Mahoney comments that Malory's book 'is full of touches that demonstrate his practical knowledge of the fighting life': 'Malory's *Morte Darthur*', 530.

[51] Another similarity is that Malory makes of chivalry an ideal as it was in the Marshal biography and Charny's book. Since the world can never quite live up to any such ideals, Malory's book, like the others, is a work of chivalric reform.

[52] In addition to the quotations which follow, all taken from Vinaver, *Malory. Works*, see the many examples drawn from Malory in Chapter 7.

[53] Ibid., 198, 24, 86, 178.

Lancelot and Queen Guinevere) take on prominence. For it is through the practice of prowess that the knights win worship—probably the highest human good in Malory's view, and a chief ingredient in nobility. Characters who have seen good displays of fighting say they have seen noble knighthood.[54]

Throughout the book worship is proved on other men's bodies. Balin says to his brother that they will attack King Rion with just this in mind: 'kynge Ryons lyeth at the sege of the Castell Terrable, and thydir woll we draw in all goodly haste to preve our worship and prouesse uppon hym.'[55] The many battle scars on Lancelot's body, evident when for a time he runs naked and mad in the woods, prove to those who see him that he is a man of worship. To fail in a fight is to get no worship from an opponent.[56]

Malory so values the military side of knighthood and the worship produced by fighting well that he emphasizes the life of prowess even at the expense of the romantic love so evident in his French sources. As scholars have argued for some time, Malory speaks in the most positive terms of stability in love, of affection arising naturally and enduring steadfastly; but he seems unhappy and even irritable when love becomes highly mannered and formalized in a cult in the manner of French *fin amors*.[57]

His recasting of the tale of Tristram and Isolde makes the point nicely. Though he tells us Tristram could not live without Isolde, 'Malory's own statement', P. E. Tucker argues, 'is not made plausible. On the other hand, much is made of Tristram's other virtues as a knight.'[58] Eugène Vinaver similarly thinks that 'love is not allowed to interfere with the customs of knight-errantry. As a true knight-errant, what Tristram values above all is not the presence of his beloved, nor the joy of sharing every moment of his life with her, but the high privilege of fighting in her name.'[59] Tucker identifies what may be Malory's key interest in the matter of the love between knight and lady. Malory 'is concerned largely with stability, that is, loyalty in love. . . . Malory finds fidelity in love praiseworthy in itself—ultimately, perhaps, because it is a form of loyalty.'[60] Sadly, love in his own day does not meet Malory's high standards: 'And ryght so faryth the love nowadays, sone hote sone colde. Thys ys no stabylyté. But the olde love was nat so.'[61]

[54] E.g. Vinaver ed., *Malory. Works*, 277.

[55] Ibid., 44.

[56] Ibid., 499, 330, 370.

[57] See the cogent argument of Tucker, 'Chivalry in the *Morte*'. Cf. Edwards, 'Place of Women'.

[58] 'Chivalry in the *Morte*', 73. In general this essay has much of interest to say on the entire issue of chivalry in Malory's view.

[59] Vinaver, *Malory. Works*, 750.

[60] 'Chivalry in the *Morte*', 81. Cf. Peter Waldron, ' "Vertuouse Love", 54–61.

[61] Vinaver, *Malory. Works*, 649.

The issue leads to a point of basic importance to understanding Malory's view of chivalry in relation to our earlier exemplars. As Tucker has noted, prowess, too, is praiseworthy in itself, and '[a]part from its inherent worth, prowess is admirable because it brings a knight reputation and honour, or what Malory calls "worship" '.[62] The chief qualities which are praiseworthy in themselves and which lead to other virtues are thus identified as prowess and loyalty, the twin pillars which upheld so much of the structure of Charny's book, the interlinked set of qualities so important to William Marshal's successful career.

'Stabylyté', Malory thinks, should be embodied in good love. Lancelot and Guinevere are true lovers because of their constant loyalty, their stability, despite all obstacles, despite doubts, misunderstandings, and quarrels. 'Stabylyté' should likewise, Malory thinks, be embodied in sound politics. Just as loyalty should bind two true lovers, the knight and his lady, so should loyalty bind together the king and his knights.[63] Lancelot, the great knight, upholds Arthur, the great king, who, in reciprocation, supports knighthood. With this great bond mortared in place like a capstone in an arch, all the realm will be whole. Could Charny have read Malory's view, would he not have agreed wholeheartedly, possibly adding one of his exclamations of 'He, Dieu!' to underscore the point? Furthermore, Charny would have agreed with Malory that to the great pairing of prowess and honour must be added the essential loyalty that makes love prosper, that makes political society work.[64]

As the Arthurian world collapses, Malory speaks out directly and with force to his audience, presenting a clear view of the problem and at least by implication a simple solution:

Lo ye all Englysshemen, se ye nat what a myschyff here was? For he that was the moste kynge and nobelyst knyght of the worlde, and moste loved the felyshyp of noble knyghtes, and by hym they all were upholdyn, and yet myght nat thes Englysshemen holde them contente with hym. Lo thus was the olde custom and usayges of thys londe, and men say that we of thys londe have nat yet loste that custom. Alas! thys ys a greate defaughte of us Englysshemen, for there may no thynge us please no terme.[65]

---

[62] Tucker, 'Chivalry in the *Morte*', 65.

[63] The splendid praise of political stability which Malory addresses to his readers ('Lo ye all Englysshemen': see Vinaver, ed., *Malory. Works*, 708) can be compared, with some interest, to a long passage in Sir Thomas Gray's *Scalacronica* (in Maxwell, tr., 75–6), and to a political sermonette on unity in *Geoffrey of Monmouth, History of the Kings of Britain* (in Thorpe, tr., 264–5).

[64] It would perhaps not be pressing a point too far to note that loyalty is here taking on more of a royalist cast, serving as a signpost to the greater emphasis on the crown as the focus of loyalty and source of honour in the centuries to come.

[65] Vinaver, *Malory. Works*, 78.

A stable political society might have a chance, in Malory's view, if it were headed by a great king who was supported by great knights. The participation of them all in the High Order of Knighthood is the key ingredient. Men of worship all working together might make the world right.

The contrast Malory draws between the kingship of Mark and of Arthur speaks to this theme repeatedly. Mark is a felon, no supporter of knights, no discriminating judge of worship in men, no personal practitioner of prowess. This heavy judgement is delivered against him by one character after another. Berluse tells him to his face that he is 'the most vylaunce knyght of a kynge that is now lyvynge, for ye are a destroyer of good knyghtes, and all that ye do is but by treson.' Dynadan adds to the charges:

ye ar full of cowardyse, and ye ar also a murtherar, and that is the grettyst shame that ony knyght may have, for nevir had knyght murtherer worshyp, nother never shall have. For I sawe but late thorow my forse ye wolde have slayne sir Berluses, a better knyght than ever ye were or ever shall be, and more of proues.[66]

The quality of prowess in a king is, of course, a key. When Lancelot learns that Mark had murdered his own knight, he opposes him; Mark 'made no differ-ence but tumbled adowne oute of his sadyll to the erthe as a sak, and there he lay stylle'. Mark's lack of the essential trait of knighthood could scarcely be clearer. Lacking prowess, he must resort to the trickery that causes Lancelot to label him 'Kynge Foxe'.[67]

Arthur splendidly reverses all these qualities in his practice of kingship. Some of the qualities praised in earlier English works reappear. The young Arthur, holding in his hands the sword just pulled from the stone, promises justice to all; he hears 'complayntes', clearly the *plaints* or *querelae* which brought so much judicial work to real-life English kings.[68]

Yet the emphasis is not placed on Arthur as governor. Malory is much more inclined to praise Arthur as 'the floure of chevalry', and to assure his readers that 'all men of worship seyde hit was myrry to be under such a chyfftayne that wolde putte hys person in adventure as other poure knyghtis ded'.[69] Speaking directly to King Mark, Gaheris later sums up this essential element in Arthur's rule, in words conveying a telling contrast: 'the kynge regnys as a noble knyght'. Arthur knows, as Mark does not, that 'a kynge anoynted with creyme [chrism] . . . sholdest holde with all men of worship'.[70]

---

[66] Vinaver, ed., *Malory, Works*, 357, 358.   [67] Ibid., 365, 380.

[68] Ibid., 10. Cf. Harding, 'Plaints and Bills'.

[69] Vinaver, *Malory. Works*, 362, 36. The tradition of the knightly king was venerable. A classic example appears in *Sir Degaré*, ll. 9–18: see Laskaya and Salisbury, eds, *Breton Lays*.

[70] Vinaver, *Malory. Works*, 333, 335.

Malory states the need for this bond between monarchy and chivalry time and again. Even the queenship of Guinevere is evaluated by this same standard. Accused of killing Sir Patrice with poisoned fruit (the unfortunate fellow 'swall sore tyll he braste'), her innocence is defended by Bors, who justifies her in terms of her overall relationship to knighthood:

Fayre lordis . . . never yet in my dayes knew I never ne harde sey that ever she was a destroyer of good knyghtes, but at all tymes, as far as ever I coude know, she was a maynteyner of good knyghtes; and ever she hath bene large and fre of hir goodis to all good knyghtes, and the moste bownteuous lady of hir gyftis and her good grace that ever I saw other harde speke off.[71]

Here, queenly largesse stands in for the prowess which bonds the king to his knights.

A veritable chorus of knights makes the case for the other half of the formula, the role of the knights themselves. The realm needs great knighthood, they say, to quote only one classic statement:

'For we all undirstonde, in thys realme woll be no quyett, but ever debate and stryff, now the felyshyp of the Rounde Table ys brokyn. For by the noble felyshyp of the Rounde Table was kynge Arthur upborne, and by their nobeles the kynge and all the realme was ever in quyet and reste. And a grete parte,' they sayde all, 'was because of youre moste nobeles, sir Launcelot.'[72]

Though Lancelot mutters polite disclaimers, the truth has been spoken.

The king and his knights, then, are joint practitioners of the religion of honour, backed, of course, by the God of Christianity. The king runs the court in which this sun shines, its rays touching knights everywhere. Knights who are at the court or who are sent out from the court settle all problems. The great ideal of the privileged is imaginatively maintained: they have a personal bond with the monarch; they basically act out of free choice; few purely royal constraints affect them.[73] A good example is set by the king and the great knights; those who will not learn lose their worship at the tip of a lance or the edge of a sword.

Regality plus knighthood yields order. The quotidian reality barely appears at all: if Malory mentions a parliament or the commons once in a while, there is nothing of the work of legal and fiscal administration, of sheriffs and coroners, of taxation, of justices and parchment rolls closely etched with the crabbed Latin record of lawsuits—all of the administrative apparatus which helped run medieval England and which had at least left its traces in earlier works of

---

[71] Ibid., 617.   [72] Ibid., 699.
[73] We will encounter this sense of personal contract or bond as late as the seventeenth century in the Epilogue.

literature in England. Did Malory, perhaps, take all this for granted in the late fifteenth century? Or was he, rather, looking behind it to what appeared to him a deeper layer of problems? He seems to be going back to what he must have considered fundamentals, stressing kingship which looks rather like warlordship writ large, alongside knighthood armed with prowess and crowned with worship. If only they would work together, the administrative apparatus (hardly fit subject for his book, and not in his sources in any case) could work quietly in the background while the trumpets sound and the horses' hoofs pound the earth as they carry their proud warriors to deeds of worship.

The tragedy, of course, is that he knows it does not really work, either in the books he reads or in the world he inhabits. But he must tell the story: Arthur and the Round Table move with unstoppable momentum towards the cliff edge, towards the fall of both the 'moste kynge' and the fellowship of the greatest knights. His book ends—despite these magnificent exemplars—in human imperfection and utter destruction.

Worship and stability are the great goals celebrated in *Morte Darthur*. Their realization, however, always seems temporary and fragile, always threatened; and in the end the great structure collapses in a cataclysm of jealousy, treachery, and murderous civil war. This bittersweet flavour of Malory's great book has surely contributed to its enduring popularity; readers have always responded to its juxtaposition of high ideals with the realities of shattered dreams. For our analysis this combination suggests at least an indirect impulse at work in the interests of reform, conceived in the broadest sense. Malory's admiration for a world of chivalry and worship, of stability in true love, and honourable governance, is so heartfelt that he need not explicitly advocate a reform programme; as in the model biography of William Marshal, the glowing description of the ideal (and constant reminders of its neglect or inversion) may be enough. Contemporary readers could well finish the text with a sense that their world should more closely approximate this ideal, that chivalry could provide a moral as well as a military and societal structure. Medieval and Tudor readers found the book deeply satisfying and hopeful. Belief in the grandeur and possibilities of linking *chevalerie* with *royauté*, blessed by the understanding practitioners of *clergie*, was far from moribund in the late fifteenth century.

Certainly, William Caxton thought so as the sheets of Malory's book came out of his printing press. As Caxton famously advised his readers in his preface to the printed book, 'Doo after the good and leve the evyl, and it shal brynge you to good fame and renomee.'[74] Whatever his doubts about the historicity of

---

[74] Vinaver, ed., *Malory, Works*, xv.

Arthur, he said outright in his edition of *Morte Darthur* that Malory could be read as a text of reform as well as a paean of praise:

And I, accordyng to my copye, have doon sette it in enprynte to the entente that noble men may see and lerne the noble actes of chyvalrye, the jentyl and vertuous dedes that somme knyghtes used in tho dayes, by whyche they came to honour, and how they that were vycious were punysshed and ofte put to shame and rebuke; humbly bysechyng al noble lordes and ladyes with al other estates, of what estate or degree they been of, that shal see and rede in this sayd book and werke, that they take the good and honest actes in their remembraunce, and to folowe the same. . . . Doo after the good and leve the evyl, and it shal brynge you to good fame and renomee.[75]

Reform to ensure Malory's ideal of knighthood is not only built into the structure and spirit of the entire work but appears in specific messages scattered throughout its pages. Malory gives continual signposts along the high road to worship. There are rules to be followed in the fighting; men who yield are to be spared; women are to be protected; jealousy is no part of true worship. Tristram announces uncompromisingly that 'manhode is nat worthe but yf hit be medled with wysdome'.[76] Lancelot is shocked when he is told about a vile knight: ' "What", seyde sir Launcelot, "is he a theff and a knyght? And a ravyssher of women? He doth shame unto the Order of Knyghthode, and contrary unto his oth. Hit is pyté that he lyvyth!" '[77] The 'oth' to which Lancelot refers is that which Arthur required of his knights at every Pentecost. At the feast which originated the custom:

the kynge stablysshed all the knyghtes and gaff them rychesse and londys; and charged them never to do outerage nothir mourthir, and allwayes to fle treson, and to gyff mercy unto hym that askith mercy, uppon payne of forfiture of their worship and lordship of kynge Arthure for evirmore; and allways to do ladyes, damesels, and jantilwomen and wydowes socour; strengthe hem in hir ryghtes, and never to enforce them, uppon payne of dethe. Also, that no man take no batayles in a wrongefull quarell for no love ne for no worldis goodis.[78]

It is a practical oath. The reform goals are not wild: no outrages, murder, treason, no fighting for immoral causes in hope of gain, no rape (at least none committed against gentlewomen); knights are, instead, to help ladies.

All such efforts, finally, came with the stamp of divine approval. Malory, no less than William Marshal and Geoffroi de Charny, combines a belief in God

---

[75] Printed in ibid. A characteristic English social broadening is at work here; reformed chivalry is not limited to an exclusive caste, but is considered a guide to life for all honourable men.

[76] Ibid., 428. The powerful pull of prowess appears a few pages later, however, when Malory tells us that two brothers 'were men of grete prouesse; howbehit that they were falsse and full of treson, and but poore men born, yet were they noble knyghtes of their handys': p. 437.

[77] Ibid., 160.   [78] Ibid., 75.

as the author of chivalry with a fairly independent attitude towards specific clerical restraints. He knows God can have no quarrel with prowess per se. As the quest for the Holy Grail begins, no knight, Malory says, found a 'braunche of holy herbe that was the signe of the Sancgreall . . . but he were a good lyver and a man of prouesse'.[79] The combination of virtues calls to mind Charny's belief in living 'by force of arms and good works'.[80]

Malory is willing at times in this tale to follow his sources and to emphasize absolute faith over prowess. Lancelot, coming to the entrance to Corbenic, guarded by lions, has the sword he has drawn struck from his hand. A voice tells him: 'O, man of evylle feyth and poure byleve! Wherefore trustist thou more on thy harneyse than in thy Maker? For He myght more avayle the than thyne armour, in what servyse that thou arte sette in.'[81] Yet Malory's Grail quest is not that of his thirteenth-century French source (examined in Chapter 12), with its strict and judgemental comparison of mere earthly chivalry with the true, heavenly chivalry.[82] As Richard Barber observes, if he thinks of the Grail quest as 'the greatest of all the quests undertaken by Arthur's knights', it 'still remains an adventure, and not an integral part of the Table's purpose. And this tells us a great deal about Malory's attitude to chivalry.'[83] He may think of chivalry as ideally a high order, with genuine mission and high dignity, but (as P. E. Tucker observes) his ideal is more like a great secular order than the celibate and highly ecclesiastical Order of the Temple as catechized by St Bernard of Clairvaux. In Malory's view, chivalry may be right or wrong in its practice, and stands thus in need of constant reform, yet it is all 'worldly' chivalry to him. The division falls, in other words, not between earthly and heavenly, but between right chivalry and wrong chivalry in the world.[84]

In fact, like so many late medieval Englishmen, Malory's concern for religion regularly translates into an attempt to practise morality in the quotidian world. A hermit tells Gawain that 'whan ye were first made knyght ye sholde have takyn you to knyghtly dedys and vertuous lyvyng'.[85] This is exactly what Malory's Lancelot tries to do. As a fallible man in the world, he fails, of course, but that failure does not diminish him in Malory's eyes. The goal remains a virtuous life in the practice of chivalry—in the world. The perfection of Galahad, much though it must be admired, is not for most men, and so is not really a

---

[79] Vinaver ed., *Malory, Works*, 81.   [80] Kaeuper and Kennedy, *Book of Chivalry*, 160.

[81] Vinaver, *Malory. Works*, 596.

[82] For a range of points of view, see ibid., 758–60; Benson, *Malory's Morte Darthur*, 205–22; Mahoney, 'Truest and Holiest Tale'; Atkinson, 'Malory's Lancelot'; Shichtman, 'Politicizing the Ineffable'.

[83] Barber, 'Chivalry', 34.   [84] Tucker, 'Chivalry in the *Morte*'.

[85] Vinaver, *Malory. Works*, 535. The parallel with being a 'good lyver and a man of prouesse', quoted just above, is striking.

practical model for knights trying to live in the world.[86] It is to encourage and steer these noble knights living in the very real world that Malory wrote.

Texts that are especially close to knighthood in the world, then, show us again that the chivalry of strenuous knights was not simply practice—how knights acted—but also how they thought about practice, and with what enthusiasm they spoke their hopes for an ideal that was so largely of their own making— or at least of their own choosing. Emphases changed over time as our writers responded to perceived changes in their society. Charny focused on a decline in prowess in an age marked by disastrous defeats of French knighthood. Malory said much about loyalty and political stability in an age of dynastic strife in England, and much about personal morality at a time when the focus of lay piety was directed at virtuous living in the world.

Yet the similarities linking William Marshal's *Histoire*, Charny's manual, and Malory's great *summa* are instructive. These three works particularly value the prowess that secures honour; the knights in these texts live by loyalty, the needed complement to prowess; if love of a lady is not the centre of their lives, they accept, or even praise love as a spur to prowess, as its just reward; and if they stoutly keep watch over their rights where the clerics are concerned, they thank God heartily as the source of the highest patronage given so freely to those who live the strenuous life and hazard their bodies, their honour, their all, in the great game of chivalry.

Both Ramon Llull and Raoul de Hodenc likewise testify to this conception of chivalry, though they both oppose it. Their books reveal lively fears that active, practising knights will place excessive belief in prowess. Raoul de Hodenc worries that the constellation of beliefs centred on prowess will smother liberality and courtesy; from first-hand experience, Llull fears that prowess will engender pride and disruptive violence.

For William Marshal, Geoffroi de Charny, and Sir Thomas Malory, however, this set of values rightly shapes the world they find honourable. Their books offer praise for that world and press forward the hope that all will be well if only their fellow knights adhere to such ideals even more closely.

---

[86] See the thoughtful discussion of Tucker in 'Chivalry in the *Morte*'.

EPILOGUE

✦✦✦

NEAR the end of *A Connecticut Yankee in King Arthur's Court*, Twain's time traveller, backed by a force of only fifty-two boys in a cave stronghold, confronts the host of twenty-five thousand knights that has come to wipe out the source of trouble in Camelot. Efficient military technology destroys the knights en masse. Attacking in the darkness, they die in droves on concentric rings of electrified fences; others are shot down from platforms mounting electric lights and rapid-firing Gatling guns; finally, all that remain drown when a mountain stream is directed into the great ditch filled with the fleeing chivalry.

Whatever the complexities of Twain's views regarding knighthood and 'modern' technology by this stage in his own life,[1] this horrific and unforgettable tableau captures the popular, simplistic explanation of the end of chivalry: knighthood died with its shining armour blackened by gunpowder. The technology of the unheroic killed off the heroes from a prudent distance.[2]

Of course a contrary popular view, though probably a minority opinion, suspects that despite improved military technology, chivalry was never quite done in, or at least was never so safely interred as to be immune from one revival or another. 'Chivalry is not dead': the old tag is usually said in a voice caught between the mockery and nostalgia we feel for ideas and behaviour that seem so immovably a part of our past. In this view chivalry took a leisurely route to its own quasi-demise in the post-medieval European world, expiring slowly and in such good form that the process recalls the slow and stately end of its great twelfth-century exemplar William Marshal, as told unforgettably by Georges Duby.[3] Even an image of death almost operatic in its pace and

---

[1] See Kaplan, *Mr. Clemens*, which elaborates the linkage between Twain's view of technology in this novel and the failure of the typesetter in which he had invested heavily.

[2] At the scholarly level, however, debate over the role of technology in late medieval and early modern warfare is anything but simplistic, though the debate is beyond the scope of this book. For an overview, with many citations, see Rogers, ed., *The Military Revolution Debate*. Evaluation of the debate from a late medieval perspective, is provided by Rogers's essay in this volume, 'The Military Revolutions of the Hundred Years War', by the introduction of Ayton and Price, eds., *The Medieval Military Revolution*, and by Prestwich, *Armies and Warfare*. Cf. claims for an even earlier period in Bartlett, 'Technique militaire'.

[3] Duby, *Guillaume le Maréchal*, 1–23.

formality may be too abrupt, for who would not be reluctant to sign a specific, dated death warrant to mark the end of so persistent and so complex a phenomenon?

Explaining this process of transformation need not be attempted here. But briefly following our lines of investigation to their conclusion in the post-medieval period will help us to see the issues more fully, by seeing their entire lifespan. What happened to the complex and powerful mixture of knighthood, public order, licit violence, lay piety, ecclesiastical authority, and royal sovereignty? Two incidents transpiring within a generation of each other early in the seventeenth century will help to direct our enquiry.

The Essex Rebellion and the Bouteville Affair

The famous revolt of Robert Devereux, second Earl of Essex, in 1601, has been termed 'the last honour revolt' and interpreted as the swansong of chivalric culture by Mervyn James.[4] Essex himself was a famous soldier and a magnet for the iron of chivalry in others. Even among the London crowd he was popular as a paragon of chivalry, a reputation that was enhanced by cheap chivalric romance in circulation. Some romantics expected him to lead a great crusade. Chapman's first instalment of Homer, that bible of honourable violence, was dedicated to him. His body of supporters included many duellists and showed in general a 'strongly military orientation', including as it did a 'considerable representation of swordsmen with a taste for violence'. Through Essex these men 'made contact with the glamorous overtones of Tudor monarchical chivalry in which the earl played a prominent part'.[5]

There were three great professions, Essex wrote: arms, law, and religion. That he belonged proudly to the first in this list with all its 'pains, dangers, and difficulties',[6] makes him the ghostly heir of the mid-fourteenth-century writer Geoffroi de Charny, as he was more obviously the ideological companion of the contemporary poet and soldier Sir Philip Sidney.

The solidarity of the Essex group, James argues, was based on honour, even on honour as it had operated in the Middle Ages, with all the competition and latent violence, thinly cloaked in elaborate courtesy, that such a code entails. Since this culture of honour likewise 'points to the importance of will and the emphasis on moral autonomy', it leads to 'the uneasiness of the man of honour in relation to authority, seen as liable to cabin, crib and confine this same autonomy'.[7]

---

[4] James, 'At a Crossroads'. Cf. *idem*, 'English Politics', and McCoy, ' "A Dangerous Image" '.
[5] James, 'At a Crossroads', 428–9.
[6] Ibid., 429.   [7] James, 'English Politics', 314.

When his revolt failed miserably, Essex at first spoke the proud and defiant language of this culture of honour. It was, as we have already seen, the language of Ganelon in the *Song of Roland*, going back to the late eleventh or twelfth century, the language of the knight Bertelay in *The Story of Merlin*, from the thirteenth century.[8] Essex justified his degree of autonomous action in the honourable pursuit of a private feud; he noted that even natural law allowed force to repel force, after all. He had done nothing against the queen herself, or against God. He was merely 'the law's traitor, and would die for it'.[9]

Yet almost as soon as he was condemned, Essex abandoned the language and culture of honour utterly, and all the way to the scaffold embraced a view which Lacy Baldwin Smith found common to those defeated in attempts to overthrow or severely constrain the Tudor monarchy: he adopted whole-hearted submission with a sense that his revolt had been judged and defeated by the will of the Almighty.[10] He thus became a late convert to what James calls providentialist religion, a believer in the divine purpose that could be effected as England achieved wholeness under its queen. Honour was hers to distribute, not his to win in showy independence; even those as chivalrous and great-hearted as he could not act as autonomous agents. His only success was posthumous. Later writers portrayed Essex as almost saintly, a victim of the pedantic snares of the law and of jealous enemies, a true chivalric and Protestant hero in the service of his country.

James's argument is powerful and fascinating. Even without entering into all its implications, students of medieval chivalry may take the Essex revolt of 1601 as a significant signpost. It points away from ideas whose societal effects we have studied; it points toward basic transformations of those ideas by the early seventeenth century.

Our French incident, taking place a quarter of a century later, shows fascinating similarities. The Bouteville affair of 1627 began with a duel and ended with two French noblemen going to the scaffold.[11] Not only did the Comte de Bouteville and his cousin the Comte des Chapelles fight in violation of the royal prohibition against duelling (a law on the books since 1602), they chose to thumb their nose at such regulation by conducting their fight in the Place Royale, the largest square in the capital and one with clear royalist associations. This was the twenty-second duel the twenty-eight-year-old Bouteville had fought in defence of his honour, but fighting in the Place Royale (rather than in some remote alley or rural lane) showed a deliberate defiance of the laws.

    [8] Brault, ed., tr., *Chanson de Roland*, laisse 273; Pickens, tr., *Story of Merlin*, 339–41; Sommer, ed., *Vulgate Version*, II, 310–13.

    [9] James, 'At a Crossroads', 455.   [10] Smith, *Treason*.

    [11] Billacois, *Le Duel*, 247–75.

In the flood of argument and petition that reached Louis XIII and Cardinal Richelieu on behalf of the young noblemen before their execution, the line of defence taken by their fellow nobles is highly revealing. The two had done nothing against the king or the state, these appeals stated. There had been no fracture of the essential and honourable man-to-man bond uniting king and nobleman. The two duellists had simply violated an edict (a distinction recalling Essex's claim that he was merely 'the law's traitor', not a traitor to his sovereign). Surely, their essential noble service as warriors ready for the king's service ought to count for more than breaking of such regulations. The effort was unsuccessful. This time the pardon so frequently sought and so regularly obtained was not forthcoming.

After their deaths the two men were highly praised by all (including the royal administration, with one eye on their influential families and friends); some even managed to portray them as ideal Christians undergoing a species of martyrdom. During his trial des Chapelles had told his judges that he was willing to shed his blood, if that sacrifice was necessary for the king to establish his kingdom. Yet he added that he did know that 'in antiquity [he means the Middle Ages] men had fought and that kings of France had tolerated it up to the present'.[12]

This trial and the somewhat mystified statement of the condemned des Chapelles will remind us of a trial that took place in Paris three hundred years earlier. In 1323 Jourdain de l'Isle Jourdain, lord of Casaubon, a notorious violator of the peace, was finally brought to justice after he had killed two men under royal safeguard and then murdered the unfortunate royal serjeant sent to arrest him. On his way to the gallows (denied the nobler death by beheading allowed the men of 1627), Jourdain confessed repeatedly that he deserved death for his many misdeeds; but in each case he added, with a puzzlement like that of des Chapelles, his quasi-defence based on old custom: 'but it was in war'. Though there was no movement to consider Jourdain anything like a martyr, he carried cherished relics on his body as he went to his death, including what he believed to be a piece of the true cross.[13]

---

[12] 'Ledit sieur dit que . . . si'l faut que le Roy establisse son royaume par le sang, il se sacrifie. Mais qu'il est vrai que . . . dans l'antiquité on se battoit, et que cela a duré jusques à maintenant et les Roys de France l'ont toleré': ibid., 274–5.

[13] Langlois and Lanhers, *Confessions et jugements*, 37–9, print the confession; cf. Cutler, *Law of Treason*, 46, 144–5, and Kicklighter, 'Nobility of English Gascony'. Kicklighter notes that his executioners clad Jordain in a robe bearing the papal arms to mock the papal efforts for a pardon.

Dissolving the Fusion of Chivalric Elements

Chivalry came into being as a powerful, mutually reinforcing fusion of several major functions, roles, and rights. Above all, the chivalrous defended honour through the violence of personal prowess; to this fusion they added a formal and rather independent piety, asserting God's blessing on their demanding and violent lives; they claimed an elite, usually noble, status and established their nobility by the practice of a chivalric way of life; they sought to regulate relationships between males and females on their own terms, exclusively linking love, too, with prowess and honour.

As in Gothic of another sort, many buttresses supported these chivalric structures. The chivalrous claimed they were set apart from others by the loyalty which guided their prowess, by the largesse which prowess supplied: they possessed castles, or at least fortified dwellings of some sort; they pictured themselves fighting from the backs of noble warhorses; they enthusiastically participated in the defining sport of tournament; they displayed appropriately refined manners in a court, or in a bedroom; they provided patronage and audience for literature of a specific, and ideally exclusive sort. Equally important, all these traits showed and helped form a generous measure of lay independence, even a powerful degree of autonomy in the face of developing institutions of governance. We saw this autonomy in the belief that knights could join the emerging state on their own terms, that they could practise a piety only partially controlled by the clerical caste, and that the cultural space in their lives could in no small measure be furnished with ideas of their own choosing.

Between the fifteenth and seventeenth centuries, however, this durable synthesis of power, status, piety, and cultural ideas came apart. Some elements largely disappeared, others underwent considerable transformation, but above all the interlocking, mutually strengthening fusion of elements dissolved. It is this dissolution rather than the disappearance of any one characteristic that marks the demise of chivalry. The revivals could only breathe life into selected aspects of chivalry; they could not revitalize the complex and powerful organic whole.

The long survivals claim our attention first. Since chivalry had long functioned as the distinguishing badge of the elite, it is not surprising that some of its more showy secondary characteristics continued into the period well beyond the traditional Middle Ages. Chivalric literary forms provide a clear case in point. Many old chivalric texts were reworked and issued in print for even wider audiences; new chivalric works were written to meet the demand from obviously avid readers.[14] Notions of 'courtly love' seem to have lasted so

[14] Cooper concluded that 'far from waning, interest in things chivalric increased manifold during the sixteenth century in France'. He supports this assertion with an outline bibliography of

long and carried enough chivalric glamour that some modern literary treatments of the culture of post-medieval Europe seem almost to assume that this is what chivalry was.

Jousting and the tournament, likewise, though in increasingly stylized form, survived well beyond the fifteenth century. The monarchs who had once prohibited tournaments or regulated them closely, fearing their show of armed independence and nervous about their potentialities for disorder, became in the end their proud sponsors, having converted tournaments into celebratory ceremonies of regality. 'The tournament survived into the second decade of the seventeenth century in a form which the knights of three centuries earlier might still have recognized as their favourite sport', Richard Barber and Juliet Barker note, but they add that on the continent the Thirty Years War (1618–48) and the changing attitudes of princes brought an end to the tradition.[15]

Towards the close of its life, tournament was undoubtedly being transformed not only in degree but in kind; parade and spectacle outweighed combat, which itself gradually became only the mock combat of the 'carrousel' or the 'horse ballet'. One so-called tournament held at night in the courtyard of the Louvre in 1606 involved 'pure spectacle, symbolism and just a little real jousting'.[16]

In England, Henry VII and Henry VIII likewise sponsored numerous tournaments, and Queen Elizabeth was honoured by Accession Day Jousts. The association of English kings with tournament lingered on a while longer, in fact, before dying out only in the early years of Charles I.[17]

Ideas and forms unmistakably recognizable as chivalric thus survived as late as the seventeenth century. But the changes are more important for basic issues of public order. How had essential elements in the formative chivalric fusion—responsible for its seemingly endless strength—weakened and separated? Meltdown in the chivalric alloy was not sudden; the furnaces had actually been fuelled by the very medieval efforts to constrain and reform chivalry which we have followed throughout this book. The trial of Jourdain de l'Isle Jourdain noted above, reinforces that point. But as trends already clear in the Middle Ages (such as the growth of state power) continued in the new conditions of early modern Europe (especially the changes in its social hierarchy), chivalry itself was utterly transformed. We can observe this

works on chivalry printed in France before 1600; the list runs to forty-six pages: 'Nostre histoire renouvelée', quotation at 175.

[15] Barber and Barker, *Tournaments*, 209.
[16] Ibid, 210.
[17] Gunn, 'Chivalry'; McCoy, *Rites of Knighthood*; Ferguson, *Chivalric Tradition*.

transformation in three of the constitutive elements, or fusions of elements, that had created chivalry.[18]

Prowess and Honour

In the first place, the essential linkage of violence with honour slipped. The value of honour, of course, did not diminish. Who could doubt that belief in honour continued in early modern European society, or that it drew strength from its medieval predecessor? 'The Renaissance cult of honour and fame', Malcolm Vale observes, 'owed more than it was prepared to acknowledge to the medieval cult of chivalry.'[19] The argument here is, rather, that prowess was no longer so regularly fused to this concept of honour, no longer the universally praised personal means of attaining honour, edged weapons in hand.

State-formation played a key role in this change, probably aided by changes in military technology. Stated in the baldest terms, the state finally achieved the working monopoly of licit violence within the realm that had been its distant goal for centuries—or at least it came to a new and undoubtedly significant step on its movement towards that victory.[20] Much larger armies, equipped with siege trains of much larger cannon, figure prominently in most analyses.[21] Historian are, of course, wisely cautious about hurrying noblemen off the stage too precipitously. As Malcolm Vale has noted, 'the nobility in England and on the Continent adapted themselves to changes dictated by new

---

[18] The fourth key to chivalric strength (suggested in Chapter 10) was the role of chivalry in establishing relationships between the genders. This Epilogue suggests basic changes in the view taken of prowess and in its links with honour, piety, and status. The link between love and prowess, too, must have altered in the post-medieval era; but it would be prudent to leave treatment of such a topic for specialists in the history of gender relationships in early modern Europe.

[19] Vale, *War and Chivalry*, 174.

[20] The classic argument appears in Stone, *Crisis of the Aristocracy*, 199–270. Even if current scholarship opposes the general thesis of a crisis, and of royalist triumph, the evidence Stone mustered in support of growing royal control of the means of violence seems significant. Bonney, *Political Change*, 441, suggests that '[t]he nobles were defeated as a political force acting independently of the crown and resorting to the sanction of armed rebellion'. In *Rebels and Rulers*, II, 221, Zagorin, speaking of the princes and *grands*, argues that 'if they still possessed substantial social and political power over their inferiors, they had largely lost their ability and will to maintain armed resistance against royal sovereignty'. Hale writes of the 'civilizing' and 'demilitarizing' of the 'armoured castes of western Europe: *War and Society*; Schalk suggests (to a medievalist, perhaps too starkly) a move from a medieval view of nobility linked with the function of fighting to a view, by the late sixteenth century, of nobility as pedigree: *From Valor to Pedigree*. James argues that the Tudor state monopolized chivalric violence: 'English Politics'.

[21] For the military revolution and state formation in various countries, see Downing, *The Military Revolution*. Black argues for the importance of the period after 1660 (i.e. beyond the usual terminal date for the military revolution) and for the absolutist state as a cause of military change rather than a consequence: *A Military Revolution?* On the role of military innovation, see Rogers, 'Military Revolution'; Parker, *The Military Revolution*; Eltis, *The Military Revolution*.

techniques of war and military organization'.[22] Even when belief in the key role of heavy cavalry in warfare had succumbed to battlefield facts, the chivalrous could still happily command units (even infantry units, supplied with firearms) in the ever-larger national armies raised to fight the king's wars. If standing armies were coming into being on the continent from the mid-fifteenth century, the crown continued to rely on militant nobles to raise soldiers, put down internal rebellion, and act as military governors.[23]

Historians likewise recognize that the generous measure of state triumph in warlike violence involves the way people thought as well as the way they waged war. Beyond recruitment and supply, taxes, tactics, and technology, we need to consider the altered self-definition of the nobles, their increasing acceptance of a cluster of ideas about violence and honour.[24] The Duc de Trémoille in mid-seventeenth-century France copied into his letterbook a description of the Duke of Parma, a famous captain of the previous generation; he notes that the duke was engaged in 'making war rather with his wits and speeches than with the force of his arms'.[25] The nobles were even coming to see chivalry (whether vocation or status) as closely linked to the crown; it meant service in what might almost be termed a 'national chivalry'.[26] This was the lesson learned by the Earl of Essex, the Comtes de Bouteville and des Chapelles, as we have seen, only at the very end of their lives. Honour need not be acquired and defended by personal acts of violence; it comes from the sovereign rather than from autonomous displays of prowess.

The very assumptions and actions of men like Bouteville and des Chapelles may, however, seem to deny these changes. From roughly the mid-sixteenth century a veritable cult of duelling stands as a remembrance of things past that is all but immovable in the face of all other changes taking place. Tournament was gone, or as near as mattered, and judicial combat was likewise on its way into memory, but autonomous individuals could still remove any stain to their sacred honour by spilling an opponent's blood in the duel, the obvious descendant of these forms. Duelling certainly demonstrates at least a partial

---

[22] Vale, *War and Chivalry*, 162. Hale, *War and Society*, 94–5, similarly argues that '[i]t has been suggested that the adoption of unchivalrous gunpowder weapons and the declining importance of cavalry led to a decreasing appetite for military service among the aristocracies of Europe. Neither assumption can be taken seriously.' Hale likewise discounts 'the case for the suggestion that artillery was an instrument centralizing power': p. 248.

[23] Hale, *War and Society*, 247–8; Vale, *War and Chivalry*, 162–3.

[24] Discussed in Vale, *War and Chivalry*, 100–74; Contamine, *War in the Middle Ages*, 132–72.

[25] Quoted in Dewald, *Aristocratic Experience*, 57. Of course, many medieval captains used their wits well, but the shift of emphasis away from prowess is fascinating. Some contemporary observers noted the same phenomenon, but were on the other side. At Elizabeth's court, the poet Samuel Daniel regretted the lowered 'virilitie' of an age in which 'more came to be effected by wit than by the sword' and decried 'all-drowning Sov'raintie'. Quoted in McCoy, *Rites of Knighthood*, 105, 118.

[26] Keen, *Nobility, Knighthood*, 167–70.

continuance into the early modern era of the old chivalric theme of a defence of honour through violence, and the old chivalric sense of political and even ethical autonomy as well. This survival of the chivalric obsession with honour and the perhaps even heightened assertion of personal independence seemed to the participants not so much an illegal as an extra-legal practice, a statement of their freedom from troublesome restraints in important matters of their own choosing.[27]

Of course the institutional force of both Church and State formally opposed the duel, and sometimes even took genuine steps to restrain it. The pattern will look familiar to anyone who has studied the arguments and measures directed at other troublesome chivalric practices, such as private war or the early tournament. The sense of a genuine opposition of ideals is obvious, as is the caution that the governors knew must accompany any clash with the deeply held beliefs of those whose support was still essential to successful governance. Royal legislation sometimes explicitly raised the issue of sovereignty and (as we have seen) royal administrations sometimes insisted that spectacular violators suffer the full punishment of the law; but the crown seldom pressed the issue to its logical and rigorous conclusion. As François Billacois suggests concisely, 'Duel is the supreme affirmation that aristocracy and monarchy are essentially opposed associates in a coherent political system.'[28]

Yet we must recognize that duelling is not the same social practice as its ancestor, private war. Perhaps the crown was all the more willing to look the other way because duel involved only individuals in private combat; the days of calling out a veritable army of armoured relatives and tenants and going to war, pennants flying, had come down to a few men with pistols or rapiers in a dark alley or a convenient field. Public order was, of course, still threatened in theory, but was obviously less threatened in fact; the public stance of those in charge could be maintained by growling and occasionally making examples of spectacular offenders.

In fact, insistence on the right to duel may inversely illustrate the degree of success the state was achieving in the separation of prowess and honour. Duelling, from this point of view, represents a reaction to growing royal control over violence on a grander scale. Such a view is finely illustrated in the statement of a sixteenth-century French nobleman, appropriately named Guillaume de Chevalier, that duelling had increased among his contemporaries because nobles were doing less fighting on the battlefields as a result of stronger monarchy.[29]

[27] See in general Billacois, *Le Duel*; Kiernan, *The Duel*; Schalk, *From Valor to Pedigree*, 162–74.
[28] Billacois, *Le Duel*, 391.
[29] Quoted in Schalk, *From Valor to Pedigree*, 169–70. Cf. Vale, *War and Chivalry*, 165–7.

Prowess and Piety

Another limitation on duelling brings us to analyse a second fusion of basic chivalric elements. The Church and religion, no less than the State, opposed duelling. Although some friends of the duel might claim religious justifications (interpreting the fight of David and Goliath as a duel being one of the more imaginative arguments), attempts to win religious backing in fact won few successes. Billacois's comment is once again pithy: duelling 'is not a counter-religion; it is another religion'.[30] Evidently most duellists confronted with religious criticism simply shrugged their shoulders and went on, showing the most sturdy sense of the lay autonomy and independence which by now was centuries old.

Yet we should take special note. This independence is not simply a continuance of a chivalric trait. In fact, a change of the greatest significance has taken place: the link between piety and prowess, always present if always under tension in the Middle Ages, has stretched to breaking point. The medieval Church had blessed knightly personal prowess, though at times with hands clasped in hope, arguing only that the violence must be directed towards proper ends. No one by the post-medieval period really thought duelling was one of those proper ends. Duelling, in other words, represents the totally secular end point of a long and tension-laden interplay between personal piety and personal violence. Since this connection of personal prowess with honour and with piety had formed one of the truly significant strengths of chivalry, the breaking of this bond represents one of the clearest causes for the general transformation of chivalry. If an old bond is snapped, a new one is created; a significant shift in the beneficiary of the religious valorization of violence has taken place. We have seen that clerics long suffered doubts about the blessing of God claimed for the violence inherent in chivalry. Over time their doubts all but disappeared, however, as the claim to licit violence came from the State. In one part of Europe after another, royal administrations more effectively and more globally asserted their supervision over licit violence; by the seventeenth century the process represented half a millennium of gradual pressure and a significant degree of success.

Constant clerical insistence on reform and restraint where chivalric violence was concerned contrasts significantly with the clerical willingness to sanctify one royal campaign after another through the later Middle Ages and early modern era.

---

[30] Billacois, *Le Duel*, 391, 350.

Of course the king's wars, no less than any knight's warlike violence, had to be just. Yet it was even harder, more futile, more clearly at odds with the divine plan to doubt the royal justifications than to debate those of the knights. Thus the Church, which had once in the distant past relied on pious rulers (Christian Roman emperors, Carolingian kings), could return—after the fireworks of the Gregorian Reform and the struggle over investiture—to an easy reliance on royal power. Were kings not God's anointed rulers for all the business involving bloodshed and violence, sadly necessary in an imperfect world? Were robbers not to be apprehended and hanged? Were the robbers who happened to wear crowns in neighbouring kingdoms not similarly to be stopped from evil?

Noble descendants of the medieval chivalrous might still play key roles in the military, but the change of religious valorization is significant. Religious justification for violence now descended not on the blessed ranks of the chivalry, but on agents of the State and, in theory and over time, of the nation.

Prowess and Status

In one final way we can see the breakdown of the durable fusions that had formed medieval chivalry. Chivalry ceased to function as the undoubted indicator of nobility.

The trappings of chivalry were at least in part appropriated by increasing numbers of people from non-noble social levels. The process was old and had already made considerable strides—and created significant tensions—within medieval centuries. Each effort to use chivalric culture as a barrier against lesser beings naturally generated even more interest on the part of the sub-chivalric to scale or breach that wall. Borrowed chivalric forms unmistakably reappeared beyond the inner circle of those who could proudly claim to be knightly or noble; aspirants in surrounding social circles eagerly brought these forms into their lives. Bourgeois interest in reading romance, in jousting, and in heraldry is well known. In the mid-fourteenth-century crisis of French chivalry, brought about most directly by repeated battlefield defeat, Geoffroi de Charny heaped praise—and urged greater valour—upon all those who lived by the profession of arms, not on the nobles alone. In England the fifteenth-century readers of Sir Thomas Malory's great work, though far from simply the bourgeois body once claimed, seem to have covered a wide social range. By the seventeenth century even London apprentices described themselves in chivalric language and participated in what William Hunt has termed civic chivalry.[31]

---

[31] Hunt, 'Civic Chivalry'.

As the social pyramid broadened, increasing numbers of the elite originated in legal and administrative families 'of the robe' rather than the older military families 'of the sword' (to use language from France).[32] Service to the State (even in the humdrum matters of diplomacy and administration, as well as in the rigours of war) proved to be an acceptable means of continuing influence. Living well, in comfortable and costly, if unfortified, country houses, or at court, even proved to be a seductive substitute for the very rigours of campaign and combat that Charny extolled in the mid-fourteenth century as the key to true superiority. Even education might be desirable; and if medieval aristocrats would have laughed at the idea that they were not educated, knowing that they had carefully learned what they needed to know, their late sixteenth- or seventeenth-century successors would have meant something different by the term.[33]

Thus *chevalerie* and its complex relationships with *clergie* and *royauté*, which have formed the core of this study, were transformed. The autonomy of chivalry and its private violence gradually disappeared, swallowed up by the growth of state power and public violence, blessed by the Church.[34] These processes were not, let it be said again, sudden and post-medieval, but, rather, the outcome of trends at work for half a millennium of European history. In one dimension the process left a stubbornly resistant residue of autonomous violence in the devotion to the duel. But the State had progressed towards sovereign control of warlike violence within the realm and the Church had made its peace with the sort of war that the State continued to lead with enthusiasm beyond its borders. After the break-up of the medieval Church, any lingering impulse for crusade could well be absorbed in the holy war against Christians with incorrect theological views.

Like a massive steel cable gradually coming unwound, the strands of chivalry, twisted tightly into place from the twelfth century, were pulled apart by the host of cumulative changes so actively at work. Change was evident in such diverse agencies as royal courts and armies, political and religious thought, mercantile companies, battlefield techniques, the classroom, the myriad of forms marking the social hierarchy. Over several centuries the

---

[32] See the similar language of Sir Robert Naunton at Elizabeth I's court in England: he claims her nobles were divided into *militi* and *togati*: see McCoy, *Rites of Knighthood*, 10.

[33] Schalk argues, for example, that the mid-sixteenth-century French nobility was not educated (in a bookish sense) and that only gradually did education become a *marque de noblesse*; by the mid-seventeenth century the nobles were associated with the culture that comes with education: *From Valor to Pedigree*, 174–5. Hale notes the endless popularity of Castiglione's *The Courtier* and the founding of military academies from the 1560's: *War and Society*, 97–8. Cf. Motley, *Becoming a French Aristocrat: the education of court nobility, 1580–1715* (Princeton, 1990).

[34] The independent piety of knights obviously intersects with Reformation themes. I am working on a general study of the religion of knights.

BIBLIOGRAPHY

✦✦✦

Actes du Parlement de Paris, 1st ser., 1254–1328, ed. E. Boutaric, 2 vols (Paris: 1863–7); 2nd ser., 1328–50, ed. Henri Furgeot, 2 vols (Paris: 1920, repr. Neudeln, Liechtenstein, 1977).

Adams, Alison, ed., tr., *The Romance of Yder* (Cambridge, 1983).

Akehurst, F. R. P., tr., *The Coutumes de Beauvaisis of Philippe de Beaumanoir* (Philadelphia, 1992).

Allen, Rosamund, tr., *Lawman. Brut.* (New York, 1992).

d'Alverny, Marie-Thérèse, *Alain de Lille, Textes inedits* (Paris, 1965)

Anglo, Sydney, ed., *Chivalry in the Renaissance* (Woodbridge, Suffolk, 1990).

Arnold, Ivor, ed., *The Roman de Brut de Wace*, 2 vols (Paris, 1938–40).

Asher, Martha, tr., *The Merlin Continuation*, [Post-Vulgate Part I] in Norris Lacy, gen. ed., *Lancelot–Grail*, IV (New York, 1995).

Asher, Martha, tr., *The Merlin Continuation (end)* [Post-Vulgate Part I], *The Quest for the Holy Grail* [Post-Vulgate Part II], *The Death of Arthur* [Post-Vulgate Part III], in Norris Lacy, gen. ed., *Lancelot–Grail*, V (New York, 1996).

Atkinson, Stephen C. B., 'Malory's Lancelot and the Quest of the Grail', in James W. Spisak, ed., *Studies in Malory* (Kalamazoo, MI, 1985).

Ayton, Andrew, *Knights and Warhorses: Military Service and the English Aristocracy Under Edward III* (Bury St Edmunds, 1994).

—— and J. L. Price, eds, *The Medieval Military Revolution: State, Society and Military Change in Medieval and Early Modern Europe* (London, 1995).

Bachrach, Bernard S., 'Caballus and Caballarius in Medieval Warfare', in Howell Chickering and Thomas H. Seiller, eds, *The Study of Chivalry* (Kalamazoo, MI, 1988).

Baldwin, John W., *The Government of Philip Augustus: Fundamentals of French Royal Power in the Middle Ages* (Berkeley, 1986).

Barber, Richard, 'Chivalry and the *Morte Darthur*', in Elizabeth Archibald and S. S. G. Edwards, eds, *A Companion to Malory* (Woodbridge, Suffolk, 1996).

—— *The Knight and Chivalry*, 2nd edn (Woodbridge, Suffolk, 1995).

—— and Juliet Barker, *Tournaments, Jousts, Chivalry and Pageants in the Middle Ages* (Woodbridge, Suffolk, 1989).

Barbero, Alessandro, *L'aristocrazia nella societa francese del medioevo* (Bologna, 1987).

Barker, Juliet, *The Tournament in England* (Woodbridge, Suffolk, 1986).

Barron, W. R. J., *English Medieval Romance* (London, 1987).

—— 'Knighthood on Trial: The Acid Test of Irony', in W. H. Jackson, ed., *Knighthood in Medieval Literature* (Woodbridge, Suffolk, 1981).

Barrow, G. W. S., *Robert Bruce and the Community of the Realm of Scotland* (Berkeley, CA, 1965).

Bartlett, Robert J., 'Technique militaire et pouvoir politique, 900–1300', *Annales ESC* 42 (1986).

Baumgartner, Emanuel, *L'Arbre et le pain: essai sur la Quieste del Saint Graal* (Paris, 1981).

—— *La Mort le roi Artu* (Paris, 1994).

Becquet, Jean, ' L'Érémitisme clerical et laïc dans l'ouest de la France', in *L'eremitismo in Occidente nei secoli XIe et XII: atti della seconda Settimana internazionale di studio, Mendola, 30 agosto–6 settenbre 1962* (Milan, 1965).

Benson, Larry D., ed., *King Arthur's Death: The Middle English Stanzaic Morte Arthur and Alliterative Morte Arthure* (Indianapolis, IN, 1974).

—— *Malory's Morte Darthur* (Cambridge, MA, 1977).

—— 'The Tournament in the romances of Chrétien de Troyes and *L'Histoire de Guillaume le Maréchal*', in Larry D. Benson and John Leyerle, eds, *Chivalric Literature* (Toronto, 1980).

Benton, John F., *Self and Society in Medieval France, the Memoirs of Abbot Guibert of Nogent* (New York, 1970).

Berry, Virginia Gingerick, ed., tr., *Odo of Deuil, De Profectione Ludovici VII in Orientem* (New York, 1965).

Billacois, François, *Le Duel dans la société française des XVIe- XVIIe siècles* (Paris, 1986).

Black, Jeremy, *A Military Revolution? Military Change and European Society, 1550–1800* (Atlantic Heights, NJ, 1991).

Blake, E. O., 'The Formation of the "Crusade Idea" ', *Journal of Ecclesiastical History* 21 (1970), 11–31.

Bloch, Marc, *La Société Féodale* (Paris, 1939–40), tr. L. A. Manyon, *Feudal Society*, 2 vols (Chicago, 1961).

Bloch, R. Howard, *Medieval French Literature and Law* (Berkeley, 1977).

Bogdanow, Fanni, ed., 'An Interpretation of the Meaning and Purpose of the Vulgate *Queste del Saint Graal* in the light of the Mystical Theology of St Bernard', in *The Changing Face of Arthurian Romance: Essays on Arthurian Prose Romances in memory of Cedric E. Pickford* (Woodbridge, Suffolk, 1986).

—— 'La Folie Lancelot: A Hitherto Unidentified Portion of the Suite de Merlin Contained in MSS B. N. fr.112 and 12599', *Beihefte zur Zeitschrift für Romanische Philologie* (1965), 1–21.

—— *The Romance of the Grail* (Manchester: Manchester, 1966).

—— ed., *La Version Post-Vulgate de la 'Quest del Saint' et de la 'Mort Artu'* (Paris, 1991–).

Bohna, Montgomery, 'Royal Lordship and Regional Power: The King's Affinity and Informal Government in Lincolnshire, 1460–85', (Ph.D. dissertation, University of Rochester, 1994).

Bonner, Anthony, *Selected Works of Ramon Llull*, 2 vols (Princeton, 1985).

Bonney, Richard, *Political Change in France Under Richelieu and Mazarin* (Oxford, 1978).

Boulton, D'Arcy Dacre Jonathan, *The Knights of the Crown: The Monarchical Orders of Knighthood in Later Medieval Europe, 1325–1520* (New York, 1987).

Boutet, Dominique, 'Arthur et son mythe dans la mort le roi Artu: visions psychologique, politique et théologique', in Jean Dufournet, ed., *La Mort du roi Arthur ou le crépuscle de la chevalerie* (Paris, 1994).

—— 'Carrefours idéologique de la royauté arthurienne', *Cahiers de Civilisation Médievale* 28 (1985), 3–17.

—— 'Les chansons de geste et l'affermisement du pouvoir royal (1100–1250)', *Annales ESC* 37 (1982), 3–14.

—— 'La politique et histoire dans les chansons de geste', *Annales ESC* 31 (1976), 1119–30.

—— and Armand Strubel, *Littérature, politique et société dans la France du Moyen Age* (Paris, 1979).

Bradbury, Nancy Mason, 'The Traditional Origins of *Havelok the Dane*', *Studies in Philology* 90 (1993), 115–42.

Brandin, Louis, ed., *La Chanson d'Aspremont* (Paris, 1970).

Brault, Gerald J., ed., tr., *La Chanson de Roland* (University Park, PA, 1984).

Brereton, Geoffrey, tr., *Froissart. Chronicles* (Baltimore, MD, 1968).

Breul, Karl, ed., *Sir Gowther: Eine englische romanze aus dem XV jahrhundert* (Jena, 1886).

Brewer, Derek, ed., *Malory, the Morte Darthur* (Evanston, Ill, 1974).

—— 'Malory: the Traditional Writer and the Archaic Mind', in Richard Barber, ed., *Arthurian Literature I* (Woodbridge, Suffolk, 1981).

Brock, Edmund, ed. *Alliterative Morte Arthure* (London, 1871: repr. London, 1961).

Brooke, Christopher, ed., *Medieval Church and Society* (New York, 1974).

Brundage, James, 'Holy War and the Medieval Lawyers', in Thomas Patrick Murphy, ed., *The Holy War* (Columbus, OH, 1974).

Bryant, Nigel, tr., *The High Book of the Grail: A Translation of the Thirteenth-Century Romance of Perlesvaus* (Cambridge, 1978).

—— tr., *Perceval: The Story of the Grail* (Woodbridge, Suffolk, 1982).

Bühler, Curt F., ed., *The Epistle of Othea*, tr. Stephen Scrope (London, 1970).

Buist-Thiele, Marie Louise, 'The Influence of St. Bernard of Clairvaux on the Formation of the Order of the Knights Templar', in Michael Gervers, ed., *The Second Crusade and the Cistercians* (New York, NY, 1992).

Bunt, G. H. V., ed., *William of Palerne: An Alliterative Romance* (Groningen, 1985).

Burgess, Glyn S., *Contribution à l'étude du vocabulaire pré -courtois* (Geneva, 1970).

—— 'The Term *chevalerie* in Twelfth-Century Old French', in Peter Rolfe Monks and D. D. R. Owen, eds, *Medieval Codicology, Iconography, Literature and Translation: Studies for Keith Val Sinclair* (Leiden, 1994).

Burns, E. Jane, tr., *The Quest for the Holy Grail*, in Norris Lacy, gen. ed., *Lancelot–Grail*, IV (New York, NY, 1995).

—— and Roberta Krueger, eds, *Courtly Ideology and Woman's Place in Medieval French Literature (Romance Notes XXV)* (1985).

Busby, Keith, ed., *Raoul de Hodenc, Le Roman des Eles. The Anonymous 'Ordene de chevalerie'* (Amsterdam, 1983).

—— and Eric Kooper, eds, *Courtly Literature: Culture and Context* (Amsterdam, 1990).

Byles, Alfred T. P., ed., *The Book of the Ordre of Chyvalry Translated and Printed by William Caxton* (London: EETS, 1926).

Cable, James, tr., *The Death of King Arthur* (Harmondsworth, 1971) .

Calin, William, 'Contre la *fin'amor*? Contre la femme? Une relecture de textes du Moyen Age', in Keith Busby and Eric Kooper, eds, *Courtly Literature: Culture and Context* (Amsterdam, 1990).

—— *A Muse for Heroes: Nine Centuries of the Epic in France* (Toronto, 1983).

—— *The Old French Epic of Revolt* (Geneva, 1962).

—— '*Raoul de Cambrai*: un univers en décomposition', *Actes du XVIe congrès de la société Roncesvals* (Aix-en-Provence, 1974).

—— 'Rapport introductif: Rapports entre chansons de geste et roman au XIIIe siècle', in *Essor et fortune de la Chanson de geste dans l'Europe et l'Orient latin*, 2 vols (Modena. 1984), II.

Campbell, David., tr., *The Tale of Balain, from the Romance of the Grail, a 13th-century French prose romance* (Evanston, IL, 1972).

Campbell, James, 'Reflections on the English Government from the Tenth to the Twelfth Century', *Transactions of the Royal Historical Society* 25 (1975).

Cardona, Marti Aurell, 'Chevaliers et chevalerie chez Raymond Lulle', *Raymond Lulle et le Pays d'Oc* (*Cahiers de Fanjeaux* 22, Toulouse, 1987).

Carman, J. Neale, 'The Symbolism of the Perlesvaus', *Proceedings of the Modern Language Association* 61 (1946).

Carroll, Carleton W., ed., tr., *Erec and Enide* (New York, 1987).

—— tr., *Lancelot Part II*, in Norris Lacy, gen. ed., *Lancelot–Grail*, II (New York, 1993).

—— tr., *Lancelot Part VI*, in Norris Lacy, gen. ed., *Lancelot–Grail*, III (New York, 1995).

Cazel, Fred, 'Religious Motivation in the Biography of Hubert de Burgh', *Studies in Church History* 15 (1978).

Cazelles, Raymond, *Société politique, noblesse et couronne sous Jean le Bel et Charles V* (Geneva, 1982).

Chaney, William A., *The Cult of Kingship in Anglo-Saxon England* (Berkeley, CA, 1970).

Chase, Carol J., tr., *The History of the Holy Grail*, in Norris Lacy, gen. ed. *Lancelot–Grail*, I (1993).

Chênerie, Marie-Luce, *Le Chevalier errant dans les romans arthuriens* (Geneva, 1986).

—— 'Preudome dans le mort artu', in Jean Dufournet, ed., *La Mort du roi Arthur ou le crépuscle de la cheneriechevalerie* (Paris, 1994).

Chibnall, Marjorie, *Anglo-Norman England* (New York, 1986).

—— ed., tr., *The Ecclesiastical History of Orderic Vitalis*, 6 vols (Oxford, 1969–80).

—— 'Feudal Society in Orderic Vitalis', *Proceedings of the Battle Abbey Conference on Anglo-Norman Studies 1978* (Ipswich, Suffolk, 1979).

Chickering, Howell, and Thomas H. Seiler, *The Study of Chivalry* (Kalamazoo, MI, 1988).

Chodorow, Stanley, *Christian Political Theory and Church Politics in the Mid-twelfth Century* (Berkeley, CA, 1972).

Clanchy, Michael, *From Memory to Written Record*, 2nd edn (Oxford, 1993).

—— 'Law and Love in the Middle Ages', in John Bossy, ed., *Disputes and Settlements* (Cambridge, 1986).

Cline, Ruth Harwood, tr., *Perceval: or the Story of the Grail* (Athens, GA, 1983).

Cloetta, Wilhelm, ed., *Les Deux Redactions en verse du Moniage Guillaume*, 2 vols (Paris, 1906–11).

Colvin, H. M., gen. ed., *The History of the King's Works*, I, *The Middle Ages*, eds, R. Allen Brown, H. M. Colvin, and A. J. Taylor (London, 1963).

Combarieu, Micheline de, 'La Violence dans *La Couronnement de Louis*', in *Mélanges de Littérature du Moyen Age au XXe siècle*, 2 vols (Paris, 1978), I.

Constans, L., and E. Faral, eds, *Le Roman de Troie en prose* (Paris, 1922).

Contamine, Philippe, *War in the Middle Ages*, tr. Michael Jones (Oxford, 1984).

—— ed., *La Noblesse au Moyen Age, XIe-XVe siècles: essais à la mémoire de Robert Boutruche* (Paris, 1976).

Cooper, Richard, ' "Nostre histoire renouvelée": the Reception of the Romances of Chivalry in Renaissance France', in Sydney Anglo, ed., *Chivalry in the Renaissance* (Woodbridge, Suffolk, 1990).

Corley, Corin, tr., *Lancelot of the Lake* (Oxford, 1989).

Coss, Peter, 'Aspects of Cultural Diffusion in Medieval England: the Early Romances, Local Society and Robin Hood', *Past and Present* 108 (1985).

—— *The Knight in Medieval England, 1000–1400* (Stroud, 1993) .

Coupland, G. W., *Letter to King Richard II: A plea made in 1395 for peace between England and France* (Liverpool, 1975).

—— ed., tr., *The Tree of Battles of Honoré Bonet* (Liverpool, 1949).

Cowdrey, H. E. J., 'The Genesis of the Crusades: the Springs of Western Ideas of the Holy War', *Popes, Monks and Crusaders* (London, 1984).

—— 'The Peace and Truce of God in the Eleventh Century', *Past and Present* 46 (1970).

—— 'Pope Gregory VII's Crusading Plans of 1074', in *Popes, Monks and Crusaders*, (London, 1984).

Crane, Susan, *Insular Romance* (Berkeley, 1986).

Crosland, Jessie, *William the Marshal: the Last Great Feudal Baron* (London, 1962).

Crouch, David, *William Marshal, Court, Career and Chivalry in the Angevin Empire, 1147–1219* (London, 1990).

—— *The Image of Aristocracy in Britain, 1000–1300* (London, 1992).

Cusimano, Richard, and John Moorhead, trs., *Suger, The Deeds of Louis the Fat* (Washington, DC, 1992).

Cutler, S. H., *The Law of Treason and Treason Trials in Later Medieval France* (Cambridge, 1981).

Daniel, Norman, *Heroes and Saracens: An Interpretation of the Chansons de Geste* (Edinburgh, 1984).

Davis, R. H. C., *King Stephen* (London, 1967).

—— *The Medieval Warhorse: Origin, Development and Redevelopment* (London, 1989).

Davis, Wendy, and Paul Fouracre, eds, *The Settlement of Disputes in Early Medieval Europe* (Cambridge, 1986).

Denholm-Young, Noel, 'Feudal Society in the Thirteenth Century: the Knights', *History* 29 (1944).

DeVries, Kelly, *Infantry Warfare in the Early Fourteenth Century* (Bury St Edmunds, Suffolk, 1996).

Dewald, Jonathan, *Aristocratic Experience and the Origins of Modern Culture* (Berkeley, 1993).

Dhont, Jan, 'Les 'Solidarites' médievales. Une société en transition: la Flandre en 1127–1128', *Annales ESC* 12 (1957), 529–60; tr. Fredric Cheyette, 'Medieval 'Solidarities': Flemish Society in Transition, 1127–1128', in *Lordship and Community in Medieval Europe* (New York, 1968).

Dickinson, John, ed., tr., *The Statesman's Book of John of Salisbury* (New York, 1963).

Downing, Brian M., *The Military Revolution and Political Change* (Princeton, 1992).

Duby, Georges, *The Age of the Cathedrals: Art and Society 980–1420* (Chicago, 1981).

—— *The Chivalrous Society*, tr., Cynthia Postan (Berkeley, 1977).

—— 'Dans la France de Nord-Ouest. Au XIIe siècle; les 'jeunes' dans la société aristocratique', *Annales ESC* 19 (1964), 835–46; tr. Fredric L. Cheyette, 'In Northwestern France: The 'Youth' in Twelfth-century Aristocratic Society', in *Lordship and Community in Medieval Europe* (New York, 1968).

—— *The Early Growth of the European Economy* (Ithaca, 1974).

—— 'Guerre et société dans l'Europe féodale: la morale des guerriers', in Vittore Branca, ed., *Concetto, storia, miti, e immagini del Medio Evo, atti del XIV corso internazionale d'alta cultura* (Florence, 1973).

—— *Guillaume le Maréchal, ou le meilleur chevalier du monde* (Paris, 1984); tr. R. Howard, *William Marshal, Flower of Chivalry* (New York, 1986).

—— *Les Trois Ordres, ou l'imaginaire du féodalisme* (Paris, 1978); tr. Arthur Goldhammer, *The Three Orders: Feudal Society Imagined* (Chicago, 1980).

Ducoudray, Gustav, *Les Origines du Parlement de Paris et la justice aux XIIIe et XIVe siècles* (Paris, 1902).

Dufournet, Jean, ed., *La Mort du roi Arthur ou le crépuscle de la chevalerie* (Paris, 1994).

Edwards, Elizabeth, 'The Place of Women in the *Morte Darthur*', in Elizabeth Archibald and A. S. G. Edwards, eds, *A Companion to Malory* (Woodbridge, Suffolk, 1996).

Ehrstein, Stephen F., 'Gentry Behavior in Fourteenth-Century Lancashire', (MA thesis, University of Rochester, 1996).

Elias, Norbert, *Über den Prozess der Zivilisation: soziogenetische und psychogenetische Untersuchungen*, 2 vols (Frankfurt-am Main, 1939; reissued 1997). I: *The History of Manners*, tr. Edmund Jephcott (New York, 1978); II: *Power and Civility*, tr. Edmund Jephcott (New York, 1982).

Eltis, David, *The Military Revolution in Sixteenth-Century Europe* (London, 1995).

Ennen, Edith, *The Medieval Town*, tr., Natalie Fryde (Amsterdam, 1979)

Erdmann, Carl, *The Origins of the Idea of Crusade*, tr., Marshal Baldwin and Walter Goffart (Princeton, 1977).

L'eremitismo in Occidente nei secoli XIe et XII: *atti della seconda Settimana internazionale di studio, Mendola, 30 agosto–6 settenbre 1962* (Milan, 1965).

Evans, G. R., *The Mind of St. Bernard of Clairvaux* (Oxford, 1983).

Evans, Joan, tr., *The Unconquered Knight. A Chronicle of the Deeds of Don Pero Niño, Count of Buelna* (London, 1928).

Ferguson, Arthur B., *The Chivalric Tradition in Renaissance England* (Washington, DC, 1986).

Ferrante, Joan, M., ed., tr., *Guillaume d'Orange: Four Twelfth-century Epics* (New York, 1974).

Field, P. J. C., *The Life and Times of Sir Thomas Malory* (Cambridge, 1993).

—— *The Works of Sir Thomas Malory*, 3rd edn, ed., Eugène Vinaver, revised by P. J. C. Field (Oxford, 1990).

Flori, Jean, *L'Essor de chevalerie: XIe-XIIe siècles* (Geneva, 1986).

—— 'L'Historien et l'épopée française', *L'Epopée* (*Typologie des sources du Moyen Age*), director, Léopold Genicot (Turnhout, 1988).

—— *L'Idéologie du glaive* (Geneva, 1983).

—— 'Sémantique et idéologie. Un cas exemplaire: les adjectifs dans *Aiol*', in *Essor et fortune de la Chanson de geste dans l'Europe et l'Orient latin*, 2 vols (Modena, 1984), I.

Foerster, Wendelin, ed., *Les Mervelles de Rigomer von Jehan*, 2 vols; I: *Der Altfranzösischer Artusroman des 13. Jahrhunderts* (Halle, 1908); II: Foerster and H. Breuer, eds, *Einleitung, Anmerkungen, Glossar, Namenverzeichnis, Sprichworter* (Dresden, 1915).

Fossier, Robert, *L'Enfance de l'Europe*, 2 vols (Paris, 1982).

—— 'Fortunes et infortunes paysannes au Cambrésis à la fin du XIIIe siècle', in *Économies et sociétés au moyen âge* (Paris, 1973), 171–82.

Fraher, Richard M., 'Preventing Crime in the High Middle Ages: the Medieval Lawyer's Search for Deterrence', in James Ross Sweeney and Stanley Chodorow, eds, *Popes, Teachers and Canon Law in the Middle Ages* (Ithaca, 1989).

—— 'The Theoretical Justification for the New Criminal Law of the High Middle Ages; "Rei publicae interest, ne crimina remaneant impunita" ', *University of Illinois Law Review* 3 (1984).

Frappier, Jean, *Les Chansons de geste du cycle de Guillaume d'Orange*, 2 vols (Paris, 1965).

—— *Chrétien de Troyes. L'homme et l'oeuvre* (Paris, 1968).

—— *Étude sur la mort le roi artu* (Geneva, 1961).

—— 'Le Graal et la chevalerie', *Romania* 75 (1954).

—— 'La mort Galehot', in *Histoire, mythes et symboles: Etudes de littérature francaise* (Geneva: 1976).

—— ed., *La Mort le roi Artu*, 3rd edn (Geneva: Droz, 1964).

—— *Étude sur Yvain ou le Chevalier Au Lion de Chrétien de Troyes* (Paris: Société d'Enseignement Supérieur, 1965).

Frappier, Jean, 'Vues sur les conceptions courtoises dans les littératures d'oc et d'oïl au XIIe siècle', *Cahiers de Civilisation Médiévale* 2 (1959).

Fresco, Karen, ed., and Colleen P. Donagher, tr., *Renaut de Bâgé, Le Bel Inconnu* (New York, 1992).

Garmonsway, G. N., tr., *The Anglo-Saxon Chronicle* (London, 1953).

Gaudemet, J., 'Les collections canoniques, miroir de la vie sociale', *Mélanges en l'honneur de Jacques Ellul* (Paris, 1983).

Geary, Patrick, 'L'Humiliation des saints', *Annales ESC* 34 (1979).

—— *Living with the Dead in the Middle Ages* (Ithaca, 1994),

—— 'Vivre en conflit dans une France sans état: typologie des mécanismes de règlement des conflits (1050–1200)', *Annales ESC* 41 (1986).

Gervers, Michael, ed., *The Second Crusade and the Cistercians* (New York, 1992).

Gicquel, Bernard, '*Le Jehan le Blond* de Philippe de Rémi peut-il être une source du *Willehalm von Orlens?*', *Romania* 102 (1981).

Gillingham, John, 'Richard I and the Science of War in the Middle Ages', in J. Gillingham and J. C. Holt, eds, *War and Government in the Middle Ages* (Cambridge, 1984).

—— 'War and Chivalry in the *History of William Marshal*', in P. R. Coss and S. D. Lloyd, eds, *Thirteenth-Century England II* (Woodbridge, Suffolk, 1988).

—— 'William the Bastard at War', in Christopher Harper-Bill, Christopher J. Holdsworth, and Janet L. Nelson, eds, *Studies in Medieval History presented to R. Allen Brown* (Wolfsboro, NH, 1989).

—— '1066 and the introduction of chivalry into England', in George Garnet and John Hudson, eds, *Law and Government in Medieval England and Normandy* (Cambridge, 1996).

Gist, Margaret Adlum, *Love and War in the Middle English Romances* (Philadelphia, 1947).

Given-Wilson, Chris, *The English Nobility in the Later Middle Ages: the Fourteenth Century Political Community* (London, 1987)

Gold, Penny Shine, *The Lady and the Virgin: Image, Attitude, and Experience in Twelfth-Century France* (Chicago, 1985).

Göller, Karl-Heinz, *The Alliterative Morte Arthure: A Reassessment of the Poem* (Bury St Edmunds, 1981).

Gouron, André, and Albert Rigaudiere, eds, *Renaissance du pouvoir legislatif et genese de l'etat* (Montpellier, 1988).

Grabois, Aryeh, '*Militia* and *Malitia*: The Bernardine Vision of Chivalry', in Michael Gervers, ed., *The Second Crusade and the Cistercians* (New York, 1992).

—— 'De la trêve de Dieu à la paix du roi: étude sur les transformations du mouvement de la paix au XIIe siècle', in P. J. Gallais and Y. J. Riou, *Mélanges offert à René Crozet*, 2 vols (Poitiers, 1966).

Gravdal, Kathryn, *Ravishing Maidens: Writing Rape in Medieval French Literature and Law* (Philadelphia: University of Pennsylvania Press, 1991).

Grave, J. J. Salverda de, ed., *Eneas, Roman du XIIe siècle*, 2 vols (Paris, 1925, 1929).

Green, Richard Firth, *Poets and Princepleasers* (Toronto, 1980).

Greenia, Conrad, tr., *Treatises III: On Grace and Free Choice. Praise of the New Knighthood* in *The Works of Bernard of Clairvaux. Volume Seven*, trs., Daniel O'Donnovan and Conrad Greenia (Kalamazoo, MI, 1977).

Gunn, Steven, 'Chivalry and the Politics of the Early Tudor Court', in Sydney Anglo, ed., *Chivalry in the Renaissance* (Woodbridge, Suffolk, 1990),

Hackett, Mary, 'Le climat moral de *Girart de Roussillon*', *Études de philologie romane et d'histoire littéraire offerts à Jules Horrent* (Liege, 1980), 165–74.

—— 'Knights and Knighthood in *Girart de Roussillon*', Christopher Harper-Bill and Ruth Harvey, eds, *The Ideals and Practices of Knighthood II* (Cambridge, 1988), 40–45.

Haidu, Peter, *The Subject of Violence: The Song of Roland and the Birth of the State* (Bloomington, IN, 1993)

Hale, J. R., *War and Society in Renaissance Europe, 1450–1620* (New York, NY, 1985),

Hallam, Elizabeth, *Capetian France, 987–1328* (London, 1980).

Hanawalt, Barbara, *Crime and Conflict in English Communities, 1300–1348* (Cambridge, Mass, 1979).

Hanning, R. W., 'The Audience as Co-Creator of the First Chivalric Romances', in G. K. Hunter and C. J. Rawson, eds, *The Yearbook of English Studies* 11 (1981).

—— 'The Social Significance of Twelfth-Century Chivalric Romance', *Mediaevalia et Humanistica* 3 (1972).

—— *The Individual in Twelfth-Century Romance* (New York, 1977).

—— and Joan Ferrante, trs., *The Lais of Marie de France* (Durham, NC, 1978).

Harding, Alan, 'Early trailbaston proceedings from the Lincoln roll of 1305', in R. F. Hunnisett and J. B. Post, eds, *Medieval Legal Records edited in memory of C. A. F. Meekings* (London, 1978).

—— *The Law Courts of Medieval England* (London, 1973).

—— 'Plaints and Bills in the History of English Law, Mainly in the Period 1250–1350', in Dafydd Jenkins, ed., *Legal History Studies 1972* (Cardiff, 1975).

Harper-Bill, Christopher, 'The Piety of the Anglo-Norman Knightly Class', *Anglo-Norman Studies* 2 (1979).

Hasking, Charles Homer, *The Renaissance of the Twelfth Century* (Cambridge, MA, 1927).

Hawkes, Emma, 'Bibliography of Legal Records Related to Rape and Ravishment in Medieval England', *Medieval Feminist Newsletter* 21 (Spring, 1996).

Head, Thomas, and Richard Landes, eds, *The Peace of God: Social Violence and Religious Response in France around the Year 1000* (Ithaca, NY, 1992).

Helmholz, Richard H., 'Crime, Compurgation and the Courts of the Medieval Church', *Law and History Review* 1 (1983).

Henneman, John B., *Olivier de Clisson and Political Society in France Under Charles V and Charles VI* (Philadelphia, 1996).

Heuckenkamp, Ferdinand, ed., *Le Chevalier du Papegau* (Halle, 1897).

Hewitt, H. J., *The Organisation of War Under Edward III* (Manchester, 1966).

Hillgarth, Jocelin, *The Spanish Kingdoms, 1250–1516* (Oxford, 1976).

—— *Ramon Lull and Lullism in Fourteenth-Century France* (Oxford, 1971).

Hilton, Rodney H., *A Medieval Society: The West Midlands at the End of the Thirteenth Century* (London, 1966).

Hindman, Sandra, *Sealed in Parchment: Rereadings of Knighthood in the Romances of Chrétien de Troyes* (Chicago, 1994).

Hofmeister, A., ed., *Monumenta Germaniae historica . . . Scriptores Rerum Germanicarum* (Berlin, 1912).

Hoggan, David, tr., *The Crowning of Louis*, in Glanville Price, ed., *William, Count of Orange: Four Old French Epics* (London, 1975).

Holden, A. J., ed., *Guillaume d'Angleterre* (Geneva, 1988).

—— ed., *Le Roman de Rou de Wace*, 3 vols (Paris, 1970–3).

Holdsworth, Christopher J., 'Ideas and Reality: Some Attempts to Control and Defuse War in the Twelfth Century', *Studies in Church History* 20 (1983).

Holzermayr, Katarina, 'Le "mythe" d'Arthur: la royauté et l'idéologie', *Annales ESC* 39 (1984).

Hopkins, Andrea, *The Sinful Knights: A Study of Middle English Penetential Romance* (Oxford, 1990).

Housley, Norman, 'Crusades Against Christians', in Peter W. Edbury, ed., *Crusade and Settlement* (Cardiff, 1985).

Hubert, Morton Jerome, tr., and John L. La Monte, notes and documents, *Crusade of Richard Lion-Heart, by Ambroise* (New York, 1941).

Hucher, Eugene, ed., *Le Saint-Graal*, 3 vols (Mans, 1875–8).

Hughes, C. W., 'Local and National Politics in Staffordshire in the Reign of Edward II' (MA thesis, University of Rochester, 1990)

Huizinga, Johan, *The Autumn of the Middle Ages* [1919], tr., Rodney J. Payton and Ulrich Mammitzsch (Chicago, 1996).

Hunt, Tony, 'The Emergence of the Knight in France and England 1000–1200', in W. H. Jackson, ed., *Knighthood in Medieval Literature* (Woodbridge, Suffolk, 1981).

—— 'L'inspiration idéologique du *Charroi de Nimes*', *Revue Belge de philologie et d'histoire* 56 (1978).

Hunt, William, 'Civic Chivalry and the English Civil War', in Anthony Grafton and Ann Blair, eds, *The Transmission of Culture in Early Modern Europe* (Philadelphia, 1990).

Hurnard, Naomi, *The King's Pardon for Homicide* (Oxford, 1969).

Jackson, Rosemary, *Fantasy: the Literature of Subversion* (London, 1981).

Jackson, W. H. ed., *Knighthood in Medieval Literature* (Woodbridge, Suffolk: 1981).

—— *Chivalry in Twelfth-Century Germany: The Works of Hartmann von Aue* (Bury St. Edmunds, 1994).

Jaeger, C. Stephen, 'Notes Toward a Sociology of Fear in Courtly Society', *Journal of English and Germanic Philology* 81 (1984).

—— *The Origins of Courtliness: Civilizing Trends and the Formation of Courtly Ideals: 930–1210* (Philadelpia, 1985).

James, Bruno Scott, tr., *St Bernard of Clairvaux. Letters* (London, 1953).

James, Mervyn, 'At a Crossroads of the Political Culture: The Essex Revolt, 1601', in *Society, Politics and Culture* (Cambridge, 1986).

—— 'English Politics and the Concept of Honour, 1485–1642', in *Society, Politics and Culture* (Cambridge, 1986).

James, M. R., ed., *The Romance of Alexander* (Oxford, 1933).

James, M. R., ed., tr., revised, C. N. L. Brooke, and R. A. B. Mynors, *Walter Map. De Nugis Curialum, Courtiers' Trifles* (Oxford, 1983).

Johnson, Charles, ed., tr., *Dialogus de Scaccario: The Course of the Exchequer by Richard Fitz-Nigel*, revised by F. E. L. Carter and D. E. Greenway (Oxford, 1983).

Jordan, William, *Louis IX and the Challenge of the Crusade* (Princeton, 1979).

Kaeuper, Richard W., 'An Historian's Reading of the *Tale of Gamelyn*', *Medium Aevum* 52 (1983).

—— 'Law and Order in Fourteenth-Century England: The Evidence of Special Commissions of Oyer and Terminer', *Speculum* 54 (1979).

—— *War, Justice, and Public Order: England and France in the Later Middle Ages* (Oxford, 1988).

—— and Elspeth Kennedy, *The Book of Chivalry of Geoffroi de Charny: Text, Context and Translation* (Philadelphia, 1996).

Kaplan, Justin, *Mr Clemens and Mark Twain, A Biography* (New York, 1966)

Katz, Blanche, tr., *La Prise d'Orange* (Morningside Heights, NY, 1947).

Kay, Sarah, *The Chansons de Geste in the Age of Romance* (Oxford, 1996).

—— ed., tr., *Raoul de Cambrai* (Oxford: Clarendon Press, 1992).

Keegan, John, *A History of Warfare* (New York, 1993).

Keen, Maurice, *Chivalry* (New Haven, 1984).

—— 'Chivalry and Courtly Love', in *Nobles, Knights and Men-at-Arms in the Middle Ages* (London, 1996).

—— 'Chivalry, Nobility and the Man-At-Arms', in C. T. Allmand, ed., *War, Literature and Politics in the Later Middle Ages* (Liverpool, 1976)

—— *The Laws of War in the Late Middle Ages* (London, 1965).

—— *Nobles, Knights and Men-at-Arms in the Middle Ages* (London, 1996).

—— (with Juliet Barker), 'The Medieval English Kings and the Tournament', in *Nobles, Knights and Men-at-Arms in the Middle Ages* (London, 1996).

Kelly, Thomas E., *Le Haut Livre du Graal: Perlesvaus: A Structural Study* (Geneva, 1974).

Kennedy, Angus, 'The Hermit's Role in French Arthurian Romance (*c.* 1170–1530)', *Romania* 95 (1974).

—— 'The Portrayal of the Hermit-Saint in French Arthurian Romance: The Remoulding of a Stock-Character', in Kenneth Varty, ed., *An Arthurian Tapestry. Essays in Memory of Lewis Thorpe* (Glasgow, 1981)

Kennedy, Beverly, *Knighthood in the Morte Darthur* (Woodbridge, Suffolk, 1985).

Kennedy, Elspeth, 'King Arthur in the First Part of the Prose *Lancelot*', in *Medieval Miscellany Presented to Eugène Vinaver* (Manchester, 1965).

Kennedy, Elspeth, 'The Knight as Reader of Arthurian Romance', in James P. Carley and Martin R. Shichterman, eds, *Culture and the King: The Social Implications of the Arthurian Legend: Essays in Honor of Valerie Lagorio* (Albany, 1994).

—— 'The Quest for Identity and the Importance of Lineage in Thirteenth-Century French Prose Romance', in Christopher Harper-Bill and Ruth Harvey, eds, *The Ideals and Practice of Medieval Knighthood II* (Cambridge, 1988).

—— *Lancelot and the Grail* (Oxford, 1986),

—— ed., *Lancelot do Lac*, 2 vols (Oxford, 1980).

Kibler, William W., ed., tr., *Chretien de Troyes: Lancelot or, The Knight of the Cart* (New York, 1981).

—— tr., *The Knight with the Lion, or Yvain (Le Chevalier au Lion)* (New York, 1985).

—— *Lancelot Part V*, in Norris Lacy, gen. ed., *Lancelot–Grail*, III (New York, 1995).

—— 'La "chanson d'aventure" ', in *Essor et fortune de la Chanson de geste dans l'Europe et l'Orient latin*, 2 vols (Modena, 1984), II.

Kicklighter, Joseph, 'The Nobility of English Gascony: the Case of Jourdain de l'Isle', *Journal of Medieval History* 13 (1987).

Kiernan, V. G., *The Duel in European History* (Oxford, 1988).

Knight, Stephen, and Thomas Ohlgren, eds, *Robin Hood and Other Outlaw Tales* (Kalamazoo, MI, 1997).

Koziol, Geoffrey, 'The Making of Peace in Eleventh-Century Flanders', Thomas Head and Richard Landes, eds, *The Peace of God: Social Violence and Religious Response in France around the Year 1000* (Ithaca, NY, 1992).

Krueger, Roberta, tr., *Lancelot Part IV*, in Norris Lacy, gen. ed., *Lancelot–Grail*, III (New York, 1995).

—— 'Misogny, Manipulation, and the Female Reader in Hue de Rotelande's *Ipomedon*', Keith Busby and Eric Kooper, eds, *Courtly Literature: Culture and Context* (Amsterdam, 1990).

—— *Woman Readers and the Ideology of Gender in Old French Verse Romance* (Cambridge, 1993),

Lachet, Claude, 'Mais où sont les tournois d'antan?', in Jean Dufournet, ed., *La Mort du roi Arthur ou le crépuscle de la chevalerie* (Paris, 1994).

Lacy, Norris, gen. ed., *Lancelot–Grail: The Old French Arthurian Vulgate and Post-Vulgate in Translation*, 5 vols (New York: Garland, 1993–6).

Lacy, Norris, J., tr., *The Death of Arthur*, in Norris Lacy, gen. ed., *Lancelot–Grail*, IV (New York, 1995).

Lalande, Denis, ed., *Le Livre des fais du bon messire Jehan le Maingre, dit Bouciquaut* (Geneva, 1985).

Langlois, Charles Victor, *Le Regne de Philippe III le Hardi* (Paris, 1887).

Langlois, Ernest, ed., *Le Couronnement de Louis* (Paris, 1924–5).

Langlois, M. and Y. Lanhers, *Confessions et jugements de criminels au Parlement de Paris (1319–1350)* (Paris, 1971).

Larmat, Jean, 'L'orphelin, la veuve et le pauvre dans le *Couronnement de Louis*', in *Charlemagne et l'épopée romane*, 2 vols (Paris, 1978), I.

Larner, John, 'Chivalric Culture in the Age of Dante', *Renaissance Studies* 2 (1988).

Laskaya, Anne, and Eve Salisbury, eds, *The Middle English Breton Lays* (Kalamazoo, MI, 1995).

Leclercq, Jean, 'The Monastic Crisis of the Eleventh and Twelfth Centuries', in Noreen Hunt, ed., *Cluniac Monasticism in the Central Middle Ages* (London, 1971).

—— *Monks and Love in Twelfth-Century France* (Oxford, 1979).

—— 'Le poème de Payen Bolotin contre les faux ermites', *Revue Benedictine* 58 (1958).

—— 'L'amour et le mariage vus par des clercs et des religieux, spécialement au XIIe siècle', in Willy Van Hoecke and Andries Welkenhuysen, *Love and Marriage in the Twelfth Century* (Louvain, 1981).

—— and Rochais, eds, *Bernard of Clairvaux. Opera* (Rome, 1963)

Leyser, Henrietta, *Hermits and the New Monasticism: A Study of Religious Communities in Western Europe, 1000–1150* (New York, 1984).

Leyser, Karl, *The Ascent of Latin Europe* (Oxford, 1986).

Life, Page West, *Sir Thomas Malory and the Morte Darthur: A Survey of Scholarship and Annotated Bibliography* (Charlottesville: 1989).

Little, Lester, *Benedictine Maledictions* (Ithaca, NY, 1993).

—— 'Pride Goes Before Avarice; Social Change and the Vices in Latin Christendom', *American Historical Review* 76 (1971).

Lodge, R. Anthony, ed., *Etienne de Fougères. Le Livre des Manières* (Geneva, 1979)

Logan, F. D., *Excommunication and the Secular Arm in Medieval England* (Toronto, 1968).

Loomis, R. S., 'Arthurian Influence on Sport and Spectacle', in Loomis, ed., *Arthurian Literature in the Middle Ages* (Oxford, 1959).

—— 'Chivalric and Dramatic Imitations of Arthurian Romance', *Medieval Studies in Memory of A. Kingsley Porter* (Freeport, NY, 1969).

—— 'Edward I, Arthurian Enthusiast', *Speculum* 28 (1953).

Lopez, Roberto, *The Commercial Revolution of the Middle Ages* (New York, 1971).

Lorenz, Konrad, *On Aggression*, tr. Marjorie Kerr Wilson (New York, 1971).

Löseth, E., ed., *Robert le Diable: roman d'aventure* (Paris, 1903).

Lot, Ferdinand, 'La Mesnie Hellequin et le comte Ernequin de Boulogne', *Romania* 33 (1903).

Luce, Siméon, ed., *Chroniques de J. Froissart*, 4 vols (Paris, 1869–99).

Luttrell, Claude and Stewart Gregory, eds, *Chrétien de Troyes. Cligés* (Bury St Edmunds, 1993).

Maddicott, John, *Simon de Montfort* (Cambridge, 1994).

—— 'Why Was England Different?' (Unpublished paper).

Maddox, Donald, 'Les Figures romanesques du discours vépique et la confluence génerique', in *Essor et fortune de la chanson de geste dans l'Europe et l'Orient latin*, 2 vols (Modena, 1984), II.

—— and Sara Sturm-Maddox, 'Le chevalier à oraison: Guillaume dans le *Couronnement de Louis*', in *Charlemagne et l'epopée romane*, 2 vols (Paris, 1978), II.

Magne, Augusto, ed., *A Demanda do Santa Graal* (Rio de Janeiro, 1955).

Mahoney, Dhira B., 'Malory's *Morte Darthur* and the *Alliterative Morte Arthure*', in Howell Chickering, and Thomas H. Seiler, eds, *The Study of Chivalry* (Kalamazoo, MI, 1988).

—— 'The Truest and Holiest Tale: Malory's Transformation of La Queste del Saint Graal', in James W. Spisak, ed., *Studies in Malory* (Kalamazoo, MI, 1985).

Maitland, Frederick W., *Roman Canon Law in the Church of England* (London, 1898).

Marchalonis, Shirley, '*Sir Gowther*: The Process of a Romance', *Chaucer Review* 6 (1971–2).

Marchello-Nizia, Christiane, 'Amour courtois, société masculine et figures du pouvoir', *Annales ESC* 36 (1981).

Mason, Emma, 'Timeo Barones et Donas Ferentes', *Studies in Church History* 15 (1978).

Matarasso, Pauline, *The Redemption of Chivalry: A Study of the Queste del Saint Graal* (Geneva, 1979)

—— tr., *The Quest of the Holy Grail* (Harmondsworth, 1969).

—— *Recherches historiques et littéraires sur Raoul de Cambrai* (Paris, 1962).

Maxwell, Sir Herbert, tr., *Scalacronica. The Reigns of Edward I, Edward II and Edward III as recorded by Sir Thomas Gray* (Glasgow, 1907).

McCarthy, Terrence, *Reading the Morte Darthur* (Woodbridge, Suffolk, 1988).

McCash, June, 'Mutual Love as a Medieval Ideal', in Keith Busby and Eric Kooper, eds, *Courtly Literature: Culture and Context* (Amsterdam, 1990).

McCoy, Richard, ' "A Dangerous Image"; The Earl of Essex and Elizabethan Chivalry', *Journal of Medieval and Renaissance Studies* 13 (1983).

—— *The Rites of Knighthood; The Literature and Politics of Elizabethan Chivalry* (Berkeley, 1989).

McDiarmid, Matthew P., James A. C. Stevenson, eds, *Barbour's Bruce*, 3 vols (Edinburgh, 1980–5).

McKim, Anne M., 'James Douglas and Barbour's ideal of knighthood', in W. H. Jackson, ed., *Knighthood in Medieval Literature* (Woodbridge, Suffolk, 1981).

McMillan, Duncan, ed., *La Chanson de Guillaume* 2 vols (Paris, 1949–50).

—— *Le Charroi de Nîmes* (Paris, 1972).

Mehl, Dieter, *The Middle English Romances of the Thirteenth and Fourteenth Centuries* (New York, 1969).

Meyer, Paul, ed., *L'Histoire de Guillaume le Maréchal*, 2 vols (Paris, 1891, 1894).

—— ed., tr., *Girart de Roussillon* (Paris, 1884; repr. Geneva, 1970).

Micha, Alexandre, ed., *Lancelot, Roman en prose du XIIIe siècle*, 9 vols (Paris, 1978–83).

Micha, Alexandre, ed., *Merlin: roman du XIIIe siècle* (Geneva, Droz, 1979).

Michel, Francisque, ed., tr., *Chronicle of the War Between the English and the Scots in 1173 and 1174 by Jordan Fantosme* (London, 1840).

Mierow, Charles C., tr., *The Two Cities by Otto, Bishop of Freising* (New York, 1966).

Mieszkowski, Gretchen, 'The Prose *Lancelot's* Galehot, Malory's Lavain, and the Queering of Late Medieval Literature', *Arthuriana* 5 (1995).

Mills, Maldwyn, ed., *Six Middle English Romances* (London, 1973).

Morris, Colin, '*Equestris Ordo*: Chivalry as a Vocation in the Twelfth Century', *Studies in Church History* 15 (1978).

—— *The Papal Monarchy: The Western Church from 1050–1250* (Oxford, 1989).

Muir, Lynette, tr., *The Capture of Orange*, in Glanville Price, ed., *William, Count of Orange: Four Old French Epics* (London, 1975).

—— *The Song of William*, in Glanville Price, ed., *William, Count of Orange: Four Old French Epics* (London, 1975).

Nederman, Cary J., tr., *Policraticus* (Cambridge, 1990).

Newth, Michael A., ed., tr., *The Song of Aspremont (La Chanson d'Aspremont)* (New York, 1989).

Nicholas, David, *Medieval Flanders* (London: Longman, 1992).

Nitze, W. A., and T. A. Jenkins, eds, *Le Haut livre du Graal: Perlesvaus*, 2 vols (Chicago, 1932).

Noble, Peter, 'Anti-Clericalism in the Feudal Epic', in Peter Noble, Lucie Polak, and Claire Isoz, eds, *The Medieval Alexander Legend and Romance Epic: Essays in Honour of David J. A. Ross* (Millwood, NY, 1982).

Novelli, Cornelius, *Sir Gowther* (PhD thesis, University of Notre Dame, 1963).

Ordonnances des roys de France de la troisième race recueillies par ordre chronologique, eds E.-J. Lauriere *et al.* (Paris, 1723–1849).

Orme, Nicholas, *From Childhood to Chivalry* (London, 1984).

Orpen, G. H., ed., tr., *The Song of Dermot and the Earl* (Oxford: Clarendon Press, 1891).

Owen, D. D. R., 'Aspects of *Demesure* (Chanson de Roland, Raoul de Cambrai, Girart de Roussillon)', in L. M. Patterson and S. B. Gaunt, eds, *The Troubadours and the Epic: Essays in Memory of W. Mary Hackett* (Warwick, 1987).

Paden, William D., jr, Tilde Sankovitch, and Patricia H. Stäblein, eds, trs., *The Poems of the Troubadour Bertran de Born* (Berkeley, 1986).

Painter, Sidney, *French Chivalry* (Baltimore, 1940).

—— *William Marshal: Knight-Errant, Baron and Regent of England* (Baltimore, 1933).

Paris, Gaston, ed., *L'Histoire de la guerre sainte: histoire en vers de la troisième croisade (1190–1192) par Ambroise* (Paris, 1897).

—— and Jacob Ulrich, eds, *Merlin: Roman en prose du XIIIe siècle*, 2 vols (Paris, 1886).

Paris, Matthew, *Chronica Majora*, ed., H. R. Luard, 7 vols (London: Rolls Series lvii, 1872–84).

Parker, Geoffrey, *The Military Revolution: Military Innovation and the Rise of the West, 1500–1800* (Cambridge, 2nd edn, 1996).

Patterson, Lee, *Chaucer and the Subject of History* (Madison, 1991).

Pauphilet, Albert, ed., *La Queste del Saint Graal* (Paris, 1923).

Peristiany, J. G., and J. Pitt-Rivers, eds, *Honour and Shame: the Values of Mediterranean Society* (Chicago, 1970).

Peters, Edward, *The Shadow King: Rex Inutilis in Medieval Law and Literature, 751–1327* (New Haven, 1970).

Piel, Joseph-Maria, ed., *A Demanda do Santo Graal* (Lisbon, 1988).

Pickens, Rupert T., tr., *The Story of Merlin*, in Norris Lacy, gen. ed., *Lancelot–Grail*, I (New York, 1993).

Pirenne, Henri, *Economic and Social History of Medieval Europe* (New York, 1937).

Pirenne, Henri, ed., *Histoire du meurtre de Charles le Bon, comte de Flandre* (*1127–1128*) *par Galbert de Bruges* (Paris, 1891).

Pitt-Rivers, Julian, 'Honour and Social Status', in J. G. Peristiany, ed., *Honour and Shame: the Values of Mediterranean Society* (Chicago, 1970).

Poly, J., and E. Bournazel, *The Feudal Transformation, 900–1200* (New York, 1991).

Pope, Mildred, and Eleanor Lodge, eds, *Life of the Black Prince by the Herald of Sir John Chandos* (Oxford, 1910).

Postan, M. M., *The Medieval Society and Economy* (Berkeley, 1972).

—— *Medieval Trade and Finance* (Cambridge, 1973).

Pounds, N. J. G., *An Economic History of Medieval Europe* (New York, 1974).

Prestwich, Michael, *Armies and Warfare in the Middle Ages* (New Haven, 1996).

—— *Edward I* (Berkeley, 1988).

Price, Glanville, tr., ed., *William Count of Orange: Four Old French Epics* (*Crowning of Louis, The Waggon-Train, The Capture of Orange, The Song of William*) (London, 1975).

Ramon Llull. Obres essencials 2 vols (Barcelona, 1957–60).

Raynaud, Christiane, *La Violence au Moyen Âge; XIIIe-XV siècle* (Paris, 1990).

Régnier, Claude, ed., *Les Rédactions en vers de la Prise d'Orange* (Paris, 1966).

Revard, Carter, 'Courtly Romances in the Privy Wardrobe', in John Thompson and Evelyn Mullally, eds, *The Court and Cultural Diversity* (Woodbridge, Suffolk, 1997).

Reynolds, Susan, *Kingdoms and Communities in Western Europe, 987–1300* (Oxford, 1984).

Rezak, Brigette Bedos, 'Medieval Seals and the Structure of Chivalric Society', in Howell Chickering and Thomas H. Seiller, eds, *The Study of Chivalry* (Kalamazoo, MI, 1988).

Richter, E., ed., *Decretum Magistri Gratiani*, 2 vols (Graz, 1959)

Rider, Jeff, ed., *De multro, traditione, et occisione Gloriosi Karoli Comitis Flandriarum. Galbertus Notarius Brugensis* (Turnholt, 1994).

Riley-Smith, Jonathan, *The Atlas of the Crusades* (New York, 1991).

Roach, William, ed., *The Didot Perceval* (Philadelphia, 1941).

—— ed., *Le Roman de Perceval ou Le Conte du Graal* (Geneva, 1959).

—— and Robert Henry Ivy, eds, *The Continuations of the Old French Perceval*, II, (5 vols, Philadelphia, 1949–83).

Robertson, Elizabeth, 'Comprehending Rape in Medieval England', *Medieval Feminist Newsletter* 21 (Spring, 1996).

Robinson, I. S., *The Papacy 1073–1198* (Cambridge, 1990).

—— 'Gregory VII and the Soldiers of Christ', *History* n.s. 58 (1971).

Robinson, J. A., *Gilbert Crispin, Abbot of Westminster* (Cambridge, 1911)

Roche-Mahdi, Sarah, ed., tr., *Silence: A Thirteenth-Century French Romance* (East Lansing, MI, 1992).

Rodes, Robert E., *Ecclesiastical Administration in Medieval England* (Notre Dame, IN, 1977).

Rogers, Clifford, ed., *The Military Revolution Debate* (Boulder, Colorado, 1995).

—— 'The Military Revolution of the Hundred Years War', in Clifford Rogers, ed., *The Military Revolution Debate* (Boulder, CO, 1995).

Rollason, D. W., 'The Miracles of St Benedict: A Window on Early Medieval France', in Henry Mayr-Harting and R. I. Moore, eds, *Studies in Medieval History Presented to R.H.C. Davis* (London, 1985).

Rosenberg, Samuel N., tr., *Lancelot, Part I*, in Norris Lacy, gen. ed., *Lancelot–Grail*, II (New York, 1993).

—— *Lancelot Part III*, Norris Lacy, gen. ed., *Lancelot–Grail*, II (New York, 1993),

Ross, D. J. A., 'L'Originalité de "Turoldus"; le maniement de la lance', *Cahiers de Civilisation Médiévale* 6 (1963).

—— 'Pleine sa hanste', *Medium Aevum* 20 (1951).

Ross, James Bruce, tr., *The Murder of Charles the Good, Count of Flanders* (New York, 1960).

Rossi, Marguerite, 'Epopée française et épopée non française', in *Essor et fortune de la chanson de geste dans l'europe et l'orient latin*, 2 vols (Modena, 1984).

—— 'Le Duel judiciaire dans les chansons du cycle carolingien: structure et fonction', in *Le chanson de geste et le mythe carolingien: Mélanges René Louis*, 2 vols (Paris, 1982), II.

Roussineau, Gilles, ed., *La Suite du Roman de Merlin*, 2 vols (Geneva, 1996).

—— 'Ethique chevaleresque et pouvoir royal dans *Le roman de Perceforest*', in *Actes du 14e congrès international arthurien*, II (2 vols, Rennes, 1985).

Rumble, Thomas C., ed., *The Breton Lays in Middle English* (Detroit, MI, 1965).

Russell, Fredric, *The Just War in the Middle Ages* (Cambridge, 1975).

Rychner, Jean, ed., *Les Lais de Marie de France* (Paris, 1966).

Sainéan, L., 'La Mesnie Hellequin', *Revue des traditions populaires* 20 (1905).

Salmon, A., ed., *Philippe de Beaumanoir: Coutumes de Beauvaisis*, 2 vols (Paris, 1899–1900).

Saly, Antoinette, 'Perceval-Perlesvaus, La figure du Perceval dans le "Haut Livre du Graal" ', *Travaux de linguistique et de Littérature* 24 (1986).

Sands, Donald B., *Middle English Verse Romances* (New York, 1966).

Saul, Nigel, *Knights and Esquires: The Gloucester Gentry in the Fourteenth Century* (Oxford, 1981)

Scattergood, V. J., ed., *The Works of Sir John Clanvowe* (Cambridge, 1975).

Schalk, Ellery, *From Valor to Pedigree: Ideas of Nobility in France in the Sixteenth and Seventeenth Centuries* (Princeton, 1986).

Schmolke-Hasselmann, Beate, 'Henry II Plantagenêt, roi d'Angleterre, et la genêse d'Erec et Enide', *Cahiers de Civilisation Médiévale* 24 (1981).

Scott, Paul C., *Domination and the Arts of Resistance: Hidden Transcripts* (New Haven, 1990).

Shaw, M. R. B., tr., *Joinville and Villehardouin, Chronicles of the Crusades* (Baltimore, 1963).

Shichtman, Martin B., 'Politicizing the Ineffable: The *Queste del Saint Graal* and Malory's "Tale of the Sankgreal" ', in Martin B. Shichtman and James P. Carley, eds, *Culture and the King: The Social Implications of the Arthurian Legend. Essays in Honor of Valerie M. Lagorio* (Albany, NY, 1994).

Skells, Dell, tr., *The Romance of Perceval in Prose* (Seattle, WA, 1961).

Smalley, Beryl, 'Capetian France', in J. M. Wallace-Hadrill and John McManners, eds, *France: Government and Society* (London, 1970).

Smith, Lacey Baldwin, *Treason in Tudor England: Politics and Paranoia* (London, 1986).

Solente, S., ed., *Le Livre des fais et bonnes meurs du sage roy Charles V par Christine de Pisan*, 2 vols (Paris, 1936).

Sommer, H. Oskar, ed., 'Die Abenteuer Gawains, Ywains, und le Morholts mit den drei Jungfrauen', *Zeitschrift für Romanische Philologie, Beihefte* 47 (1913).

—— *The Vulgate Version of The Arthurian Romances, Edited from Manuscripts in the British Museum*, 7 vols (Washington, DC, 1909).

Southall, Aidan, 'The Peace in the Feud', *Past and Present* 8 (1955).

Southern, R. W., *Medieval Humanism and Other Studies* (New York, 1970).

—— *Western Society and the Church* (Harmondsworth, 1970).

Spiegel, Gabrielle, 'History, Historicism and the Social Logic of the Text in the Middle Ages', *Speculum* 65 (1990).

Spisak, James, W., ed., *Studies in Malory* (Kalamazoo, MI, 1985).

Staines, David, tr., *Complete Romances of Chrétien de Troyes* (Bloomington, IN, 1990).

Stanesco, M., 'Le Chevalier dans la ville: le modèle romanesque et ses métamorphoses bourgeoises', in Giovanna Angeli and Luciano Formisano, eds, *L'Imaginaire courtois et son double* (Naples, 1991).

Statutes of the Realm (London: Record Commission, 1810–28).

Stephenson, Carl, and Frederick George Marcham, *Sources of English Constitutional History* (New York, 1937).

Stone, Lawrence, *The Crisis of the Aristocracy* (Oxford, 1965).

Strayer, Joseph R., *Medieval Statecraft and the Perspectives of History* (Princeton, 1971).

—— *On the Medieval Origins of the Modern State* (Princeton, 1970).

—— *The Reign of Philip the Fair* (Princeton, 1980).

—— 'The State and Religion: A Comparison in Various Cultures', *Medieval Statecraft and the Perspectives of History* (Princeton, 1971).

Strickland, Matthew, *War and Chivalry* (Cambridge, 1996).

Strohm, Paul, *Hochon's Arrow: the Social Imagination of Fourteenth-century Texts* (Princeton, 1992).

Stroud, Michael, 'Malory and the Chivalric Ethos', *Medieval Studies* 36 (1974).

Stubbs, Willam, *Select Charters*, 9th edn, ed., H. W. C. Davis (Oxford, 1962).

Suard, François, ed., *La Chanson de Guillaume* (Paris, 1991).

Subrenat, Jean, 'Moines mesquins et saint chevalier', in *Marche Romane: Mélanges de philologie et de littérature romanes offerts à Jeanne Wathelet-Willem* (Liege, 1978).

Sullivan, Richard, 'The Carolingian Age: Reflections on its Place in the History of the Middle Ages', *Speculum* 64 (1989).

Switten, Margaret, '*Chevalier* in Twelfth-century French and Occitan Vernacular Literature', in Howell Chickering and Thomas H. Seiller, eds, *The Study of Chivalry* (Kalamazoo, MI, 1988).

Taylor, Michael, 'A Critical Edition of Geoffroy de Charny's "Libre Charny" and the "Demandes Pour La Joute, Les Tournois et la Guerre" ' (PhD thesis, University of North Carolina at Chapel Hill, 1977).

Tellenbach, Gerd, *Church, State, and Christian Society at the Time of the Investiture Contest* (Oxford, 1956).

Thoms, William J., ed., *Early English Prose Romances* (London, 1924).

Thorpe, Lewis, tr., *Geoffrey of Monmouth, History of the Kings of Britain* (Harmondsworth, Middlesex, 1968).

Tobler, Adolf, and Erhard Lommatzsch, *Altfranzösisches Wörterbuch* (Wiesbaden, 1954).

Topsfield, Leslie T., *Chrétien de Troyes. A Study of the Arthurian Romances* (Cambridge, 1981).

Trempler, Volker, 'Robert der Teufel. Ein Beitrag zur Untersuchung des destruktiven Narzissmus in der Adoleszenz', *Psychotherapeut* 39 (1994).

Tucker, P. E., 'Chivalry in the *Morte*', in J. A. W. Bennett, ed., *Essays on Malory* (Oxford, 1963).

Twain, Mark, *A Connecticut Yankee in King Arthur's Court* (New York, 1982).

Upton-Ward, J. M., *The Rule of the Templars* (Bury St Edmunds, Suffolk, 1992)

Vale, Juliet, *Edward III and Chivalry* (Woodbridge, Suffolk, 1982).

Vale, Malcolm, *War and Chivalry* (Norwich: Duckworth, 1981).

Vanderlinde, Henry, 'Sir Gowther: Saintly Knight and Knightly Saint', *Neophilologus* 80 (1996).

Van Engen, John, 'The Crisis of Cenobitism Reconsidered', *Speculum* 61 (1986).

Verbruggen, J. F., *The Art of Warfare in Western Europe During the Middle Ages*, tr., Sumner Willard and S. C. M. Southern (Amsterdam, 1977).

Vesce, Thomas, ed., tr., *The Knight of the Parrot (Le Chevalier du Papegau)* (New York, 1986).

—— tr., *[Jehan]. The Marvels of Rigomer* (New York, 1988).

Vinaver, Eugène, ed., *Malory. Works*, 2nd edn (Oxford, 1971).

Wailly, Natallis de, ed., *Joinville. Histoire de Saint Louis*, 2nd edn (Paris, n.d.).

Waldron, Peter, ' "Vertuouse Love" and Adulterous Lovers: Coming to Terms with Malory', in D. Thomas Hanks, jr, ed., *Sir Thomas Malory: Views and Re-views* (New York, 1992).

Wallace-Hadrill, J. M., and John McManners, eds, *France: Government and Society* (London, 1970).

Waquet, Henri, *Suger. La Vie de Louis VI le gros* (Paris, 1929).

Waugh, Scott, 'The Profits of Violence: The Minor Gentry in the Rebellion of 1321–1322 in Gloucestershire and Herefordshire', *Speculum* 52 (1977).

Webb, C., ed., *Ioannis Saresberiensis Episcopi Carnotensis Policratici* (Oxford, 1909, repr. Frankfurt, 1965),

White, Lynn, jr, *Medieval Technology and Social Change* (Oxford, 1966).

White, Stephen, ' "*Pactum . . . Legem Vincit et Amor Judicium*", The Settlement of Disputes by Compromise in Eleventh-Century Western France', *American Journal of Legal History* 22 (1978).

Whiting, B. J., 'The Vows of the Heron', *Speculum* 20 (1945).

Wienbeck, Eric, Wilhelm Hartnacke, and Paul Rasch, eds, *Aliscans* (Halle, 1903).

Willard, Charity Cannon, 'Christine de Pisan on Chivalry', in Howell Chickering and Thomas H. Seiler, eds, *The Study of Chivalry* (Kalamazoo, MI, 1988).

Williams, Mary, and Marguerite Oswald, eds, *Gerbert de Montreuil: La Continuation de Perceval*, 3 vols (Paris, 1922).

Wright, Thomas, ed., tr., *Historical Works of Giraldus Cambrensis* (London, 1887).

Yeandle, F. G. ed., *Bertrand de Bar-sur Aube, Girard de Viane* (New York, 1930).

Yunck, John, A., tr., *Eneas: A Twelfth-Century French Romance* (New York, 1974).

Zagorin, Perez, *Rebels and Rulers*, 2 vols (Cambridge, 1982).

INDEX

Printed in the United States
91537LV00001B/50/A